Metamorphosis:

The Reality of Existence and Sublimation of Life

(Volume 1)

The Unsolved Mystery
of Life and Death

Shan Tung, Chang

美商EHGBooks微出版公司
www.EHGBooks.com

EHGBooks 公司出版
Amazon.com 總經銷
2023 年版權美國登記
未經授權不許翻印全文或部分
及翻譯為其他語言或文字
2023 年 EHGBooks 第一版

Table of Contents

Chapter 3: The slow and lingering "trampled to death by the geese" of Kierkegaard..................................162

Chapter 4: Nietzsche: The God of Wine and the God of the Sun...194

Preface

We come into the world naked and leave empty-handed, taking nothing with us between our coming and going, which makes one wonder what is the true meaning of the existence of life itself in the universe? In the infinite space of all celestial bodies in the universe and in the long history of the earth, it is the great question of mankind about the existence of life itself for thousands of years.

It is also a mystery of the existence of life in the universe, and a philosophy of life that has been explored in metaphysics, philosophy1, science, theology, and religious philosophy.

What is the meaning of life? To put it plainly, it is the purpose of life, and to put it plainly, it is the reason why people live. This is a seemingly simple, yet not simply paradoxical, philosophical question.

It not only reflects a person's value trend, but also

highlights the extent to which a person consciously and voluntarily carries out or voluntarily pursues the overall long-term goals of the task, the basic foothold for people to deal with, in the end it is a question of life and values.

In the memory of each of us, all knowledge of life and death cognition comes from others' description of the process of birth and death, and in the memory of our own thinking and consciousness, we cannot search for the knowledge that we had.

Therefore, many people only know that they will die in the future, but they do not think that they will die, especially right away.

However, when we have a chance to calm down, look back and think deeply about our past life journey, we realize that our life is like a blank sheet of paper. From the moment we are born to the end of our lives, we are always drawing our own destiny.

In the end, it all comes back to nothing. It is a frightening and worrying thing that one's life is just a sudden blossoming of the colors painted by the brush, because one is completely unaware of the life experiences one has had, and therefore, like a "frog boiled in warm water", one is unaware of the unexplained mystery of the existence of life in the universe.

It is because all the objects or phenomena that exist objectively in the natural world always maintain a certain appearance so that we can know their "existence". All the things we see, hear, or touch, and all the objects or phenomena we know that exist objectively in nature, we personally use our senses, perceptions, thoughts, memories, and other mental activities to perceive and understand the state of our body and mind and the changes of people, things, and objects in the environment, and we will cling to the idea that they are real and concrete.

This includes the air we breathe and the water we drink. We all think that these are natural, real objects or things that have real content and are firmly in our control. Is this really true?

For example, rain: when it rains from the clouds in the sky, you think there is rain in this world. Is there an entity in this rain? No, there is not. "Rain" is just water.

It is the water on the ground by the sunlight, then turned into water vapor; water vapor up in the sky called clouds; clouds in the air floating around, encountering cold air will condense into water droplets, water droplets more and more collection, more and more heavy, then from the sky down, forming rain.

Because of this effect, you can feel the existence of "rain". So you give it a name. Under this name, you think that there is "rain" falling down. Is there really a thing called rain in this world? Not at all. When those drops fall to the ground, they become rivers, streams, and eventually the water you drink.

Everything in the world exists objectively in nature, all objects or phenomena are not only "impermanent", but also "egoless". It means that there is no independent and unchanging entity or master of all the existing and non-existing laws.

What we are talking about here refers to all objects or phenomena that exist objectively in the universe, including material phenomena and mental activities, and is a generic term for the visible and invisible matter, reason, color and mind.

We generally think that the so-called "I" means master and entity; "I" is a constant and unchanging entity with the function of self-mastery; "I" is an independent, autonomous and unchanging master. However, is there such a single, independent, self-existent, self-determining and eternal thing in the world?

On the contrary, religions in general hold a positive view of this. For example, Brahmanism in India believes that the world was created by the Great Self, and Catholicism in the West believes that there is an all-powerful God who created the world, created mankind, and is sovereign over everything.

However, there are other sects that do not believe this, such as Buddhism, which says that in the process of knowing all things or phenomena, people can reflect reality observation by means of concepts, judgments, and reasoning.

All objects and phenomena in the natural world are created by cause and origin, and if they are brought together, they exist, and if they are dispersed, they perish. Therefore, it is said that all objects or phenomena that exist objectively in nature are not under our control.

For example, the amount of money, the size of power, and the level of ability do not represent the existence of life itself, and the purpose of existence of life is only to realize a certain ideal, or to achieve a certain purpose, and consciously work for it, and it does not represent the value of life itself.

However, to deny the value of the whole without asking the reason, to generalize, and to deny the value of the whole by only one's own opinion, will certainly hurt the self-esteem of countless people, because this is their dream, their life of glory and wealth, and also their ultimate goal to realize a certain ideal or achieve a certain purpose, and to live for it consciously.

However, since they have come to this world, they should let themselves live in a spirit of freedom, clarity and meaning, consciously transcending life and death, and transcending all worries.

Chapter 1: The meaning of life's existence

I. The Essence of Life

In the philosophical viewpoint, the essence of life (English: Essence) is an everlasting attribute that makes a distinguishable, independent entity, the spirit, within itself, its very essence.

It is an objective law that does not depend on the will of man and necessarily exists, without which it would lose its proper identity. It cannot be isolated from all the objects or phenomena that exist objectively in the natural world.

Only by integrating the egoic life into the larger universe, by consciously working for a certain ideal or a certain purpose, and by associating it with nature, can we know the origin and context of life, and then the nature of life.

Only in this way can we find the awakening of life consciously, transcend the spiritual trust of life existence, and realize the truth of life's metamorphosis and ascension, and achieve the spiritual destination of transcending life and death, transcending all troubles and pains, and living eternally.

I am born to be useful

Li Bai, a poet of the Tang Dynasty, wrote in his poem "The Music of the House - The Wine of the General": "Life should be enjoyed to the fullest; do not let the golden bottle be empty to the moon. I was born to be useful, a thousand pieces of gold will be scattered and come back. In the poem, the phrase 'born with my talent will be useful' means that I was born with my talent, there must be a need for me.

After the money is used up, these lost things will still come back later. Li Bai's highly optimistic character and his ability to see through life are fully reflected in his profound perception of the nature of life.

When we recognize the essence of life, we will not be confused by the different forms of quenching that we experience in our daily lives. For example, the amount of money, the power, the ability, etc., are all differences in the external environment and in the enjoyment of material life, but the essence of life is not different at all.

When we recognize the human meaning of life, we will not be tempted and stimulated by society and lose ourselves. For example, the reputation is only the evaluation of the society, not the only measure of self-worth.

The nature of life has a wide range of common qualities, not limited by time and space, therefore, the existence of life itself, the real meaning of life existence, is that a person in a limited life, can show off the light of life without any cover, not just confused life confused death, like a dull black dwarf star.

Therefore, the essence of the meaning of life does not lie in the length of life itself, but in the contribution and contribution of the consciousness of self-liberation in the limited existence of life, the awakening of one's inner self-discovery and outer innovation.

Zhuangzi's view of life and death

The journey of life, the impermanence of birth, old age, sickness, and death, is like the change of four seasons: spring, summer, autumn, and winter, and all objective existence in nature, all objects or phenomena, thoughts and feelings change with the change of environment.

The [supreme happiness] is the eighteenth book of [Zhuangzi]; the supreme happiness is the highest happiness, or the extreme happiness in common parlance. It discusses the possibility of supreme happiness, identifies what the world calls happiness as not supreme happiness, and explains the changes in all things and the feelings of life and death.

The essay begins with several questions: Is there the highest happiness in the world, or "extreme happiness" as the saying goes? Is there a principle and a way to live on? If so, on what basis? And how to do it? What should we strive for? What to avoid? What do you like and what do you dislike?

Story 1.

Zhuangzi lost his wife in his old age. When Huish heard the news, he rushed to mourn the dead and console the living. He was an old friend of Chuang Tzu's, and at that time he was no longer the prime minister of Liang, so he no longer had to put up an official show. So Huishi got off the car at the entrance of the alley, and walked into the narrow alley.

Zhuangzi's eldest son knelt outside his home to greet those who had come to mourn the dead, and Zhuangzi's eldest son said, "I thank my uncle on behalf of my mother.

Huishi picked up the mourning son, said a few words according to the etiquette, and then, with a sad and sympathetic look on his face, he entered the gate solemnly and walked into the hearse.

Zhuangzi was sitting beside the coffin with his legs spread out in a figure-eight shape, resembling a dustpan for garbage, which was very unpleasant, and his hands were clapping on the tile basin to accompany him.

She raised your children and grew up for you, and now she has died of old age. You are looking at it lightly, do not cry is fine. But you, alas, even knocked up a tile basin and sang a song. Don't you feel that you have gone too far in your behavior now?

Zhuangzi said, "Duke Hui! You are wrong. I am also a human being, and I can't help but be saddened. But I can't be dominated by my feelings all the time, but I have to be calm and think more deeply and thoughtfully. I remembered that once upon a time, when she was not yet born, not yet formed into life.

At an earlier time, not only had she not become a living being, but she had not even formed a zygote. Even earlier, not only had the embryo not yet been formed, but there was not even a soul. Later, in a trance, the yin and yang mating, into a wisp of soul gas. And then later, the soul gas into a body, so there is an embryo.

And then later, the embryo became a baby, she was born and became an independent living entity. During her existence, she experienced various hardships in life, and then returned to death. Looking back at her life of birth, aging, sickness and death, it reminds me of the evolution of the four seasons: spring, summer, autumn and winter, which are so similar.

Now she is about to move from my house to this big house in the universe, with a calm mind and no worries, lying peacefully. If I don't sing a song to send her off, instead of wailing and crying, then I don't know the truth of life's origination and destruction. When I thought of this, I unconsciously sang a song, beating on a tile pot.

Huishi handed over a bag of money and put it into the tile basin, cursed himself and said, "Damn it!

Story 2.

A disabled man, Zhi Li Shu, whose surname is Zhi Li, means a disabled person. The definition includes people with long-term physical, mental, intellectual, or sensory impairments that interact with various barriers that may prevent people with disabilities from participating fully and practically in society on an equal basis with others.

The last name of the skinny person, Uncle Slipkick, means that the bones choke without flesh. The two of them are not adapted to do their best and use all they have to make extreme efforts to achieve their goals in society. Retreating from monasticism, they traveled together to the ghost town where the tomb of the Yellow Emperor is located in the Kunlun Mountains, where they came to watch the process of changes in the life and death of all things in order to understand the secrets of nature.

Watching the process of life and death can lead to enlightenment, which is a must. The two of them walked around the ghost town and watched. On both sides of the main road, there are all kinds of life and death changes of everything and human beings, and they are quickly reproduced here.

Of course, they are all phantoms, and silent. He lifted his long sleeve and saw a small tumor emerge from the itchy spot, which quickly swelled into a large tumor, causing severe pain. He was shocked, panicked, irritable and disgusted. This is a malignant tumor, it will kill you!

The handicapped man, Uncle Zhi Li, said, "Do you dislike or dislike this tumor very much?

The skinny man, Uncle Slippery, said, "No, I can't dislike or dislike it extremely. I borrowed this life for temporary use, and sooner or later I have to return the debt to others. The soul is borrowed from Yin and Yang. The flesh, borrowed the gold, wood, water, fire and earth. It is clear that my existence is an illusion. Now this tumor is coming to me again, and it is false again and again, just like the dirty things that accumulate on the human body or on the object, such as mud.

Falsehood is not real, and the malignant tumor will kill me, but I need not be troubled. Life and death are like the cycle of day and night, and the end is the beginning, so let's wait for the arrangement. I came to the ghost town with you to watch the process of change of life and death of all things, and now it has been transferred to me, so I have to accept my fate. How can I be extremely disgusted or dislike it?

At this time, the large tumor on the left arm quickly swelled into a giant tumor, collapsing and bleeding. The skinny man, Uncle Slippery, lay down calmly and was no longer frightened. Uncle Zhi Li watched him, respectfully and cautiously watching the process of life and death of all things. Only when he died in peace did he leave alone.

Story 3.

Zhuangzi rode a weak horse on the ancient road leading to the state of Chu. The cold west wind pounded Zhuangzi's thin face and lifted his long, white, flowing hair. As Zhuangzi looked around, he saw the sad scene after the war and the chaos. When the sun went down in the west, the twilight gradually closed, lacking light, the surrounding area became dark, only the near area could still barely be seen, and all around was gradually dark.

When Zhuangzi first came to Chu, he was in the middle of nowhere and lost the right direction. It was near dusk and there was no place to stay. Zhuang Zi went to an old tree tangled with dead vines and was surprised by a few ravens circling up the tree, making a lot of noise. After tying up his horse, Chuang Tzu wanted to find a rock to sit down and rest. While searching around, he glimpsed a human head in the grass, decayed and damaged, with the corners of the skull still visible.

The color of the bones was white, so it was clear that it had suffered from the wind and rain for many years. Zhuangzi struck the white skull with his whip, sounding as if he was recalling a time of vicissitudes in the world.

After tapping the skull twice, Chuang Tzu asked, "Is it because you are greedy for life that you have fallen ill for the sake of sensual pleasures? Did you fall ill and cry out?"

When he struck the skull twice, he asked, "Or was it because his country was broken and his family was killed, and he was caught by the enemy and killed by the sword and axe?

After hitting the skull twice, he asked, "Sir, did you commit suicide because you were ashamed of your parents and wife and were afraid of disgracing your wife and children because of your scandalous deeds?

Then he struck the skull twice and asked again, "Or did you come to this state because you were poor, had no food or clothing, and were suffering from hunger and cold, and freezing and dejection?

Then he struck the skull twice, and finally asked, "Have you lived long enough, or are you dying? Did you die of natural causes?"

After asking the question, Chuang Tzu set up a wood-burning fire in a wilderness or open area and stayed outside or in the countryside. He used a human skull as a pillow and slept on his side, but he fell asleep as soon as he could because he was tired and weary from his journey.

In the middle of the night, Zhuangzi dreamed that he saw the master of the skeleton, fully clothed and well-groomed, standing in front of him, smiling and saying, "I heard you talk with great eloquence, as if you were a good debater.

But you ask those sad things, only you living people, hanging in the heart. Once a person dies, all worries are now in the past. No dead person is interested in answering the questions of the living, so forgive me for not answering you. But would you like to hear about the joy of death?

Zhuangzi said, "Yes.

The master of the skeleton said, "Once a person enters the realm of death, there is no pressure from the top of the sovereign to control him, and there are no ties of responsibility from the bottom, social equality is realized, and the difference between rulers and subjects is abolished. The climate is neither cold nor hot, and there are no four seasons. The spring plowing, the summer plowing, the autumn harvesting, the winter hiding, all kinds of hard work, have been relieved.

There is no need to worry about the scruples of old age, and everyone can have fun for a long time. That kind of joy is even more joyful than being a king!

Chuang Tzu was suspicious and guessed that this guy was advertising for the ghost town, so he tried to say, "Sir, I have a friendship with the god of the ghost town, so I can ask him privately to allow you to be reborn, to provide you with a full set of flesh and blood for free, to transfer you back to your hometown, and to return your parents, wife, children, neighbors and friends. Will you do it?

The master of the skeleton thought or behaved in a controlled manner, did not indulge in smiling, frowned deeply and forced to ask: "Do you want me to give up the joy of being a king and go back to live and suffer? I'll tell you later.

From the point of view of the way of survival, the most basic way of survival is that I love the principle and method of sticking to the way to live. Principles are the essential, basic framework that tells me what I can and cannot do.

The method is the way of doing things under the principle, the same goal can have many methods, also can have many choices. But to survive under the general principle. A clear distinction between right and wrong is the most basic way of survival.

From the point of view of the nature of life, the existence of life itself is only a part of the universe's conscious effort to realize a certain ideal or achieve a certain purpose.

From the beginning, it is defined as "the sum of the existence of the universe," or all the things that existed in the past, present, and future, (or our existence of life itself is but a part of the orbit that the universe consciously strives to run in order to realize a certain ideal, or to achieve a certain purpose,)

Therefore, the real meaning of the universe's conscious effort to run its course in order to realize a certain ideal or achieve a certain purpose

It is to realize the true meaning of the existence of life itself and the existence of life from the quenching of the experience of the daily life of the universe, and to realize the snare of the existence of life itself.

2.The meaning of life

The meaning of the existence of cosmic life or the meaning of the life of cosmic life is related to the meaning of the life of existence in general or the meaning of the transformation of life existence.

In a narrow sense, it is divided into two aspects of inquiry: first, it studies the relationship between the universe and life, between people and people or between people and things, of a certain nature. Second, it explores the evolution of species and environment, especially the purpose and value of the existence of Homo sapiens.

In a broad sense, it is also divided into two aspects of

inquiry: one, including the existence of the universe itself, the purpose of existence, that is, in order to achieve a certain ideal, or to achieve a certain purpose, and consciously strive to run the track for it. Secondly, the true meaning of the existence of the universe life itself, the existence of existence, in order to achieve the wise man's conscious realization of the reality of truth, the realization of the ideal of transcending the existence of the universe life and metamorphosis sublimation.

This concept is embodied through many questions related to actual existence, or reflecting the objective existence in nature, the whole with actual content, or to all objects or phenomena, etc., in the form of intrinsic thinking.

For example, "Where did I come from?", "Why was I born here?", "Where will my life go after I die? What is the true meaning of life?", "What is the true meaning of life?", "What is the true meaning of life? What is the true meaning of the existence of life in the universe? What is the true meaning of the existence of life in the universe?" and "Where is the ultimate destination of my life?

It is a question that cannot be answered directly through perception. It is a question that can be answered through rational logical reasoning under a priori conditions, and cannot be contradicted by empirical evidence.

It is the search of human reason for the most universal aspects and ultimate causes of things. It is the philosophy of life that has been explored in metaphysics, philosophy, science, theology, and religious philosophy.

Therefore, the beliefs or behaviors (folk customs) that have been passed down from one group or society to another with symbolic or special meanings, in different cultural environments and ideological contexts, have given rise to many diverse speculations.

And according to the predetermined, all the objects or phenomena that exist objectively in nature, the specious explanation, that is, according to the known scientific facts and scientific principles, on the natural phenomenon studied and its regularity, the speculation and explanation.

It is a doctrine of faith or trust in human things or concepts, and it is used to teach the world, to make people believe in a temporary, but acceptable explanation.

For example, religions will claim that wine is the blood

of God and bread is the body of God, so that people can feel and experience it, and after the rituals have been passed down for many years, they will extend the so-called rituals and moral norms, and develop customary culture until they are enlightened and transformed into the current laws and social norms.

In the beginning, these were just a few people, for their own benefit, the fictitious concept of an objective existence in nature, all objects or phenomena, and worship, and worship as a rule and guide for speech and action.

Therefore, different cultures and different people have different views on the real meaning of life existence itself, or the value of life existence, or the understanding of the general life experience, or the purpose of life existence.

This question is often intertwined with philosophical, religious, and scientific reflections on and explorations of the existence of life itself, the interactions and interactions between human relationships, the state of consciousness and happiness, and concepts such as symbols, ontology, values, teleology, ethics, good and evil, free will, the existence of God, the concept of God, the soul, and life after death.

Science is the study of all objects or phenomena that exist objectively in the natural world, and it is based on experimentation and logical reasoning to find unified and exact objective laws and truths.

It also studied the formation of recommendations for the pursuit of happiness and related moral concepts. Another humanist formulation is "What is the meaning of my life existence itself?

This question of the self of the existence of life in the universe has been interpreted differently by countless philosophers throughout history, from ancient Greece to the Middle Ages to modern and contemporary times.

The concept of philosophy of life was first inspired by the works of scholars such as Artur Schopenhauer, Soren Aubert Kierkegaard, and Friedrich Nietzsche, and was born in 19th century Germany as a response to the rise of positivism and the theoretical focus of post-Confucianism. The philosophy of life movement is indirectly related to the subjective philosophical system of vital impulse, which was proposed by Henri Bergson and focuses on direct experience].

The first step to insist on is to avoid adopting the

doctrines of any one established religion, and its particular interpretations, as our starting point. We may then follow in their footsteps. Let us discuss them from several perspectives

(01) The De Mocritian view of life in happiness

This is a naturalist philosopher from the northern Aegean coast of ancient Greece, Democritus (Greek: Δημόκριτος, 460 BC-370 BC or 356 BC, English: Democritus).

He was the founder of "atomism", from which he started to establish epistemology. Democritus gained the knowledge or skill of natural scientists from many practices, and was the first encyclopedic scholar. An important representative of ancient materialistic thought. He advocated the theory that all matter in the universe is made up of tiny particles of atoms, and that atoms are the limit of separability of matter.

He believed that every object or phenomenon that exists in nature is composed of atoms, and that the essence of the whole world (in philosophy, essence) is an eternal attribute or set of attributes that make an entity or substance what it is.

And it necessarily exists, without which it loses its identity), just atoms and emptiness. The atoms are indivisible, not identical, and are the result of the highest logical thinking in the early days of analytical thinking to inquire and reflect on fundamental questions about life, knowledge, and values.

At the same time, it was one of the symbols of the flourishing of ancient Greek philosophy in the study of the universe, the principles of life, and the learning of principles (economic or business). Democritus believed that the origin of everything is the content, structure and development of the world of space-time itself, which is presented in the form of "atoms" and "emptiness".

The atom is the last indivisible particle of matter. All objects or phenomena in the universe that exist objectively in nature are composed of atoms in motion in the void. All objectively existing objects and phenomena are created by the union of atoms.

The atom is in perpetual motion, i.e., the motion is original and inherent to the atom itself. "Emptiness" is nothingness that exists independently of any condition and is constant and unchanging, and is a field of motion.

The atom is called "existence" and the "void" is called "non-existence", but "non-existence" is not the same as non-existence, only that the "void" is non-substantiated compared to the atom which is substantiated. In contrast, when measuring all objects or phenomena that exist objectively in nature, there is a basis or criterion for measuring things.

Moreover, the standard of the basis or criterion for measuring things changes, so that when you measure the objectively existing objects or phenomena in nature, the relativity presented is conditional, constrained, special, and changeable in meaning.

Therefore, the existence of any objectively existing object or phenomenon in nature, or the determination of its characteristics, properties, or authenticity, is not a mere, absolute determination, but must be considered in relation to another thing.

Therefore, from a certain position or perspective, the view of a thing or problem. Both "non-existence" and "existence" are real. The world is created by "atoms" in the swirling motion of emptiness. There are countless worlds in the universe that are constantly "created" and "destroyed".

The world in which man exists is nothing but the overall orbit of the universe, in which all the objects or phenomena that exist objectively in the natural world are in a new state of form or nature. Therefore, he claimed that man is a small universe (small world).

Therefore, he founded the happinessist view of life, in which he advocates that human beings, after careful consideration of all the evidence, deduce reasonable conclusions (rational atoms) by means of reasoning that is smooth and refined.

The two kinds of atoms constitute two kinds of understanding of the way a person thinks about and disposes of things, and they also form two kinds of happiness and joy, namely, physical happiness and mental happiness and joy.

Democritus considered necessary material pleasures to be reasonable. He said: "A life without feasting is like a long road without an inn. He also said: "One should deeply appreciate the vagaries of life.

It is often disturbed by many misfortunes and difficulties, by the disturbances it suffers, so that one should only arrange for a moderate fortune and limit one's great efforts to what is serious, not relaxed and necessary in observing the rules or mastering the standards.

But, according to Democritus, happiness and pleasure are not mere [sensual pleasures] and [material stimuli]; unrestrained material desires are dim and coarse atoms, and the result of stimulation refers to something that is unconditioned in the mind, unbounded in space and time, without beginning or end.

The infinite can exist only through the finite, but it cannot be reduced to a finite, simple quantity, which adds up to the total, or to the entire content, and therefore, although sometimes necessary, often brings about consequences contrary to the desire for human happiness. The purpose is to avoid the infinite consequences contained in this finite.

Without the will, there is no pursuit, and without the motivation to pursue, one will lose the goal of life, and without the goal, one will live in confusion and die in confusion, becoming a walking corpse, and without the soul, the existence of life will have no meaning.

Therefore, the will of personal love has always been endless, because everyone is trying to perfect himself.

Therefore, Democritus believed that the first thing to do is to abstain from desire. He says: "Temperance increases pleasure and makes enjoyment more intense. All unprofitable pleasures should be rejected.

Secondly, it is necessary to achieve peace of mind and tranquility. He believed that the purpose of life is the peace of the soul. This is not the same thing as happiness, which some people have misunderstood and confused with DeMarculite's mind.

Because of this peace, the soul lives in peace and tranquility, not without any reason: for example, fear of unverifiable, irrational, false beliefs without moral value, or other psychological reactions to external stimuli, such as joy, anger, grief, fear, love, hatred, etc.

Democritus believed that every object or phenomenon that exists objectively in nature is composed of atoms, and that the essence of the whole world [in philosophy, essence (English: Essence) is a kind or set of eternal properties that make an entity or a substance its root, and that it necessarily exists, without which it would lose its identity], is just atoms and emptiness.

It is just atoms and emptiness. The atoms are

indivisible and not identical. In nature, everything that happens has an innate cause, and this cause originally, that is, exists in the very being of all objects or phenomena that exist objectively in nature.

The enjoyment of the mind is the result of the action of smooth and refined atoms, which is true happiness and joy, while the pursuit of material enjoyment is a false happiness and joy.

The atoms that constitute reason are sublime and permanent, while the latter are low and transient. The purpose and criterion of life is to seek spiritual happiness and to abstain from material desires.

The position on which Democritus based his study and analysis or criticism of problems and issues is not only different from the theistic view, that is, the view that spirit is everything, but also different from vulgar hedonism, but a rational happinessism, a happinessism based on moderation.

(02) The opposing views of life of the Cynics and the Cyrillicists

The founder of the Cynics was Antisthenes, who lectured in a stadium called Kunosarges, hence the name of the Cynics. Kuno is the Greek word for "dog".

At the same time, the name "cynic" signifies their way of life. In fact, the cynicism is a school of thought that has a distrust of the world and a negative attitude toward any object or phenomenon that exists in nature.

01.The Idea of Conformity

Why? Why did Antisthenes create the cynicism school? Because in his later years he lost confidence in the orthodox philosophy of analytical inquiry and reflection on the fundamental questions of life, knowledge, and values, and at that time he was no longer young and despised the things he had valued before. He did not want anything more, and wanted Greece to return to its original, original society.

Inspired by the result of this thinking, or cognitive mental process, Diogenes (a disciple of Antisthenes), almost naked, and without any supplementary offerings or equipment, traveled throughout Greece, enjoying all the gifts of nature, such as sunlight and warmth.

He gathered thousands of converts to his ideas and told them how extremely wrong and unconscionable this society was, and how it deserved to be exposed and criticized by metaphors and exaggerations of people or events.

The philosophers of the Cynic school, led by Antisthenes and Diogenes, proposed absolute personal spiritual freedom, despised all social falsehoods, polite and packaged customs and cultural norms, and lived an ascetic and simple life, and were ridiculed as poor dogs by the world at that time. Later on, it also refers to people with these characteristics in general.

What is the outcome of the cynic's thinking, or the main idea of the mental process of cognition? The main dogma of the cynic school is that one must get rid of worldly interests and pursue the only good worth having.

Cynics believe that true happiness is not based on the seemingly noble and elegant advantages of fleeting external circumstances. Happiness is available to everyone, and once possessed, it can never be lost again.

One does not need to worry about one's own health, nor does one need to worry about the suffering of others. Therefore, they advocate living a simple and pure life, returning to the so-called natural state, being self-sufficient, living independently, and imagining that one can leave the reality of society and live a life of poverty and contentment.

The cynical school of thought is the idea of being at peace with one's surroundings. It is similar to the story of Li Defu, who is recorded in the Chinese book "The Boat Studio". When he was an official in Jinling (now Nanjing and Jiangning County), he built several adjacent study rooms on the east side of his official residence, which looked from both sides as if they were in a boat, hence the name "Boat Studio".

One of the guests said after visiting: "You are said to be a hermit, but you are loyal and righteous, and have the intention of merit and fame; but you are not, but you are fond of the mountains and waters, and you are good at reading books, unlike ordinary officials.

De Fu smiled and replied, "I see the rituals of loyalty, filial piety and friendship as a vast, cloud-covered expanse of water, and my place of peace as a boat to carry me.

Once upon a time, Feng Yi was able to travel the great rivers with ease, and when the fisherman finished speaking, he left with the reeds. Both Feng Yi and the fisherman were high achievers who, having mastered the essence of the natural way, were able to live in peace with their situations.

In this way, he illustrates that his behavior is not contradictory, but rather, he returns to his original natural state, responds to the changes in the environment with his true nature, and then expresses it in his behavior in accordance with the circumstances.

It is because he understood the philosophy of following the path that he was able to "respond to the environment and be content in any situation".

Later on, the phrase "to be content with the situation" evolved and was used as a metaphor to describe the ability to be content with the environment in which one finds oneself. In fact, it refers to one of the challenges in life. Everyone's life is full of countless opportunities, but the key lies in whether one can be at peace with the situation, without any small desires in one's mind, so as to move forward as usual.

Therefore, it is impossible to judge by the general form of "hidden" or "not hidden". It is also because he understands the way of living by the way of life that he can be at ease with his situation. This reflects the gradual decline of the slave-holding system in the Greek city-states, and the negativity of their thinking.

02. Sensual hedonism

In the 4th century B.C., a Greek philosophy of sensual hedonism, the Cyrenaic school (English: Cyrenaics or Kyrenaics) (ancient Greek: Κυρηναϊκοί; Kyrēnaïkoí), was founded on the experience, facts, perceptions, and tested laws of nature and social phenomena.

But it was given its proper name by his eponymous grandson, Aristippus the Younger, but was founded by Aristippus of Cyrene, hence the name Cyrene.

This place is also the birthplace of Aristippus. This is one of the earliest doctrines of Socrates' Square. The Syllanites proposed that the only good that is inherent in the individual or in all objects and phenomena that exist objectively is happiness, which means not only the absence of pain, but also the feeling of positive pleasure.

In this case, short-lived pleasures, especially physical pleasures, are stronger than expected or remembered pleasures. But they do realize the value of social obligation and can derive pleasure from [altruistic] behavior.

Some people think that in today's society, people are

indifferent and the world is getting worse, and that hedonism is like materialistic hedonism, the idea of "living in confusion and dying in confusion".

What do they think is the meaning of life? What does a person come to this world for decades for? We seek to maximize the total amount of happiness in life, not the enjoyment of a certain moment, but the total amount of happiness in a lifetime.

The enjoyment mentioned here is not only material, but also includes spiritual and subjective satisfaction. It is not just about "having wine now and getting drunk today", caring only about the present and not about the future; it is about "having wine now and getting drunk today", caring not only about the present but also about the future. People should pursue a long and healthy life, because people who live long live longer, and of course they may get more happiness. Stay away from harmful environment and substances, these foods will reduce your happiness. Consider the consequences of your actions. The desire for a moment of pleasure may lead to endless consequences.

In their [altruistic] behavior, they are also willing to help others to enjoy their lives. Why? They believe that the success or failure of life often depends not only on themselves, but also on the environment, or on "others.

If the "others" go against each other in every way, it is bound to be unsuccessful. In their eyes, the so-called "gentleman's beauty of being an adult. If you know how to help the "other" to be happy, you will have an environment to create happiness in the "here", and it is easier to realize happiness together, so that the goal of mutual use is established and the total amount is maximized. The idea of helping the "other" to enjoy is both altruistic and self-serving in the act of altruism.

As the Greek philosopher Iberoglossus argued, life is ultimately about pleasure. However, pleasure here does not mean sex and drugs, but rather the absence of pain. He believes that there are two kinds of happiness, one short-lived and the other long-lasting. A thirsty person feels happy when he drinks water, and a tired person feels happy when he lies down to rest.

In addition to this short-lived happiness, there is also a lasting happiness, which leads to a truly happy life. This lasting happiness means a state without pain and without intense deprivation.

Therefore, this view of the Cyrillic school: the act of helping others and altruistic behavior, we can still see in everyday life, this lasting happiness, still prevails, on the bus, we can see young people get off the bus, help pregnant women and elderly people to carry things, also have seen many people give their seats to women holding children, also from time to time encounter kind people, help to guide the way, and, tirelessly explain the route These people have a common characteristic after helping others, and that is a positive feeling of joy from the heart.

It is obvious that after helping others, these people appear happy and indescribably happy. In fact, we can often experience this positive feeling of joy, a warm and comforting feeling that comes over us after helping others. Why, then, does helping others make people happy?

The happiness we are referring to here is not, of course, decadent nihilism, but the happiness that comes from temporarily paralyzing oneself with sex and drugs, drinking, dancing, and gambling, that is, the happiness that has after-effects.

The Cynicism of the same period as the Cyrannian school holds the opposite view. As stated above, the Cyrannians were hedonists who believed that happiness was the highest of all the things that people did, thought, and felt every day, especially physical happiness.

Especially physical happiness, which they consider more intense and desirable than spiritual happiness. Happiness is the only good in life, and pain is the only one who behaves improperly and fiercely.

Socrates considered noble moral behavior, and good moral qualities, as the only good for mankind, but he also accepted utilitarianism to a limited extent, making pleasure a secondary goal to the norms and standards of behavior and conduct that should be followed in the common life of mankind.

Aristippus and others who rely on common interests or beliefs, perform specific tasks, or follow specific standards in the pursuit of common organizational goals, seize this point and make enjoyment the only ultimate goal of life, denying that virtue has any substantial intrinsic value hidden within things.

03. The inquiry into the forms of thinking that reflect the nature of happiness is divided into four general categories.

For this kind of study of the things that are the target

of certain actions or thoughts, the objective laws and truths based on experiments and logical reasoning, as well as the positive thinking about the meaning of the existence of the self and the search for a bright and positive life oriented to the position of liberation, the necessity of recognizing this kind of lasting happiness refers to the state of no pain and no strong deprivation.

It is the happiness that comes from a positive feeling of joy in the heart. It is a form of thinking that reflects the nature of happiness by deconstructing the "whole", and is divided into four general categories.

03-1. The existence of the "altruism" gene

Researchers have found that there is an "altruism" gene in humans, which can promote the acceptance of "dopamine" by the human body, thus giving a good feeling to the brain, therefore, the kind of happiness that humans experience after helping others may originate from this gene, causing the receptors (also known as receivers, a biochemical concept, refers to a class of molecules that can transmit extracellular signals and produce specific effects in dopamine").

Dopamine is a neurotransmitter in the hypothalamus

and pituitary glands, a chemical used to help cells transmit impulses that have the effect of transmitting excitement and happy information.

Why some people are addicted to sweets and others are addicted to gambling, this may be related to the psychological effects of dopamine. There is a "nucleus accumbens" in the deep part of our brain, which is our "pleasure center" and is responsible for releasing "dopamine" in our brain.

In fact, dopamine is not the same as happiness, but the reason for feeling happy is the "reward prediction error". This wave-like dopamine movement encodes reward-related information in a hierarchical manner, thereby enhancing dopamine for learning and producing more efficient and accurate motivation.

When we feel happy about something, the brain stores the memory, and the next time we are faced with it, we quickly release the signal that it will make you happy, and when you do it, you will feel happy again.

At the same time, the human body has a reward mechanism, when you experience the pleasure, the brain will remember the pleasure, and at the same time to give the experience of operating again, this is also the dopamine has an addictive effect.

Once a large amount of dopamine is secreted, the object of the impulse slowly becomes something that is important to you, that is, "dopamine" will begin to hijack your attention, the brain will only think about how to get.

For example, you feel happy after exercising, and the brain will motivate you to do the next activity in order to get this comfortable emotional experience again, or if someone feels happy in a cigarette, then it is very addictive after repeated behavior.

03-2. "Self-worth" is realized

Self-worth refers to the relationship between a person's life and social activities in which he or she contributes to society and then society and others affirm his or her existence as a human being. It includes the dignity of the person and the material and spiritual conditions to affirm the dignity of the person.

After helping others, one's own behavior improves the situation with others, which makes the helper feel that one's self-worth has been affirmed and one's behavior is meaningful, which will undoubtedly give one a positive experience.

In the evolutionary process of life's metamorphosis and sublimation, the "ego" structure arises from the need to evaluate one's own ability. In an environment where individuals compete with each other for certain purposes, whether they "compete with others for their own benefit" or "leave quickly to avoid danger or unfavorable situations" requires a mechanism to evaluate their own ability. If you are better than the other person, then you "fight with them for your own benefit".

If one is inferior to the other, then one "leaves quickly in order to avoid danger or unfavorable situations". However, if a person always chooses to "avoid", he will also lose the opportunity to win with each other for a certain purpose.

But the problem is that in the process of survival and adaptation, competition for a certain purpose can be seen everywhere and anytime.

For this reason, human beings have evolved the need for self-improvement and higher self-worth, and higher self-affirmation gives us the courage to engage in various affairs, to realize certain ideals or to achieve certain purposes, and to consciously work for the psychological state. It is also the maintenance and development of the nature of human consciousness that is the true realization of freedom.

The inner life itself has the contradiction between the consciousness and the material essence, which constitutes the inner essence of man, and its basic attribute is the neurological reaction of man, which is a combination of self-feeling, self-existence and feeling to the outside world, and the consciousness of maintaining and developing the self.

This makes the self-worth, the play of certainty, their own behavior, is meaningful, which will undoubtedly give people a positive experience.

03-3、The pleasure of relaxation by reducing stress

When people see others in pain and distress, sometimes put themselves in the shoes of the person suffering similar negative emotional experience, at this time if the victim is not helped, said also strange fast, the bystander worried about the emotional pressure, and personally experienced the anxiety and pain experience, also can not disappear, so this feeling will prompt people to make the impulse to help others behavior, in order to obtain internal relief and relief.

Sometimes parents are more anxious than those who have lost their children; for example, many parents have the experience of losing their children, and the moment they leave their sight, their children are inexplicably gone, and that moment always makes people's heart beat fast, their minds empty, and they are disillusioned and in a trance.

According to a survey conducted by the Child Welfare League, as many as 70% of parents have lost their children, with children aged 2 to 4 years old being the most likely to get lost. Although most children can be found within 15 minutes of being lost, it is becoming increasingly difficult to locate them as the time of loss lengthens.

Amusement parks, hypermarkets, food markets, supermarkets, and crowded places are really the easiest places to lose a child, and an excited child may run off to play with the amusement facilities in an instant.

Sometimes in a crowded place, small children get lost in a panic, holding their parents' hands wrongly, so every holiday there are always at least 20 or 30 broadcasts looking for their mothers.

Especially when you go to a big store to buy things and check out, your attention is mostly focused on the accounting with the cashier, and sometimes you neglect to pay attention to your children. Similarly, when a family goes to the mall.

It is always when they hear the announcer calling for a lost child that they are alerted to immediately dial their cell phones and call the parents who are looking for their child. When the child saw the mother, she cried out for her mother and immediately threw herself into her arms.

The anxiety and pain that the helper experienced when she saw the stranger reunite with her child must have made her realize the joy of the child's mother who was relieved and crying with joy.

3-4、The additional experience brought by helping behavior

Technology is becoming more and more prosperous, and social civilization is changing rapidly. Values determine, regulate, and constrain the needs, motives, and desires of personal tendencies in the middle and lower levels, and it is the intention of human motives and behavior patterns.

Once determined, they in turn influence and regulate the further needs of people. For example, some adolescents with inadequate self-esteem nowadays will increase their appearance scores (vanity) by various means, such as buying brand-name products, worshipping movie and song stars, being strange and different, forming groups of friends and people, and doing all kinds of out-of-the-ordinary behaviors.

These signs of vanity often influence the psychology of human values and continue into adulthood. Until an idea is absolutely denied, the perspective, context, judgment, and meaning of that idea are all influenced by the idea.

The value of an idea lies in the degree to which it is recognized and its meaning, which is the most simple and real assessment of the human mind.

This is the simplest and most real assessment of human thinking. It also determines whether an idea is great and whether it can be a source of value. Therefore, the analysis of self-worth is self-confidence, self-love, and self-esteem. These three are in this order; self-confidence is built before self-love can be built.

Self-esteem can be built only after self-love is established. Self-confidence is trusting in one's own ability. Ability to bring positive value to a person, anything that can bring a lot of value and meaning to oneself, one will usually cherish and love very much.

For example, sometimes helping someone does not necessarily bring us much happiness, but the praise, encouragement, or improved personal image that comes from helping someone brings us a great deal of happiness. Values are a system of psychological tendencies that people use to distinguish between good and bad, right and wrong, and their importance.

It reflects man's evaluation of the rights and wrongs of objective things and their importance, unlike animals, which can only passively adapt to the environment.

Unlike animals, which can only passively adapt to the environment, human beings not only have the ability to recognize the environment and self, and the clarity of cognition, but also know what to do and what to choose, discover the meaning of things to themselves, design themselves, and determine and achieve their goals. These are the things or phenomena that have a positive meaning for the individual, for the person or group, that are valued by people, or that make people feel fulfilled.

It becomes a value that people respect or are interested in pursuing. Therefore, it is a psychological process in which an individual's behavior is affirmed and recognized by a certain person or group, and praised in terms of behavior and value standards, so that he or she and others or groups tend to be in agreement. Only when we cherish and care for it will we respect the existence of a sense of self-worth and identity.

03-4-1. Theory of Knowledge

The Cyrannian school is known for its philosophical skepticism. They reduced logic to a basic doctrine of standards of truth. They believed that we can interpret known facts and principles and principles in our own words, texts, or other symbols, with immediate sensory experiences (e.g., I have a sweet sensation right now), but that these sensations lead us to know nothing about the nature of objects (e.g., honey is sweet).

They also deny that we can understand, not only understand the matter, but also see it from the other person's point of view and understand the experience of others.

They also believe that all acts of "knowing" and "recognizing" a subject, in order to know with certainty, and that these knowings have the potential to be used for specific purposes. It means that the ability to become familiar with something through experience or association is a direct result of one's own feelings, which are purely subjective, whether they are painful, indifferent or pleasurable.

These are things that exist objectively in all objects or phenomena of nature, whether they are violent, calm or mild, according to the concrete facts and conditions that exist in front of them.

In addition, they are the comprehensive perception and cognition of the individual's state of mind and body and the changes of people, events and things in the environment by using mental activities such as sensation, perception, thinking and memory, and can never objectively describe the world.

Therefore, sensation is the act of "cognition" and "recognition" of a certain subject in order to be sure of the knowledge, which is the thinking activity of the human brain to reflect the characteristics and connections of objective things, and to reveal the meaning and effect of things on people, and these knowings have the potential ability for a specific purpose, and this is the only standard of use and behavior, so the only goal of each person should be happiness.

03-4-2. Ethics

The Cyrannian brings a universal goal for all people, and that is happiness. In addition, all reactions to individual characteristics of objective reality (sounds, colors, smells, etc.).

A certain stimulus from the material world acts directly on certain sensory organs of the organism, such as light causes vision, sound waves cause hearing; the nerve impulses caused by the stimulus in the senses are transmitted by the sensory nerves to certain parts of the cerebral cortex to produce sensation.

The sensations are all the same and short-lived. It is thus clear that past and future pleasures are not real to us, while present pleasures are not different in kind. As for the higher pleasures, which Socrates speaks of as the best and purest, the Cyrannians deny that there is such a distinction, and emphasize that bodily pleasures are clearer, more uncomplicated, more powerful, more immediate, and more worthy of study or praise.

Thus, short-lived pleasures, especially physical pleasures, are the only benefits for human beings. However, some of these acts that bring immediate pleasure can also bring pain.

Therefore, a wise person should control pleasure instead of abusing it, otherwise it will lead to pain. This requires an individual to use mental activities such as feeling, perception, thinking, and memory, and to be aware of, recognize, and judge the state of one's body and mind and the changes of people, events, and things in the environment, in order to evaluate the various kinds of pleasure in life.

We should be aware of the ideas, culture, morals, customs, arts, institutions and habitual behaviors that have been passed down from generation to generation and from history. We should pay attention to laws and customs that have an invisible influence and control over people's social behavior, because even if these things themselves do not have a substantial connotation of value hidden within things, failure to conform to laws, rules, customs, etc., can lead to the imposition of unpleasant punishments on others.

However, in the process of cognitive activities, such as analysis, synthesis, judgment, and reasoning based on images and concepts, logic must abandon what is considered wrong or unjust.

The individual makes a choice based on his or her own memory or external senses such as sight, smell, hearing, and touch, and then makes a judgment based on his or her own worldview, morality, and values that he or she has developed over the years.

On the contrary, friendship (an emotion that comes from a two-way (or reciprocal) relationship, i.e., an emotion that is shared by both parties and must be maintained together; any unilateral show of affection or deviation cannot be called friendship) and justice (righteousness that is in accordance with the righteousness of the heart) are useful because of the pleasure they provide.

Thus, the Cyrillicists believed in the hedonistic value of [social obligation] and [altruistic] behavior. Like many modern utilitarians, they combined a psychological distrust of universal, right and wrong judgments, and a firm belief in all these distinctions.

They believe that all these distinctions are based on laws and practices of thought, culture, morality, custom, art, institutions, and behavior that have been handed down from generation to generation and from history, and that this is an unwavering principle that wise people should pursue pleasure.

3.There are three general points why the value of self-affirmation is important.

When self-affirmation, self-improvement, and maintaining high self-worth become a need, it will motivate us to enhance our self-worth by improving our skills, or winning the appreciation of others, while promoting personal growth and progress.

But it can also make us feel physically or mentally uncomfortable when our self-affirmation is low, so the value of self-affirmation is important in three ways.

First, the first manifestation of why self-affirmation is

important:.

One, the first manifestation of why self-affirmation is important is that when people are low in self-affirmation, things do not go well, they feel very painful physically or mentally, and they want to enhance their self-affirmation.

Therefore, when our external image, mental outlook, personality characteristics and behavioral performance and other aspects of recognition, appreciation and affirmation of self-evaluation is low, we do not dare to engage in a lot of work, do not dare to compete, but also gave up a lot of opportunities to train, less opportunity to train, the ability not to improve, many needs can not be met, ultimately leading to lower self-worth, forming a vicious circle.

Second, the second reason why self-worth is important.

To engage in any work, we need a certain amount of self-worth and self-affirmation (refers to the individual's recognition, appreciation and affirmation of their external image, mental outlook, character traits and behavioral performance, but also self-evaluation of whether a specific job can be used), if self-worth and self-affirmation is not enough, we dare not to engage in a lot of work, many needs can not be met, but also can not go to realize their We are unable to realize our full potential.

Third, the third reason why self-worth is important.

Self-affirmation directly affects our perceptions, emotions, and behaviors toward objects. In a competitive situation, if our self-worth and self-affirmation are high and we believe we can handle the situation on our own, we will feel less threatened by the opponent in terms of cognition and less nervous and scared in terms of emotion.

On the contrary, if you feel that you cannot handle the situation on your own, you will cognitively feel that the opponent is too strong and may not be able to succeed, so you will be very nervous and scared, resulting in poor performance, and even want to run away and give up.

Whether it's giving up or failing, it will further reduce self-worth and self-affirmation effectiveness.

Some people may take the easy way out to maintain superficial self-esteem and make themselves feel better, but this also deprives them of the opportunity to improve their self-worth and self-affirmation, keeping them at their original level of timidity and weakness.

But the problem is, if we want to engage in more challenging and difficult work in the future, a higher sense of self-worth and self-affirmation is a prerequisite for us to take risks.

Although the environment we live in is completely different from the environment our ancestors lived in during the evolutionary process, the environment we need to adapt to, the work we do, the people we interact with, and even ourselves, are not our "competitors".

Our self-worth directly affects our perceptions, emotions, and behaviors toward the environment, our work, our friends and family, and ourselves, and these are the foundations of our success and happiness.

4. Later Cyrene School

The later Cyrannian school changed under Anneliese, Hegesias, and Teodorus. For Anneliese, happiness is achieved through personal acts of fulfillment, which arise for the purpose of seeking satisfaction. But Anneliese valued family, country, friendship, and gratitude as providing happiness even when these things demanded sacrifice.

Hegesias believed that happiness is impossible to achieve. Therefore, the goal of life became the avoidance of pain and sorrow. If traditional values such as [wealth], [poverty], [freedom] and [slavery] lack emotion, interest and concern, they produce more happiness than pain. For Hegesias, the Cyrannian school was only the most irrational strategy for taking measures, countermeasures, to cope with the existing painful conditions of life.

For the atheist Theodorus, the goal of life was [spiritual] pleasure, not [physical] pleasure, and he placed greater emphasis on the need for moderation and righteousness. He was also known as an atheist.

In fact, all of these philosophers strove to challenge the Iberian school, which succeeded in establishing a philosophical system that was more comprehensive and complex than the views they advocated.

In the time of Hegesias, the Syriac school had developed in the form of skepticism, Ibigülism, and in a manner similar to Buddhist teachings. In fact, it bears a striking resemblance to the Buddhist doctrine (English:

dogma), also translated as theorem, creed, faith, dogma, doctrine, thesis, a principle or group of principles attributed to an authority that is considered absolutely correct and indisputable, especially the concept of the Four Noble Truths and suffering. Thus, it is possible that Hegesiades was directly influenced by Buddhist teachings.

The basic philosophical tenet of this school is sensationalism. Its founder, Hieronymus, believed that the purpose of life is to find happiness, and was therefore called the "Only Sense of Happiness". By happiness, they meant both physical and spiritual happiness.

However, they believed that the important happiness is physical happiness and immediate and present happiness. Happiness is not uncontrolled, and people should be the masters of happiness, but not let happiness dominate people, otherwise they will get pain.

The reaction to an objective reality with individual characteristics (sound, color, smell, etc.). The nerve impulses caused by stimuli in the senses are transmitted by the sensory nerves to certain parts of the cerebral cortex to produce sensations, which is an important feature of this school of thought.

5. Iberian Happiness Theory of Life

A distant parallel to the Hellenistic school is the late Greek philosopher Ibigüel, who advocated a happinessist view of life. He believed that it is human nature to seek happiness and avoid suffering, and when it comes to happiness, he said: Happiness is the beginning and purpose of a happy life. Because we believe that happiness is the highest good, we start from happiness in all our choices.

Our ultimate goal is to be happy, and we judge all goodness by the perception that comes from contact with all objects or phenomena that exist objectively in nature and are reflected in the human consciousness through the activity of thought.

Epicurus (Ἐπίκουρος, 341 BC-270 BC) was an ancient Greek philosopher and founder of the Epicurean school. Epicurus succeeded in developing the hedonism of Aristippus and combining it with the atomism of Democritus. The main purpose of his doctrine was to achieve a state of undisturbed tranquility.

Iberoglossus is well known for his hedonism, but the word "hedonism" often gives the wrong impression that he lived a life of unchecked debauchery, but in fact his life was the exact opposite of what we imagine.

Strictly speaking, Iberoglou is indeed a hedonist, but he is the result of a process of cognitive activity based on the analysis, synthesis, judgment, and reasoning of images and concepts.

This is a psychological process in which an individual uses his or her senses, perception, thinking, memory, and other mental activities to become aware of and understand his or her own physical and mental state and the changes in people, events, and objects in the environment.

In terms of the discipline of analyzing and reflecting on the fundamental issues of life, knowledge, and values, this is indeed hedonism. But the happiness he seeks is completely different from the small, insignificant happiness that we often associate with happiness.

According to Ibigülı, all happiness is good and good. His view, in logic, is that authenticity requires the judgment that happiness itself must be good, even though some of the actions that accompany it may be bad.

Ibbijuel argues that the positive purpose of human life

is happiness, and that happiness is the criterion for judging human good and bad. Ibbijuel does not present any reasons or evidence to support or deny certain matters in order to prove this point. He only said: "Happiness is something that all human beings are born to feel.

This is the only basis for his statement. Upon hearing these statements, one might be tempted to think that Iberoglou meant that happiness is all that exists in life, as if he were promoting the supremacy of happiness.

However, a closer look at the actual meaning of Ibbi Guru's words reveals that his definition is somewhat unique, separate, and different from others, and that he subdivides happiness into [worthy] and [unworthy] pleasures.

According to the philosophy of Iberoglossus, the premise of Iberoglossus' hedonism begins with "the exclusion of the need for physical or mental suffering", so he sets the state of "no physical or mental suffering" as the state of "already feeling happiness".

Thus, in the same vein of thinking and consciousness, to exclude all physical or mental suffering we have is to satisfy the most basic and intense of needs. Happiness is the satisfaction of a need.

Therefore, the most important happiness is the satisfaction of this intrinsic need. And the importance of happiness must be determined by what needs it can satisfy. That is, what is the most basic and strongest of all our needs? It is to be able to be happy by eliminating the physical or mental feeling of being very uncomfortable.

This type of happiness can be obtained by getting rid of painful states such as hunger, thirst, cold, etc. It is also called static happiness, which means the state of happiness that is near or has been reached after the physical or mental suffering has been eliminated.

On the other hand, the happiness obtained by satisfying a need other than the original one, for example, the use of a certain food, not simply to relieve hunger, but to satisfy the desire to eat a particularly delicious food.

The happiness derived from this is called dynamic happiness because it is the feeling of happiness felt while satisfying the desire. Whether it is unpalatable food or delicious food, after eating it, you will be satisfied with the food you eat and drink, and you will be satisfied from the bottom of your heart.

However, only delicious food can bring us the pleasure of eating something that is materially or spiritually satisfying at the same time. In fact, the need for such dynamic pleasure is not necessarily necessary for us.

Even if we want to eat fried chicken for dinner today instead of rice and noodles, there are no serious consequences of not eating fried chicken; even if there is no fried chicken to eat, there are still many kinds of food that can satisfy our hunger.

Not only does Ibigülü believe that there are differences in the importance of happiness, but also in the magnitude of happiness felt. He believes that non-essential, dynamic happiness is not greater than static happiness.

Therefore, Iberoglou advocates that the happiness we should seek and value is the static happiness that can be obtained by relieving the body or mind of a very uncomfortable state. To further clarify, the release from a state of great physical or mental distress is not only the removal of physical pain from the concrete facts and conditions that exist in front of us.

Static happiness consists of "ataraxia," which is the

absence of mental turmoil, and "aponia," which is the absence of pain in the body. With a little bit of organization, it becomes clear why Iberoglossus is not the culinary expert we think he is.

If he had been a gourmet who loved luxurious food, he would have been more interested in dynamic pleasures, but Ibbi Guru says that we should be looking for static pleasures.

Ibbi Guru believes that in the long run, if a pleasure causes great physical or mental distress, it is better to give it up, no matter what kind of pleasure it is; even if the present physical or mental distress is great, if it produces great pleasure in the long run, then such physical or mental distress is worth enduring.

This means that in order to attain the ultimate true happiness, one should not now cling to the pleasures that come in the blink of an eye, as in the case of delicious food.

What we need is moderation that brings us greater joy afterwards, even if we have to endure temporary physical or mental hardship. Here is the reason why Ibigülü's hedonism cannot be defined simply by the word "pleasure".

Interestingly, the general impression of philosophers as rigid and unadapted is that they seem to be highly capable of judging and analyzing an event or person and then concluding that all intellectual fields are of value, but Iberoglou is different.

He believed that the act of "knowing" and "identifying" a subject, by which to know with certainty, and that these knowings have the potential ability to be used for specific purposes, including the need to study learning and philosophy, is not necessary, as is dynamic pleasure.

Likewise, he does not consider the pursuit of truth to be important. In contrast, Iberoglossus believed that there was no need for the deliberate pursuit of knowledge and emphasized that by living according to his own teachings, one could achieve a state of life in which no physical or spiritual feelings were very difficult and in which one became permanently happy and harmonious.

From the preceding analysis, it is clear that Ibigülü divides the zone of happiness into [dynamic happiness] and [static happiness]. Dynamic pleasure is the pleasure that arises when a desire is satisfied (e.g., the pleasure of eating a good meal), while static pleasure is the pleasure of being calm after a desire has been satisfied (e.g., the pleasure of eating a good meal).

At the same time, Iberoglou emphasizes that when we consider whether an action is interesting, curious or joyful, we must also consider the side effects that it entails. While seeking short-term pleasure, we must also consider the possibility of greater, longer-lasting and more intense pleasure.

He also emphasizes that while physical pleasures are mostly imposed on us, spiritual pleasures are at our disposal, so that making friends, appreciating art, etc., is also an ideal state and a passion for inner joy in the pursuit of a goal.

Self-desire must be restrained, and a peaceful state of mind can help us endure physical or spiritual suffering. According to Ibbi Gurudev, the highest state of ataraxia is reached when one is free from anything that causes great physical or mental suffering and when all desires are satisfied.

Ibigüérico believed in Democritus' atomic theory, but he did not believe that the movement of atoms, which is governed by various rules that arise of their own accord, is consistent with the implementation and development of instincts and does not have to be governed by natural laws through human institutions.

Ibigülü denies that the religion that takes advantage of man's wonder and awe at the mysteries of the universe and life, and constitutes a doctrine that exhorts good and punishes evil, and is used to teach the world and make people believe, denies that God is the author of the supreme law.

Therefore, it also belittles the principle of the inevitability and certainty of the connection and development of all objects or phenomena that exist objectively in nature, as well as their regular and definite tendency, under certain conditions.

Epicurus also agrees with Democritus on the "soul-atoms" that after death, the soul-atoms leave the body and are scattered everywhere, so that there is no life after death. He said, "Death has nothing to do with us, because as long as we exist, death will not come, and when death comes, we will no longer exist. Ibero-American, the author of the book

Therefore, Iberoglou thinks that the fear of death is irrational. It is because the activity of thinking about one's own death, which reflects the identity and connection of objective things and reveals the meaning and effect of death on human beings, is ignorance of death itself.

In short, the happiness and well-being that Ibigülü's point of view describes is conditional, first of all, on the satisfaction of certain material desires; but, in his view, the search for happiness does not require the satisfaction of all wishes and demands to obtain something, or to achieve a certain purpose.

It requires only a conscious desire for something that gives pleasure or satisfaction, or for an experience that is necessary for the preservation of life and health, and that is sufficient for all objects or phenomena that exist objectively in nature.

Iberoglossus also believed that in addition to material happiness, there should be spiritual happiness, which is a greater happiness in terms of the ideas and truths contained in certain things.

It is clear that Iberoglossus' happiness is different from the indulgence of the never-ending pursuit of contact with all objects or phenomena that exist objectively in nature, which produces perceptual enjoyment, but requires the maintenance of "physical health" and "tranquility of the soul.

This kind of happiness or satisfaction is the satisfaction of immediate material and spiritual needs, and the longing for future goals of life, the expectation of satisfying higher material and spiritual needs. The highest ideal state of life is also the expression of morality.

He says that "health of the body" and "tranquility of the soul" are the purpose of a happy life. It is for this purpose that we strive to avoid things that cause great physical or mental distress and a strong unpleasant emotion for perceiving or identifying danger or threat.

Once we reach this situation, the "disturbance of the soul" will disappear and disperse. The doctrine of Ibigüeyuru has not developed the tradition of studying a certain object as the scope of study, and seeking to obtain unified and exact objective laws and truths based on experiments and logical reasoning.

However, its attitude of analyzing, synthesizing, judging, and reasoning freely on the basis of images and concepts, and its practice of opposing superstition, were always respected by some members of the upper classes in the early Roman Empire.

Using a form of thinking that deconstructs the "whole" to reflect the nature of happiness, we can clearly see that Iberoglossus' doctrine of happiness refers to a state in which there is no great physical or mental distress or intense deprivation. It is happiness that comes from a positive feeling of joy in the heart.

However, today, the hedonism of Epicureanism has distorted the doctrine of Epicurean pleasure, and without the limitations of individualism, the practice of pleasure does not have to be limited to the pursuit of personal pleasure or satisfaction; this "pleasure" can include activities based on human relationships and group structures, from which people can derive satisfaction.

Thus, "pleasure" is understood to be the pleasure of being drunk today, and is primarily concerned with physical pleasures, such as eating, drinking, and sexual gratification. Therefore, it is transformed into a meaning of disapproval or bad evaluation, and is used ironically to describe those who only know how to pursue sensual pleasures without knowledge and ignorance of reasoning.

6. The humanist's philosophy of life

The ancient Roman writer Cicero has already used this word. The German philosophers of the Enlightenment era referred to human beings collectively as humanity, and the humanists of that time called themselves humanists.

Humanism, however, did not appear until 1808. Humanism was the central idea of the Renaissance, the first prototype of humanism.

Humanism in its entirety refers to the more medieval ideas that have been used in European history and philosophy, mainly to describe and visualize things using various rhetorical devices between the 14th and 16th centuries.

As a generalization of history, the idea of an unimaginable, widespread, and common nature, is a form of thinking that serves to specify the actual existence of an object, or the actual existence of an area or class of things, events, or relationships with actual content, reflecting the nature of things.

Humanism, a term that actually emerged very late,

comes from the Latin humanitas, which affirms the normal emotions and rationality of human beings, things or phenomena that have a positive meaning for people or groups, are valued by people, or can make people feel satisfied, become objects of respect or interest, demand the joy of the human world, demand the emancipation of human personality and freedom and equality, and promote the idea of human nature. It demands the enjoyment of human happiness, personal liberation and freedom and equality, and the promotion of human sensual experience and rational thinking.

Generally speaking, today's historians regard the period from the 14th to the 16th centuries as a period reflecting a European intellectual and cultural movement (from the existentialist perspective, culture is the description of the way of being of a person or group of persons.

People exist in nature, but also in history and time; time is an important platform for a person or group of people to exist in nature) and social changes during this period are called the Renaissance, and a social movement with the direct aim of affecting the physical and mental development of people is called Humanism.

From another point of view, humanism is not a unified, but a brief and complete expression of an abstract, universal idea that serves as a specification of an entity, an event or a relationship, or a synthesis of many identical or similar people and things into a category, a language or word that is distinguishable and within itself, but independent of human consciousness, of something in the objective material world.

For, in the period between the 14th and 16th centuries, there were many different people who called themselves or were called humanists, and their worldviews, and their conceptions of people, could be very different.

Some humanists, because of their cultural backgrounds or life experiences, form perceptions and opinions about people and things that are very contradictory to each other (English: Contradiction) is the inconsistency between two or more concepts, perspectives, ideas or actions of people who express things, facts or say things in a structured way, and there is a big difference. There are humanist schools of thought [in liberal democracy] and [in Protestantism] or [in Catholicism].

Even at the time of Rome, there was what today can be called humanism, the objective existence of which is reflected in the consciousness of man, the result of the activity of thought, or the formation of a trend of views and systems of concepts. Humanism at that time was, of course, very different from the humanism of the Renaissance or the Enlightenment.

The humanism of Johann Wolfgang Goethe and Friedrich Schiller is often called historicism, while the humanism of Wilhelm von Humboldt, which reflects the nature of things, is completely different from the humanism of the Enlightenment.

The philosophy of the Renaissance period was regarded as the result of the reflection of objective existence in human consciousness through thinking activities, or as the basis of the formation of viewpoints and systems of concepts, while the science of William von Humboldt's period was regarded as the reflection of objective existence in the individual's use of sensory, perceptual, thinking, memory and other mental activities, the comprehensive awareness and knowledge of his own physical and mental state and the changes of people, things and objects in the environment. The result is produced through thinking activities that reflect the nature of things.

Humanism is a disciplinary theory that analyzes and reflects on fundamental questions about life, knowledge, and values. For example, "Is there an objective standard of morality?" , "What is science?" and a viewpoint and basic cognitive orientation of an individual or society toward society as a whole and personal knowledge.

Humanism takes as its starting point the interests, values, and dignity of the human person, especially the individual. For humanism, tolerance, non-violence, and freedom of thought are the most important principles of interpersonal relations.

Especially in the fifteenth and sixteenth centuries, the period known as the Renaissance of Europe. At this time, the object of holistic, fundamental, and critical inquiry into the realm of reality and man shifted from being oriented toward God to being oriented toward man and nature.

In the midst of the struggle to criticize theology and philosophy of the academy, humanism and natural philosophy, centered on human beings and nature, flourished, opening up a new historical stage in Europe for the study of fundamental questions of life, knowledge, and values through analytical reflection and introspection.

The basic spirit of humanism is to elevate the status of man and to depreciate the status of God. They praise the positive meaning and usefulness of the human object in relation to the subject, that is, the first two phrases in contrast to each other from two contradictory aspects, expressing the opposite and opposing the meaning of human contempt.

To praise the reality of a society in which man has bad manners, and the life of an attitude of evaluation towards it, and to oppose a means of achieving certain specific ends by depriving certain basic needs and desires, especially the prohibition of sexual desires, is the manifest use of this 'term', especially in reference to asceticism associated with religion

It is the ability of a person in a normal state of mind to face a situation with confidence and courage and to perform it effectively in order to obtain the desired result, and the act of "knowing" and "identifying" a subject in order to have a confident knowledge that is used for a specific purpose.

It is the ability to become familiar with, and to understand, something through experience or association, and to oppose blind faith; it promotes the liberation of the individual, the shackles and the feudal hierarchy.

Enjoying the reality of happiness in the concrete facts and situations that exist in front of us, pursuing physical happiness, and satisfying the objective existence of things or situations of earthly life, is what humanists understand.

This is the nature of human beings to reflect their love and attachment, and it is also the important content of the essential thought form of life, and more importantly, the most basic way of existence of the universe and life itself.

Petrarch exclaims: I do not want to become God, or to live in eternity, or to hold heaven and earth in my arms, the kind of glory that belongs to man. For me, that is enough. This is all I seek. I am a mortal myself, and I ask only for mortal happiness.

The Decameron

In 1348, a terrible plague broke out in Florence, Italy. Every day, even every hour, large numbers of corpses were transported outside the city. From March to July, more than 100,000 people died of the disease. The formerly beautiful and prosperous city of Florence, which was crowded with people, was now filled with corpses, deserted, and filled with graves.

This event left a deep impression on Boccaccio, a great Italian writer of that time. In order to remember this terrible human disaster, he wrote one of the most famous Italian short stories of the time, The Decameron, using the plague as a backdrop.

The stories in the Decameron are drawn from a wide range of sources, from historical events, medieval legends, and Eastern folk tales such as the Book of the Seven Philosophers and the Thousand and One Nights.

However, Boccaccio transplanted the plot of these stories to Italy and reworked and recreated them with humanist ideas. It was a common feature of humanist writers during the Renaissance period to criticize the corruption and decadence of the Church.

But compared to the forerunner Dante, Boccaccio's thought was more advanced and his criticism was more pointed.

In many of his stories, Boccaccio directs his criticism at the Catholic Church and religious theology, unmistakably unveiling the sacredness of the Church and exposing to the world's eyes all the dark deeds of the monks, such as extravagance, extortion, priesthood trading, and heresy suppression.

It is noteworthy that in the first two stories of the Decameron, Boccaccio, with a sharp and unmistakable brush, mocks the corruption and decadence of the Church.

A notary who has done so much evil and has lost his conscience is beatified by the Church after his death, after he has confessed his sins and made up a lot of nonsense.

A Jewish man, who visits Rome in secret, learns from what he hears and sees that from the Pope, the bishops to the clergy, all of them are drunkards, unscrupulous, lustful, and traffickers in human beings, and that Rome has become a "melting pot of all sins" and "Christianity is full of sin and darkness. These two stories set the tone for the entire work.

But Boccaccio does not only mock the monks' vices, but also attacks their hypocrisy and treachery. He reveals vividly, in many interesting stories, that the monks chastise the priests for their lustful thoughts in order to scare them away so that the black-robed wolves can take advantage of the situation and seduce the virtuous women.

The servants of the gods condemned the usurers, saying, "After death, those who exploit with heavy interest will be sent to hell for eternity," just to make others spit out their ill-gotten gains so that they could fill their pockets.

Boccaccio did not only attack the personal character of monks. He analyzes wrong or reactionary thoughts, words, and deeds with reason and justification, and then rejects them and portrays them in depth. He gets to the bottom of the matter and is unrelenting, pointing his finger at the Holy See and religious doctrine.

He shows in some stories that the monks are moral, full of righteousness and morality, but in their bones they are thieves and hypocrites. The root cause of this is the canon of the Church, the hypocrisy and anti-humanity of the canon. Boccaccio's criticism of the Church expresses the dissatisfaction of the urban commoners with the supreme divine authority of the time.

The story of love between a man and a woman plays an important role in the Decameron. Boccaccio recounts many vivid and interesting stories that illustrate that medieval asceticism, which preached love as a sin and divine love and heavenly happiness, was contrary to the laws of nature and stifled human nature.

"Of all the forces of nature, the power of love is the most unrestrained and unstoppable. True love is not a sin, but a reasonable, humane, noble and valuable thing. Therefore, divine love is no substitute for love, and man has the right to enjoy love and happiness in this world.

The Decameron also attacked feudal privileges and the inequality between men and women. Boccaccio is convinced that the nobility of man is not determined by his birth, but by his talent. Even the horseman who served the king was as well mannered and intelligent as the king.

Many stories describe how in the struggle for happiness, people of humble origins often defeated feudal lords and nobles with their own wisdom and perseverance. Boccaccio reveals the following truth.

"Poverty does not erode the noble qualities of man," "A dignified and beautiful appearance cannot conceal folly,"

"Sages often emerge from the poor," but "nobility makes people lose their ambition," and "the sons of the emperor's family are only worthy of herding pigs and sheep.

Boccaccio also rejects the medieval monasticism, which tainted the stereotype of women as sinners, and praises women as beautiful creatures of nature, advocating that women should enjoy equal status with men.

The concept of comprehensive human development is also embodied in the Decameron. In Boccaccio's rational and logical thinking, in order to obtain the desired result, man must have the confidence and courage to face the present situation calmly, and quickly and comprehensively understand the reality, analyze a variety of feasible solutions, then judge the best solution, and implement it effectively.

Therefore, it is emphasized that people should be well-educated, versatile, harmoniously developed, healthy, handsome, intelligent and brave. This was the ideal of human being during the Renaissance.

In addition, there is another aspect, which is called indulgence. Boccaccio said: Among the forces of nature that exist, the power of love is unrestrained and unstoppable. Theology holds that the demand for the realization of man's physical happiness is short-lived, false, a manifestation of evil and foolishness.

Humanists, on the other hand, believe that the survival and meaning of man lies in the fulfillment of this nature, which is entirely appropriate and a prerequisite for the existence of the world.

It can be said that the humanist, being in a relatively unfavorable position in the existing organization, social state, or mode of operation, is strongly dissatisfied, thus generating the concept of negation and urgently seeking a radical change of the status quo.

Therefore, the objectively existing social consciousness is reflected in the individual's self-consciousness, and through the process of analysis, synthesis, judgment, reasoning and other cognitive activities on the basis of social consciousness images and concepts, and the results or the formation of views and conceptual systems.

It is a "great reaction" to medieval theological asceticism. Its influence and results are so far-reaching and extensive that it has become an integral part of traditional Western culture and spirituality.

However, this awakening to the meaning of the existence of life is still at the stage of the awareness of the meaning of the existence of the will of the individual, and has not yet entered the stage of the awakening to the meaning of the existence of the will of the individual, that is, the "philosophy of life" which is a holistic, fundamental and critical inquiry into the real world and human beings.

7. The Awakening and Emergence of Life.

The philosophy of life in Western traditional culture and spirituality is a deep inquiry into the fundamental questions of life existence, cognition, and the value and meaning of existence through analytical thinking and reflection.

It was not until the nineteenth century that it really entered the germination stage of the awakening of the meaning of life existence by freeing the will of the individual, that is, the stage of the gradual formation of nihilism in Western culture.

The most influential figure in the practical development of the philosophy of life was the French philosopher Henri Bergson (October 18, 1859-January 4, 1941). Henri Bergson's philosophy advocates the idea of durée, the reality of change.

He believed that not only the nature of things change (blue things become red, young things become old), but also the substance of life itself; moreover, he considered concepts to be static and one-sided.

When we try to analyze all the objects or phenomena that exist objectively in nature, we already distort and change all the objective objects and phenomena; we judge things according to our own perceptions, without trying to fit the actual situation, but adopt one point of view and abandon the other.

Freezing the time of things without understanding their development, i.e., the "life" of things. Analysis necessarily brings with it one's own thoughts and emotions to judge a matter, which is, in short, not very fair and unsatisfactory, because there are infinite perspectives and endless moments.

Henry Bergson Bergson's "creationism" emphasizes

that creation and evolution are not mutually exclusive, because the universe is a big will "life impulse" in operation, and everything is dynamic.

He opposed the mechanistic, psychological determinism and idealism of using a certain object as the scope of study and seeking for a unified and exact objective law and truth based on experiment and logical reasoning. He believed that human life is a "continuum" or stream of consciousness, a whole and indivisible into small units of causality.

Henri Bergson not only changed the analytical approach, but also insisted that the study of the universe, the principles and principles of life, should reject analysis altogether.

He tells us that for questions that cannot be answered directly through perception, it deduces the answer through rational logical reasoning under a priori conditions, and cannot contradict empirical evidence. It is a discipline that "dispenses with character" and, therefore, the metaphysician is in the difficult position of having to express the "inexpressible".

Moreover, Henri Bergson rejects not only the notion of

simple facts, simple things, and the action of the intuitive senses, but also the notion that philosophy contains facts, things, and the action of the senses.

His basic ontology is the ontology of change, in which the object of action or thought is not all objects or phenomena that exist objectively in nature, or all objects and phenomena that exist objectively as changes in nature, but change itself, change as a whole.

Bergson uses his term "durée" in The Evolution of Creation to refer to an individual, subjective experience of time, as opposed to the mathematical, objectively measurable time of the clock.

In The Evolution of Creation, Bergson argues that the experience of time "durée" is a creative intuition rather than a knowing (a philosophical term for the ability to provide innate concepts to synthesize sensory material into knowledge. It is also called "enlightenment". (A general term for the possession of knowledge, rationality, etc.). It is the ability to create. The "continuum" is the free creative consciousness, whose upward movement creates the spirit and the form of life.

Thus, the evolutionary process of living beings is also

the process of creation of consciousness and will, and matter that has weight, occupies a place in space, and can be known to exist by the senses, is "stagnant".

It is also a psychological process, an objective reality that cannot exist without relying on human subjective consciousness, and has no absolute movement that is relatively static.

Henri Bergson Bergson laid down a more mature explanation for the "philosophy of life" with the term "creationism".

Therefore, "philosophy of life" refers to a kind of idealistic philosophical doctrine or school that tries to explain the knowledge and culture of the universe by the occurrence and evolution of life, and to attribute life to a certain spiritual force, and philosophers try to summarize a kind of law of the regularity of life that organizes all the developments of the universe, including human beings, creatures ......, etc. The philosophers have attempted to summarize a law of life that organizes all the developments of the universe, human beings, creatures, etc., and to present an analytical reflection on the fundamental questions of existence, cognition, and the value and meaning of existence.

Henry M. Bergson Bergson's "creationism" has laid down a more mature explanation for the "philosophy of life".

In addition, Schopenhauer's "Survival voluntarism" (Survival voluntarism is the desire for survival) and Nietzsche's "Der Wille zur Macht" (The Will to Power) are also about "discovering the meaning of the question" and understanding why the question should be asked.

In other words, to understand the relevant "power" of the question", and Darwin's "Biologische Evolution", which is the evolutionary development of organisms under the effect of variation, genetics and natural selection, the process of species elimination and species emergence. It is generally regarded as a "philosophy of life".

As early as the ancient Greek period, there were scholars who held to a philosophy of life perspective to analyze and reflect on fundamental questions about life, knowledge, and values.

But a more structured and coherent narrative, which explains the relationship between certain observed phenomena, concepts, variables, definitions, and propositions, is a systematic and combined philosophy of life, which sprang up in the 18th century in the philosophical and literary movement of Romanticism in Germany, and flourished in Germany and France in the late 19th and early 20th centuries.

In the nineteenth century, the rise of disciplines that study universal and fundamental issues, including existence, knowledge, value, reason, mind, and language, was mainly in reaction to Cartesianism, which had emphasized objectivity and reason since the Enlightenment in the seventeenth century, and to the mechanism caused by natural science and technological progress.

Philosophy differs from other disciplines in that it has a unique way of thinking. Scholars who advocate a philosophy of life usually oppose the mechanistic and static viewpoint, and advocate that life is a process of constant movement and change.

Life can only be grasped through inner experience and intuitive methods. "Reason" can only grasp static things, which are sufficient to understand natural phenomena, but cannot grasp the universe, human nature, and human spiritual culture.

Therefore, it is necessary to give prominence to will, emotion, and intuition in disciplines and psychiatry that use analytical thinking to inquire and reflect on fundamental questions about life, knowledge, and values, in order to avoid the negation of humanity, personality, and freedom.

Arthur Schopenhauer (1788~1860) and Friedrich Nietzsche (1844~1900) opposed rationalism and mechanism, the suppression of human emotions and the complete separation of human beings from their nature.

He affirmed the importance of the "will to live" (Wille zum Leben), and regarded the will to live and the will to be strong as the essence of life as the origin of existence or the highest value standard, and believed that "culture" is the inner expression of the inner experience of the heart and soul, which is hidden in the substance of things, and is expressed by the constant flow of emotional power.

From the viewpoint of "philosophy of life," we have formed a research orientation that is different from that of the Enlightenment, which emphasizes the supremacy of reason, and our interpretation of education is different from the "empirical and analytical" model, which requires objectivity, rationality, and empirical evidence.

Rather, it is the understanding and interpretation of educational phenomena from the perspective of the "wholeness of life", which is the "interpretation and understanding" of educational research, emphasizing the form of thinking that reflects the nature of things and is a value-creating activity based on inter-subjectivity.

The "philosophy of life" perspective research refers to the understanding of a consensus normative system rather than a purely causal inquiry into the formation of laws; its research paradigm is based on the presumption of the wholeness of life and emphasizes the intersection of life and vision among each other.

However, this research orientation, because it does not emphasize the understanding of individuality and subjective meaning, is based on the general principle of holistic and universal knowledge, emphasizing the integration of subjective and objective consciousness, and moving toward a philosophical view of the wholeness of life, while also emphasizing the meaning of the unique ideology behind society and culture, rather than becoming a tool for rationalizing the interpretation of the current situation.

The term "philosophy of life" has two meanings, as

written in the book "From God of Wine to Superman".

First, it refers to the actual life of the concrete facts and conditions that exist in front of us, in order to analyze and reflect on the fundamental questions of life, knowledge, and values, in an attempt to provide an interpretation of the meaning of life.

Second, it deals with the question of what is life, which refers to the existence and activity of living organisms, and the nature of all objects or phenomena that exist objectively in nature.

For example, Bergson's élan vital, which includes nature and human beings.

Chapter 2: Lifting the Veil of Schopenhauer's Moiety

Indian religions and philosophies believe that there exists an omniscient and omnipresent entity "Brahman" (also known as the Big Self, which is similar to the meaning of Taiyi mentioned by Nietzsche) in the universe.

Everything in this world is the manifestation of Brahman. The greatest purpose of life is to attain liberation of the self through painstaking practice, and to achieve unity with Brahman, which is called "unity of Brahman and self" (also called "unity of Brahman and self"). After achieving unity with Brahman, one can be free from the suffering of reincarnation and attain eternal life.

Therefore, Māyā is a very important concept in Indian religious philosophy. In this sense, we must lift the veil of Schopenhauer's Māyā and see the truth of individualization, that is, we must see through the appearance of life.

But in fact, in Indian religious philosophy, the relationship between Māyā and Brahman is very complicated. Although māyā is translated as "illusion," it is not an illusion, nor is it a fantasy, nor is it an illusion, but it is itself a manifestation of Brahman, and therefore a kind of Brahman, and therefore a reality. Māyā is a necessary experience, and it is essential to the realization of Brahman.

1. Schopenhauer: Life is like a pendulum

In modern times, the study of universal and fundamental issues is a discipline that includes the fields of existence, knowledge, value, reason, mind, and language. It is the philosophy of the subject of consciousness, and most philosophers regard the subject as [pure reason] and [the subject of knowledge].

However, in Arthur Schopenhauer's view, man is certainly the subject of reason and cognition, but he is, in a more fundamental sense, a subject of instincts, impulses, desires and longings.

Hence, Schopenhauer's significance for the development of a Western discipline of analytical thinking that explores and reflects on fundamental questions about life, knowledge, and values. For example, "What is life?" "Is there an objective standard of morality?" and "What is the meaning of life's existence? and

The meaning of life lies in the ideas, cultures, morals, customs, arts, institutions, and ways of behavior that have been handed down from generation to generation and from history to history. The criticism of rationalism, the tangible and intangible influence and control of people's social behavior, and the irrational orientation of the subject of mediation.

Schopenhauer was deeply influenced by Immanuel Kant's philosophy, but his forward line is different from that of the German philosophers J. G. Fichte, F.W.J. Schelling and G.W.F. Hegel, who took the approach of abolishing the thing-in-itself (das Ding an sich/thing-in-itself). The approach of das Ding an sich/thing-in-itself is different. He retains the thing-in-itself and sees it as a will (der Wille).

Since Schopenhauer believed that man and the world are hidden within things, and that the essence of substance is will, his philosophy is more concerned with the irrational aspects of man, such as emotions, desires, and bodily reactions.

After Schopenhauer, many philosophers began to pay attention to the irrational aspects of human beings. For example, Friedrich Nietzsche, in his book Schopenhauer as Educator, treats Schopenhauer as his own philosophical teacher who analyzes, thinks about, explores, and reflects on the fundamental issues of life, knowledge, and values. Schopenhauer as Educator.

Schopenhauer's irrational philosophical thinking is captured in the philosophical development of Chinese and Western studies on the principles and principles of the universe and life.

01. The World as Appearances

The World as Will and Representation is one of Schopenhauer's important works. Schopenhauer inherited Kant's distinction between the "thing-self" and the "phenomenon/appearance".

He believed that human cognition is based on the form of subject-object opposition. The world of experience and science, or the world known by sensory experience and reason, belongs to the world of appearance that is perceived by the subject.

In other words, it is the process of knowing external things, or the process of processing information about external things acting on human sensory organs.

It includes sensation, perception, memory, thought, imagination, and speech, and refers to the process of cognitive activity, i.e., the process of information processing in which an individual receives, detects, converts, simplifies, synthesizes, encodes, stores, extracts, reconstructs, forms concepts, makes judgments, and solves problems.

In psychology, it is the process of retrieving knowledge through mental activities such as concept formation, perception, judgment, or imagination, i.e., the mental function of information processing by the individual's mind

Schopenhauer means that any object of experience that is known is constructed by the subject's a priori cognitive ability.

02. Schopenhauer in "On the Fourfold Root of the Law of Sufficient Reason"

Therefore, from Schopenhauer's philosophical point of view, when people see the sun, the sun is only presented in people's personal use of sensory, perceptual, thinking, memory and other mental activities, the comprehensive awareness and knowledge of their own physical and mental state and the changes of people, things and objects in the environment, the sun in a certain time and space, the sun is only the sun of the cognitive ability of the environment and self, and the clarity of cognition.

The object exists in the comprehensive awareness and cognitive consciousness of the human individual's state of mind and body and the changes of people, things and objects in the environment by using mental activities such as sensation, perception, thinking and memory, and it is constituted by the cognitive ability of the subject.

In On the Fourfold Root of the Principle of Sufficient Reason, Schopenhauer believes that human beings have four kinds of ability to construct cognitive objects.

First, the reason of existence means that things must be in the intuitive form of time and space.

Second, the reason for change means that the change of things must obey the law of cause and effect.

Third, the reason of behavior refers to the behavior of things have their own motives.

Fourthly, the reason of cognition means that people should obey the laws of reason and logic when they know.

It can be seen from the above that Schopenhauer believes that in the framework of subject-object opposition, "object" always exists relative to the subject, and in a certain sense, the object exists as a product of the subject.

He pointed out that the essential form of "object" is the subject-object opposition of people, things, and objects touched by all human activities, and that the form of object is in all kinds of objects or phenomenal forms existing in nature (i.e., in the subject) according to the law. The following is a brief outline of Schopenhauer: the fourfold root of the law of sufficient reason.

03. The law of sufficient reason has four roots.

The basic proposition of Schopenhauer's Fourfold Law of Sufficient Reason is that the ordinary world is composed of four types of "objects", all of which are "objects". The first category consists of "real objects", such as tables, chairs and stones; the second category is the forms of thought that reflect the nature of things, and the judgments that are made through the combination of these concepts; the third category is time and space; and the fourth category is human behavior. The existence of these four categories of "objects" must have a basis or reason.

Thus, it can be said that each of these categories is subject to a particular form of the law of sufficient reason. In its most general form, the law of sufficient reason declares that everything has a reason or explanation as to why it is what it is and not what it is not.

These four "forms" of the law of sufficient reason are thus.(1) every change in a real object has a cause; (2) the truth of every true judgment is based on something outside it; (3) all mathematical properties are based on other mathematical properties; (4) every Every action has a motive. To put it more succinctly, in the ordinary world, there are four necessary connections, each of which constitutes a root of the Law of Sufficient Reason.

To put it more succinctly, in the ordinary world there

are four necessary connections, each of which constitutes a root of the law of sufficient reason. Thus, the law of sufficient reason [in its universal, extensive form] has four roots.

In the following, we will explain each of these four necessities.

(1) Causality: The Law of Sufficient Reasons for Change

Schopenhauer first describes the first class of objects as some intuitive, complete, empirically real objects. Compared with concepts, they are special. The explanatory principle of causality applies only to such objects.

Much of the Fourfold Root is devoted to the explanatory principle of causality. The principle of causality declares that in a world made up of material things, every change must have a cause, and that "every occurrence must follow or be caused by a change that precedes it. (The Fourfold Root, v. 53). There are no exceptions to this principle.

That which we usually call the cause of an event is only a particular change preceding that event, but that change itself must follow on from a previous change.

Cause and effect are linked in this way: if the first occurs, then the second cannot fail to occur.

This role or influence on all objects or phenomena that exist objectively in nature is regarded as an unavoidable and necessarily exclusive and fixed, unshakable kind of development and change.

Necessity is the reasonableness of thinking or judging something from different viewpoints or perspectives, the nature of a thing that exists independently of subjective thought or consciousness, corresponding to "subjectivity".

Objective facts are not influenced by subjective means such as human thoughts, feelings, tools, and calculations, but can maintain their truthfulness. To know the necessity of things is to know the nature of all things and objects that exist objectively (as opposed to "contingency").

Schopenhauer insists that the cause of an event can only be another event: the cause cannot be an object or a state of affairs. Objects and states are sequences linked together in a causal way, in a sequence of ranks.

The subsequent effects or stages of the development of things at the end of the state, brought into or introduced into existence, and all these objects or phenomena that exist objectively in nature together, constitute the ongoing history of the natural world, that is, the entire physical world.

A simple example will illustrate his idea. I use a tool that moves or deforms an object, breaks a glass, and distorts a stainless steel pot. The movement of the tool (hammer, or hammer), i.e. a relevant change in the state of the tool (hammer, or hammer), is the cause.

The movement of the broken glass, which distorts the stainless steel pot, i.e. a relevant change in the state of the broken glass, which distorts the stainless steel pot, is the result.

In this simple example, the cause and effect are specific facts and conditions that exist in front of us, some changes in the real object. Schopenhauer considers the same to be true for the cause and effect of all objects or phenomena that exist objectively in nature.

The change, and only the change, of all objectively existing objects or phenomena in nature is the cause and effect; therefore, when acting or thinking, the thing that is the goal is neither the cause nor the effect itself.

His reasoning is that the concrete facts and conditions

that exist in front of us, the things that are the object of real action or thought, are entities, that is, they are constituted by the nature of matter, and since the nature of matter is eternal and unchanging.

Therefore, he believes in something that is distinguishable and exists independently within itself. But it need not be a physical being. In particular, abstraction is considered to be an entity that has no beginning and no end.

The conclusion is that the concrete facts and conditions that exist in front of us, the reality that acts or thinks as the goal, all objects or phenomena that exist objectively in nature are not changes, and therefore are neither causes nor effects.

However, there is a temptation to misunderstand that what is the object of real action or thought is the cause, for example, that a tool (a hammer, or hammer) is the cause of breaking a glass or deforming a stainless steel pot.

However, a moment's reflection shows that this is not true. If the (hammer, or hammer), which is the object of action or thought, is the cause of the breaking of the glass, or of the pot of deformed stainless steel, then it is impossible to explain why the movement of the (hammer, or hammer) occurs after the movement of the (hammer, or hammer), and not before, while it is still such a (hammer, or hammer) before the (hammer, or hammer) begins to move.

It was because Schopenhauer believed that the change of all objects or phenomena that exist objectively in nature, and only the change of all objects or phenomena that exist objectively in nature, is the cause and effect, that he called the law of cause and effect "the law of sufficient reason for change".

According to this law of evidence, in the state of a real object, each change is a result, which follows the occurrence of a change in front of it, and this previous change is the sufficient basis of the material nature, which constitutes its cause.

This cause is a complex of many events; the material nature of those events is necessary for each material nature, and those events must come together as conditions for the material nature to be sufficient.

Since the cause itself is also a suspended change, it can produce other things or phenomena, and there is also a cause that produces things or phenomena, and this cause has a cause, and so there is an effect in the cause, and a cause in the effect, and so on, to infinity.

For example, most people have probably played the game of using a magnifying glass (convex lens) to gather light to light a match, but this can only be done under sunlight, that is, only when the sunlight is concentrated to a point, there can be a high enough temperature to light a match, so if the moonlight is concentrated to a point under moonlight, can also light a match?

No one should have done such a thing, really do it may not be successful, but from a theoretical analysis, in fact, this is also possible to light a match. Because from the perspective of thermodynamics, the process of gathering light with a magnifying glass is a process of increasing energy at a point, as long as the energy can be pooled to a certain limit, to reach the ignition point of the match can be lit.

However, some people may question that the light source of moonlight is from the sun's refraction, its temperature is different from the sun's direct light, but the sun's light shines on the moon, the reflected light, which is a kind of cold light, its own temperature is very low, how can it light a match?

However, light itself is a kind of electromagnetic energy wave, it does not have any hot and cold, as long as enough light can be converged together, then the energy is bound to increase, so the light source is not the key, and the essence of the magnifying glass convergence of light is to increase the density of energy at the convergence point, which is reflected in the material at the convergence point, that is, the increase in temperature.

Whether it is sunlight or moonlight, they are a kind of light, are electromagnetic waves, the accumulation of energy will increase the density. And in fact, the temperature of sunlight itself is not enough to light a match.

But because of the convergence of a large area of sunlight on a point, the energy density accumulated at this point is many times that of the same area of sunlight, resulting in the temperature of the surface of the match head to reach the ignition point, which ignites the match.

What are the conditions needed to ignite a match?

Matches are a kind of fire-making tool made according to the principle of frictional heat generation. Here is an example of a safety match. A match consists of a small wooden stick and a match head, which is usually made of a mixture of potassium chlorate ($KClO_3$), manganese dioxide (MnO_2) and sulfur (S), and has a flash point of about 400 degrees Celsius.

The ignition point of the wooden stick on the match is slightly lower than that of the match head, and the ignition point of the wood is not fixed and has a wider range, about 200 to 300 degrees Celsius. The paper used to burn the matches on both sides of the match box is made of red phosphorus (P), antimony trisulfide (Sb_2S_3) and glass powder, and the red phosphorus ignition point is only 260 degrees Celsius, which is used as a primer to ignite the match head.

From this point of view, in fact, the use of moonlight is the same, as long as the convergence of enough moonlight, energy can also be increased to the ignition point of the match.

In fact, not only the moonlight can, as long as the conditions needed to ignite the match to receive, and focus the convergence of the area of light sources enough, that is, starlight can also light the match.

Data show that the light intensity under direct sunlight in summer can reach 60,000 to 100,000 lx; while the light intensity under the full moon at night is only 0.2 lx, which is equivalent to the illumination of a 100-watt incandescent lamp at a distance of 20 meters.

By comparing the data, we can find that the intensity of moonlight is about one 400,000th of the intensity of sunlight. Although the Moon can reflect sunlight, the Moon's reflectance is only about 10% and the remaining 90% is absorbed by the Moon.

However, since the density of moonlight and starlight is too low compared to the energy of sunlight, it takes many times more area than sunlight to receive the light and focus it together to reach the ignition point of a match (the ignition point of red phosphorus in a match is 250 degrees Celsius).

So what size magnifying glass is needed? In good weather conditions, the sunlight received on Earth is 400,000 times the intensity of moonlight, and it takes at least 6 square centimeters of magnification to light a match.

If the sunlight is replaced by moonlight, then at least

240 square meters (8.8 meters in radius) of magnifying glass is theoretically needed to light a match.

Such a large magnifying glass, to do is to do, in order to curvature of the mirror and light transmission rate to pass, it is more expensive and time consuming.

As far as I know, there is no optical telescope in the world with a diameter (diameter) of more than 10 meters. Perhaps it is more convenient to replace the ordinary convex lens with a Fresnel lens. With such a large diameter magnifying lens, and considering the light transmission problem, there must be energy loss when the moonlight penetrates the lens.

In the full moon state, it should take a magnifying glass with a radius of 10 meters to gather enough moonlight to light a match.

In addition to the match in the continuous heat dissipation, the focus of the magnifying glass needs a large enough energy power, but also need a certain amount of time to make the temperature of the match head to reach the ignition point using moonlight, it is estimated that the full moon in a clear night sky, the diameter of 5 to 10 meters of convex lens to do, such a large convex lens is not found.

And moonlight through a convex lens will have a light attenuation effect, so in practice it is difficult to use moonlight to light a match, although theoretically possible, but basically no realistic possibility of implementation.

We use a magnifying glass to focus the sunlight on the tip of a matchstick, and after a period of time the match starts to burn, we would be inclined to say that it was only because I put the convex lens in the right place that caused the tip of the matchstick to catch fire, however, this is wrong.

Because, if there was a cloud blocking the light of the sun, in the conditions of the loss of light source, then the stick of the matchstick or not on fire.

That piece of cloud as long as a little move away, the stick of the matchstick began to smoke and fire, so that only the movement of the clouds is the reason for the fire of the stick of the matchstick, but this is not right, because we also need to know what makes the displacement of the clouds.

Obviously, the cause and effect, the cause and effect,

and so on, under this kind of inquiry are endless, that is to say, the causal chain of cause and effect, and the cause and effect are endless loops.

(2) Logical Necessity: The Law of Sufficient Reason for Knowledge

Those objects that make up the representations of the second category are concepts. Concepts are abstract forms of thinking that reflect the essence of things, and are general, subsuming countless special existences under themselves.

Concepts of forms of thought reflecting the nature of things are useless in isolation, but only when combined to form estimates (such as qualities, behaviors, or persons) of degree, power, value, or character,

And express the belief that the act of "recognition" and "recognition" of a subject is based on, and that these perceptions have the potential ability to be used for a specific purpose. It means that through experience or association, it is useful to be familiar with and then to understand something.

But the affirmation or denial of whether the object of thought exists, whether it has a certain attribute, and whether there is a certain relationship between things, can not provide anything from its own resources;

That is to say, there is no judgment hidden in the substantive connotation of things, and it is true. Schopenhauer maintains that every estimate (such as quality, conduct, or person's) degree, power, value, or character must have some reason external to it that constitutes its grounds of truth.

Schopenhauer divides the reasons that constitute the basis of truth into four categories, according to which he asserts that there are four categories of truths: logical, empirical, transcendental, and metalogical truths.

First, logic, logic is knowledge, an important thinking tool.

Logic is not only a knowledge, but also an important tool for thinking. Even people who have not studied logic can realize its importance.

For example, "someone's statement is illogical", "someone's theory is illogical", "someone's behavior is so exaggerated that it is completely illogical", etc. are some of the statements that we often encounter in our daily life. In our daily language, "logic" is a very popular term.

But what is logic? "What are the qualities of logic?" Many people do not know the answers to questions such as "What is logic?

There was a very popular view that logic is the science of the laws of thought. This view is probably due to the fact that logicians like to call some logical principles, such as uniformity, the law of alignment, and the law of contradiction, as "laws of thought". However, this view of logic has the following drawbacks:

First, it does not distinguish logic from other disciplines, such as psychology or cognitive science. The purpose of psychology and cognitive science is also to study the "laws of thought" of human beings. So what is the difference between what they study and what logic studies?

Second, it is misleading. It gives the impression that logic is the study of the actual patterns of human thought and the laws that must be followed in the course of human thought.

But under what circumstances and in what patterns do humans think? What are the laws that govern human thought? These are questions of empirical fact. The object of study of logic is obviously not directly related to empirical facts.

Third, logic is the study of the principles and methods used to distinguish correct reasoning from incorrect reasoning. This view is quite popular in academic circles. However, logical reasoning can usually be divided into three types: inductive reasoning, retrospective reasoning, and deductive reasoning. Scientific methods are all inductive reasoning and have no inevitability. Mathematics, on the other hand, belongs to deductive reasoning.

In philosophy, logic is used in most of the major fields: metaphysics/cosmology, ontology, theory of knowledge, and ethics. In the narrower sense, logic is the study of the principles and methods of deductive reasoning or proof."

This view places the study of logic on things such as "correct/incorrect reasoning", "correct and proper argumentation", and "proof". This view is more appropriate than the "logic is the science of laws of thought" view mentioned earlier.

At least it does not mix logic with other disciplines such as psychology, brain science, semantics, and law, which are the study of the processing of human thought and reasoning, and treats them as the same thing.

However, there is still a flaw in this view. Logic is certainly the study of how to distinguish correct reasoning from incorrect reasoning. But logic is about more than that. For example, logic is also about how to distinguish between contradictory sentences and propositions that are true under any interpretation. However, determining whether a statement is a contradiction or a proposition that is true under any interpretation is not the same thing as determining whether an inference is correct.

For a statement is true for all possible values of its propositional variables, which is called tautology, while a conclusion from a known or assumed premise, or an inference from a known result of an answer to its justification, are not treated as the same thing.

From this point of view. The view mentioned earlier that "logic is the study of the principles and methods used to distinguish correct reasoning from incorrect reasoning" is not comprehensive enough. Let us now look at another, more "unconventional" view.

The famous American philosopher W.V. Quine defined

"logic" as "the systematic study of logical truth.

Quine's definition places the object of study of logic above logical truths, meaning that a judgment with logical truths is a judgment based on the truth of another logical judgment or judgments.

For example, Hegel's trivium dialectic, a trivium based on the truth of two of its premises, has truth.

Second, empirical, rules of thumb are principles that are widely applied.

Empirical, rules of thumb are principles that are widely applied, but are themselves simplified and not guaranteed to be strictly accurate or reliable in all cases. For example, the Rule of 72 is a rule of thumb. Rules of thumb are generally approximations to calculate or memorize specific values, or to make decisions, and are easy to learn and apply in practice.

The basis of the rule of thumb is the practical application, not the logical inferential summation of natural and social phenomena according to existing empirical knowledge, experience, facts, laws, cognition, and tested hypotheses, through generalization and deductive reasoning.

It is a judgment of empirical truth, an affirmation or denial of the existence of an object of thought, of a certain attribute, and of a certain relationship between things, based on a world made up of empirical reality.

For example, "Successful people learn from other people's experiences, while unsuccessful people learn only from their own experiences, but usually unsuccessful people have few experiences, and most of them are unsuccessful. Successful people know how to learn from others' experiences and turn them into their own knowledge and wisdom.

Those who fail learn only from their own experience, but because most of them are failures, they often keep failing" has an empirical truth because it is based on this fact.

Thirdly, the a priori is a philosophical thought.

A priori is a kind of philosophical thinking. It believes that the concepts and notions formed by the human mind have an autonomous nature of existence, and denies that they are only the temporal reflection of people's changing experience.

It gives great strength and power to the human

intellect, and considers that experience is actually, to a large extent, constructed by the human mind, or formed by the concepts generated by it, in its extreme form: the belief that the only pillar of the universe is the human mind.

An object of experience reality (successful people learn from other people's experience, and failed people learn only from their own experience, but usually failed people have little experience, and most of what they have are failed experiences.)

The successful person learns from the experience of others and replaces it with his or her own knowledge and wisdom, while the failing person learns only from his or her own experience, but because most of it is a failure, he or she also fails all the time.

Generally speaking, when we can know the truth of a proposition without examining experience, the proposition is a priori proposition, and a judgment with a priori truth is a judgment based on the existence or nature of time, space, and causality (forms of perception and understanding).

For example, "For example, "A triangle has three

angles" is an a priori proposition based on the nature of space; "If there is no cause and condition for an event to occur, there is no effect that enables it to occur" is also an a priori proposition based on the nature of causality.

Fourth, Meta Logic, the study of the metatheory of logic.

Meta Logic is the study of the meta-theory of logic. While logic studies the use of logical systems to construct valid and rational arguments, meta-logic studies the properties of logical systems.

Logic is concerned with the truths that can be derived from the use of logical systems. Meta-logic is concerned with the truths that can be derived from the language and systems used to express them.

The basic objects of meta-logical research are formal languages, formal systems, and their interpretations. A judgment with meta-logical truths is a judgment based on the formal conditions of all thought.

It is the law of identity that things and themselves are equivalent to each other, that "self" cannot be "not self"; that things cannot be "yes" and "no" at the same time. It is the law of non-contradiction that things can only have two states of being or not being, and there is no other intermediate state.

(3) Time and Space Necessity: The Law of Sufficient Reason for Existence

The objects that constitute the third category of representations are time and space. Time and space, given that they depend on the intellect to exist, are the same as real objects and concepts, and are the external features of some objective things, which are reproduced in the image of human brain perception, and are the higher forms of perceptual awareness.

Time and space are forms of internal and external perception, which exist in the brain, and are added to all objects or phenomenal materials that exist objectively in nature, so that the perception of real objects can begin.

However, from the standpoint of another research analysis or criticism of problems, issues, etc., as the projection of perception outward, time and space themselves are also perceived, and it is the composition of time and space that describes the pure, unadulterated, non-experienced or pre-experienced knowledge, and those objects that are directly perceived.

This being so, time and space are special beings independent of human consciousness, the objective abstract world, but abstract, universal ideas, not entities that act as specified entities, events or relationships, or as kinds of entities that consist of a combination of many identical or similar persons and things.

It is something that is distinguishable from a particular existence and exists independently within itself. But it need not be a physical being. In particular, abstraction is usually regarded as an entity, like time and space.

These abstract physical parts are systematically interconnected and constitute the third form of the root of the law of sufficient reason, called the law of sufficient reason for existence.

Time is composed of an infinite number of abstract entities, well-ordered moments, rather like points of abstract entities on a line, each moment being related to other points and dependent on other points, and having a definite and unshifted position, all together forming the sufficient reason for the abstract entity time.

In contrast, space is composed of an infinite number

of abstract entities, well-ordered points, forming lines, angles, areas, volumes, all of which are where they are and are what they are, because the other points, lines, angles, areas, volumes of abstract entities are also where they are and are what they are.

In other words, any given geometric property of a spatial part of an abstract entity has a sufficient reason to be the geometric property of one or more other parts of the spatial part of the abstract entity.

Further, the relevant sufficient reason is neither causal nor conceptual in nature, but existential in nature (ontological). That is, if we ask how any spatial part of an abstract entity is what it is as it is, then on what principle we can find the answer to the abstract entity, which is simply that other spatial parts of abstract entities are what they are.

For example, if we ask why the three angles of a given triangle are what they are, we find that it is because the three sides are what they are.

So also known as a triangle, it is a closed plane geometric figure composed of three line segments connected first and last in sequence, or three points that do not share the same line connected two by two, is the most basic and least edge of the polygon.

Schopenhauer argued that the existence of numbers, and therefore of arithmetic, depends on the possibility of counting in time.

From this, he concluded that arithmetic is a hierarchical whole of time relations, with different dimensions of indicators at different levels, forming a certain order, a clear system of logical relations between indicators at the same level, and between indicator levels and indicator levels, and a direct grasp of space, direct senses, formed by generalizing from direct experience of other properties and relations, which is the same as the grasp of spatial relations. This is the same reason that geometry is achieved by the grasp of spatial relations.

(4) Motivation and behavioral necessity: the law of sufficient reason for behavior

The object that constitutes the fourth type of representation is our individual self. In the experience of the individual self using sensory, perceptual, thinking, memory and other mental activities, the comprehensive awareness and knowledge of one's physical and mental state and changes in people, events and things in the environment.

Self-consciousness (self-cognition or ego) is a multi-dimensional, multi-level complex psychological phenomenon, which consists of three psychological components: self-knowledge, self-experience, and self-control, and the things that we target when we act or think.

It is the most basic psychological process of human beings that we can directly acquire knowledge or apply knowledge, or information processing process. However, although we can know ourselves so directly, we do not see ourselves as the subject of knowledge.

Rather, we see ourselves as the subject of our desire for something, or as the subject of a mental state that we consciously strive for in order to realize a certain ideal or to achieve a certain goal.

In other words, in self-consciousness, we face ourselves, but we do not see ourselves as the object we should know, but always see ourselves as something that makes a decision to achieve a certain purpose and produces a psychological state, which is often expressed in words or actions.

Schopenhauer tenaciously argues for his belief in the truth of the thesis that it is impossible for a being with a unique consciousness and a unique personal experience, or another entity external to itself and related to it, to recognize that they are persons who recognize the ability to know and practice the object, because if something is known, it is recognized as an object.

Another way to express this point is that the object is something that exists independently of the mind, and only the object or object in philosophy means anything that can be perceived or imagined, including both objectively existing and observable things, as well as imaginary things.

The object corresponds to the concept of the subject that is known; therefore, when we know ourselves, the self we know is not the self that we know, but something else; it is some will, according to Schopenhauer.

According to Schopenhauer, this does not mean that each of us has two different existences: a body and a will. On the contrary, each of us is one, and indivisible.

Yet, while we are one, we know ourselves in two separate ways.

First, self-consciousness is a condition for knowing objective things in the outside world. If a person does not know himself, and cannot distinguish himself from his surroundings, he cannot know the external objective things.

We know ourselves from the outside, and it is necessary to know from this perspective what belongs to our body; we also know ourselves from the inside of the hidden things, from the inside of the inner substance, and from the perspective of this flexible way, we know what belongs to our own will.

Thus, this distinction between ourselves as bodies and ourselves as wills is an epistemological distinction, not an existential one.

Schopenhauer later adds that the subject knows itself as a mental state that consciously strives for the realization of a certain ideal or the achievement of a certain goal.

However, he says that the ultimate unity in the universe is impossible to think on the basis of observation, to explain reasonably the causes of changes in things, the connections between things, or the laws of development of things; it can appear and be given in the immediate knowledge.

Here, the reason why it is impossible to explain is that all objects or phenomena, processes, states, reasons, etc. that exist objectively in nature are described to explain their meanings, causes, reasons, etc., and must be about all human activities, the people or things to which they refer, as well as the explanation of the interactions and interconnectedness between objects and things.

But the problem here is the equivalence between what is the object of an action or thought, and what is not necessarily the person or thing to which all human activities are directed.

For this equation of different things as the same thing is simply beyond explanation, and we can only speak of it as the most remarkable of many miracles.

Schopenhauer's explanation of behavior completes and consolidates the act of "knowing" and "recognizing" from a subject in order to know with certainty, and these knowings have the potential ability to be used for a specific purpose.

It means to be able to be familiar with and to

understand, through experience or association, the perspective of something, the dual existence of the conditions that cause ourselves to cause a certain result, or to cause another thing to happen.

Schopenhauer thinks in this way, on the basis of observation, to justify the causes of changes in things, the connections between things, or the regular behavior of their development.

We know correctly and practically that in front of every action, something happens, called the motive. Indeed, we find it difficult to conceive a concrete image of something that is not in front of us, using past memories or similar experiences, if there is no motive for an action, which is the same as a dead body that has no signs of life, but moves for no reason.

The reason we think so is that the inner mental processes or internal dynamics of individual activity, directed, motivated, and sustained by a goal or object, which underlie most human behavior, are the causes: the motive seems to be the cause from the inside, just as the will is the body when viewed from the outside.

Most instances of causality, i.e., mechanical,

chemical, etc., we know that causality will be there, and we can even see the inevitable and inevitable trend in the development and change of things.

However, we have no idea of the nature of the substance of the things that are hidden inside of them, when we put certain attitudes or actions on the outside of people or those events.

However, when it comes to our own behavior, our perception of things will be different in our mindset. We do have the act of "knowing" and "recognizing" a subject from the outside of our own behavior, in order to know with certainty, and these knowings have the potential to be used for specific purposes.

It means to be familiar with something through experience or association; but for their cognition, we also have the act of "knowing" and "recognizing" a subject from the inside, with the knowledge of certainty, and these knowings have the potential to be used for specific purposes.

"We can say that we stand behind the situation and are able to discover the occurrence of a cause, the result of it, and the most insidious, yet profound nature of the process.

The relationship between motive and action is thus the same as the relationship between cause and effect in real objects; however, since the former is the thinking activity of the human mind that reflects the characteristics and connections of objective things in different ways, and reveals the meaning and effects of all objects or phenomena that exist objectively in the natural world.

Schopenhauer considers it to constitute the basis of a unique form of the Law of Sufficient Reason, which he calls "the Law of Sufficient Reason of Action". It firmly asserts that there is a motive behind every action.

The words of Schopenhauer about the mental state of an individual determined to achieve a certain end, often expressed in words or actions of will, link him to an obvious reason for what he requires.

Such an objective existence is reflected in the individual's use of sensory, perceptual, thinking, memory and other mental activities, the state of his body and mind, and the environment, people, things and objects in the comprehensive awareness and understanding of changes, through the activities of thinking, and the results, or the formation of views and systems of concepts, is very important.

If the mental state that arises from the decision to achieve a certain end, often expressed in words or actions, is equivalent to the body, then it is possible to seek or establish rules and evidence for the complex mental history that supports or determines a belief, decision, and action: like other real objects, the will is a creature of the intellect.

Therefore, it cannot provide direct knowledge of something that exists outside of knowledge, and is absolutely unknowable.

At the same time, if motivation and action are the cause and effect, then motivation and action are some changes in the reality of action or thought, in the things that are the object, in relation to which rules and evidence are sought or established to support or determine a belief, decision, and action, and the inference of the complex mental history is that

The corollary of the complex mental history is that changes in some actions or thoughts, in what is the target, lead to changes in other actions or thoughts, in what is the target, and so on, and never beyond.

There is another reason, which is of no apparent importance to the system of thought described by Schopenhauer. Our body, from the inside, is our will, and he tells us that this fact forms the cornerstone of his "whole metaphysics.

What he means by this is that the direct knowledge of our self as will provides us with a grasp not only of the internal nature of our own body, but of the internal nature of any appearance, of reality.

Each of us can act as one, revealing the concrete and microscopic parts of the whole. He also believes that this knowledge can lead us to grasp what exists beyond recognition, and which is absolutely unrecognizable.

It is the basis of phenomena, and one who acknowledges that one can know phenomena must recognize the existence of the Self as the basis of phenomena; for "this Self, the root of all apparent phenomena, is not something else, but we know it directly and very intimately, and we find it in our internal will.

This act of "cognition" and "identification" of a subject

from the knowledge of the will of the many bodies leads to the knowledge of certainty, and these knowings have the potential to be used for specific purposes.

It is possible to sublimate the metamorphosis of learning and experience acquired in the process of learning and practice, because the individual consciously strives for the mental state in order to realize a certain ideal or to achieve a certain purpose. It is the objectification of the only will, and it is also a certain kind of revelation of the only will.

In summary, the four aspects of the law of sufficient reason, that is, the four kinds of necessity that exist in the immediate facts and conditions, are philosophically defined by the intrinsic nature of things, the decisive connection or trend.

In the process of development of things, necessity and contingency are linked to each other, interact, and transform each other under certain conditions.

01. The World as a Will

Schopenhauer points out that the world has two different aspects, one is the world that is represented, i.e., the world that is in the phenomenal level, in which the individual knows and understands things through the mental process of the individual's comprehensive awareness and knowledge of his physical and mental state and the changes of people, things and objects in the environment by using mental activities such as feeling, perception, thinking and memory.

The other is the world that is not represented, but is independent of the mental process of knowing and understanding things by the individual's cognitive ability and clarity of cognition of the environment and the self.

Schopenhauer points out that in the way of knowing by the law of sufficient reason, both the self and the world exist in relation to each other.

In this sense, if the human mind is engaged in the world, reflecting the characteristics and connections of objective things, and revealing the meaning and effect of all the objects or phenomena that exist in nature, the process of acquiring knowledge by forming concepts, perceptions, judgments or imaginations, i.e., the world of the mental function of information processing by the mind, can only be the world of the representational, phenomenal level. The world of the mental function of information processing by the mind can only be the world of representations and phenomena.

If we carry out the process of acquiring knowledge by forming concepts, perceptions, judgments, or imaginations, i.e., the mental function of the mind to process information, the self we obtain can only be the represented self, i.e., our body.

But the ego also has another aspect, which is independent of the process of acquiring knowledge by mental activities such as forming concepts, perception, judgment or imagination, i.e., the mental function of thinking to process information, which, according to Schopenhauer, is the human will.

But Schopenhauer thinks that this does not mean that, as the external features of objective things, the image reproduced in the human brain perception, is the will (body) of the higher forms of representation of perceptual cognition, and as in a kind or a group of everlasting properties, they make an entity, or matter, its fundamental place, and it necessarily exists.

Without it, the will (essence) which loses its identity is two wills, both of which are in fact the same will, but presenting different aspects in relation to the perspective from which the subject is viewed.

Schopenhauer points out that the physical body, which is the mental process of knowing and understanding things through the activity of the individual's consciousness, is the external expression of the mental state for which the individual consciously strives in order to realize a certain ideal or achieve a certain purpose, so the human body is the visible expression of the human will.

Schopenhauer cites the example that the delivery of the intestines is a thing, independent of the influence of consciousness, and the nature of hunger exists independently; the response of the genitals is a thing, independent of the influence of subjective thought, and the nature of sexual desire exists independently.

The whole body is the external manifestation of the mental state of the will to realize a certain ideal, or to achieve a certain purpose, and to consciously work for it.

That is, the body, as the object of human awareness, needs to obey the law of sufficient reason, but in order to realize a certain ideal or to achieve a certain purpose.

The state of mind itself is independent of the law of

sufficient reason. It can be said that the state of mind in which the will consciously strives for the realization of a certain ideal or the achievement of a certain goal is in itself blind and incessant.

Its various desires, cravings, and instincts are not based on rational thought, but on the fact that they are not the basis for the conclusion of the matter.

Schopenhauer goes to great lengths to point out that the nature of the individual is a mental state that consciously strives for the realization of a certain ideal, or the achievement of a certain purpose, and then he uses analogies to point out that since the individual is a mental state of will that consciously strives for the realization of a certain ideal, or the achievement of a certain purpose, and that there is a will outside the individual.

In addition to the individual, there are many other things, whose essence should be the mental state of consciously striving for the realization of a certain ideal or the achievement of a certain purpose, and even the whole world is hidden within the substance of things.

The inner essence is also the will to consciously work for the realization of a reasonable vision or hope for something in the future, or to achieve a certain purpose.

Therefore, in the world, every individual is essentially a small will that consciously strives for the realization of a certain ideal or the achievement of a certain purpose, and the world itself is a big will.

The world as a whole, from the level of the appearance of being known, all the objects or phenomena that exist objectively in nature in the world are very different, but they are only the external manifestation of the same great will that consciously strives for the realization of a certain ideal or the attainment of a certain purpose.

Schopenhauer believes that there are hierarchical differences in the manifestation of the will, the mental state that consciously strives for the realization of a certain ideal, or the achievement of a certain purpose.

He said that the mental state of the will that consciously strives for the realization of a certain ideal or the achievement of a certain purpose has the lowest level in inorganic beings and then a higher level in organic beings and animals, and that the mental state of the will that consciously strives for the realization of a certain ideal or the achievement of a certain purpose reaches the highest level in human beings.

Finally, in human beings, it reaches the highest level of expression. But what is the will that consciously strives for the realization of a certain ideal or the achievement of a certain purpose, if it is clear by comparison with all the objects or phenomena that exist objectively in nature, so that there is no need to repeat the expression?

02. Human life and will

The will to live is also known as the "will to live". It is a philosophical concept that advocates the perfection of human existence through the hard work of the will. The German philosopher Schopenhauer proposed it. It is the opposite of Kant's "good will".

The former believes that the spiritual life is the result of the impulse to work consciously for the realization of a certain ideal or the achievement of a certain purpose, while the latter believes that the spiritual life is a rational expression of the norms and guidelines that human beings should follow in their conduct and behavior when living together.

According to Schopenhauer, the will is the constitutive principle of the inner world and the basis for understanding the meaning of the existence of life itself, and is the source of a life full of sin, misery and suffering. One cannot break free from the will, but can only wear out the will to determine one's own ability to act, in order to achieve the spiritual state of transcendence of life and death and transcendence of all worries through the practice of austerity.

In Schopenhauer's view, every living being has the will to make conscious efforts for the realization of a certain ideal or to achieve a certain purpose, and the will to make conscious efforts for the realization of a certain ideal or to achieve a certain purpose is actually the will to exist.

As the degree of objectification of the will varies, all kinds of objectively existing objects or phenomena in nature, the cognitive ability of man to the environment and self and the clarity of cognition, to the clarity of his own will varies.

Man is to achieve a certain ideal, or to achieve a certain purpose, and consciously strive for the mental state. The highest expression of objectification.

Therefore, only human beings have the most clear understanding of their own will, that is, they have the deepest understanding and comprehension of their own will in order to realize a certain ideal or achieve a certain purpose, and they consciously work for it, and therefore have greater suffering.

The state of mind in which the will consciously strives for the realization of a certain ideal or the attainment of a certain goal is manifested in man as an endless, never-ending desire, which is infinite, but limited in what it desires.

Therefore, man is bound to feel pain. Schopenhauer does not deny the existence of happiness and joy, but he believes that pain is more fundamental than happiness and joy, and is closer to the original nature of the world as a conscious effort to realize a certain ideal or to achieve a certain purpose.

Happiness and pleasure are only short-lived desires that are satisfied, and once the feeling of satisfaction subsides, greater suffering appears immediately. Sometimes even when people get long periods of satisfaction and happiness, they fall back into boredom.

And when desires are not satisfied, people find themselves in a state of mind where they consciously work to achieve a certain ideal or purpose, and there are things between what they want and what they desire that hinder their desires, causing pain and agitation.

Schopenhauer once described the situation or encounter of life as extremely painful and heartbreaking with a metaphor of a specific form or gesture that can cause human thoughts, or emotional activities: life is like a pendulum, always swinging back and forth between pain and boredom.

Schopenhauer believes that the degree of awareness of the mental state that people consciously work for in order to realize a certain ideal or achieve a certain purpose, the brain's overall view and understanding of the external world when external stimuli act on the senses, organizes and interprets the sensory information of the external world most clearly for us, so people feel the pain of life more than inorganic, organic and animal.

But Schopenhauer points out that among people, the higher the degree of intelligence, the more they can feel pain than others; in this way, people with genius are the ones who suffer the most.

People with higher degrees of intelligence and genius

are often good at abstract thinking, and their general ideas, or the organization of ideas in their thinking, is so broad that they include both the future and the past in their thinking.

And the main reason for suffering is that these people often do not want to rest in the status quo, but put their thoughts and energy into the past that no longer exists, and the future that does not yet exist, to make unnecessary regrets, and to feel anxious and fantasy about the future.

2. Schopenhauer: How to get rid of the painful and pessimistic life

Schopenhauer is an important representative of the irrationalization of the will in the history of Western philosophy. This concept embodies the core of Schopenhauer's philosophical thought, which has a significant impact and effect on people or things by reflecting on the European rationalist tradition.

Schopenhauer takes up Kant's concept of the phenomenon and essence, and expands and complements it. In Schopenhauer's system, the Great Will, which is the essence of the whole world, is the "one" outside of time and space, and it has integrity and uniqueness.

When a person perceives and understands things through the mental process of consciousness, different phenomena will emerge, resulting in the existence of different, objective objects or phenomena in the world, which is what Schopenhauer called "the principle of individuation".

The magnetic force, gravitational force, and human activities on the earth are in fact the external and individualized expression of the will to realize a certain ideal or to achieve a certain purpose, and to work for it consciously.

This manifested world is the world in which all objects or phenomena that exist objectively in nature by the subject act directly on the human sense organs and the human brain reflects the objective things as a whole.

The great will (essence) expresses "itself" as a variety of phenomena, but the phenomena and essence are related to each other, and the phenomena do not conceal an eternal attribute or a group of attributes, they make an entity, or a substance, its essence.

And it necessarily exists, without it, it would lose its identity. The external form, the observable fact or event that things take in their development and change is always a manifestation of the essence.

The different phenomena of the world create oppositions between people and things, and within the oppositions, competition tends to arise. Schopenhauer believes that the reason for this is that every individual thinks that the will to achieve a certain ideal, or to achieve a certain purpose, and to consciously work for it, is the ultimate will itself.

Individuals tend to be self-centered and often turn a blind eye to the will of others, sometimes even imposing their own will on others, thus creating tragedies.

In addition, all the objects or different phenomena that exist in the world objectively in the natural world also bring people a series of endless opposites of suffering. People have to face the trouble of the division between [finite and infinite], [sensibility and reason], [existence and nothingness].

The Great Will is independent of time and space, but people are limited by their ability to know all the objects or phenomena that exist objectively in nature within a certain, limited space-time limit.

In order to realize a certain ideal, or to achieve a certain purpose, people consciously work for the mental state of the will, but drive people to desire infinity.

However, the process of acquiring knowledge by forming concepts, perceptions, judgments, or imaginations, which is the mental function of the mind to process information, is only a phenomenon of the world objectively existing in all objects in nature, not the essence of the world, which is the irrational and ever-desiring will.

In other words, people's ability to form concepts, make judgments, analyze, synthesize, compare, reason, and calculate can hardly teach them to see the nature of the world and guide their lives.

Finally, even though people try to seek happiness and maximize their own desires, they cannot escape from the fate of death and emptiness in the end.

In other words, all the events, all the situations, all the good times, all the bad times, all the things that people have at the moment, in the end, always come to nothing.

01. The Way of Liberation

Schopenhauer was not only influenced by Kant's philosophy, but also by Eastern thought. The Hinduism and Buddhism, the view that life is ultimately nothingness, and the view of things or problems from a certain position or perspective, inspired Schopenhauer to think analytically and reflect on the fundamental issues of life, knowledge and values.

The mainstream of Hinduism, Brahmanism, in the Veda and Upanishad, puts forward the view that life is nothing and the bráhman is real.

The concept of "impermanence" (impermanence) proposed by Buddhism is a concept of ideas, culture, morals, customs, arts, institutions, and ways of behavior that have been passed down from generation to generation and from history.

Schopenhauer, who was dissatisfied with the tangible and intangible influence and control role of rationalism on people's social behavior, provided valuable resources of objective existence, reflected in human consciousness, through thinking activities, and the results, or the formation of views and systems of concepts.

Since Schopenhauer proposed that the essence of the world is the will to realize a certain ideal or to achieve a certain purpose and to consciously work for it, the way to liberation lies in the mental state of will denying, to realize a certain ideal or to achieve a certain purpose and to consciously work for it.

Schopenhauer points out that there are two ways to deny the will: one is through philosophy and art, but this can only alleviate the suffering of life; the other is through abstinence, which is the only way to achieve complete liberation from suffering.

Schopenhauer believed that the genius has the ability to engage in philosophy, to know the inner nature of things independently of the law of sufficient reason, and to see the "principle of individuation". The genius has the intuitive ability to see directly into the nature of the world, that is, the incessant, never-ending will to desire.

All the objects or phenomena in the world that exist objectively in the natural world are colorful, complex, and objective, and all the things that exist in the natural world are only superficial phenomena of the mental state that the will consciously strives for in order to realize a certain ideal or achieve a certain purpose.

Once people can explain the known facts, principles and principles in their own words, texts or other symbols, they can understand that all objects or phenomena in the world exist objectively in nature.

All things, like ourselves, have a common root, and all belong to the same great will to work consciously for the realization of a certain ideal or the achievement of a certain purpose, transcending for a short time the opposition with others and reaching the spiritual realm where everything is one.

Secondly, people can obtain temporary liberation through artistic aesthetics. Schopenhauer pointed out that contemplation is the key to achieving freedom of mind and body through artistic aesthetics by relieving oneself of worries and fetters.

Kant believes that people's aesthetic activities do not carry utilitarian, cognitive purposes and motives. Schopenhauer's view of aesthetics is similar to Kant's. He also advocates that in aesthetic contemplation, people should give up their everyday rationality and acquire knowledge through mental activities such as forming concepts, perceptions, judgments, or imagination, i.e., the mental function of the mind to process information.

The way of objectively existing all objects or phenomena in nature, no longer considering when and where things are.

And not to let the abstract concept of knowledge dominate one's own personal use of sensory, perceptual, thinking, memory and other mental activities, the state of one's body and mind and the environment of people, things and changes in awareness and knowledge of the consciousness, but should be fully focused on the object itself.

Schopenhauer believed that the intuition of genius and the meditation of art can transcend the form of time and space, get rid of the concept of knowledge, and immerse oneself completely in the meditation.

It can be said that in the meditation, the subject has a unique personal awareness and knowledge of his own physical and mental state and the changes of people, things and objects in the environment by using sensory, perceptual, thinking and memory activities, and the existence of a unique personal experience, or the complete disappearance of another entity external to and related to him.

Things that include objective existence and can be subjectively perceived (concrete things such as trees and houses, abstract things such as prices and freedom) completely fill the subject's vision, and for a moment, the subject and object seem to be one.

For example, when we gaze at a fireplace, once we have watched it for a long time, we will find that we and the fireplace seem to be one, that is, we enter a state of oblivion. Attaining this state, one can temporarily forget one's own existence, that is, one temporarily forgets one's own desires and sufferings.

Although one can achieve a certain kind of freedom of mind and body by analyzing the philosophies and arts of inquiry and reflection on the fundamental issues of life, knowledge, and values, one can achieve a certain kind of freedom from distress and fetters.

But Schopenhauer did not consider these two paths to be radical, but only temporary relief from suffering. He argues that only abstinence can enable us to achieve complete release from troubles, freedom from fetters, and thus freedom of mind and body, and that the highest state of life is to have no desire and no want.

The prerequisite for abstinence is that people need to understand the nature of things, the will to consciously work for the realization of an ideal or the achievement of a certain purpose, and the will to see the nature of the will to consciously work for the realization of an ideal or the achievement of a certain purpose, so that they can control their desires and impulses. In addition, when people suffer from the pain of not being able to get what they want, they can also be motivated to take the path of "clearing their minds and desires".

As long as one realizes that there are different kinds of suffering in the world, [those that harm and those that are persecuted], [those that torment and those that are tormented], although they exist objectively in all objects or phenomena in the natural world.

Although all the objects or phenomena that exist objectively in nature are different in the level of phenomena, they are essentially of the same general will. The process of acquiring knowledge by forming concepts, perceptions, judgments, or imagination is the mental function of the mind to process information.

Then people can achieve a non-differentiated mind, no desire, no want, and embark on the road to freedom of mind and body by releasing the worries and fetters, which can be said to be very close to the Buddhist idea of "exodus".

02. Schopenhauer's [Maya's Veil]

Schopenhauer was a famous pessimist philosopher in the 19th century. He held a negative attitude toward the life of the universe and the existence of life, and thought that life was not worth living. He believed that life has no meaning, life is suffering.

As long as people live, they cannot be freed from suffering. Since life is painful and has no meaning, it is not worth living.

He says that it is a mistake to be born with the desire to live with a smile on one's face and to look very happy. The world is a land of doubt, error, sin, madness, and life is mostly a dream, a journey to death.

History is a long and difficult dream for mankind. Everything is relative and temporary, only desire is eternal. Fundamentally, man is something that should not exist.

Death is the correction of the mistake of the desire to

live after a painful experience, and it is also a punishment for the mistake of people's existence.

The so-called pursuit of happiness is only blinded by the veil of Moyer. Schopenhauer categorically declares that life, the whole of it, is suffering, every history of life is the history of suffering, life is suffering, the world is hell.

Schopenhauer finally points out that to obtain permanent liberation, the will to live must be completely denied. The best way to do this is to give up one's will completely in a life of abstinence, as Christian ascetics and Buddhists actually practice, in order to attain a life of abstinence from the world and transcend suffering. The specific way is divided into three steps: voluntary renunciation of sexual desire; willingness to suffer; and death and silence.

Schopenhauer's will to live and pessimism catered to the pessimism and anguish of the German bourgeoisie after the defeat of the 1848 revolution, and laid the foundation for voluntarist philosophy.

The "will to power" theory of idealism and the superman philosophy, i.e., the will to power, evolved from Schopenhauer's "will to live" as the essence of the superman, and was a further development of the concept of the superman philosophy put forward by Nietzsche to confront the secular mediocrity of the human group.

Chapter 3: The slow and lingering "trampled to death by the geese" of Kierkegaard.

1. The transformation and rise of confidence

As for the metamorphosis and sublimation of the "philosophy of life," let us begin with the father of existentialism, the Danish writer Søren Aabye Kierkegaard (1813-1855), the "father of existentialism. He sees only each individual."

He believes that true faith must come from the heart of the "individual" and lead directly to the God of his faith, not from external indoctrination and social pressure.

Søren Kierkegaard took the religion of man as the object of his study of all human activities, touching people, things, and objects, and paid great attention to the experience of the individual in the practice of knowing all objects or phenomena that exist objectively in nature.

After the death of Chikgo

His philosophical ideas, which were originally confined to Denmark, became known in 1877 when G.M.C. Brandes, a Danish literary critic, discovered and promoted his ideas.

As a result, this nineteenth-century thinker influenced not his time, but more the twentieth century.

For example, the Existentialism of Scharthe and the Protestant theologian Karl Barth were inspired by the holistic, fundamental, and critical inquiry into the real world and the human being.

The process of analysis, synthesis, judgment, reasoning and other cognitive activities on the basis of images and concepts has been further updated and developed.

01. The solitary person

If we look deeper into the three stages of the aesthetic philosophical thinking of Kierkegaard, we will find that, to a considerable extent, Kierkegaard's philosophical thinking began with the criticism of Hegel. He was dissatisfied with the absolute rationalism of Hegel's philosophical system and its tendency to emphasize the importance of the "whole" over the "individual".

Kierkegaard thought that Hegel had created a huge structure of philosophical system that was not related to his life experience, just like a man who built a huge palace but did not live in it.

He also believes that the more grandiose a philosophical system is, the more likely it is to follow the path of abstraction without realistic fantasy, and the more it leaves the concern for the actual problems of personal existence.

In his early years, he stood on the side of Hegelian holism and criticized Socrates, accusing him of ignoring the whole and seeing only the existence of the individual. In his diary, he said, "The greatness of Socrates was that even though he was accused and had to face the accusations of the community, he did not see the community, but only the individual in his eyes.

At this time, Socrates, in the eyes of Kierkegaard, was busy with a more profound and thoughtful thought process: what is the meaning of life as a human being?

Socrates realized that Socrates' thought was a

profoundly objective description of the actual state of existence, that is, of natural and social phenomena.

For human beings, each individual has his own strong experience of daily life, and thus the individual's experience of existence is always more real than the concept of the group.

On the contrary, what is the mass? At best, it is just a number, which does not mean anything. The millions of people who live and die in a muddle are not social entities formed by a number of individuals or groups with a common goal and certain boundaries.

In a broad sense, an organization is a system of many elements linked together in a certain way. In a narrow sense, an organization is a collective or group of people working together to achieve a certain goal, without a structured and organized arrangement of the constituent parts.

It is a social matrix of illusions, illusions, disturbances, and noises that gather people together in a specific physical or virtual space and time.

02. The Subjectivity of Truth

Another point of dissatisfaction with Hegel's philosophy (the fundamental questions of life, knowledge, and value are explored and reflected upon by analytical thinking) is that Hegel's holistic, fundamental, and critical system of inquiry into the real world and human beings emphasizes objectivity too much.

The true meaning of philosophy is as a way of inquiry, not just as a specific, specialized body of knowledge. By taking objectivity as a criterion for the pursuit of truth, the actual individual is sacrificed.

In 1846, the Danish sensationalist tabloid The Corsair published drawings and articles mocking Kierkegaard, portraying him as a comical eccentric, walking down the street and being pointed at and ridiculed by people for what he called his slow and tardy "death by goose trampling.

This unpleasant experience made Kierkegaard more aware of the dangers of the "crowd". He called these ignorant masses "mobs" and "opinionless rabble".

In his mind, the "crowd" brings blindness and error, and only the "individual" is the path to truth.

In the philosophical level, the subject refers to the person who has the ability to practice and know, while the subjectivity of the "individual" refers to the person who is in opposition to the objectivity, and the subjective-energy, which is the active response to the object world, replaces the objective way of thinking.

Here, Kierkegaard makes the famous proposition that truth is the subjectivity, the reality, of the "individual". What he means is that values are closely related to the individual, and one should choose a value that can [live and die for] the subjectivity of the "individual" and live.

03. Mutual Subjectivity

This is a requirement of the empirical science method. It means that empirical science is a practical science with an emphasis on the description of empirical facts and clear and concrete facts, and generally less on abstract theoretical generalizations.

The research method is mainly inductive, with more blind observations and experiments, and only statements of observations that can be verified by researchers of each discipline can be included and accepted.

By observation, the researcher means to scrutinize all

the objects, phenomena, and movements that exist in nature; it must be repeatable by everyone, i.e., to scrutinize all the objects, phenomena, and movements that exist in nature, not only by one or a few people with special gifts, but also by expressing them in words.

Strictly speaking, the first scrutiny of phenomena and movements and their verification are not mutually subjective, because any scrutiny of phenomena and movements is necessarily the work of a subject.

In philosophical terms, it means a being with a unique consciousness and a unique personal experience, or another entity external to itself and related to it.

Only through the medium of language and the communication between different subjects can the phenomena and motives of the scrutiny of things be verified as the subjectivity of each other as "individuals".

In addition, all the information obtained by scrutinizing the phenomena and movements of things must, without exception, be concrete facts and conditions that exist in front of us and belong to the external world of external images or environment, which is also the common structure of different subjects.

Some scholars believe that the a priori proposition that human beings reason out reasonable conclusions after careful consideration of various evidence has the validity of mutual subjectivity, because in principle, every cognitive subject has rationality belonging to abstract thinking activities such as concepts, judgments, and reasoning, and can realize the universal validity of rational a priori propositions.

Finally, anthropologists, who have made a holistic, fundamental and critical inquiry into the real world and human beings, often regard mutual "individual" subjectivity as the characteristic of human beings, because as subjects, human beings always point to others and depend on others.

For those who study the structure of experience and consciousness, the mutual "individual" subjectivity in philosophical phenomenology has a special and different meaning.

In discussing the question of the origins of the act of "cognition" and "identification" of a subject in order to ascertain knowledge, and the potential capacity of such knowledge to be used for specific purposes, phenomenologists argue that people live in groups in the world and that there are various relationships between people.

The most fundamental is the act of "cognition" and "recognition" of a subject by which cognition can be ascertained; it is the activity of thinking in which the human mind reflects the properties and connections of objective things and reveals their meaning and effects on people.

In a broad sense, cognition includes all cognitive activities of a person, i.e., the collective term for the mental phenomena of perception, memory, thought, imagination, language comprehension, and production, and these cognitions have the potential ability to be used for specific purposes, meaning that through experience or association, one is able to become familiar with and further understand something.

It means that a person, as a subject of practice and knowledge, is conscious of his or her own subject status, subject ability and subject value.

It is the relationship between the conceptual expression of the subject's conscious initiative and creativity, and the consciousness of one or more other subjects. Each of them reflects the characteristics and connections of objective things, and reveals all the objects or phenomena that exist in nature objectively, and the cognitive role of thinking about the meaning and role of human beings, that is, mutual "individual" subjectivity.

A. Schutz synthesizes the mental processes of thought or cognition of M. Weber and Ed. Husserl, the originator of phenomenology, and constructs his sociology to explicate Husserl's statement of "mutual subjectivity".

It emphasizes that each individual has an a priori ego and the ability to cognize ourselves through the mental process of knowing and understanding things through the activity of consciousness, thus constituting a mutual cognitive commonality or homogeneity, and that the expression and representation of this social consciousness in social reality is also the expression of mutual "individual" subjectivity.

Therefore, Kierkegaard does not deny that there are objective truths in the world, such as physical laws and mathematical axioms. However, he believes that although these truths are factual and transcend personal emotions and opinions, they can only tell us what is true, not how to live.

If the truth stands before me, cold and naked, not caring whether I recognize it or not, what good does it do me?

It can be said that the real truth that Kierkegaard considers is not the kind of physical laws or mathematical axioms that have nothing to do with personal experience, but rather the values that are imprinted with personal choice and emotion.

But since truth belongs to the subjectivity of the "individual" and lacks absolute objectivity, truth is full of uncertainty for the individual, because one never knows whether what one chooses is correct and whether it can be recognized by others.

Zygmunt says that truth is subjective and requires the subject's choice of ideal values and the passionate handing over of destiny to others.

It is the tendency to look at all the objects or phenomena that exist in nature with the subject's own needs as the basis of vision, and it is the viewpoint, experience, consciousness, spirit, feelings, desires or beliefs that an individual or a particular subject in a group can have.

Its fundamental characteristic is that it exists only within the subject and belongs to a being with a unique consciousness and a unique personal experience, or to another state of consciousness that is external to and related to the entity itself.

It can influence human judgment and the element of truth, becoming consistent with objective facts, true and not false. Truth is precisely an adventure, an adventure that chooses objective uncertainty by virtue of an infinite passion.

04. A state of awareness or action

The mission of Kierkegaard's philosophy is to find a good life, so we need to return to human existence, to understand the limited purpose that human beings can achieve, to understand human anxiety, fear, and sensuality, and to find in them the possibility of living a life of peace.

The emphasis on truth is essentially a free choice of objective uncertainty and a passionate handing over of destiny to others. Thus, Kierkegaard turns to the religious belief in a religion, or a doctrine, that is believed, worshipped, and held as a rule and guide for speech and action.

He pointed out that the relationship between the individual and God is in fact the relationship between the individual and objective uncertainty. He points out that if the individual can objectively grasp God, there is no need to trust God; it is because the individual cannot grasp God that he must trust.

Trusting God means that you do not get into heaven by yourself, but by God. We cannot get to heaven by doing good deeds, thinking that doing them makes us acceptable to God.

Once we believe that God forgives our sins, a new life begins - "If anyone is in God, he is a new creation; old things have passed away, and they have become new. This person then becomes a follower of God. As a follower of God, this person relies on God in all aspects of his life, not just on God's forgiveness of sins.

For example, the apostle Paul rebuked the Galatian believers for not recognizing this very important principle.

They had begun by trusting in Christ, but because of the pressure of the legalists they had gone into the realm of "spiritual advancement by human effort through religious works". In fact, he saw their failure to understand this as the result of their confusion. This is undoubtedly the product of Satan's deception. (Gal. 3:1-5)

O ignorant Galatians, who has confused you, when the crucifixion of Jesus Christ has been painted alive before your eyes? I only ask you this: Did you receive the Holy Spirit because of the law? Did you receive the Holy Spirit because you believed in the gospel? Did you enter by the Holy Spirit, and are you now made perfect by the flesh? Are you so ignorant? Have you suffered so much, and all in vain? Is it really in vain? He who gave you the Holy Spirit, and did miracles among you, did he do them because you practiced the law? Is it because you have heard the gospel? Trust in the power and plan of God is absolutely necessary.

God is the One who knows all truth, so He wants us to build our lives on His truth. Jesus said ...... "Therefore, whoever hears these words of mine and does them is like a wise man who built his house on the rock; and when the rain falls, or when the water rushes, or when the wind blows, or when it hits the house, it does not fall down, because the foundation is built on the rock. (Matthew 7:24-25)

Kierkegaard believes that the greater the uncertainty, the greater the risk to the believer's "trust", but also the greater his faith. Objective uncertainty can mean something that is logically impossible and contradictory.

In other words, objective uncertainty can sometimes even mean absurdity. For Kierkegaard, faith is a decision to trust God by one's own will, regardless of the existence of God and the absurdity of the Christian religion (that the divine, all-powerful God could become incarnate and die on the cross).

Zikgoh has cited the story of Abraham in the Christian religion who was commanded by God to kill his son and sacrifice him to "trust" as an example of what true "trust" faith is all about. When God saw that Abraham was old and childless, he was so merciful that he gave him a son named Isaac.

One day Abraham heard God calling him to offer Isaac as a sacrifice. If Isaac was sacrificed, Abraham's wife Sarah would not be able to bear it.

Abraham chose not to tell Sarah and took Isaac to the mountain to prepare for the sacrifice. To the casual observer, Abraham was unfaithful to his wife, and possibly guilty of murder, plus how could Abraham "trust" that the voice calling him was really God and not some other evil spirit?

The most important thing is that Abraham's "trust" had to face the tension between ethics and religion, in terms of ethics he could not kill, but in terms of religion he needed to "trust" to kill his son for sacrifice.

In the end, Abraham chose to sacrifice, and Kierkegaard believes that the greatness of Abraham was that he "trusted" and loved God so much that he offered the best he had to God. That best thing was his son, and even though a father has the highest moral responsibility for his son, he still offered his own son in order to "trust" the uncertain test that God had given him.

In other words, Abraham's "trust" manifests its greatness in the tension between ethics and religion.

Ziklag believes that man has gone from the ethics of the various moral standards of human interaction to the use of human wonder and awe at the mysteries of the universe and life to constitute a doctrine of persuasion for good and punishment for evil.

The religious transition of faith requires the individual

to make a "leap of faith", i.e., one must "trust" with passion, and leap from one stage of existence to another. The three stages of life in Zygmunt.

2. Kierkegaard: Three Stages of Aesthetics

According to Kierkegaard, man believes in the supernatural, superhuman mystical realm and power that dominates nature and society, and thus is infinitely revered and worshiped. On the way to religious belief, one may pass through three stages of existence: the aesthetic, ethical, and religious stages.

The difference and transition between the aesthetic and ethical stages is explained more clearly in Either/Or, while the distinction between the ethical and religious stages is explained in more detail in Fear and Trembling.

The aesthetic stage is the initial and immediate stage of life, the ethical stage is the intermediate stage of transition, and the religious stage is the highest stage of life. The three stages of life can be seen as a person's journey toward God.

01. Aesthetic Stage

The aesthetic stage is characterized by a person's feelings, impulses and emotions in life. In this stage, a person "lives for himself or herself", using mental activities such as sensation, perception, thinking, and memory, and is aware of his or her physical and mental state and the changes of people, events, and things in the environment, and adopts a way of life that aims to directly satisfy his or her desires.

Therefore, they tend to indulge in carnal pleasures, and their lives are full of corruption, moral corruption, and shameless behavior.

In other words, it can be said that people at this stage are hedonists. Sometimes people in this stage will romanticize their own depravity.

For example, the artist would say that this is a way of life, that this life will bring some pleasure to people. Don Juan is a typical example of the aesthetic stage, according to Chicco.

Don Juan is a well-known legendary figure in Spain, and many people regard him as a synonym for "holy man of love" and "flirt". Don Juan was fond of pursuing young and beautiful women, and was eager to have one-night stands with wild dogs and to have sexual relations with them, but never thought of making any promises to women, raising children or being with them for the rest of his life, assuming ethical and moral responsibilities.

Chikgo also points out that Don Juan's lifestyle eventually leads to emptiness, despair and boredom. Because the repetition of pleasure is tiresome, and it is unlikely that one will be able to live a life of pleasure without stopping.

If one is to try to leave things behind, to be free from the dilemma of constraint, one needs to pursue another way of life. That is, ethics, meaning the ethical and moral reasoning of human beings, refers to the way of life in which people live with each other with various moral standards.

At this time, individuals wish to accept the guidance of universal ethics and moral law, that is, from the aesthetic stage, jumped to the ethical stage.

02. Ethical stage

The ethical stage is characterized by the individual's willingness to be guided by one's own knowledge and the ability to realize one's own will according to the law. In other words: people are guided by certain values, guided by respect for natural laws and social laws, restrain their personal desires, and combine their desires with social obligations.

In this stage, people "live for the sake of others", and individuals must think of others and no longer only care about their own interests. Since this stage requires the individual to assume certain responsibilities for others, the individual forms an ethical relationship with others.

The individual no longer disregards his ethical responsibilities to others, like Don Juan in the aesthetic stage. The representative figure of this stage is Judge William, the character of "Either/Or".

He pays special attention to a certain thing or idea, or puts emphasis on it to express his struggle for freedom and for others, and to remind himself to be a good husband.

At first glance, Don Juan in the aesthetic stage and Judge William in the ethical stage are two aspects of the human being, mutually exclusive or opposing poles, or even unrelated.

The actual state of being (the likeness), the objective description of natural and social phenomena, the ethical stage, is sublimated by the aesthetic stage.

Romantic love in the aesthetic stage, through a certain leap of the individual who chooses to assume ethical and moral responsibilities, rises to the love of a spousal relationship between two people who are married.

However, the ethical stage is not the highest stage of life. At this stage, although the individual makes himself subordinate to the universal ethical and moral laws, ethics and morality belong to all objects or phenomena that exist objectively in the natural world.

When the two kinds of irreconcilable cognition or action exist, they sometimes inevitably produce a state of discomfort or tension for the individual.

The individual, in the presence of dissonance, is driven to alleviate or eliminate this uncomfortable state of mind caused by the conflict of mental processes of awareness and understanding through the activities of the consciousness of the individual.

In this case, the individual has a subjective experience of consciousness in which he or she feels guilty for violating family, religious, or social norms, either in actual behavior or in imagination, which triggers internal conscience condemnation.

Kierkegaard believes that an individual generates an internal emotional feeling. When a person wants to do or has done a certain act and this act contradicts the moral standards and values that constitute his conscience.

The experience of guilt and shame cannot be explained by ethics and morality, because the feeling of guilt belongs to the religious sphere, and the way to free oneself from the experience of subjective consciousness of guilt caused by the internal condemnation of one's conscience for violating family, religious or social norms, either in actual behavior or in imagination, is to go to God.

From the ethical stage of human relationships and dealings, which are of a certain nature, between people and people or between people and things, to the religious stage of believing that what rules nature and society is supernatural and superhuman mysterious realms and powers, and therefore infinitely revered and worshiped.

In the process of moving from a certain status and state to another status and state, Kierkegaard believes that one needs to make a leap of faith, i.e., you fully embrace "trust" in your faith and are willing to do anything for it, even if it requires you to pay a great price.

03. Religious stage

The religious stage is characterized by a belief in and worship of a certain religion or a certain doctrine as a guideline for one's words and actions.

It is no longer governed by the desires of the aesthetic stage, nor is it governed by the things of the ethical stage, which have a wide range of common qualities and are not limited by time and space, with ethics and moral laws as the norms of behavior.

It can be said that in the religious stage, which believes that the supernatural and superhuman mysterious realm and power dominates nature and society, and therefore is infinitely revered and worshiped, man "lives for God".

In other words, at this stage, man is in absolute relationship with the Absolute, and places God in the highest position, and believes in a certain religion or doctrine as a standard and guide for speech and action, above personal enjoyment and universal moral obligation.

The religious stage of believing in the supernatural, superhuman mystical realms and powers that dominate nature and society, and thus infinite awe and worship, is higher than the ethical stage of human relationships and rules for handling them, which shocked many people.

If we say that the ethical stage of human relations and the rules for handling these relations is the stage where individuals realize their own knowledge and laws, the rational stage where they consciously work for the realization of certain ideals or the achievement of certain purposes.

The irrational stage is the religious stage where one believes that the supernatural and superhuman mysterious realm and power dominates nature and society, and therefore is infinitely revered and worshiped.

When man wants to establish a one-to-one relationship with God, God may have to test the individual. These tests sometimes go beyond the boundaries of the moral laws of time and space, which are widely shared, to the point where a person seems to be called by God to do something unethical.

It is easy to see that the representative figure of this

stage is Abraham. His greatness lies in the fact that he had to choose between human relationships and the ethical norm of "Thou shalt not kill" and the religious test of "Loving God" to "trust", to be convinced of a certain religion or a certain doctrine, to worship it, and to hold it as a rule and guide for his words and actions.

If so, Abraham was faithful when he was called by God and simply fulfilled a requirement that did not exceed the moral law, he was faithful.

But what made Abraham great was that he set aside the requirements and effects of the moral law and chose to kill his son for the sake of "trusting" God. That is to say, his greatness was in choosing between the tensions of ethics and religion, and choosing to "trust" in a religion or a doctrine that he believed in, worshiped, and held as a rule and guide for his words and actions.

Ziklag does not totally reject human sensibility and rationality, but he believes that faith in a religion or a doctrine that is obeyed, worshiped, and held as a rule and guide for speech and action is higher than the first two.

In other words, faith in God cannot be operated rationally by logic, scientific method, etc. One can only "trust" in God by believing in and worshiping a certain religion or a certain doctrine as a rule and guide for speech and action. Even faith in God, or the "trust" that God gives, requires absurdity.

Belief in God means the possibility of going beyond reason into a mystical and absurd spiritual realm. That is why Kierkegaard said of the belief in "trust": "I believe because it is absurd (credo quia absurdum).

He was posthumously named the father of existentialism because he had the courage to stand up for himself and refute the wrong ideas or words and actions, as represented by Hegel, the dehumanization of Western rationalism and the complete detachment of philosophy from the realm of "existence", which became a castle in the air.

But Kierkegaard's position is always purely and completely Christian: he emphasizes the subjectivity of the individual, exposes the absurdity, anxiety and despair of human "existence", and believes that only in the relationship between man and God can man's "trust" realize himself. The focus of later existentialists, however, is often only on the interception of their analysis of existence.

He offers many criticisms of the social and Christian reforms of his time, criticizing the faults and shortcomings of ideas, cultures, morals, customs, arts, institutions, and ways of doing things that have been passed down through the generations and through history, in order to correct them, and to make significant breakthroughs in the philosophy as a way of inquiry, not just as a specific, specialized body of knowledge.

In particular, his criticism of Hegel and Romanticism laid the groundwork for the development of modernism. He also gave a modern meaning to the role of the Bible and had a great influence on twentieth-century theology and philosophy of religion.

It was only years after his death that he was honored with the title of "Father of Existentialism," a title bestowed upon him by philosophers of religion, as he lamented that he had "never had a confidant" in his life and had not been recognized by the intellectual community.

The reason why philosophers of religion gave him this title is that he shifted the focus of the discussion of universal and fundamental issues, including existence, knowledge, values, reason, mind, and language, from the exploration of the external world and the construction of knowledge systems to human existence itself.

Existentialism's Being refers to the existence of human life itself. If the question is: Did the egg come first, or did the chicken come first? If the question is: The occurrence of tides is basically related to the gravitational force of the Earth and other celestial bodies, and the main influence comes from the Moon, then the Sun itself is more massive than the Moon, so why is it the Moon and not the Sun?

This question is meaningless, because whether you ask this question or not, these physical phenomena are the same, will not change.

But the existence of human beings will change. Human existence is not dead, but living, vital and free to choose.

In other words, existence is a choice, the possibility of choosing to be oneself. The first is to choose not to be oneself, and the second is to choose to become oneself.

The first is to choose not to be oneself, obviously easier, in this case we are used to disguise ourselves, hide our true feelings, play the role expected by others, and never make a sincere choice, because we are afraid that a sincere choice will bring us into conflict with others.

The second is the choice to be ourselves. This is the philosophical reference to autonomy, which means self-restraint or self-management. Isaiah Berlin, in his famous speech 《The Two Concepts of Freedom》, clearly explains the quality of autonomy: "I want my life to be determined by me, not by external factors. I want to be a subject and not an object. ...... to be an actor, a decider and not a decider.

I want to be a self-directed person and not an external object, or an animal or slave playing the role of a human being. ...... I want to be a conscious, thinking, willful and active person who can take responsibility for my own choices and can explain the decisions I make with my own ideas and purposes."

It is clear that autonomy implies a resistance to being determined. And, as Imm. Kant points out, freedom is the ability to resist being determined. The relationship between autonomy and freedom can be seen.

According to Kant, with freedom one is no longer dependent on the law of cause and effect, nor is one subject to the body or the senses. G.W.F. Hegel applied freedom not only to thinking but also to living.

R. Peterson argues that freedom of mind is necessary for thought to transcend. In essence, freedom means freedom of the will, and with freedom of the will comes responsibility for one's own actions. To be responsible for one's own actions is an expression of autonomy.

Thus, Kierkegaard brings out the connotation of free choice in the "existence" of the individual. He argues that although only human beings are qualified to use the word "existence" among all things in the universe, few people actually use it.

As a vivid analogy, Kierkegaard once mentioned that life is like a drunken farmer driving a wagon home in a state of consciousness close to unconsciousness, apparently the farmer is driving the wagon forward, but in fact the old horse is dragging the drunken farmer home. Because the farmer was drunk and had no sober consciousness at all, the old horse knew the way and was able to drag the drunken farmer home.

Most of the time, one has a strong desire to sleep and is in a state of consciousness close to unconsciousness, which is not easy to awaken.

It is only when one is awake that one can decide what path one wants to take and be one's true self. But this awakening to the meaning of life's existence is still the awakening to the meaning of life's existence of the individual's will, the awakening to the autonomy of the individual.

Chapter 4: Nietzsche: The God of Wine and the God of the Sun

However, the awakening of the individual autonomy of the meaning of life existence, the awakening of the meaning of the liberation of individual willed life existence, is still in the stage of the awakening of the external autonomy of the body or spirit, and has not yet entered the stage of the awakening of the meaning of life existence itself, that is, the awakening of the overall, fundamental and critical inquiry into the real world and human beings. The "philosophy of life" stage.

Friedrich Wilhelm Nietzsche (October 15, 1844 - August 25, 1900) was a German philosopher and thinker who studied the principles and principles of the universe and life, the meaning of the existence of individual will, and the awakening of individual autonomy.

His posthumous manuscript "The Will to Power" contains the phrase: "Doubts about present morality will sweep the world! It seems to be a prediction of what will happen in the future (in the present). The most widely known of Nietzsche's writings is "Thus Spoke Zarathustra".

Nietzsche's original name was Friedrich Wilhelm Nietzsche. Wilhelm Nietzsche (October 1844) Nietzsche (October 15, 1844 - August 25, 1900) was a famous German philosopher, thinker, poet and composer who is considered to be the founder of modern Western philosophy.

He was born on October 15, 1844, on the birthday of Frederick William IV, then King of Prussia. The father asked for permission to name his son after the king, which was granted. His grandfather was a devout Christian who wrote theological works, and his mother was a Polish nobleman of noble blood.

However, the God they believed in did not always "love" them. When Nietzsche was five years old, his father, whom he regarded as the goal of his life, died of cerebral tenderness, and two months later his brother, who was only two years old, died.

As for his enlightenment in philosophy, it started

when he was 20 years old and bought Schopenhauer's book "The World as Will and Representation" at an old bookstore.

At that time, Nietzsche was very confused: Why would a genius like Schopenhauer be abandoned by the world and his great work be in an obscure corner?

From that time on, Schopenhauer became an icon in Nietzsche's mind, and later he was also considered as the successor of Schopenhauer's "voluntarism".

In philosophy, it is a philosophical theory that proposes that a person's will is the necessary and ultimate basis for his or her [conduct] and [achievement of values]. Philosophers who have theories similar to this theory include Pascal, Kierkegaard, Schopenhauer, and Nietzsche.

Voluntarism "places the will in a more dominant role than the intellect in the metaphysical or psychological system," or "considers the will as the fundamental element of cosmic nature and human activity.

Nietzsche's philosophy, which at that time was considered a "philosophy of action," is in fact an act performed to achieve an end. A philosophy that claims to maximize the individual's demands and desires. A typical action theory treats behavior as the result of human interaction with the environment.

His philosophy has the grandeur of being proud of everything and critical of everything. This is one of the important reasons why his philosophical thinking is appreciated by post-modernism.

Perhaps it was because Nietzsche needed to resist the little demons within him, and to become a doctor after a long illness, that he often presented himself as a psychologist, believing that he had a special, different and special gift, and was familiar with what he called the breakdown of things and concepts into simpler components.

He was familiar with what he called the "art of psychoanalysis" of breaking down things and concepts into their simpler components and examining them separately to find their intrinsic properties and their connections with each other. After that, he lived for another ten years, but became totally incapacitated and died in 1902.

In Nietzsche's hands, psychology was a method and a

weapon for critically discussing thinkers he disagreed with (such as Plato, Rousseau, and Kant) and the results of their sublime thinking or cognitive mental processes, for uncovering the evil, poorly understood, and semantically unclear energy of the individual, for triggering the activity of the individual, for sustaining and promoting that activity toward a fixed goal (such as the concrete presence of an immediate event). Nietzsche saw).

The psychological disorder caused Nietzsche's mental disorder and caused him to lose his teaching position at the University of Basel and to have to retire at the age of thirty-five with a small pension.

He spent the next few years wandering alone, writing works that are now famous, but were unknown at the time. There has never been a definitive conclusion as to the cause of Nietzsche's illness. Nietzsche insisted that pain and illness were blessings that stimulated the imagination and gave sick people a depth that healthy people did not have.

Post-modernism has either rejected and denounced, or eliminated and excluded, traditional philosophies that are out of step with the times and modern philosophies. Postmodernism, however, is particularly fond of

Nietzsche's philosophical thinking, and postmodernists have taken in everything they need from Nietzsche's philosophy.

This includes Nietzsche's fundamental ideas of holistic, fundamental, and critical inquiry into the real world and people, and even Nietzsche's analytical style of philosophy.

Nietzsche's tendency toward elimination and exclusion has become the spiritual pillar of postmodernism and, in effect, the theoretical precursor of postmodernism.

For Nietzsche, his philosophy of holistic, fundamental, and critical inquiry into the real world and human beings does not require the deduction of conclusions from known or assumed premises, or the inversion of reasons from known answers to results based on argumentation, without a systematic framework.

Nietzsche's philosophical view is that, as Schopenhauer said, life is like a pendulum swinging back and forth between pain and boredom, so his philosophy is not a theoretical system at all, but his most sincere and direct perception of the experience of pain and joy in life.

Among Nietzsche's "late works," Jenseits von Gut und Böse. Vorspiel einer Philosophie der Zukunft (The Other Side of Good and Evil: A Prelude to the Philosophy of the Future), published in 1886, comes closest to the style of his middle period.

In this book Nietzsche, by ironically listing the basic properties of an event or an object to describe or regulate the meaning of a word or a concept, defines the conditions that a true philosophy should possess: imagination, self-assertion, danger, creativity, and the "creation of values"-all other conditions that he considered incidental.

From here Nietzsche is prompted to question some important assumptions of the philosophical tradition, such as the concepts of "self-consciousness," "knowledge," "truth," and "free will," which are often used by many philosophical schools.

Nietzsche criticizes these concepts of thought, culture, morality, customs, art, institutions, and ways of doing things, which have been passed down through the generations and through history, as insufficiently substantiated. A universal morality exists in the human world.

In his famous "Master-Slave Moralism," Nietzsche reassesses the humanist tradition that has long dominated Western philosophy by judging and analyzing an event or a person, and by arguing that even when domination, possession, or even harm is inflicted on the weak, it does not mean that anyone who considers himself superior is entitled to blame or to be blamed.

In this book, Nietzsche completely and fully puts the arguments of moral relativism and perspectivism into practical and effective action.

Nietzsche, in his first academic work, The Birth of Tragedy, begins to understand the ideas that have been handed down from generation to generation, from history, in favor of the process of acquiring or applying knowledge, or the process of processing information, which is the most basic mental process of human beings.

It includes sensation, perception, memory, thought, imagination and language, and the critique of humanism, invention and creation that is adapted to the objective world, in line with human spiritual pursuits, and recognized and accepted by the vast majority of people.

He believes that despite the increasing prosperity and

progress of human material civilization, people have not achieved true freedom and happiness.

Moreover, the scope of study is based on certain objects, and experiments and logical reasoning are used to find unified and definite objective laws and truths, mechanically crushing human personalities and rigid frameworks, depriving people of the passion for free thought and limiting the impulse to create culture.

He declares: "Great suffering will eventually liberate the mind. He believed that his most prolific writings coincided with his most painful moments of physical and psychological suffering, and he used the language of disease to "diagnose" modern civilization, trying to replace the language of good and bad, good and evil, with that of "sickness and health" and "weakness and strength".

In 1882, in The Gay Science, Nietzsche used the metaphor of a "madman" to illustrate his prophecy of a new age, proclaiming to a confused public that "God is dead".

At a time when the West has lost its faith in Christ God, nihilism is a condition that he believes must and should be overcome, and the antidote to this condition is the "superman," a brilliant genius, overflowing with creativity and the will to power, who can only break free from morality, a social ideology.

It is the sum of the norms of behavior that regulate the relationship between people and individuals, and between individuals and society. It is only after breaking free from the fetters of morality (a social ideology that regulates the relationship between people, between individuals and society.

All the gods are dead, and Nietzsche argues that Western civilization is on an open sea, without the moral shackles of ideas, cultures, morals, customs, arts, institutions, and ways of behavior that have been handed down from generation to generation and from history, good and bad things are possible again.

Without the entanglement of mental illness, Nietzsche might never have come to this important insight, at least in his own opinion. Perhaps it was because Nietzsche needed to fight his inner demons that he often presented himself as a psychologist, believing that he had a special gift and was well versed in what he called "the art of psychoanalysis.

Sigmund Freud Sigmund Freud and Carl Jung were the first to write about psychoanalysis. Freud even avoided going deeper, using a planned and systematic method of data collection, analysis, and interpretation to obtain Nietzsche's work, because he knew that his own knowledge of natural and social phenomena, based on existing empirical knowledge, experience, facts, laws, cognition, and tested hypotheses, would be used as a basis for his work.

Nietzsche's work is based on his own empirical knowledge, experience, facts, laws, cognition, and tested hypotheses, and logical inferential summaries through generalization and deductive reasoning.

Attracted by psychology, Nietzsche was so disappointed with traditional philosophy that he replaced it with psychology. He liked to first psychoanalyze the results of thinking or the psychological processes of cognition, and then "refute" the results or systems of ideas and concepts that are reflected in human consciousness through the activities of thinking.

In Nietzsche's hands, psychology is a method or weapon for discussing the thinkers he disagrees with (e.g., Plato, Rousseau, and Kant) and their noble ideas, or for organizing the ideas in the course of reflection, revealing the evil and unconscionable motives behind them (e.g., the concrete facts and conditions that exist in front of him as Nietzsche sees them).

Nietzsche regarded the views that these people held about things or problems from a certain position or perspective as symptoms of an underlying mental illness. "A thinker not only transforms his physical body into the highest level, the act of "knowing" and "recognizing" a subject in order to know it with certainty, but also these knowings have the potential ability to be used for specific purposes.

The act of transformation is the study of the universe, of the principles and principles of life," meaning the ability to become familiar with the form of understanding something through experience or association, when nothing else is necessary.

However unjust this approach to a holistic, fundamental, and critical inquiry into the real world and human beings may be.

Nietzsche's writing is full of language that is caustic, humorous, to the point, and to the point. At the same time, it is persuasive, penetrating, linguistically straightforward, deeply centered in psychological insight and brilliant analysis, and often alert and perceptive, quick to perceive changes in situations, and deeply penetrating in the psychological relationship between human beings and their own minds.

This analytical skill was very effective in Nietzsche's own case, and he was the first person to admit that analysis was effective in his own situation.

1. The God of Wine and the Sun God

In his first academic work, The Birth of Tragedy, Nietzsche originally dedicated this book to Wagner, whom he still admired at the time, to explore the nature of beauty, the relationship between art and reality, and the general laws of artistic creation.

But there are still many personal insights, and these insights have become the objective reflection of Nietzsche's future philosophical thinking in which he explores and reflects on the origins of the fundamental questions of life, knowledge, and value, and of the system of concepts.

He received a major insight into the meaning of human affairs from Schopenhauer, who believed that the essence of the world is the will to live.

The will is the psychological state in which a person consciously strives for the realization of a certain ideal or the achievement of a certain purpose. The will as the ideology of philosophical thinking is inseparably related to Nietzsche's philosophical view of literary thinking as the background of philosophical logical thinking.

His aesthetic view is based on the study of universal and fundamental issues, including the fields of existence, knowledge, value, reason, mind, and language, etc. He analyzes in detail and in order, from the process of learning or applying knowledge, or the process of processing information, which is the most basic mental process of human beings.

It includes the sensory, perceptual, memory, thinking, imagination and language understanding, understanding the meaning of the ancient Greek mythology, Apollo, the sun god, and Dionysus, the god of wine, not directly saying the name of the thing to be said, but using the name of another thing related to it, instead of them to interpret the origin of the tragedy.

We not only understand the matter, but also see it from the other side's point of view, and understand the cause and effect of the whole matter, and we agree with his disciplinary idea of analyzing and reflecting on the fundamental issues of life, knowledge, and values.

I also agree with his idea of analyzing and reflecting on the fundamental issues of life, knowledge, and values, as well as the development of human civilization. The god of the sun and the god of wine are both sons of Zeus. The god of the sun is the god of logic and reason, while the god of wine is the god of chaos and emotion.

The book is ostensibly about the origins of tragedy, but in fact it is about the over-emphasis in modern society on the ability of people to form concepts, make judgments, analyze, synthesize, compare, reason, calculate, and so on, bringing about cultural things or phenomena that have a positive meaning for people or groups, are valued by people, or can make people feel satisfied, and become a crisis that people respect or are interested in pursuing.

In his book, Nietzsche points out that the rational tradition of human beings, which developed from the ancient Greek era, reasoned and deduced reasonable conclusions (symbolized by the Apollonian art) after careful consideration of all evidence.

To a large extent, it is the tendency to look at things from the perspective of the subject's own needs, and it is the attribute of view, experience, consciousness, spirit, feelings, desires or beliefs that an individual can have.

Its fundamental characteristic is that it exists only within the subject and belongs to the subject's state of mind. It can influence the feelings and intuitions of human judgment and truth factors, while also denying and escaping from the fact of human tragedy and madness. The god of wine represents sensuality, or irrationality, which is precisely the affirmation of humanity and truth without falsehood, and is also needed in this era.

Nietzsche, in his later autobiography, "Look! In his later autobiography, Behold the Man, Nietzsche pointed out two of the greatest things about the book that were not easily understood: first, the discovery of the spirit of the god of wine as the power of salvation in life; and second, the emergence of Socrates as the cause of the decline of ancient Greek culture.

Nietzsche pointed out that in order to cure the disease

of modern civilization, the instinct of human will to live must be restored and given a new soul, and a new explanation must be given for the true meaning of life.

2. The Birth of Tragedy

The Birth of Tragedy" is ostensibly an exploration of the origins of tragedy, but in fact it is a discussion of modern society, which places too much emphasis on logical reasoning to observe things. It is not easy to show emotion, not good at sympathy, and does not care about the harmony of interpersonal relationships, which brings about the crisis of cultural values.

In his book, Nietzsche pays special attention to a certain thing or idea or expresses it in a solemn way, in order to revive the artistic spirit of the ancient Greek era, in order to save the decay caused by the supremacy of reason in modern times. In this book, he proposes the spirit of the god of wine and the spirit of the god of the sun to transcend Schopenhauer's "pessimistic and world-weary" philosophy.

The spirit represented by Apollo, the god of the sun, appeals to the beauty of all objects or phenomena that exist objectively in nature, while the spirit represented by Dionysius, the god of wine, appeals to the substance of tragedy or music hidden within things.

It also represents silence and intoxication and passion respectively. The Birth of Tragedy is an objective reflection of the will of human consciousness in general, the result of life experience and thought, and the existence of a conceptual system, which obviously comes from the inquiry and contemplation of the world and life by the "art of tragedy".

The book The Birth of Tragedy begins with a discussion of the birth of Greek "tragedy" and develops a view of art and aesthetics. The ideas in the book are strongly influenced by Schopenhauer and Wagner.

However, it is a "pessimism" that overcomes the lack of confidence in life or the development of all things, and believes that art is not a liberation from life's troubles and fetters, and thus from physical and mental freedom, but rather a mental state that arises from the decision to achieve a certain goal, often expressed in words or actions of conquest.

The Greek "tragedy" arises from the [confrontation

and reconciliation] of the spirit of Apollo, the god of the sun, and the spirit of Dionysus, the god of wine, and is dominated by the spirit of the "god of wine".

The book has shown the tendency to change Schopenhauer's "psychological state in which life consciously strives to realize a certain ideal or achieve a certain purpose" to "psychological state in which power decides to achieve a certain purpose", and advocates that in the art of "tragedy", one should perceive beyond pain, metamorphose and sublimate into a higher, conquering joy, and realize that life is eternal beauty.

1. Schopenhauer's pessimistic worldview.

Nietzsche is based on Schopenhauer's "pessimistic" worldview. In German, "Weltanschauung" (worldview) means "looking at the world above", a term used in German intellectual theory, and refers to a "broad world concept".

Weltanschauung refers to a basic framework of human perception through which the individual can understand and interact with the world. It refers to Nietzsche's personal view of society as a whole and Schopenhauer's personal knowledge and basic cognitive orientation to explain the nature of [Greek nature] and [Greek culture].

It is an aesthetic and intuitive theoretical description of Schopenhauer's irrational will to live, and as a way to free oneself from troubles and fetters, and thus to obtain freedom of mind and body, and to give a single or generalized exposition of a certain or many problems, events, studies, etc., and to propose problems or solutions.

The ability to explain known facts, principles, and principles in one's own words, texts, or other symbols, and to talk about [access] and [comprehend] in a general and organized description and account of people, events, and circumstances.

The key to Schopenhauer's philosophical thought is to recognize that Schopenhauer first talks about "epistemology" and then "ontology", which is exactly the opposite of metaphysics that first talks about "ontology" and then "epistemology", and opens the way from "knowledge" to "ontology".

The term "epistemology" is derived from the combination of the Greek word "knowledge" and "doctrine", which is a doctrine of knowing (or knowledge); it is defined as: "epistemology" is a theory of the principles and principles of the universe and life, which is concerned with the nature of knowing and the laws of development.

In other words, it is a philosophical doctrine that examines the premise and foundation of human knowledge, the process of occurrence and development of knowledge and its laws, the relationship between knowledge and objective reality, the standard of truth of knowledge, and the nature and structure of knowledge, also known as the theory of knowledge.

01. There are two definitions of philosophy.

"Epistemology is the rational and active process of reflection of the human mind on the real world or any object in the form of "inward dialogue".

The so-called inward dialogue is like talking to oneself without the condition of the listener, and is one of the themes of inquiry and reflection on fundamental questions about life, knowledge, and values.

First, it is a theory that explores the origin, nature, limits, and validity of knowledge.

It is a theory that explores the origin, nature, limits, and validity of knowledge, which uses textual metaphors to analyze how and why an event or an action is possible, to explain what is not known into what is known, and to define the meaning of a thought, thing, or name, so that "epistemology" is used in the same way as Gnosiology. The second is the theory of knowledge.

Second, it is regarded as the Theory of Knowledge

The theory of knowledge is the act of "knowing" and "recognizing" a subject in order to have confident knowledge, and these knowledges have the potential ability to be used for specific purposes.

It means the ability to become familiar with something through experience or association; this fact or state is called knowledge, and it includes knowing or understanding a science, art, or technique. A systematic analysis of the concepts of knowledge that people use to understand the world.

"Epistemology" can be divided into a broad definition and a narrow definition, with the narrow definition only addressing the validity of knowledge.

In the first definition, epistemology is the study of the

relationship between knowledge and reality, and therefore [the process of cognition] and [the validity of cognitive outcomes] become the subject of analysis, synthesis, reasoning, judgment, and other thinking activities, exploring issues such as how humans know, where knowledge comes from, how knowledge is formed, the functions of reason and mind in knowledge, whether truth exists, and the concepts of belief, knowledge, truth, opinion, and fact. and the difference between the concepts of belief, knowledge, truth, opinion, and fact.

In the second definition, "epistemology" broadly analyzes various acts of "cognition" and "identification" of a subject in order to determine the knowledge of certainty, and these knowledges have the potential to be used for specific purposes, and the concepts used to explain the world, so that "epistemology" has a critical function, focusing on different objects as the scope of study, and based on experiments and logical reasoning, to find unity and certainty. The basic concepts of objective laws and truths and the methods used, including the exploration of propositions, are based on experimental and logical reasoning.

On the surface, Schopenhauer seems to have not gone

beyond the scope of Kant's philosophy, but in fact he has changed the Kant's form of a priori knowledge in two ways.

On the one hand, he shifted to "egoism" (the idea that the ego is the only existence, and that the things in the external world and the mental states of others are only the contents of the ego consciousness, and exist in dependence on the ego mind, but do not really exist in themselves.) The ego, on the other hand

On the other hand, there is a shift to non-rational "intuition" (also known as intuition, which usually refers to a direct thought, feeling, belief, or preference that emerges quickly without much thought process. When a person has a belief, but does not know the reason for it, it is usually attributed to an intuition).

Schopenhauer rooted his irrational philosophy of the will to live in a certain range of objectively existing objects or phenomena in nature [irrational will] and [intuition of will] as expressed by Schelling and Fichte.

Schopenhauer considered the distinction between Kant's "phenomenon" and "object-object" reasonable, and held a different view from Fichte, Schelling, and Hegel, who abolished "object-object" in the same era.

Schopenhauer believed that the "object-self", which is an unknowable and absolutely unknowable being, can be known through direct thoughts, feelings, beliefs, or preferences that can emerge quickly without much thought process. Both "reason" and "knowledge" are subsidiary (i.e., will).

Once one enters the aesthetic (a special form of human understanding of the world, which means that one forms a state of non-utilitarian, figurative and emotional relationship with the world (society and nature).

Aesthetics is a state of mind (will) that consciously strives for the realization of a certain ideal or the achievement of a certain purpose when contemplating the existence of the world in the rational and emotional, subjective and objective knowledge, understanding, perception and judgment), they escape from this aesthetic process.

Life is originally accompanied by suffering, and the mental state of consciously striving for the realization of a certain ideal or the achievement of a certain purpose is dominated by the decision to achieve a certain purpose.

The state of mind that arises from the decision to

achieve a certain goal, often expressed by words and actions, is instead abandoned by the state of a non-utilitarian, figurative and emotional relationship between man and the world (society and nature), and how painful and empty it is.

It is a feeling of frustration and discouragement that arises because the "will" expects too much from itself and others, but does not reach the desired level.

Nietzsche, who originally respected Schopenhauer's "will to live", said: "The great suffering of the individual is the result of the deviation of the mental process of knowing and understanding things through the activity of consciousness of the human individual.

The unreliability of ultimate cognitive knowledge, the inequality of knowledge and skills that individuals use to effectively respond to particular circumstances and situations, all of these things make it necessary for the individual to have aesthetic value for natural objects and science, for everything that man produces.

What Nietzsche calls "aesthetic", especially the tragic art, can make people forget about death and time, and take the individual's life will power as the main body, so that all the phenomena and objects that exist objectively in nature can come out from and be governed by the individual's life will power.

The essence of the art of tragedy, which is also the core of the inner substance of things, is to make people perceive something sacred, to dissolve the suffering that human beings have to go through, and to bring them the joy of being freed from the sire bondage after removing the pain.

At the same time, it is believed that aesthetics is the only special form of human understanding of the world, a state of non-utilitarian, figurative and emotional relationship between human beings and the world (society and nature).

Nietzsche, who used aesthetics to know, understand, perceive and judge the world in terms of reason and emotion, subjectivity and objectivity, to express concepts with images and sounds, and to express the existence of things with aesthetic value, and to turn suffering into joy, has to a great extent departed from Schopenhauer's "pessimistic" thought.

02. The art of tragedy compensates for the shortcomings and limitations of human nature.

The great suffering of individuals, the inconsistency of human understanding, the unreliability of ultimate knowledge, and the inequality of abilities all make individuals need art, and the art of tragedy is the best way to compensate for this human flaw and limitation.

In the first chapter of The rule of metaphor, Paul Ricoeur identifies the themes that the Poetics and the Rhetoric want to address.

Although they are both based on metaphor, the role of the tragedy is to evoke pity and fear in the audience and then to purify these emotions (catharsis), while the role of rhetoric is to convince others, which makes them fundamentally different from each other.

In Nietzsche's The Birth of Tragedy, too many concepts are open to inspiration to be used as referential expressions, much less as expressions with real conditions. If the tragic arts need to be applied in a precise terminological context (e.g., scientific theory), then their role is purely one of enlightenment, i.e., they are meant to serve an end, or as a means of aiding understanding, rather than a means by which their true or false value can be assessed.

Rather than being able to assign truth conditions to their true or false values. The core of the tragedy lies in the interaction between the subject words, which in turn provides a condition of insightful meaning, and the words of this tragic art are not independent of the metaphorical context.

The purpose of the tragedy, therefore, is to show metaphorically the fall of the hero, thereby arousing the sympathy and fear of the audience, who must therefore be a figure for whom the public can identify. Aristotle then further explains that the emotion of pity is caused by innocent misfortune, while the emotion of fear comes from the heart of the average person.

He then defines the ideal tragic protagonist. The protagonist of a tragedy is usually somewhat nominal but not divine, and the doom that befalls him is not the result of his evil but of his own indecisiveness and weakness.

At the same time, the hero's actions cannot contradict the audience's sense of morality. According to these definitions, Aristotle says that Oedipus is a representative of the typical tragic figure. Nietzsche argues that it is wrong to inquire into the true conditions of tragedy, because "in tragedy we are aroused to the truth.

For "most of what attracts our attention in the tragedy is not propositional in character," that is, the tragedy is a prompting of thought that cannot be reduced to a set of real conditions, nor can it be subsumed within them.

The role of the tragedy is to "let the dramatic tension of the statement provoke or suggest an insight" that allows us to understand something else in the way that the language of the play, the question, speaks, and to understand one of the real things.

To understand something else in a way that one can explain the known facts and principles and principles in one's own tongue, words or other symbols, is not to admit some truth or fact. Therefore, to try to give a literal and true expression to the content of a tragedy is to be misled by the virtual reality of metaphor.

According to Nietzsche, we are in the metaphor of the tragedy, or we are the role-players in the metaphor of the tragedy: our existence is not derived from a Platonic eternal essence, nor from a Cartesian process of analysis, synthesis, judgment, reasoning, and other cognitive activities on the basis of images, concepts, and so on.

Rather, it is the interaction of forces of checks and

balances between competing internal drives or perspectives, between the abstract and the concrete, between the totality and the individual, between the narrow and the broad meaning of words, etc., that emerge in the way that we can, at best, call our own.

We are accustomed to think of truth as the act of "knowing" and "identifying" a subject by which knowledge is ascertained and which has the potential to use correspondence with reality for specific purposes.

It means to be able to become familiar with something through experience or association; it includes knowing or understanding an art, a science, or a technique. Nietzsche claims, however, that truth is revealed in "metaphor, metonymy, and the dynamic host of the human as the divine".

Because of the fundamental metaphorical nature of the conceptual construction of tragedy, there is a series of creative leaps that the drama makes from the neurological stimulation of retinal images (the first metaphor) and that enable (the second metaphor) forms of thought that reflect the nature of things, resulting in concepts that are as solid as they are reliable.

The metaphors and judgments we form through the art of tragedy can never correspond to the thing itself, because they are formed through a series of transformations that ensure that there is "no causality, correctness, or expression" in the association of the first (stimulus) and second (concept) stages.

02. The problem of science itself.

For the first time, science was seen as a problematic and questionable east. Nietzsche opposed all kinds of positivism and scientism produced by modern society, which is mainly marked by industrial civilization: he opposed the combination of mathematics and scientific experiments, a mechanical mode of thinking, to interpret the way people face the reality of life, and to look at art in a superficial way.

He was profoundly aware that people facing such a social framework of high-sounding talk often lose their imagination, passion and creativity, and their lonely and painful emotions and lonely souls cannot be properly settled.

Therefore, Nietzsche proposed in "The Birth of Tragedy" that one should learn to examine science through the eyes of an artist, and to examine the proposition of art through the eyes of the secret planning and direction of an event.

Schopenhauer in "The World as Will and Image" says: "The real driving force in the present world, which drives the rise of everything tragic, is the state of mind that arises from the recognition of a decision to achieve a certain end. That is, a life that does not give us true satisfaction and, therefore, does not deserve our loyalty to it, and this is where the spirit of tragedy lies, which leads people to do what they are told. Nietzsche

Nietzsche says that with this tone he corrupted the Dionysus spirit and the great Greek problem by mixing it with what is in vogue nowadays.

At the same time, he argues that the Romantic movement of the ontological state of modernity, with the will-to-power position it represents, leads to a variety of solidified formats that increasingly lose their power to confront the vulgar social status quo, and ultimately form a kind of nihilism.

Our philosophy and culture cannot get rid of this narrow-minded perspective, but reveal an anti-subjective orientation, and lose the multiple possibilities that inspire people to think about the meaning of life.

They only know how to watch the joy and criticism of human beings, but they cannot penetrate into the center of the great sorrow of human nature. Science and modern industrial civilization cannot bring us happiness and another world of spiritual longing.

03. What does ethics and morality mean through the mirror of life?

The tragic metaphor is valued because it does not conform to the accepted semantics of truth conditions, which determine the truth or falsity of a statement.

Literally, the phrase "the birth of tragedy" is wrong, if not absurd. But the statement is a metaphor for tragedy, which is meaningful and may even be true, even if it is far from clear in one sense.

Metaphorical contrastive theory holds that the true value of tragedy can be illustrated by citing the "spirit of the god of wine" and the "spirit of the god of the sun," two similar aspects of all of them, for example

The birth of the tragedy is formed by the interplay of the "spirit of wine" and the "spirit of the sun", but the two occur in different roles and positions. The spirit of the god of wine represents the primordial pain, and the spirit of the god of the sun, through active imagery, completes the crucial step of elevating the spirit of the god of wine, which represents the primordial thing that makes the body or spirit feel very bad, into a tragedy.

Tragedy, as an art, needs to have the characteristics of art, so the key factor of the birth of tragedy is the spirit of Apollo, which is the process of artistic transformation.

Nietzsche asks: What does ethics and morality mean through the mirror of life? The decadent forms of philosophy, morality, and religion stifle the temporal world of man, its own content, structure, and vigorous drive to develop, even its primitive and wild vitality.

Therefore, when an individual has a need, whether it is a secondary need or a primary need, he or she will act as much as possible to try to alleviate the anxiety of the need in order to satisfy it.

This force that compels the individual to take action causes the omission or failure and deviation or reversal of the existence of the individual will of life, or the social identification of the individual identity, and the normal position of the body or mind to feel very uncomfortable and painful.

He further criticizes the doctrine of "being", one of the foundations of Western philosophy. From the ancient Greek philosopher Parmenides, in On Nature, he proposed the proposition that "thought and being are one and the same": "You cannot know what does not exist, it is impossible, and you cannot say it, because what can be thought and what can be thought is the same.

For what can be thought and what can exist are the same thing", to the modern Western doctrine of Existentialism (i.e. man is thrown into the world, we exist, but no one can understand the meaning of existence).

The way of truth "existence" makes people realize that the world of the senses is illusory, that the world known and proved by the senses is false, and that this world is only a world that is accommodated and used by human reason.

Behind it is a real world that exists in itself, a real world that can only be understood, known and proved with our knowledge.

Nietzsche also acknowledges that this form of

metaphysical argument pioneered by Parmenides profoundly influenced Socrates and Plato, and that subsequent philosophers have invariably asked a series of questions about "existence.

But Nietzsche also felt a great logical guilt that rolled over his life. In The Birth of Tragedy, he pointed the sharp edge of his criticism directly at Socrates, who proposed the supremacy of logic, and pointed out that what led to the demise of tragedy was moral Socratism, dialectic, and conceptualism.

Nietzsche feels that Socrates' virtue, knowledge, insight, and virtue as knowledge need to be rethought and reassessed.

The result of this rational and active process of reflection of the human mind on the real world or on any object, in an "inward dialogue", and of measuring the existing or future effects of solutions according to predetermined criteria, in order to determine their feasibility for selection or improvement, is a deep reflection on "what does ethics mean through the mirror of life? The result is a deep reflection on the question "What does ethics mean through the mirror of life?

04, Nietzsche: Platonism will eventually lead to nihilism

Nietzsche believes that Plato is a faithful follower of Socrates' logical inferential summary of natural and social phenomena in accordance with existing empirical knowledge, experience, facts, laws, cognition, and tested hypotheses, through generalization and deductive reasoning.

His "ideas" are inseparable from Socrates' "concepts". In this way, virtue, concepts, knowledge, reason and insight form the core of Plato's doctrine, which will eventually lead Platoism to "nihilism.

Nietzsche opposed "nihilism", Platonism, and metaphysics. He treated Platonism as a traditional metaphysics, and in opposing Platonism, he saw the great logical sin committed by men like Parmenides.

In The Birth of Tragedy, Nietzsche begins to think about tragic thought and consciousness, all the way to "eternal reincarnation," "the will to power," "the death of God," and "beyond good and evil" to Zarathustra's "theory of the superman," all of which are based on opposition or confrontation with the results achieved by traditional philosophy.

The concept of "spirit of the sun" and "spirit of wine" in

The Birth of Tragedy laid the aesthetic foundation of Nietzsche's philosophy, and the dichotomy of "spirit of wine" and "spirit of the sun" was finally integrated into the general system of his "philosophy of the superman".

05. The Spirit of Apollo, the God of the Sun, and Dionysus, the God of Wine

Nietzsche's philosophy is shaped by two major spirits, namely the "spirit of the god of wine" and the "spirit of the god of the sun". The metaphysical consolation represented by the spirit of Dionysus, the god of wine, does not produce artistic impulses, which originate from the principle of individuation represented by the spirit of Apollo, the god of the sun, which manifests itself in the form of temporality and repetition.

Finally, the spirit of Apollo, the god of the sun, is the key factor in the birth of tragedy through the coexistence of time and eternity. Therefore, it can be said that the spirit of Apollo is the key factor in the birth of tragedy.

In his book, Nietzsche explores the origins of ancient Greek tragedy as a clue and elaborates on the fundamental differences between the pre and post-Greek cultures, with Socrates as a turning point.

The former creates the illusion of appearance by rational meditation to preserve the individual body in order to obtain the meaning of survival; the latter returns to the original impulse of life as the origin of the world by means of personalized destruction, so as to obtain the highest aesthetic pleasure and the meaning of survival. The unification of the two gave rise to ancient Greek tragedy; aesthetics is the only value on which man relies for survival.

Dionysus was the patron god of Greek tragedy, but in more ancient times he was the god of instinct and wine, the god of drunken ecstasy and madness, and the god of music.

The spirit of wine precedes the spirit of the god of the sun in an even more ancient way, as Nietzsche says: "The spirit of wine is not as a personality, but as the unity of all beings, to which we are intimately linked by its affiliation with the instinct of procreative joy. In the sense of emotional expression, the spirit of the god of wine is not as a personality, but as a whole of beings.

In terms of emotional expression, the spirit of the spirit of wine is a kind of primitive instinctive impulse, an anti-rational emotional outburst of life, which causes the uninterrupted movement of the will to live, constantly generating a great destructive force to destroy individual life, and in the midst of continuous destruction, giving birth to new and more vigorous individual life, so that the life of the universe can be born and "eternally reincarnated".

Therefore, in Nietzsche, the deconstructive power of the spirit of God is to destroy old and weak individuals, while the powerful will to live, the will of the heart, constantly initiates the program of life's rotation, constantly restores individuals to their phenomenal origin and destruction, and then creates new and stronger individuals.

In this regard, Nietzsche says: "The secret to greater fruitfulness and greatest enjoyment from existence is to live in danger! An important sign of the spirit of the god of wine is to dominate yourself, to make yourself stronger and more willful, and ultimately to become a superman!

From this passage, we can see that Nietzsche has moved from the original ontology of the will to life to a "strong will" ontology. In the Greek tragedy, Oedipus, Prometheus and Antigone are all incarnations of the god of wine.

The principle of individualization of art is forgotten in Nietzsche's portrayal of the "drunkenness" of the god of wine, which merges with the primordial life, with the ecstasy and pain of existence.

Apollo, the god of light, shape, and prophecy, is also an important component of Nietzsche's philosophy. The structural power of the sun god allows the individual to withstand the impact of the deconstructive power of the god of wine, the latter being a rational individual guarded and glorified by the will to power.

These bodies (such as the images of the gods in Greek mythology) embody the image of silence and greatness with a kind of restraint. Thus, for life, Nietzsche emphasizes the value of art over truth.

From the point of view of the form of artistic creation, art must constantly break through the principle of the perfect, quintessential beauty of the sun god in the form of the god of wine. The tragic art form, as a spiritual shaping force, reconciles the dichotomy of the spirit of the god of the sun and the spirit of the god of wine in the Greek tragedy, and makes them one.

06. The relationship between the pursuit of truth and aesthetics

To establish a new concept, a new doctrine and a new spirit to destroy all old ideas and art forms; to pursue the relationship between truth and aesthetics

In The Birth of the Tragedy, Nietzsche defended the aesthetics of the world and life by "art", especially "tragic art", and he did not agree or disagree with the high reverence and fervent pursuit of scientific reason prevailing in German society at that time.

He thought that the scientific spirit was a germ that was destroying our society, and that the pursuit of unified and exact objective laws and truths based on experiments and logical reasoning, with certain objects as the scope of study, was beyond the reach of man.

It is only when one is driven by the insatiable desire for "optimism" to know, when one is driven by logical reasoning in a continuous cycle, and when one finally bites one's own tail, that one realizes that if one wants to endure the pain and boredom of life, one needs the protection and treatment of art.

In order to master the true meaning of life, one should not indulge in the abyss of reason, as the scientist does, but should learn from the artist, who goes beyond the act of "knowing" and "recognizing" a subject in order to know it with certainty, and that these knowings have the potential to be used for a specific purpose, meaning that through the use of "aesthetic" experience or association, one can become familiar with, and thus understand and grasp, the world.

From the Nietzschean philosophical point of view, too much persistence in the pursuit of truth leads to the prevalence of agnosticism and skepticism, to the confusion of anxiety, and to the loss of the desire and passion for life.

Therefore, in order to live, people need to use "art" as a veil to conceal the truth of life; in order to love life with a will, people need a "tragic worldview" and an "aesthetic" attitude to face the birth, growth, change, and death of the objective world. The impermanent art of life is transformed into the joy of aesthetic beauty, so that the tragedy of the individual is transformed into the comedy of the whole.

As Nietzsche mentions in The Birth of Tragedy, "Only as an aesthetic phenomenon does life and the world appear to be justified", the truth of life is flawed, unsatisfactory, and existence itself is not justified.

The truth of life is flawed and unsatisfactory, and there is no good reason for existence itself. If we want to transform pessimism into a full and meaningful life, we can only do so through "art".

Besides, Nietzsche also takes the example of "tragic art" of ancient Greece, and further proves how art can cover up the truth to save life.

The prosperity of Greek art is not based on the position of the traditional academics who insist on analyzing or criticizing problems and issues, i.e., it is due to the appropriate and harmonious cooperation of the Greek people's inner heart.

The "inner pain and conflict" of the Greeks stemmed from their deep awareness of the eternal pain and conflict of the world's will (the state of conscious effort to achieve a certain ideal or purpose), and it was because they saw the tragic wood of life that they were eager to use the art of tragedy.

It was because they saw the tragic wood of life that they were so anxious to use "art" to save life, to give value and meaning to it, to use pain as a source of new expectations and joys, and to continue to endure the pain and boredom brought about by the hardening of daily life experiences.

Nietzsche was fascinated by ancient Greek culture, ancient Greek mythology, and in particular the ancient Greek gods of wine and the sun. What he wanted and saw in his heart was not only the criticism, but the total destruction of everything he did not want to see.

In fact, he wanted to break the fetters of the old world of ideas, cultures, morals, customs, arts, institutions, and ways of behavior that had been handed down from generation to generation, from history to history, and to establish a doctrine that was opposed to rationalism. There are two types of rationalism: first, mysticism and pantheism, which believe in the existence and truth of the supra-rational, the ultimate thing. Secondly, the rational and enlightened ability to know is meaningless, and further denies the ideal new world of reason.

Therefore, with the god of wine, he prefers to forget his hierarchical status and stay in the uncontrolled drinking and indulgence of desire.

Because the god of wine has the power to make the boundaries between man and nature, man and man, and man and God disappear, one can live in a world of instincts, free from troubles, free from any kind of purpose, and free from competition with each other, and thus bring the self and all events, facts, or all things and circumstances that exist objectively, or the other in the background, into a state of "nothingness.

Nietzsche praised the god of wine for its irrationality and powerful primordial wild power, which, when applied to the human mind and to the suffering flesh, causes the world's old phenomena and concepts of ideas, morals, customs, arts, and institutions, which have been passed down through history, to disappear or be destroyed completely.

In Nietzsche, the only thing that can shake and inspire us and keep our vitality and imagination alive is the spirit of the god of wine, the spirit of thought and the spirit of mental condition. The god of the sun is a symbol of perfection and fulfillment, but only by relying on the god of wine can we live our own lives and break down all the social factors that have been passed down from generation to generation and that are inherited.

For example, the old order of customs, habits, morals, beliefs, ideas, methods, etc., and the establishment of a new order. In addition to the above, there are fundamental principles and wisdoms about the universe and life. It is usually a philosophical theory about the problems of life, and it is a theoretical form of life view.

It focuses on the purpose, value, meaning, and form of life, compared to theorizing and systematizing, and it is the cognition of the fundamental questions about life, knowledge, and value that are explored and reflected upon by analytical thinking.

For example, "Is there an objective standard of morality?" and "What is the meaning of life's existence?" In The Birth of Tragedy, Nietzsche also developed several other important concepts: the will to power, the strong will (in effect, the superman), and the death of God.

His late work contains a fierce criticism of Christianity and of Christian morality, which, according to the Dictionary of Ethics, refers to "the knowledge and view of morality.

In social life, people always observe and understand all kinds of social morality from the standpoint of certain social status and specific interests". Therefore, people from different societies and classes are bound to have different moral values.

Meanwhile, on the eve of his madness, he seems to be working on a project to "reevaluate all values" (Umwertung aller Werten).

Although Nietzsche's ideas of analytic inquiry and reflection on the fundamental questions of life, knowledge, and values are often associated with fatalism and nihilism, Nietzsche's own ideas of overcoming the "problematic" of the "problematic" of the "problematic.

Nietzsche himself made the overcoming of "pessimism" and "Schopenhauerian thought" the philosophical goal of his holistic, fundamental, and critical inquiry into the real world and human beings.

3. Critical Present Agency

Nietzsche is interested in the ability of modern people, in a normal state of mind, to face the present situation with confidence and courage in order to obtain the desired result, and to analyze a variety of feasible solutions with a quick and comprehensive understanding of reality, and then to judge the best solution and to implement it effectively.

Nietzsche's ability to judge the best solution and to implement it effectively, as well as his ability to analyze wrong or reactionary ideas, words and deeds with justification, and thus to reject them. He starts with the philosophers who have reason, and he points out that

The first characteristic is the lack of a sense of history.

The first characteristic of philosophers is the lack of a sense of history. For thousands of years, everything that has been dealt with by philosophers has become a concept expressed in words or phrases, based on their perceptual understanding, framing the attributes specific to them among the many attributes of similar things.

Concepts are abstract and universal. Therefore, the mummy of the form of thinking that reflects the nature of things is formed. People's ability to form concepts, to judge, analyze, synthesize, compare, reason, calculate, etc., serves only to rigidify the flowing history and to frame the living reality with some eternal concepts.

The result is to stifle the objective existence of all objects or phenomena in the natural world, and to suppress the process of birth and death, making it impossible to survive and develop life.

This world is a world where some phenomena caused by non-essential connections in the process of development and change of things may or may not appear, may or may not appear, may or may not appear this way or that way, full of chance, volatile, and thus inscrutable. There is no such thing as a stable, unmoving or unchanging reality; everything is fluid, ungraspable and evasive.

The second characteristic is the "rejection of the evidence of the senses

The second characteristic of the philosopher is the rejection of the evidence of the senses, which refers to the organs that come from the rejection of sensation and the stimulation of all objects or phenomena that exist objectively in nature, including the eyes, ears, nose, tongue, and body.

The brain is the center of all the senses. The eyes are visual, the ears are auditory, the nose is olfactory, the tongue is gustatory, and all parts of the body are tactile sensory receptors. However, the real world and the world of false images are reversed from their original or supposed positions, and the up and down, front and back are created.

The perceptual evidence of concrete facts and conditions that exist in front of us is real and credible, but it is only when they are processed with information that lies are inserted.

The third characteristic is the confusion of the beginning and the end

The third characteristic of philosophers is that they confuse the beginning with the end. They create confusion by deliberately describing black as white and white as black. This refers to the deliberate creation of confusion so that people cannot distinguish between the two.

The process of growth that denies the gradual increase in size and weight of living organisms under certain living conditions, the phenomenon that organisms differ from one generation to another, and the evolutionary process that explains these phenomena in various theories.

Evolution is also called evolution, and the main mechanisms are genetic variation of organisms, adaptation to the environment, and competition among species.

The fourth characteristic is the "use of reason in speech"

The fourth characteristic of philosophers is the ability to use "reason" in language to force people to make mistakes in order to obtain the desired results, to face the present situation with confidence and courage, and to analyze a variety of feasible solutions with a quick and comprehensive understanding of reality, and then to judge the best solution and to implement it effectively.

The "is" is confused with the "is" and the "is", and the false becomes true and the true becomes false, deceiving the ignorant who are deceived without knowing. He thinks that it is absurd that from Socrates to modern man, there is an extremely enthusiastic appeal to intellectual reason that can identify, judge, evaluate practical reasons, and conform human behavior to a specific purpose.

The reason why man reveres reason is that it finds truth through argument and convincing arguments, and obtains conclusions, opinions, and reasons for action by logical reasoning rather than by appearances.

To be responsible for one's own existence and for a

social mission beyond oneself but inherent in it. It is expected to bring freedom and happiness; however, the opposite happens: the ability to form concepts, to judge, to analyze, to synthesize, to compare, to reason, to calculate, etc., is everywhere an enemy of human instincts and causes greater suffering.

Some of the most brilliant philosophers in history have used the weapon of truth through argument and convincing arguments to observe and understand the world. Reason is not denied by logical reasoning rather than by relying on appearances to reach conclusions, opinions, and reasons for action, which are not wrong in themselves.

It is reasonable and correct to criticize the fallacies brought by reason, but the existence of reason, its historical status and role cannot be denied. Reason is the symbol of human progress and the fruit of the progress of human civilization.

Without reason, human beings cannot know the world and the truth correctly. Without reason, human beings will fall into the terrible situation of not knowing how to choose from all the objects or phenomena (for example, life or work) that exist objectively in the natural world, without a sense of direction.

4. Criticism of traditional morality

Nietzsche is extremely powerful and violent in revealing the secrecy of Christianity, as well as in criticizing the traditional morality of Christianity and attacking modern agency. In the study of the doctrine of the origin of knowledge, the process of development, the method of knowing, and the relationship between knowledge and practice.

It can be divided into empiricism and rationalism. In terms of epistemology, Nietzsche is an extreme anti-rationalist, who does not rely on the senses to determine truth, but on reason and the methodology of deductive reasoning, or on the human understanding of natural and social phenomena.

He is the most radical critic of any theoretical philosophy that logically summarizes natural and social phenomena in accordance with existing empirical knowledge, experience, facts, laws, cognition, and tested hypotheses, through generalization and deductive reasoning.

He believes that the spiritual life of Europeans for two thousand years has been based on the belief in and worship of a certain religion or a certain doctrine, which has been taken as a guideline for words and deeds, and on the belief in God as the core.

All the values of life are delivered to God with ideals, hopes, and emotions. Although the foundation of God's existence has begun to crumble or split and separate since the Enlightenment, when man used the light of reason to dispel all obscurity, ignorance and obscurity, people still believe in God and worship Him because there is no new faith.

As an influential philosopher, the study of Nietzsche's thought is probably the area where there is the least consensus in the contemporary philosophical world. One can easily see the main concepts Nietzsche proposed and their importance, but the true meaning of these concepts and the context of the time are both very controversial.

Nietzsche famously proposed the idea that "God is dead," but Nietzsche did not propose this death of God in order to portray himself as a radical, but rather to force the reader to accept any one fact, the "truth" always being a proposition with a framework of established views.

Nietzsche also distinguishes between master-slave morality, saying that the morality of the master comes from the celebration of life, while the morality of the slave comes from the hatred of the former. This distinction directly points out the conflict between the moral standards of "good and bad" and "good and evil", which are conflicting due to different opinions.

More importantly, in terms of ideology, the opposite is true: what is called "good" in the master's morality may indeed be considered "evil" in the moral standard of the slave's view of things or problems from a certain standpoint or perspective.

Nietzsche believed that Christian ethics, the ideas, culture, morals, customs, arts, institutions, and behaviors passed down from generation to generation and from history, restrained the human mind and suppressed human instincts, and that in order to be free, one had to kill "God".

Nietzsche believed that the decline of Christianity was historically inevitable, that it had changed from the religion of the oppressed to the religious rule of an oppressor, and that its decline was the result of an intrinsically prescribed connection and a definite trend of development.

Nietzsche believed that in a world without God, people would be given unprecedented opportunities to establish new values, values centered on the will of man rather than on God, Nietzsche called himself an amoralist and the last of the anti-Christians.

He fiercely attacked the philosophy of reason and the values espoused by Western society. Nietzsche wanted to establish a new philosophy, an irrational philosophy that placed the will to live above reason. As a challenge to the ideal, he proposed to consider, discuss, accept, or adopt the "strong will" doctrine.

Replacing God with strong willpower, the core of strong willpower is the affirmation of the power of life, the affirmation of life, as opposed to traditional metaphysics that is studied through rational reasoning and logic and cannot be answered directly through perception.

It is an instinctive, spontaneous, irrational force. It determines the nature of life, the human meaning of life existence itself.

Nietzsche compares the different characteristics of "strong willpower" and "rationality". The characteristic of rationality refers to the ability to think logically, to remain calm in the midst of unexpected events, and to make an accurate judgment and analysis of the current environment, people and events, without over-exposing or mixing subjective emotions with the events.

Rational people are usually very aware of their own emotions and are familiar with where their psychological limits are, and can correctly identify and control their emotions.

They are aware of the impact their emotions and behaviors can have on others, so they have a strong ability to manage their emotions, are good at handling their emotions, know how to respond flexibly, and can remain calm under strong pressure, and can quickly adjust themselves to get out of the frustrations and troubles of life and return to their normal state.

Rational people are usually emotionally driven, they can be self-motivated, according to the analysis of their ability to find ways to achieve their goals, no matter what the goal is, they have the confidence and determination to achieve the goals set.

Even if they live in an environment where their work is

not recognized and they are treated differently, they are able to face it optimistically and find the real problems through their appearance and solve them with their own ability.

Rational people usually have good communication skills, are able to express their feelings and ideas concisely, and interact with others in a friendly manner, and have high levels of social skills.

Powerful willpower, as Nietzsche considered it, is not an ordinary force, but a very powerful one. It is dominant and ruling because it is strong. A strong will is the will to live, yet it seeks not the will to live itself, but the potential power that enables life to transcend itself.

It is this desire to work consciously for a certain ideal, or to achieve a certain purpose, that expresses life, that never-ending nature. Nietzsche called it: the inexhaustible will to live.

Strong will power originates from life and returns to life, and it is the reality of life that in its everyday application means "objective things" or "conditions that are compatible with objective circumstances.

It is the sum of all real things or existing things, as

opposed to things that are entirely imaginary. The term reality is also often used to denote the ontological state of things, including their existence or non-existence.

Although life is short, as long as one has a strong determination to achieve a certain purpose and a state of mind that is expressed in words or actions, and one becomes spiritually strong, one can realize one's value.

What Nietzsche considered to be strong will power is not an ordinary power, but a very powerful one. It is dominant and ruling because it is strong. The strong will is the will to live, but what it seeks is not the will to live itself, but the potential power that enables life to transcend itself.

It is this desire to work consciously for a certain ideal, or to achieve a certain purpose, that expresses life, that never-ending nature. Nietzsche called it: the inexhaustible will to live.

Strong will power originates from life and returns to life, and it is the reality of life that in its everyday application means "objective things" or "conditions that are compatible with objective circumstances. It is the sum of all real things or existing things, as opposed to things that are entirely imaginary.

The term reality is also often used to denote the ontological state of things, including their existence or non-existence. Although life is short, as long as one has a strong determination to achieve a certain purpose and a state of mind that is expressed in words or actions, and one becomes spiritually strong, one can realize one's value.

Strong willpower as the measure of the highest value, on the one hand, affirms the value of life, and on the other hand, defends the inequality of the human world. In Nietzsche's view, all objects or phenomena that exist objectively in nature, human beings and natural beings alike, have strengths and weaknesses, the strong are always the minority and the weak are the majority.

History and culture are created by the strong few, who rightfully rule over the weak. Nietzsche overturned the system of superiority and inferiority of God according to a certain standard, and affirmed the system of superiority and inferiority of man according to a certain standard.

Nietzsche's holistic, fundamental, and critical inquiry into the real world and man seeks to establish a new philosophy, an irrational philosophy that places the will to live above reason. As a challenge to reason, he proposed the doctrine of the powerful will.

The strong will replaces the status of God and the metaphysics of ideas, cultures, morals, customs, arts, institutions, and ways of doing things that have been passed down through the generations and through history. The core of the doctrine of the strong will is the affirmation of life, the affirmation of life.

It is not a secular power, but an instinctive, spontaneous, irrational force. It determines the nature of all objects or phenomena that exist objectively in nature, and becomes a prerequisite for the meaning of life.

01. Who killed God in the end

In Western history, God has always been the guarantor of truth for religionists, moralists and philosophers to ensure the established requirements and standards without compromise. God is the basis of religious belief, moral values and rational knowledge, and God is the ultimate guarantee of all values.

However, in 1543, before his death, Copernicus wrote his main theory in his "Treatise on the Movement of the

Heavenly Bodies". Here, in Copernicus' (Heliocentrism) Short Treatise, he summarized his principles of geodesy and proposed some theories of "heliocentric geodesy" for several decades. This was the first time that Copernicus killed God.

Later, on July 1, 1858, C.R. Darwin and A.R. Wallace presented a paper on evolution at the Linnean Society in London. In his book The Origin of Species, published in 1859, Darwin systematically expounded his theory of evolution. Darwin himself called The Origin of Species "a long controversy" which argued two questions.

First, species are mutable and organisms evolve. The vast majority of biologists who read On the Origin of Species at the time quickly accepted this fact, and evolutionary theory has since replaced creationism as the cornerstone of biological research.

Even at that time, the debate on whether organisms evolved was mainly between biologists and Christian preachers rather than within the biology community.

Second, natural selection is the driving force behind biological evolution. All organisms have a tendency to overpopulate, and since space and food are limited, organisms must "struggle for survival".

Individuals in the same population have variation, and those with favorable variation that can adapt to the environment will survive and reproduce, while those without favorable variation will be eliminated.

If natural conditions change in a directional manner, then in the course of history, after a long period of natural selection, small variations will accumulate and become significant variations. This may lead to the formation of subspecies and new species. When Darwin published his theory of evolution, God, who is the basis of faith, was declared to die a second time.

Conte says that before one knows anything, one has an innate scope of things, and that one cannot know things without an innate scope of things. This also explains the problem of how all of our thoughts are possible; without this scope, we would all be imagining things.

Kant's life can be divided into two phases, the first in 1770 and the second in 1781. In the latter phase, Kant published a series of great and original works in a wide range of fields that brought a revolution in philosophical thought at that time, including the Critique of Pure Reason in 1781, the Critique of Practical Reason in 1788, and the Critique of Judgment in 1790. Critique of Judgment (Year)

Kant's three major critiques are the Critique of Pure Reason, the Critique of Practical Reason, and the Critique of Judgment, which are three major works. These three major works are his views on cognition, ethics, and aesthetics, respectively.

In particular, the Critique of Pure Reason of 1781 marked a major shift in philosophical research from ontology to epistemology. Prior to Kant, the main direction of research in the discipline of analytic reflection on the fundamental questions of life, knowledge, and value.

It is ontology that can be traced back to Plato and Aristotle in ancient Greece, who defined existentialism as "the science of the existence of objects. Specifically, it is the study of the classification of objects, that is, the circumstances under which an object can be defined as "existing".

This includes, for example, the question of the "universal" and the "specific", the study of entities or ontologies. Postmodernist philosophers of the entity have sought to redefine each of these questions through philosophical action in different contexts, relying primarily on recent findings in biology, ecology, and cognitive science to understand how animals perceive themselves in natural and artificially provided environments.

After Kant, however, the direction of philosophical research shifted and the question of the sources of human knowledge began to be studied. The question of the source of knowledge, does it come from experience? Or is it innate knowledge, and do we have access to the right knowledge?

How is it possible to know the right knowledge, and how is it necessary to criticize knowledge itself before knowing it, are the general contents of the Critique of Pure Reason.

The question that the Critique of Pure Reason seeks to answer is: What can we know? Kant's answer is that we can only know what natural science allows us to know, and that philosophy's holistic, fundamental, and critical inquiry into the real world and human beings is to explain the question of how it is possible to know what we can know.

Kant's Critique of Practical Reason has the same general structure as the Critique of Pure Reason, but differs greatly in the details of its delineation. This is due to the difference in the tasks, objects, and goals to be achieved by the two critiques.

In the second Critique of Practical Reason, Kant focuses on the problem of the practical ethics of human beings. This refers to human relations and the rules governing these relations.

For example, the problem of freedom, the freedom of Kantian ideology, is definitely not the freedom to do whatever one wants, but the freedom to be able to do, but not to do. This kind of "freedom" is a sign of the difference between animals and the various moral standards of human beings, which is that "the power to do good without doing evil is good, and the power to do good without doing evil".

For example, giving up one's seat on a bus for the elderly, young women and children is just a matter of raising one's hand. When I see an elderly person getting on the bus, I am free to choose, to get up and give up my seat, or to act as if nothing is wrong.

Kant's view is that the freedom of choice to get up and give up one's seat when one sees an old man getting into a car is the "freedom" of human beings to practice ethics, not the freedom to do whatever one wants and pretend to be indifferent.

Kant's third critique, the Critique of Judgment, is divided into two parts, the Critique of Aesthetic Judgment and the Critique of the Judgment of Purpose, which serve as a bridge between the first two critiques.

This critique is both intellectual and rational in nature. The exchange of views between these two natures, or the unblocking of disagreements between epistemology and ethics, also completes Kant's philosophical system in accordance with its intended goal. This is also where Kant's [Three Critiques] is announced as the third death of God.

The first half of the Critique of Judgment is devoted to aesthetic judgment, which is strictly defined in four aspects: [affirmative and negative], [ordinary and particular], [necessary and contingent], [cause and effect].

The second half of the book deals with aesthetic judgment, moving from the most important and decisive aesthetic judgment of all objects or phenomena in nature to the objective judgment of nature, and describes Kant's own view of nature.

Kant's three major critiques expel God from the realm of reason, drive God into the realm of morality, and pronounce God, the ground of rational knowledge, dead.

Finally, Nietzsche abstracts from God what little room he has (abstraction is used to describe the process of having an external consciousness of yourself (or any other view).

When you think about "yourself," "stop and look," "step back and think," "take yourself out of something," "take yourself out of a situation," you are experiencing a process of being "withdrawn.) God, as the basis of moral values, was declared dead.

In 1882, in The Gay Science, Nietzsche used the metaphor of a "madman" to illustrate his prophecy of a new age, proclaiming to a confused public that "God is dead.

In the middle period, Nietzsche's The Science of Happiness (1882). He called his philosophy of this period "the philosophy of the morning. Thematically, these works of Nietzsche focus on the revelation and analysis of the phenomenon of "décadence" and its moral and religious roots.

In The Science of Happiness, in particular, Nietzsche's accusation against Christianity reaches its height, culminating in the appalling cry "God is dead! Nietzsche's accusation of Christianity reaches its height in The Science of Happiness, finally crying out "God is dead! It can be said that Nietzsche dealt God a final blow: "God is dead, but man will build a cave that will last a thousand years, and in it people will show His image. And we we must still overcome His image. (v. 108)".

Nietzsche proclaims the total death of God through the mouth of a madman. Who is the murderer? The madman replied, "We killed God! If it was man who killed God, it must be because we no longer need God or because God is hindering our progress.

The total death of God must be an epoch-making event. Nietzsche foresaw that after God's death, man could not at once reach a state of self-affirmation, of being able to create his own values.

With the death of God, all human values are left in a

vacuum. Nietzsche points out that one has to face the nihilism that comes with the loss of established values.

02. Nihilism

Friedrich Nietzsche: Nihilism and the Death of God" What does nihilism mean? The devaluation of the highest values, the lack of purpose, the absence of an answer to the question "why?   "

-The Will to Power38

Meaning

Nietzsche calls himself "the most radical nihilist in Europe," but he makes a logical and deductive conclusion about natural and social phenomena by generalizing and deducing from existing empirical knowledge, experience, facts, laws, cognition, and tested hypotheses.

It can be said to follow the line of transcendental nihilism. Nietzsche believed that the so-called values, concepts, and truths are merely man-made explanations, and that the world itself has no metaphysical truth, ultimate value, or meaning.

Nietzsche believed that the rational world (ideal state) described by Plato, the kingdom of heaven described by

Christianity, and the inevitable moral order of the world are only human beings using their senses and senses.

Nietzsche believed that the rational world described by Plato (the ideal state), the Christian kingdom of heaven, and the inevitable moral order of the world are only the products of human individuals' comprehensive awareness and knowledge of their own physical and mental states and the changes of people, events, and things in the environment through mental activities such as sensation, perception, thinking, and memory.

Nietzsche took "God is dead" as a symbol of the advent of nihilism, and this became the starting point of the philosophy of many later "existentialist" philosophers, such as Heidegger, Sartre, and Camus.

Nietzsche believed that there are two kinds of nihilism: negative, pathological nihilism and positive nihilism. Negative nihilism includes Platonism, Christianity, and Schopenhauer's philosophy. Positive nihilism, on the other hand, sees the crisis of losing ultimate values as the key to the transformation of things that can create new values.

For Nietzsche, nihilism means, in a philosophical

sense, the view that the world, and especially human existence, has no meaning, purpose, and intelligible truth and intrinsic value because all objects or phenomena that exist objectively in nature and what happens to them have no meaning, purpose, or intelligible truth.

The reason is that all objects or phenomena that exist objectively in nature, and what happens to them, have no thought or reasoning (meaningless), and are therefore a kind of humanistic nihilism. The meaninglessness of all objects and phenomena in nature is usually the indicator of whether life is worth living or not.

Voidism can be divided into at least two kinds: first, the vainism that is valid under all circumstances, i.e., life is no one's knowledge of natural or social things, it is the meaning given by human beings to the object, it is the spiritual content transmitted and communicated by human beings in the form of symbols, and it is not worth living; second, the vainism that occurs only under certain circumstances, i.e., under the influence of certain circumstances or reasons. The ideas and truths contained in the things of our life are lost, and life is not worth living.

Nietzsche is talking about the latter kind of nihilism, the nihilism that emerged at the time of the death of God.

The phenomenon of God's death, after all, can be said to be experienced in some sense by people all over the world, but not everywhere, as in Europe, by nihilism.

Therefore, it would be too arbitrary to say that the death of God leads to nihilism. The emergence of nihilism requires not only the death of God, but also the belief in God (and the values He advocates), that is, the belief in God and the death of God, which leads to the loss of values and nihilism.

According to Reginster's interpretation, in Nietzsche's philosophy, nihilism can be divided into two aspects: nihilism that teaches disorientation and nihilism that causes despair. The former is more related to Nietzsche's postulated ethics, while the latter is more related to cultural history and to the death of God.

Nietzsche's nihilism as a kind of despair has a developmental stage. It is first a pessimism, and then it develops into nihilism. The reason for this pessimism is that we do not believe that we are in a world where we can live up to the highest values we have always sought.

A good example of this is the Christian worldview that Nietzsche understood by using his mental activities such as sensation, perception, thinking, and memory, and by his comprehensive awareness and understanding of the state of his body and mind and the changes of people, events, and things in his environment.

For Christianity, the present world is a place of suffering, and the highest ideal is not here at all; what we should long for is not this life, but the kingdom of heaven beyond. So pessimism is pessimism about the present world. But if we are only pessimistic, we are not desperate, because this world is sad, but perhaps our highest values still have a chance to be realized elsewhere, so we still have hope.

The development from pessimism to nihilistic despair requires another level of thinking: on the one hand, we are pessimistic about the present world, and on the other hand, we do not believe that our ultimate purpose has a chance to be realized elsewhere.

This is the ultimate nihilism, and its despair is that we can only keep suffering between pain and boredom, but without seeing any hope. This is the result of believing in God (the feelings, perceptions, discernment, choices, etc. made on the basis of human thinking, the discriminative thoughts or attitudes of human beings towards things, and thus the values or effects manifested), but God withdraws from the scene.

With the death of God (the subject's value orientation towards himself and external people or things), man's belief in the other side of the world also collapses. In the past, life under the Christian worldview was painful, but at least we believed that there was still value and that we could make a situation that did not exist a reality somewhere else.

But since we no longer believe in the other side, there is no chance for values to be realized now. But the pessimistic situation continues to exist in front of our eyes, so that we have to believe in the reality and condition of the present world, which is still painful.

The constant suffering and the lack of a way out constitutes a complete loss of faith and despair in something. A nihilist is one who believes that the world, the existence of life, has no objective meaning, purpose, or understandable truth.

This is exactly the problem that people need to face after the death of God (the cognition, understanding, judgment or choice based on the human mind and senses, that is, the thinking or orientation of human beings to identify things, to debate right and wrong, and to realize the certain value or function of people, things and objects).

Therefore, rather than a person's publicly expressed position, it is a kind of confrontational opinion. Because, any kind of objective existence reflected in human consciousness, through thinking activities, and the result or formation of the viewpoint and concept system, before it has been absolutely denied, then the perspective, background, judgment formed by this thought, as well as its stated meaning, will have a certain degree of objective value.

This is the simplest and most real assessment of human nature in the process of analysis, synthesis, judgment, reasoning and other cognitive activities on the basis of images and concepts, which also assesses whether an idea is great, and this objective existence is reflected in human consciousness, through thinking The result of this objective existence reflected in human consciousness, through thinking activities, or the formation of views, and whether it can become the source of values.

03. Value revaluation

Nietzsche believes that there are two kinds of nihilism: negative, pathological nihilism and positive nihilism. Negative nihilism includes Platonism, Christianity, and Schopenhauer, which are philosophies that analyze and reflect on fundamental questions about life, knowledge, and values.

Nietzsche believed that even if "nihilism" comes, people can still rebuild new values through value revaluation in order to obtain a reason for survival.

Nietzsche also emphasizes that if people are to become free spirits, it is necessary to get rid of social factors that have been passed down from generation to generation, such as customs, habits, morals, beliefs, ideas, methods, and other old thinking, and to ignite the desire for some definite and eternal values. Because "the need for an unconditional affirmation and negation is a need that arises from vulnerability".

5. Nietzsche: The Death of God

Nietzsche points out that nihilism, as a philosophical meaning, is the ultimate form of skepticism. Nietzsche pointed out that nihilism as a philosophical meaning is the ultimate form of skepticism.

That is, the individual subjectively believes that the loss of the highest value, the lack of action or thought in life, as the purpose of the target thing, no one can provide the ultimate answer to the question of teleology! Faced with such a painful and boring dilemma. People with a weak will may feel pessimistic, disappointed, or even disenchanted with the world.

Modern people are generally tormented by such unexplained negative emotions (pessimism and anxiety), and they may choose to escape from their busy work schedule without rest, or they may choose to live and die in a state of confusion that allows them to adapt to their environment and be content in any situation.

Or they may choose to be conformed to the rules, not daring to change to fit in with the masses, to play different social roles, to submit to the general constraints of the whole social matrix, and to be unable to calm their own thoughts. This is what Nietzsche called "negative nihilism".

Nietzsche believed that modern man, faced with this

impractical and inscrutable dilemma, feels powerless and self-indulgent, oblivious to moral and social perceptions, demoralized and depressed.

He believed that "positive nihilism" was needed to overcome the "negative nihilism" of depression, negativity, depression, and mental depression. "Active nihilism" is a transcendence of "negative nihilism".

Nietzsche proposed "positive nihilism" with a strong will and active effort, believing that from the fundamental point of view, all objects or phenomena that exist objectively in nature and are considered by people or groups to have positive meanings, to be valued by people, or to make people feel satisfied and become objects of respect or interest. What is the reason for assuming the existence of some established, God-like supreme value?

The fundamental question of contemporary spiritual life is whether it is possible to extricate oneself from the dilemma of contemporary nihilism, which has persisted for more than a century, by being deeply obsessed with something or being in a certain state or thinking activity.

This paradoxical concept of metaphysical thinking is like rescuing the soul from the hell of suffering in the present life and asking for forgiveness of sins, relief of misfortune or elimination of karma, but not from the present life, but from the hell of suffering of the body and soul, but the soul is still living in the present life and cannot be reincarnated.

In order to understand the true meaning of the existence of the universe and life, and to witness the true nature of the truth, one has to understand and realize the Anodolite Three Seconds and Three Bodhisattvas, and to realize the Anodolite Three Seconds and Three Bodhisattvas, one has to understand existentialism, and to understand existentialism, one has to criticize nihilism.

Among the various moral codes and ethics that refer to human interaction, the "nihilist" or "nihilism" is the complete rejection of all authority, morality, and social convention; either through the rejection of all established beliefs, or through extreme relativism.

Or skepticism; the nihilist believes that those in control of power are ineffective and should be opposed and resisted. From the nihilist point of view, the ultimate source of moral values is not culture or reason, but the very meaning of the existence of individual life.

Postmodernist thought has taken cognitive and ethical systems to the extreme of relativism. These philosophers seek to deny the truths, meanings, historical processes, and humanist ideals of Western civilization, as well as the foundations upon which the Enlightenment was built. Although postmodernism, in its apparent ideological form, is considered a philosophy of nihilism.

is considered to be a philosophy of nihilism. However, it is worth noting that nihilism accepts the accusations of postmodernism. It is because nihilism is an irrational assertion of the truth of the universe, which is what postmodernism rejects.

Although postmodernism has been ridiculed by some as nihilism, it does not conform to the nihilist, defeatist perspective, to which the above nihilist formula is applied.

Postmodernist philosophers have sought to explore the power and causes of the study of the universe, the principles and principles of life in all its forms and unique human relationships.

Skepticism, on the other hand, examines and critiques these arbitrary propositions and deductions of solipsism. It does not answer the question of whether phenomena are similar to carriers or whether a non-obvious entity exists, but rather inquires into the basis for the propositions and deductions about the obvious that solipsism establishes and the reliable means by which to ensure the necessity of such knowledge.

Skepticism repeatedly asks by what means solipsism establishes that the entity behind the phenomenon is necessarily similar or necessarily dissimilar to it, and how it knows that something that is not manifest must have that particular sign or representation by which it is known.

For example, is this a question based on sensory experience? Skepticism holds that sensory experience only tells us about the properties of objects such as sound, taste, hardness, size, number, movement, etc. These properties of concrete facts and conditions that exist in front of us, no matter how they are combined, are not equivalent to the objects themselves.

Another example is that of something that is distinguishable and exists independently of itself. In particular, abstractions are usually regarded as entities or carriers, and are not known by experience.

Is this the complex mental process of seeking or establishing rules and evidence to support or determine a belief, decision, or action according to reason?

Skepticism states: "Every objective existence is reflected in the human consciousness, and the result of thought activity, or the formation of a system of ideas and concepts. It occurs either from sensation, which cannot be separated from feeling, or from experience, which cannot be separated from experience.

Or it comes from experience, but not without experience." "In a general sense, it is impossible to find in the forms of thought or in the results of thought or in the mental processes of cognition, which reflect the nature of things, anything that is not known by experience."

It is worth noting that in this historical issue of ideas, culture, morals, customs, arts, institutions, and ways of behavior, which have been passed down from generation to generation, contemporary philosophy and cultural spirit, in a strong group of people, is a kind of subcultural non-culturalism triggered by negative emotions such as decadence, pessimism, and despair.

In the irrationalistic atmosphere of a subculture

triggered by the decadent, those who witness the decadence praise nature and refinement rather than the simple skill of the snake culture, and scorn the discourse of contemporary decline by accepting the themes and styles that critics consider morbid and overly refined. Concretely, the contemporary nihilism has come full circle.

Nietzsche's late works are primarily concerned with nihilism. A volume of The Will to Power, a collection of selected notes by Nietzsche from 1883 to 1888. He named it "European Nihilism" and considered it the main problem of the 19th century.

Nietzsche defined nihilism as "a world in which man's cognitive capacity for the environment and the self, and the clarity of cognition, especially the absence of meaning and purpose in human existence, can be analyzed in detail and understood in a certain cognitive way, with an understanding of truth and intrinsic value.

Although Turgenev made the term nihilism universally known, it was first introduced by Jacobi into the field of the discipline of analytical reflection on the fundamental questions of life, knowledge, and values.

With this term, Jacobi wanted to present the rationalist character, especially Kant's holistic, foundational, and critical philosophy of the real and human world. He believed that all "rationalism" could be reduced to nothingness, so that we should try to avoid it and return to certain beliefs.

Thus, Nietzsche declared in The Will to Power that Europe had entered the age of nihilism since the middle of the 19th century. To put it more fully, nihilism did not begin to infect European spiritual culture only in modern times, but is a deep-rooted nature of European spiritual culture itself. Nihilism also has its social elements, such as customs, morals, habits, beliefs, and ideas, which have been passed down from generation to generation.

Therefore, the critique of contemporary nihilism must begin with an analysis and critique of the evolution of social factors, such as customs, morals, habits, beliefs, and ideas, which have been passed down from generation to generation and have been inherited from civilization, and which reflect the characteristics and appearance of the national culture. The purpose of this study is to analyze and criticize the various ideological and conceptual forms of national culture in the history of the nation, so that we can grasp the contemporary spiritual and cultural context of nihilism in a more fundamental way.

The ideas, cultures, morals, customs, arts, institutions, and behaviors that have been passed down from generation to generation and throughout history. Nihilism, which has invisible influence and control over people's social behavior, is essentially the existence of gods and ideas, a negation of the "existence of human life.

This negation is expressed through the religious theology, conceptualism, or idealism of ideas, morals, customs, arts, and institutions that have been passed down through history, and therefore the critique of traditional nihilism necessarily involves the critique of theology and idealism.

The "negation of man by God" and the "negation of man by the idea" are essentially similar. The similarity between God and the idea is expressed in a specific nature or phenomenon through all objects or phenomena that exist objectively in nature, or in the subjective will of man, which is expressed through things, products, works, and so on.

It is expressed as the metaphysics that the answer to the question that cannot be obtained directly through perception is deduced through rational logical reasoning under a priori conditions and cannot be contradicted by empirical evidence.

According to this analysis, thinking about God, reason, ideas, transcendentalism, and metaphysics, which inquire into and reflect on the fundamental questions of life, knowledge, and values, forms a detachment from and denial of human existence.

The mission of the Enlightenment is obviously to liberate reason from its attachment to God and to return it to man, to resist and even deprecate and reject divinity and transcendence through man and his rational power, and thus to shake the theological foundations of traditional nihilism.

For nihilists, this is a question of life that cannot be escaped by man's indifference to existence. The realization of social factors, such as customs, morals, habits, beliefs, and ideas, which have been passed down from generation to generation.

We will make use of our ability to form concepts, make

judgments, analyze, synthesize, compare, reason, and calculate in order to realize the negation of the existence of the divine to the existence of human nature, and turn to the power of reason to realize the negation of the existence of the divine to fully open modern humanism.

Modern humanism is a further completion of Enlightenment philosophy and modern humanism. Its theme is not only a further negation of God, but also a shift from reliance on reason to a questioning of reason, and even to rebellion.

Not only Enlightenment philosophy, but also French materialism in particular, formed a philosophy of "hatred", an attitude of confrontation and hatred. The philosophical theory that the basic component of the world is matter, and that all things (including mind and consciousness) are the result of the interaction of matter.

Material forms and representational processes are the main way for human beings to understand the substance hidden within things.

It is also considered a form of physicalism. The theory is based on the idea that all entities (and concepts) are a composition or expression of matter, and that all phenomena (including consciousness) are the result of the interaction of matter.

Between consciousness and matter, the matter of concrete facts and conditions that exist in front of us determines the cognitive ability and clarity of cognition of the environment and the self, and the individual uses mental activities such as sensation, perception, thinking, memory, etc. to

The individual uses sensory, perceptual, thinking, memory and other mental activities to perceive and recognize his own physical and mental state and the changes of people, things and objects in the environment, which is the objective world, the physiological response in the human brain, that is, the content, structure and development of the spatio-temporal world itself, out of the response to matter.

Therefore, the entity is the only thing that exists in fact, is distinguishable, and is within itself, and exists independently. As a human being to natural and social phenomena, according to the existing empirical knowledge, experience, facts, laws, cognition, and tested hypotheses, through the

Existentialism is the theory of the beginning of the universe and the chaotic state of man before he was born, which is also called the theory of the number of times of the world.

01. Existentialism (ontology)

Existentialism is an ontology based on dualism or pluralism, but it is different from the ontology itself. It is an expression of a philosophical theory. It has different meanings in the history of Western philosophy and Eastern philosophy respectively.

Generally speaking, ontology in philosophy is a doctrine opposed to epistemology and methodology. It is the study of the origin, nature, and beginnings of the world, also known as metaphysics. This broad ontology includes cosmology. Ontology (existentialism) in the strict sense refers to the theory of being and its nature.

The concept of "ontology" was first used by the 17th century German philosopher Rndolphus Godenins (1547-1628) in his writings. It was later used by Johaun Clautcerg and the French philosopher Jean Baptiste Duhamel (1624-1706).

Clauberg called ontology the "first science", the study

of being as "being", and believed that this study could be applied to all entities as well as to God, who created being.

The eighteenth-century German philosopher Christich Wolff (1679-1754) used ontology in metaphysics, which is the study of questions that cannot be answered directly by perception, and which derives answers through rational logical reasoning under a priori conditions that do not contradict empirical evidence.

The theory of being, which is abstract and completely universal, is called abstract metaphysics, in order to separate it from cosmology, psychology, and theology in metaphysics. Since then, ontology has taken on a special meaning in Western philosophy.

The study of the problem of "being" mentioned earlier was first proposed in Western philosophy by the ancient Greek philosopher Parmenides. He pointed out that only the existent exists, and that the non-existent does not exist, or that the existence of the non-existent is impossible.

What he called "existence" is a "general" concept formed by abstracting the unified, complete, and static side of things and exaggerating it one-sidedly.

The definition of the only true essence, in people's understanding of history, including historical thinking and historical interpretation, shows that the cognition is a progression from concrete perceptual things to general abstract concepts, which shows the deepening of human cognition and the improvement of abstract thinking ability.

Aristotle systematically established the doctrine of "being", defining "essence" as "being as being", "pure being" or "the central point of being".

The number, nature, relationship, place, time, state, condition, irrigation, and suffering of things are called dependent existence, or double existence, because they are all dependent on the being.

They are temporally dependent, cognitively dependent, and logically dependent. This study of being itself, with the being in being as the central point, is what Aristotle calls "first philosophy.

Aristotle also divides ontology into first and second ontology, with individual things being the first ontology, because only individual things are the most primitive being. The genus and species are the second ontology, because the genus and species can express individual things.

This means that individual things are primordial, and that "genus" and "species" arise from the differentiation of the subject in the process of development of things.

Aristotle says: "Ontology, in the most authentic, original, and definite sense of the word, means something that can neither be expressed in a subject nor exist in a subject, such as an individual human being or animal.

However, in the sense that all objects or phenomena that exist objectively in nature are derived from the subject in the process of development, things that include the original essence, like 'genus', are also called ontology.

Likewise, the species that includes the 'genus' is also called the ontology. ...... Man and animals are the second ontology." (Aristotle's ontology finally leads to the conclusion of a "purely formal" immovable agent, God, affirming the existence of a supra-experiential thing outside of empirical things.

This is the condition for the ontological proof of the existence of God in medieval soteriological philosophy. The ontology in Western philosophy takes into account the two contradictory properties inherent in things in the world.

The duality of two opposing properties of one thing at the same time seeks to affirm a real and eternal world outside the real world. There are similarities with the fundamental view of theology, and Kant proves for the first time the impossibility of traditional ontology.

Conception is the process of knowing all external objects or phenomena that exist objectively in nature, or the process of processing information about external things that act on human sense organs. It includes sensory, perceptual, memory, thinking, imagination, and speech abilities.

It can only be limited to the scope of experience, and can only know phenomena. The "thing-self" (the thing that exists outside of knowledge and absolutely unknowable), which is beyond the scope of knowledge or skills obtained through personal practice, is unknowable.

It is impossible for traditional ontology to know the "object-self" (something that exists outside of knowledge and is absolutely unknowable) and to attempt to establish a scientific knowledge of the "object-self" as if it were a "phenomenon".

This is because the "object" can be an object of thought, but it can never be an object for the act of "cognition" and "identification" of a subject in order to know with certainty, and these knowings have the potential to be used for specific purposes.

There are three ontologies studied in traditional philosophy: first, God, second, the soul, and third, the century as a whole. Kant proves that the knowledge of God can only be a rational ideal.

In fact, it is impossible for any human being to make logical deductive conclusions about natural and social phenomena in accordance with existing empirical knowledge, experience, facts, laws, cognition, and tested hypotheses, by means of generalizations and deductive reasoning.

Knowledge of the soul can only lead to fallacious reasoning, while knowledge of the world as a whole produces the opposite. All these prove that the "essence" is unknowable. But Kant argues that the pursuit of ontology is a necessary requirement of reason, as the act of "knowing" and "identifying" a subject in order to know it with certainty, and that these knowings have the potential capacity to be used for specific purposes.

Moreover, Kant believed that his pre-experientialism had laid the foundations of metaphysics for the study of such questions through rational reasoning and logic, which could not be answered directly through perception.

His book "Critique of Pure Reason" is the introduction to this ontology. One of the questions that Kant left to future generations is how metaphysics, which takes a certain object as its scope of study, is possible to find unified and exact objective laws and truths based on experimental and logical reasoning.

Hegel believes that traditional metaphysics is possible, and that "the ontology can be known as an object of knowledge, and the key lies in the replacement of abstract reason by dialectical reason, and of formal logic by dialectical logic.

Hegel believes that the absolute idea is the ontology, and its dialectical movement is the process of knowing itself. Therefore, he merged ontology, epistemology and logic into one, and established a huge system of dialectical logic.

The answer of modern Western philosophy to Kant's question is negative, that in order to take a certain object as the scope of study and to seek a unified and exact science of objective laws and truths based on experiment and logical reasoning, one cannot have metaphysics, and one cannot have science if one wants metaphysics.

It means that a systematic system of knowledge cannot be established for ontology, which refers to the pursuit of verifiable and transmittable acts of "cognition" and "identification" of a subject, in order to be sure of the knowledge, and that these knowledges have the potential ability to be used for specific purposes with underlying assumptions and methods.

In science, the assumption is that the entire world of experience and observation should be objectively cognizable, that there are relationships between things in the world that can be discovered, and that knowledge that is truly trustworthy must be obtained through careful observation, theorizing, and hypothetical testing, and that if metaphysics is to be studied, it cannot be done by scientific methods of proof.

They "reject metaphysics" and believe that ontology itself is a meaningless problem that arises from the confusion of propositional forms.

Once the different forms contained in a proposition are distinguished, it is clear that the problem discussed in ontology does not exist.

The school of humanism believes that metaphysics cannot be studied by natural science methods at all, but only by phenomenological methods. Heidegger believes that traditional ontologies are rootless ontologies, which replace the study of being with the study of being.

Therefore, he wants to establish a limited ontology, and the study of "being" can only begin with the "state of being" of "human life existence itself.

The phenomenal ontology proposed by Scharthe takes the irrational consciousness of man, i.e., the "I-thought before reflection", as the condition for the manifestation of ontology. As a result, modern ontology is centered on the human being, in contrast to the traditional ontology, which was centered on an absolute supernatural entity. A new face of ontology has emerged.

02.Does the soul exist?

For the ultimate nihilists, this is also a question that

cannot be avoided because of man's indifference to physical existence, and must be confronted with the question of the substance hidden within life. The soul is considered to be an immaterial thing that attaches itself to the human body as a master.

The soul is the driving force that allows the living body to manifest the phenomenon of life; the so-called phenomenon of life includes thought, desire, emotional expression and action. In the ancient disciplines of the study of universal, fundamental questions, including the fields of being, knowledge, values, reason, mind, and language, the soul was often seen as the mind or self.

This term is no longer used in disciplines that are substituted for analytical thinking to explore and reflect on fundamental questions about life, knowledge, and values.

The study of the principles and principles of the universe and life often focuses on the following issues: the elements that make up the soul, the functions of the soul, the relationship between the soul and the body, and the immortality of the soul.

The proponents of Platonism believe that the soul is

composed of immaterial and incorporeal entities. The Epicurean school believes that the soul is composed of atoms, and that there is no difference between the atoms that make up the soul and the atoms that make up the body.

R. Descartes (1596-1650) argued that the soul is composed of a thinking substance, while the matter is composed of an extended substance.

I. Kant (1724-1804) considered the soul to be a thing-in-itself, which could not be understood by human reason. The American psychologist W. James (1842-1910) believed that the soul is only a combination of many psychic phenomena and does not exist independently.

On the question of the function of the soul, social factors such as customs, morals, habits, beliefs, and ideas, which have been passed down from generation to generation, have been advocated as a mechanism to dominate the physical body; Aristotle (384-322 B.C.) believed that the soul is the driving force of life, the element that makes man different from other beings.

These views have recently been challenged by behaviorism, which advocates the study of manifest behavior through objective measures because behavior can be observed, measured, and manipulated, the most famous opponent being the English philosopher G. Ryle (1900-1976).

Regarding the relationship between the soul and the body and the immortality of the soul, the ancient Hebrews believed that the soul is the power of physical activity, which exists in the blood of a person and perishes with the destruction of the body.

Plato thought that the soul and the body are two different entities, and that the body is the prison of the soul, and that the death of the body represents the liberation of the soul, and that the best state of existence of the soul is its independent existence without being united with the body.

The soul has immortality. Aristotle believed that the soul is a function of the physical body, and that the relationship between the soul and the physical body is like the relationship between the eyes and the sight.

The exception is that the rational part of the soul (nous) is not attached to the physical body, so it can exist independently of the physical body, but Aristotle does not specify whether this part has immortality.

03. Impersonal Reason

However, the culture that believes that all facts must be observed or experienced by the senses to know the objective environment and external things in each person also has the tendency to attach importance to material things and the present life, and the present life that attaches importance to material things and concrete facts and conditions in front of the eyes is considered as a universal cultural principle.

In German classical philosophy, especially in Hegel, reason also constructs a spiritual kingdom of "self-justification" through an idea centered on "practical verification.

While Hegel saw the development of human history as a process in which impersonal reason, through human desires and passions (the things that are the goal of action or thought), realized its free nature, thus achieving a "Christian" reconciliation of the relationship between man and nature and man and society, some materialist debaters directly saw the development of history as a process of purposeful activity (will) of individuals pursuing their own interests.

Hegel, on the other hand, sees it as a state in which the free and comprehensive development of each individual is the goal. In this way, social rationality, which aims at the reconciliation of human and nature, human and social relations, is manifested in the individual's ability to realize his or her own will according to his or her own knowledge and laws.

Thus, as in Hegel's case, it points to the mutual symbiosis of individual freedom and the freedom of the common body, but the ontology or foundation of society is not Hegel's "impersonal mystical reason," but the productive activity of the action or influence of things and the state of interaction and mutual influence between things. At the same time, the question of the recognition of beings above nature and man, i.e., the question of theism, can be denied.

The completion of Hegel's rationalist philosophy also means that the nihilistic tradition has been pushed to the extreme, and God has lost his last refuge.

In this process, contemporary nihilism emerged, which is in essence the negation of man's value to himself.

This was Hegel's destiny at the beginning of modern philosophy, which led to the wave of irrationalism that still profoundly influences and even dominates contemporary spiritual culture.

With the philosophy of realism, which holds that the universe consists of many entities and is an objective and concrete existence that does not depend on the human or divine mind to understand concepts, and that the human mind has the cognitive ability to discover the true nature of some objective things, it is the accumulation of modern materialistic situations that continues to exacerbate the contemporary view of nihilism.

After Hegel, Kierkegaard (Kierkegaard), Schopenhauer, Nietzsche, and their contemporary thought have more explicitly used human practice, will, and irrationality against absolute reason to deny God, and human sensibility to deny the abandonment of transcendence.

However, these efforts do not lead to the self-affirmation and awakening of man in the direction of Western-oriented modern thought, but rather to a strong existentialism, to the anxiety of unexplained suspension, to the vanity of the decay of the individual, and to the post-modernism, to the reflection of the complete reconstruction of human autonomy.

At the same time, the scientistic idea of taking a certain object as the scope of study and seeking unified and exact objective laws and truths based on experiments and logical reasoning, as well as the holistic, fundamental and critical inquiry into the real world and human beings conducted by linguistic analysis, is the rejection of questions that cannot be answered directly through perception, which is to deduce answers through rational logical reasoning under a priori conditions and cannot contradict empirical evidence.

It is the rejection of questions that cannot be answered directly through perception, which is deduced through rational logical reasoning under a priori conditions, and cannot contradict empirical evidence, that is, to expel the transcendental metaphysics from the world of meaning, to manifest it through language, symbols, etc., and to consolidate the empirical world's verifiability or expressiveness.

The recent scientistic trend has also fallen into irrationalism and post-modernism. Even phenomenology, a holistic, fundamental and critical inquiry into the real world and human beings.

It is a movement that pursues a "strictly scientific philosophy," a study of the principles and principles of the universe and life, but it is also caught up in a negative and negative nihilistic trend.

It was also a movement that developed in the direction of a "constructive theory" hermeneutics that focuses on an international event, a trend, or a phenomenon of international interaction in the contemporary era of history, proposing theoretical hypotheses, testing them, and providing causal relationships.

In fact, after Nietzsche, the entire modern spiritual culture has been reflective and critical, questioning whether the beliefs and perceptions that we firmly believe in under the status quo are really the truth and reality.

We are always lost in our unexamined acceptance of what most people call "right", what is specious and may not be true. Therefore, instead of the "positive nihilism" described by Nietzsche, we fall into a "negative and negative nihilism", but rather into a negative and rebellious spiritual condition.

In the context of positivism at that time, nihilism was

growing exponentially, and it was not only the negation of God and divine consciousness, but also the negation of all kinds of human definitions and their ways of existence, such as humanity, history, cultural traditions, nationality, and publicness, which led to various forms of nihilism.

Among them, the following four types of nihilism are particularly prevalent and show obvious global characteristics and symptoms.

001. Human nihilism

Human nihilism. It has two main manifestations. One manifestation is a negative pessimistic attitude toward the future destiny of human beings, denying the meaning of human existence as a whole, confronting humanity with naturalness, looking at technology and modern materialistic life pessimistically, being spiritually confused, losing faith, mixing unrestrained hedonism with self-abandoned pessimism.

The spiritual soul is deeply absorbed in the pursuit of power or in the hedonism of materialistic civilization, in the realm of life or in the activities of thinking, and it is difficult to extricate oneself.

002. Collective Nihilism

Another manifestation of collective nihilism is to confront and deny the unity and diversity of human beings with specific nationalities, national consciousness, groups, and individuality. Thus, collective nihilism lacks a certain nature of connection between people and things, and a basic understanding of each other (understanding means not only understanding the matter, but also being able to see it from the other's point of view) with respect to the common body, the national social group, and the life of the public community.

It also lacks the ability to recognize the environment and the self, as well as a clear understanding of the public good, the concept of common citizenship and dedication.

Narrow nationalism, nationalism, chauvinism, imperialism, and collective nihilism all imply, to varying degrees, human nihilism, which denies the value of altruism and the value of altruism.

It is a denial of altruistic values, a denial of the unifying function of organizations, a direct view of organization as an autocratic rule that abolishes the independence of the individual, a utilitarian attitude toward the collective, a give-and-take, and anarchism. The essence of collective nihilism is individualism and egoism.

003. National nihilism

The expression of nihilism in the national question. The term nihilism is a German translation of Nihilismus, from the Latin nihil (nothingness). It was first used by the German idealist philosopher F. H. Jacobi in his Letter to Fichte. The German idealist philosopher F. Nietzsche called the phenomenon of denial of historical traditions and moral principles nihilism.

National nihilism ignores the characteristics of nations and the differences between nations, and simply sees national independence as "geo-nationalism".

It even considers "nation" as a fictional concept and denies the existence of a nation at all. The so-called supra-national cosmopolitanism and "internationalism" have been used to erase, eliminate, and exclude ethnicity, and treat ethnicity, national sovereignty, and national identity as obsolete concepts.

Historically, the reactionary ruling classes in some feudal autocracies denied the existence of other nationalities. During the imperialist era, the bourgeoisie considered the concepts of nationality and national sovereignty obsolete, and regarded the struggle of oppressed nations for national independence as "local totalitarianism".

It advocated that "individual freedom" should be based on supra-nationalism and cosmopolitanism, and deceived and induced the "geopolitical" colonial and semi-colonial peoples to leave the path of nationality and democracy. In the post-modern socialist era, communist political and economic cooperation is practiced.

Under the pretext that "the people" are the masters of the proletariat, they use people, nationalities and democratic nihilism to oppress their own people and nationalities and to invade other countries under the pretext of economic cooperation for common prosperity, and to perform political and economic national services.

004. Cultural Nihilism

Culture is the total result of human creation in the process of historical development. It includes religion, morality, art, science and other aspects; Wikipedia explains culture from a philosophical point of view, and considers culture to be the expression of philosophical thought. Culture is essentially the expression of philosophical thought. The age and region of philosophy determine the different styles of culture.

Generally speaking, changes in philosophical thought cause changes in social institutions, accompanied by the suppression of old culture and the rise of new culture.

From an existentialist perspective, culture is a description of the way of being of a person or a group of people. People exist in nature, as well as in history and time.

Time is an important platform for the existence of a person or a group of people in nature; society, state and nation (family) is another important platform for the existence of a person or a group of people in history and time.

04. Culture has many meanings. It can be divided into three.

Culture is the way people speak or express themselves, interact or behave, and become aware or cognitive in the process of such existence. Culture is not only used to describe the external behavior of a group of people, but culture especially includes the mental awareness and perception of the self as an individual.

It is a way of dialogue and observation of the self when a person returns to his or her inner world. Therefore, the term culture has a variety of meanings in its use. It can be divided into three.

First, the level of material activity. Culture is an observable fact or event that is the external form of human things in their development and change, and is a continuous process of human generation. Therefore, "culture" is the process of quenching people's daily experiences.

If culture is understood as an "objectively existing thing" or a "condition that fits the objective situation" in its daily application. Reality is the sum of all actual things or existing things, as opposed to the fact of imagining all imaginary things, and then it is the material production activity of human beings.

Second, the level of mental activity. Culture cannot be directly equated with human psychology, emotions and thoughts, but rather with their expression.

It includes political, legal, moral, artistic, religious, scientific, and other concepts, ideas, and their corresponding institutions. Thus culture refers to the construction of religion, art and philosophy, and the establishment of various customs, habits and institutions.

Thirdly, the level of words and symbols. Because the word metonym is the gathering of people's spiritual activities, it is the most concentrated manifestation of culture. It is the sum of all the social phenomena of the wisdom group and the inheritance, creation, and development of the inner spirit of the group.

It encompasses the history of the wisdom community from the past to the future, and is the foundation of all the activities of the community based on nature. Therefore, it is not surprising that people equate the study of culture with the study of writing, and that the basis of communication between cultural philosophies is the common understanding of the rules and structures behind the system of symbols and codes among the communicators. It is also called "symbolic philosophy".

In our everyday language use, these three cultural meanings may be said to be used in tandem. Perhaps the most widespread of these is the semantics of spiritual activity.

Although the external forms, observable facts or events that are manifested in the development and change of cultural things have always accompanied human history, the objective presence of culture in all objects or phenomena of nature, in all situations that can be perceived, has only become a prominent issue in the contemporary world.

This is because the long history of human beings is mainly the history of life experience activities, not the history of spiritual activities.

At the time of life experience activities, the intelligent group basically relies on the will of the person to consciously determine the purpose, and according to the purpose of the regulation of their own body, by their own actions, to overcome difficulties, to achieve the predetermined goal of mental tendencies.

The freedom of the will to create all social phenomena of the group and the inner spirit of the group, to pass on, to create, and to develop.

It is an important psychological factor in the process of cultural-philosophical decision-making mental activity, and is a concentrated expression of the dynamism of human consciousness, which means "objectively existing things" or "conditions appropriate to the objective situation" when people actively change in daily application.

It is all the actual things or the existence of things in action, the act of initiation, persistence and stop, change and other aspects of control and regulation. The will process includes two stages.

One is to take the decision stage, but also the preparation stage of the will to act. In this stage, first to solve the problem of competition for motivation, and then is to determine the goal of action and choose to achieve the goal of effective strategies, methods and means, and to develop a practical action plan.

Second, the implementation of the decision stage, which is the action plan into the realization of the process. In this stage, to firmly implement the action plan set, and strive to overcome the subjective and objective difficulties encountered in the final realization of the plan

Not only that, but traditional culture is a national culture that reflects the characteristics and appearance of the nation through the evolution of the group's civilization of will, and is a general representation of various ideological and cultural and conceptual forms in the history of the nation.

In all parts of the world, each nation has its own traditional culture of volitional civilization; it means that the culture of the contemporary world is fundamentally an information culture of volitional civilization, or media culture, such as books, movies, television, Internet, cell phones, etc., which has become the main volitional civilization of contemporary culture.

It is a nihilism that denies that history and culture are passed down from generation to generation, and that social factors such as customs, morals, habits, beliefs, and ideas are inherited and continued.

This kind of nihilism does not recognize the inheritance and continuity of history and cultural traditions, and regards the transition from traditional civilization to modern civilization as the replacement of ideas, culture, morals, customs, arts, institutions and behaviors passed down from old generations by the will of the new civilization, denying the inherent logic of historical development and treating various historical and cultural heritages lightly.

We disregard the inheritance of the human spirit and civilization from generation to generation, and the social factors of continuity, such as customs, morals, habits, beliefs, ideas, etc., and their edifying significance, and pursue commercial interests as the basis.

In order to meet the interests of post-modern fashion and popular culture, and even self-indulgence, the academic and ideological banners are used to arbitrarily smear historical materials, ridicule historical figures, and distort classics, ignoring moral and social perceptions, under the banner of hermeneutics, and open contemporaryity.

In fact, various negative and even negative contemporary values, such as relativism, skepticism, mysticism, hedonism, anarchism, fascism, and terrorism, are closely and intricately linked to nihilism.

Moreover, from a spiritual point of view, nihilism itself is the crux of the negative or even negative values that result from the failure of these will processes. Contemporary nihilism itself is strongly Western, but the critique and containment of nihilism is a global nihilism.

In the process of expanding global capitalism,

modernity, and materialization, contemporary nihilism, which emerged in Western societies, has not only dragged post-developed countries and nations into the vortex of contemporary nihilism, but has also given rise to various colonial or post-colonial phenomena.

In general, according to the basic logic of German and Russian nihilist discourse, nihilism is not a phenomenon of individual countries or regions, nor a phenomenon that occurred only in the nineteenth century, but a universal phenomenon that concerns the whole of Western history.

Nietzsche argues that nihilism has existed since the beginning of Western culture, or at least that the emergence of Christianity and Platonism, and especially the fusion of the two, led directly to nihilism.

It was only at the beginning that people did not realize that it was a problem. It is only in modern times that it has become a serious and troublesome problem. With the globalization of European civilization, nihilism would go worldwide.

According to this explanation, nihilism, which has become a serious problem, is instead the result of the completion and maturation of Western culture, the expression of the thoroughness of the modernization of human will civilization, and only when the modernization of will civilization has achieved a certain degree of success and the modernization of will civilization has become a prominent problem in the process of defeat, will nihilism manifest itself.

05. The Self-Contradiction of Nihilism

Nihilism is sometimes considered to be a belief in the non-existence of truth. This belief, in its most extreme form, is difficult to prove. It consists of a self-contradictory lie: if it is true that truth does not exist, then "truth does not exist" is itself not true, thus proving itself false.

A more complex explanation is that truth may exist, but is inaccessible in reality. Others believe that nihilists, realizing that truth exists but is impossible to achieve in practice, see the search for truth as futile.

In the West, nihilism has been around since ancient times. But it was at the beginning of the last century that the age of nihilism was officially announced. At the threshold of the turn of the century, the German philosopher Friedrich Nietzsche, who was known as a madman, made the astonishing statement "God is dead" in the mouth of the Persian prophet, "the madman, Zarathustra," which is still a historical symbol of nihilism.

According to the context of Western culture, nihilism is a state of emptiness of values in the spiritual world. Under this state, people's spirits have no place to turn to and their souls have no solace. All standards of value have collapsed and collapsed, and all the inner laws of the mind, authority, and beliefs of people have vanished into thin air.

In short, the transcendental abode of the human spirit has collapsed, and those lonely souls are either wandering or drowning in the storm. In Nietzsche's own words, this means that the highest values have lost their value and lack an answer to the "why".

In other words, if the highest values are lost, then "everything is false, everything is permissible", everything is relative, and one is the basis of one's own legitimacy. After the spiritual idols have been smashed by man's own "hammers" and stepped on their remains, people seem to be able to do whatever they want, to do nothing, to do no evil.

In summary, nihilism confronts the so-called

essentialism, which relies on absolute values, and aims to shatter its unbreakable authority and unity.

Obviously, the nihilist is a person who, as Turgenev said, "is a nihilist who does not submit to any authority, who believes in no principle with others, no matter how sacrosanct that principle is considered.

Overcoming nihilism is a problem faced by the entire modern age in terms of analyzing and reflecting on the fundamental questions of life, knowledge, and values, as well as social ideologies and the institutional and organizational structures appropriate to them, including political, legal, moral, artistic, religious, scientific, and other concepts, ideas, and their corresponding institutional spirits.

After Nietzsche, many schools of modern Western philosophy and even post-modernism have also criticized and resisted to a certain extent while expressing nihilism.

However, on the whole, the study and critique of nihilism in the Western academy is still limited by the limits of relativist values, post-theology, and the capitalist system, and has not escaped from the positivist philosophy of Comte in the 19th century.

After the First World War, it was gradually introduced into the field of international relations, and after the two World Wars and the introduction of the behaviorist, or scientific, approach to social science research in the West, the "explanatory theories" of observing objective phenomena and proposing explanations were gradually established.

What positivists think the world looks like is probably constructed by our human "concepts". That is, an "interpretation". Therefore, post-positivism can also be called a "constructive theory", such as realism, neo-realism, and neo-liberal institutionalism, which all belong to this kind of explanatory theory.

They also belong to positivism. It is also increasingly evident that the mainstream theories of international relations are conservative and even anti-modern, thus making it difficult to fully and profoundly develop an analytical critique of the nihilism of the present age.

Nietzsche believes that in order to overcome "negative nihilism", one needs to deny all the values of the past on the one hand, and to reevaluate all the values on the other.

001. Reevaluating all values

"Revaluation of all values" is the subtitle of Nietzsche's book The Will to Power. Nietzsche argues that people need to go through a painful stage of nihilism before they reach the point of revaluing all values in their own power, and then they will wake up.

Nietzsche points out that the old values have been shattered, which is also an affirmation of the power of the self. Nietzsche's other book, Twilight of the Idols, is subtitled "How to Philosophize with a Hammer," meaning that many of the concepts that have been the basis of values in Western history are considered to be idols and are to be smashed.

Nietzsche shattered all the old values. The old human playgrounds, such as the philosophical world of ideas or the religious world of the other side, were all burned to the ground. Nietzsche points out that the present world, which was previously despised by philosophers and religionists, is the place where human beings can reaffirm themselves and establish their values.

Since Nietzsche affirms the importance of the present world, he also believes that life in the present world is very important, and that people should affirm their will to live in order to realize a certain ideal or achieve a certain purpose, and to work for it consciously.

In other words, the moral value of all values must be measured by the ability of all objects or phenomena that exist objectively in nature to make the will to live strong or not.

002. The Will to Power

The concept of will to power (English: Will to power / German: der Willer zur Macht) is an extension of Nietzsche's idea of "value revaluation". Simply put, the will to power is the most basic driving force of all things, which is another term for what was called motivation in early psychology.

Motive" is the cause of behavior, and "drive" means the force that motivates behavior, which is similar to the meaning of motive, but more explicitly, the force that drives behavior in individuals. Needs include physiological, psychological and social aspects.

This internal state of arousal is caused by physiological or psychological needs and motivates the person to engage in actions that satisfy these needs.

In the early days, this concept referred only to the

physiological needs that could create a state of tension and subsequently lead to an activity that would satisfy such needs in order to reduce that tension. Later, the concept of learned endogeneity was introduced by Hull and others and was gradually extended to include the psychodynamic aspects of behavior.

In the first three decades of the twentieth century, psychologists had two approaches to drive, involving the question of "nature-nurture" and "acquired" (Nature-Nurture). In terms of drive, McDougall (1871-1938), in his Introduction to Social Psychology (1908-1926), argued that drive was an innate instinct that was present in all living things.

J.B. Watson (1878-1958) maintained his behaviorist position that drive is acquired through learning. Since then, psychologists have recognized that genetics and environment are equally important, and that there are both innate and acquired drives. However, they are divided into two categories: primary and secondary.

Primary Drives are biological instincts, such as hunger and thirst, and avoidance of pain for safety, which are innate, but can also be changed through learning, such as the way we feed ourselves in early childhood, and the degree of pain tolerance.

Secondary Drives, which are acquired drives, are mostly caused by experiences, such as the object of fear (i.e., the thing to be feared), the cause of pain, and so on.

For example, if a normal person walks alone and sees a fierce beast or a large and fierce animal, he or she will be afraid of it, while a hunting professional or a person with hunting expertise will be happy to see it.

In general, people regard bodily injury as a painful disaster, but in the Hindu religious practice, there is a way to obtain the blessing of the gods or to be liberated.

Practitioners of a certain religion, who believe that they must follow a particular external precept, religious ritual or austerity in order to be liberated because of uncertain knowledge and biased perception, and who achieve their goal through various practices that transcend nature and transcend the self, express their confidence by hurting their flesh and do not regard it as suffering.

The physical changes, biological reproduction of all objects or phenomena that exist objectively in nature, and even the ideas, cultures, morals, customs, arts, institutions, and behaviors that have been passed down from generation to generation and from history.

The social behavior of people have invisible influence and control role. In a hierarchical society, traditions have class will and national will, positive traditions promote social development, conservative and backward traditions, human psychological and cultural phenomena that hinder social progress and change, Nietzsche believes are driven by the will to power.

As mentioned above, the will to power is actually the will to life in the present world, so Nietzsche said that wherever there is life, there is the ability of human beings to decide their own behavior. However, Nietzsche's will to live is different from Schopenhauer's. Schopenhauer believed that in order to realize a certain ideal or to achieve a certain purpose, the will to live is different from the will to act.

But Nietzsche believed that the will to live should refer to the ability of human beings to decide on their own the act of pursuing life, to give full play to their own vitality, and to demonstrate their own strength.

It can be said that Nietzsche's will to live, in full

conformity with actuality or expectation, should refer to a state of mind that arises from the decision of life to achieve a certain purpose, often expressed in words or actions, and a tendency to constantly self-express, create, and expand.

Gilles Deleuze, a philosopher who studied Nietzsche, said that Nietzsche's will to power does not refer to a will that is lacking or imperfect, nor does it refer to a will to be constantly satisfied.

In the history of Western philosophy, since Plato introduced desire, it is Eros that gives it the meaning of love, lack, etc. Desire is the desire and requirement to realize a certain ideal or achieve a certain purpose.

It is the desire to consciously work for it. The desire to achieve a certain purpose that arises from human nature, the desire itself is not good or bad, the key is how to control. The most primitive and basic instinct of all animals in the world.

From the human point of view is a psychological to physical desire, satisfaction, it is essential to the existence of all animals needs. The most basic desire of all animals is to survive and exist. Simply put, it is [love and dissatisfaction], that is, the desire to be lacking in itself, the desire is always enough.

Schopenhauer believed that desire is the root of all existential misfortunes, and that people feel distressed because their desires are never satisfied. The French thinkers, however, found in the unfulfillment of desire a magical effect that made people motivated and energetic.

According to the famous French thinker Rousseau, "Self-love" (Amour-de-soi) is "the source of all human desires" and "the origin and principle of all other desires". It is also the "fundamental desire of all human beings," and "it is the original, intrinsic desire that precedes all other desires. It is "the original, inner desire that precedes all other desires, and, in a sense, all other desires are only its evolution.

That is to say, man's suffering comes from his ability, and it seems appropriate to match his inability to desire. When the ability is greater than the desire, man feels happy; when the ability does not reach the desire, and when he encounters obstacles in purposeful activity, he feels pain because he cannot achieve his purpose. Rousseau believed that "natural desires" are the most basic and limited.

Therefore, when civilized people realize that their excessive dissatisfaction does not come from "natural desires" but from false "human desires", then they can get rid of their dissatisfaction. Then people can be free from their "spiritual suffering" and achieve freedom.

Human beings, through their contact with each other and the progress of civilization, have developed "infinite desires". These unquenchable human desires give rise to "false human emotions. "Self-esteem/selfishness" drives humans to constantly compare themselves with others.

The desire to gain the attention and admiration of others is the result of the arrogance of the selfish mind. Rousseau believes that the result is that "pride/selfishness" produces "pride" in the mind of a great man, but "vanity" in the mind of a small man.

As long as the "pride/selfishness" changes and develops from small to large, from simple to complex, from low to high, the relative "I" will continue to carry out activities, and all objects or phenomena that exist objectively in the natural world will grow again from birth.

All the objects or phenomena in nature will again grow from birth to completion, a repetitive process of progress and change, and things will be constantly renewed because they are satisfied. However, when "self-esteem" is overdeveloped or suppressed, human beings become angry, cruel, inferior, paranoid, jealous, and other emotions.

Selfishness drives us to compare ourselves with others, so that there is never, never, never a time to be satisfied, because when it makes us only know how to care about our own feelings and not others' feelings, and insists that others care about us first.

It is not possible to insist that others care about us before they care about their "pride/selfishness", because paranoid and jealous dispositions arise from selfishness. People are happy precisely in anticipation, before their desires are satisfied.

In other words, we are truly happy when we are desiring. According to Jacques Lacan, another famous French spiritualist, people are indeed fully motivated when they desire.

This is because the motivation to pursue desire, to strive to improve oneself and to be worthy of one's desires, is the driving force for one's own advancement and is also necessary for the progress of society as a whole. Although excessive pursuit, neglecting the overall will, focusing on personal desires, and never being satisfied, being unaware of things, having no mastery, and not being able to control yourself, is quite terrible.

However, when you are gazing at the abyss, the abyss is gazing at you at the same time. Desire, too, will lead you step by step to the abyss. Therefore, it is believed that people sometimes deliberately avoid having their desires satisfied, because they are afraid that when they get what they desire, their life will lose the joy of expectation, the motivation of pursuit and the charm of fantasy.

To many, Rousseau and Lagan's theory of desire is undoubtedly positive, and later Westerners have inherited this "lack of desire" thesis. But if Nietzsche's desire refers to this will, the will to live is a servile will, for it is compelled to pursue material things to satisfy itself, and it confines itself to them, led by the desire for civilized enjoyment.

However, another thinker of the same period as Lagan, Gilles Deleuze, had a different view. He argues that Lagan's theory of desire is still not free from negativity, because it still presumes that man is a willed being with a desire that is lacking and to be satisfied.

Instead, he argues that desire itself is not negative, but fully productive, active, and even subversive. As a desiring being, man can actively combine with other things in order to expand his power.

Therefore, Deleuze believes that Nietzsche's will to consciously work for the realization of a certain ideal, or to achieve a certain purpose, refers more to desire and productivity, producing diversity and novelty in repeated actions. It becomes an explosive expression of power.

6. Nietzsche's understanding and criticism of Buddhism from the standpoint of religious philosophy..

In this paper, we will look directly at the position on which Nietzsche based his research and analysis or criticism of problems and issues. As mentioned above, this judgment is viewed within the context of Nietzsche's philosophy in order to understand the meaning of Nietzsche's viewpoint and to discuss whether this judgment has its own interpretation of the objective meaning of life existence.

Since Nietzsche's philosophy is unique in the Western philosophical tradition in its practical philosophical criticism, the starting point of his philosophy is not metaphysics or theory of knowledge, but the ideas that have been handed down from generation to generation and passed down through history.

Therefore, we can explore how Nietzsche and Buddha opened a new direction for practical philosophy from the perspective of practical philosophy by criticizing their metaphysics-theology tradition.

It is not surprising that Nietzsche's criticism of Buddhism was misunderstood because of the great divide between the cultural and traditional backgrounds of his life.

Moreover, Nietzsche's tendency to look at things from the perspective of the subject's own needs is an attribute of Nietzsche's personal view, experience, consciousness, spirit, feelings, desires, or beliefs. Its fundamental characteristic is that it exists only within Nietzsche, and it belongs to the subject's consciousness bias to develop his theory.

However, if we look at Nietzsche's "misunderstanding"

of Buddhism from a broader perspective, if we look at it from the perspective of the integration of Eastern and Western cultures, the integration of all aspects of knowledge and reasoning, and the value of a comprehensive and thorough understanding of spirituality as an interpretive worker to open the horizon of human wisdom, then we can have a broader perspective.

Nietzsche's purpose in dealing with Buddhism was not to make an objective examination of comparative religion. If this was Nietzsche's purpose, then it is clear that his work was poor and crude, and that his achievements were far inferior to the depth and breadth of knowledge of the German comparative religious philosophers and Indian religious philosophers of his time. In all conscience, it can be said that he was far inferior.

However, we do not think that because Nietzsche's understanding of Buddhism was not deep enough, we should be ready to conclude that Nietzsche's criticism of Buddhism is of no value.

Although his generalizations about Buddhism are crude and generalized, his broad vision and critical spirit may have penetrated directly into the mistakes of other Indian scholars or those who have long targeted the blind spots of those who have not studied Buddhism deeply enough and have been inaccurate in their interpretations.

Although Nietzsche, with the help of Professor Ritschl, was easily offered a professorship in classical philosophy at the University of Basel in Switzerland, his virgin work, Die Geburt der Tragödie (The Birth of Tragedy), was not only ignored by the classical literature community at the time, but he was also ostracized by other classical literature scholars.

But this prematurely born work has gone on to become a major success, marking a period of significance that the classical literary scholars who severely criticized Nietzsche at the time could never have imagined or expected.

Therefore, we should not judge Nietzsche's criticism of Buddhism to be absurd and unreasonable due to the lack of an objective understanding of the whole.

In particular, we must pay attention to the context in which Nietzsche's criticism of Buddhism was made and what his intentions were.

※Nietzsche's Criticism of Buddhism

In Nietzsche's lifetime, the most concentrated discussion of Buddhism appears in chapters 20-23 of Der Anitchrist, followed to a lesser extent by the third essay in Zur Genealogie der Moral, on the ideal of monastic asceticism. There are even more references to Buddhism in the manuscripts of Nietzsche's numerous notebooks.

These references to Buddhism are all within the same thematic narrative context, namely, the question of how European culture can transcend nihilism, which is the central idea of Nietzsche's later writing projects, in works of central importance, or in social activities. Its main content.

It also involves Nietzsche's personal experience of life, which is also the source of Nietzsche's creative inspiration.

In the early 19th century, German Romantic writers (such as F. Majer and F. Schlegel) began to pay attention to early Indian religion and poetry, and they were regarded by Nietzsche as pessimists of aesthetics.

Nietzsche's pessimism was the predecessor of Vorform des Nihilism, which he called "art pour l'art "Description";

and he called aesthetic pessimism "description for art's sake". ").

He considered Schopenhauer to be an "epistemological" and "phenomenalist" pessimist; Buddhism, as a "religion of compassion," is also a pessimist. As for Nietzsche himself, he admits to be a moral pessimist.

All quotations from Nietzsche (author's translation) are from the Kritischen Studienausgabe edition of the complete works of Nietzsche compiled by G. Colli and M. Montinari, abbreviated as KSA.

M. Müller, an important scholar of comparative religious philosophy at the time, interpreted Buddhism as a "nihilistic" religion.

Thus, in the preface to Nietzsche's Moral Genealogy, Nietzsche refers to what the pessimists of the time called "neo-Buddhism" (neuen Buddhismus) as "negative nihilism," an ideological content expressed in language and words.

This idea, expressed in language and words, implies that Nietzsche's personal prejudice was not the only one, but the background and conditions of the academic world at that time. However, we have to investigate the causes of things.

(1) What is Nietzsche's intention of the so-called "negative nihilism"?

(2) If Nietzsche judged Buddhism as "negative nihilism," what kind of logical thinking was this judgment based on?

(3) Does Nietzsche's criticism of Buddhism have an objective meaning? In the manuscript of the third essay of Zur Genealogie der Moral written in the autumn of 1887, we can see Nietzsche's definition of the so-called "negative nihilism". This text is a very important basis for our forthcoming discussion, and the full text is excerpted below.

(1) Nihilism is a state that occurs from time to time.

Nihilism, that is, in common usage, the term usually refers to the form of "nihilism," according to which life has no substantial connotative value, meaning, or purpose hidden within.

Other prominent positions in nihilism include the

rejection of all standards or rules and ethical perspectives that control behavior in a social context (moral nihilism), the rejection of all social and political institutions (political nihilism), the position that no knowledge can or does exist (epistemological nihilism), and the position that no knowledge can or does exist (epistemological nihilism). Epistemological nihilism.)

There are also many problematic positions that can be studied through rational reasoning and logic but cannot be answered directly through perception, asserting the non-existence of non-abstract objects (Metaphysical nihilism), the non-existence of composite objects (Mereological nihilism), and even the non-existence of life itself.

The lack of the purpose of the mental state in which the individual consciously strives for the realization of a certain concept of the perfection of something, or the achievement of a certain purpose; the lack of the answer to the "why" of the drive.

What is nihilism? It is also the self-depreciation of the highest value. Nihilism has two meanings.

01. nihilism as a sign of spiritual ascension.

That is, positive nihilism. It can be a powerful symbol. In other words, the power of the spirit may grow to such an extent that the purpose ("belief", creed) for which it has hitherto been used cannot be strictly and tightly matched.

Generally speaking, faith is a firm belief and faith in a person, an object, a thing, or a concept, including trust and reverence for an idea or a religion, which is expressed in the compulsion to submit to the authority of the conditions of existence (Verhältnissen) that make the species prosper, grow, and gain strength... ...

On the other hand, as a sign that it is not strong enough, that is, not creative enough, to set again a purpose, a reason, a belief in a certain proposition, a doctrine, a religion or a person that is highly believed and respected.

The relative power of nihilism is the comparison of one substance or whole with another substance or another whole, or the dependence on certain conditions of existence or change as a strong destructive (Zerstörung) force that reaches its maximum: that is, as positive nihilism. Its opposite is the weak nihilism, which is no longer aggressive, and whose most famous form is Buddhism, that is, nihilism as extinction.

Nihilism expresses a morbid intermediate stage (a morbid state is a state of psychological abnormality, meaning that it generalizes everything to meaningless conclusions): either by associating two or more concepts or things in a certain way

The power of the act of subjectively creating objectively generally acceptable things to achieve a certain purpose is not strong enough; or it is self-indulgent, ignoring moral and social perceptions, still hesitant, and has not yet found a cure.

02. Nihilism as a sign of spiritual decline and regression.

That is, negative nihilism: it is a sign of weakness. The strength of the spirit is so exhausted and depleted that the hitherto purpose and values are no longer appropriate, and no longer find any value of faith, and the synthesis of purpose (on which every strong culture is based) disintegrates so that between individual values there arises a measure of dissatisfaction or opinion, a strenuous resistance to the other's approval of one's claims: this is disintegration (Zersetzung).

All the things that make people tired, restored to health, and in a state of anesthesia, cloaked in all sorts of different amazement and reverence for the mysteries of the universe and life, constitute a doctrine of good and punishment for evil, and are used to educate the world, to make people believe in religious, moral, political, or, aesthetic, and other deceptive names or disguises that hide the true nature of the world, are considered important and treated seriously. (2).

(2) the premise of this hypothesis has no truth;

There is no absolute nature of any objectively existing object or phenomenon in nature, no "thing in itself". This thing-in-itself is nihilism, and it is the most extreme. It places the value of all objectively existing objects or phenomena in nature on a value that is not real, either now or in the past.

This is the reason for consciously working for the realization of a certain ideal or the achievement of a certain goal, making complex things simple.

The so-called positive nihilism, as mentioned above, means that when man's spiritual power reaches a state of fullness that is sufficient to destroy everything, it means for him that he denies all value-setters from outside himself, and thus denies God and his responsibility to man.

But positive nihilism is not strong enough to set values in a state of creation in which one consciously strives for the realization of an ideal or the achievement of an end, but it is strong enough to destroy all existing values that are inappropriate.

He questioned what the consequences would be if faith and its basis were to lose their validity. Nietzsche answered in the affirmative, for example, if one lost one's faith, could one live?

Nietzsche's answer is yes. But negative nihilism presents a worrying picture of the "loss of validity of faith," a cultural tendency to self-indulgence, to disregard moral and social perceptions, and to appear in various guises of rebellion against religion, morality, politics, or aesthetics.

Negative nihilism, as a sign of the decline of the spiritual power of the weak, is a weak and powerless state of mind that cannot consciously work for the realization of a certain ideal or the achievement of a certain purpose, and cannot affirm the creativity of its own life, its ability to set values.

And the existing values, having lost the ability to

synthesize, disintegrate on their own all the tangible material structures that exist objectively in nature, and therefore, for it, collapse, disintegration also lose their effectiveness at the same time.

The moral teachings of Socrates and Christianity, according to Nietzsche, are typical of a self-indulgent culture of disregard for moral and social perceptions.

They regarded the natural life that was born in the world as impure and sinful, and therefore subverted the order of values by means of the norms and standards of behavior and conduct that human beings should follow when they live together, and applied the anesthetics of [rationalism] and [empiricism] to the natural life that was supposed to enhance spiritual power, rendering it weak and incapable of creation.

Nietzsche believed that life itself is the instinct of growth, continuity, and accumulation of power, an instinct for power (Instinkt für Macht). He said, "Niedergang appears where the will to power (Wille zur Macht) is lacking. The so-called "morality" emerges only when a person has sufficient energy to work consciously for the realization of a certain ideal or the achievement of a certain purpose, in order to enhance life and set values.

In other words, the will to power is the source of the creative power of value setting, and the emergence of nihilism is the result of the disintegration of this source of creative power, or, as in the case of positive nihilism, although it has relatively strong power, it is still insufficient to create value setting for the purpose of consciously working for the realization of a certain ideal or the achievement of a certain purpose.

As for the negative nihilism, it is a cultural form of weakness, inability to synthesize values, self-indulgence, and disregard for moral and social perceptions.

It even inverts all objects or phenomena that exist objectively in nature and have positive meaning to people or groups, are valued by people, or can make people feel satisfied.

It becomes the order of objects that people respect or are interested in pursuing, denigrates all cultural conditions that belong to the strongest, creates power, and causes the decline of the overall culture of ideas, culture, morals, customs, arts, institutions, and ways of acting of the will that have been handed down from generation to generation and from history

(3) Nietzsche's analysis of the phenomenon of nihilism is divided into two general points.

In this way, we can summarize and draw together a series of specific facts by means of methodical deduction, and conclude that Nietzsche's points of departure in analyzing the phenomenon of nihilism can be summarized in two ways.

First, all metaphysics is not a system of truth, but a system of values.

For questions that cannot be answered directly through perception, it is not necessary to deduce the answer through irrational judgment under a priori conditions, and it is the face of human irrational thought's distrust of things, and the search of whether the object has positive meaning and usefulness to the subject's manifestation.

Secondly, any value setting is motivated by the need of life to realize a certain ideal: or to achieve a certain purpose, and to work for it consciously, so it is the setter, the marker of the power of life.

However, since the answer to a question that cannot be obtained directly through perception, it is deduced through rational logical reasoning under a priori conditions, and cannot contradict empirical evidence.

It is the beginning of human reason's search for the most universal aspects and ultimate causes of things that has set the morality of denial of life as the highest value, and the ideas, cultures, morals, customs, arts, institutions, and moral ways of behavior that have been passed down from generation to generation and from history have long ruled over the life force of mankind, and this means that the driving force of value setting is undermined.

Therefore, once the old social factors, such as customs, morals, habits, beliefs, and ideas, which have been passed down from generation to generation, collapse, and new value settings cannot be established in a short period of time, there will be a widespread failure to believe and trust in a person, an object, a thing, or a concept, including the trust and reverence for a certain idea or religion.

(4) Nietzsche distinguishes between two opposite kinds of nihilism.

At this point, only vital natures retain the ability to

create new values, and thus not only accept but actively contribute to the total collapse of old values.

Until new values are created, they are, for the time being, in a state where they do not believe in, worship, and hold a religion or a doctrine as a rule or guide for their words and actions. But it is not the same as the state of faithlessness, which is the weakness of life and nature. Accordingly, Nietzsche distinguishes two opposite kinds of nihilism.

First, positive nihilism (deraktiveNihilismus): nihilism as a sign of increased spiritual power.

Second, derpassiveNihilismus: nihilism as the decline and regression of spiritual power.

(5) Nihilism is a normative state.

"It can be a strong sign that the spiritual force can grow to such an extent that for it the goals (beliefs, creeds) so far are not proportionate; on the other hand it can be a sign that is not strong enough to set values, even now, and recreate for itself a goal, a why, a belief. "

[A] Nihilism as a normative phenomenon.

Nihilism as a normative phenomenon can be a

symptom of growing strength or growing weakness. On the one hand, the power of creation, the power of will, grows so much that it no longer needs this total explanation and placement of meaning.

On the other hand, the weakening of the power to create meaning is transformed into a disappointment with the dominant state. The inability to believe in meaning is faithlessness.

Again, faithlessness is of opposite origin and nature. Positive nihilism has its origin in the strength of spiritual power, and therefore does not require faith. Negative nihilism has its origin in the weakening of spiritual power.

Therefore, it is impossible to believe. The former is above all beliefs, like a man who peers into the secrets of idols and looks down on them from above. The latter, however, is always a slave to faith, still depressed by the loss of faith in the mood of a believer.

In Nietzsche's view, the negative nihilist is the same type of person as the old metaphysicians and Christians, but in a more impoverished class, no longer possessing the ability to explain and create fictions.

[B] The active nihilist does not need a "real world

If the active nihilist does not need a "real world" and dares to accept the meaningless reality of the world, the Christian does, and can still make up a "real world".

Then, the negative nihilist needs but is not able to imagine a "real world" and does not have the courage to accept the real world, so he or she is in a dilemma where there is no way forward or backward. Schopenhauer's pessimism is a typical form of this kind of negative nihilism.

Generally speaking, nihilism is a state of transition from the collapse of old social factors, such as customs, morals, habits, beliefs and ideas, which have been passed down from generation to generation, to the establishment of new beliefs. On the one hand, because "creativity is not strong enough", new beliefs cannot be established yet.

On the other hand, because "self-indulgence and disregard for morality and social values continue, and no alternative means of relief have yet been found," social factors that have been passed down from generation to generation, such as customs, morals, habits, beliefs, and ideas, continue to have a corrupting effect.

Positive nihilism is the position taken by the strong

during this transitional period. In the void of faith, the weak are frightened, drowning and climbing the grass (people in critical situations do not have time to judge the object, but by impulse to recklessly seek to rely on) and casually climbing the "ideal" to comfort themselves.

But Nietzsche says: "We look at what we call the "ideal" with mocking indignation; we only despise the state of mind in which people cannot, at any time, consciously work for the realization of an ideal or the achievement of a certain end, and suppress the absurd excitement of the so-called "idealism".

[C] For Nietzsche, "idealism" is the cause of nihilism. For, philosophically, it means the theory that human life, in addition to desire and happiness, sets a higher purpose in the spirit and strives for its realization in order to achieve the true meaning of life.

Therefore, how can one rely on it to escape from the nihilistic consequences that would otherwise arise from it? If a philosopher can be a nihilist, he is one, because he finds nothingness behind his imagination or hope (mostly well-founded and reasonable, as opposed to imagination and fantasy) of all things to come.

Not even an unrealistic, inscrutable nothingness, but something worthless, absurd, morbid, cowardly, exhausting.

Like the dregs of pain, anguish, and boredom poured out of the drained glass of life, what is defended is the reality that man, in the life he consciously strives for in order to realize an ideal or to achieve a certain purpose, sets a higher purpose in the spirit, beyond desire and happiness, and strives for its realization, in order to achieve the true meaning of life, and always defends it.

The freethinkers of the future, representing the reality of the human life, are looking at the reality of the human life in which, in addition to desires and pleasures, a higher purpose is set spiritually and strives for its realization in order to achieve the true meaning of life.

At this transitional stage, he dares to live without any belief in or worship of a particular religion or a particular doctrine, and to hold it as a rule and guide for his words and actions. Nietzsche repeatedly said, "The degree of unbelief, the degree of permitted "spiritual freedom," is the expression of the growth of vitality.

The extent to which we can guarantee to ourselves the

inevitability and certainty of the development and change of illusions and lies, without destroying them, is caused by physical or psychological needs.

This is the measure of the state of awakening that arises from the physical or psychological needs and motivates one to engage in actions that satisfy these needs; the extent to which one can "endure living in a meaningless world" is "a measure of willpower.

The knowledge of natural or social things is the meaning that man gives to the object, to bear patiently without fearing all the objects or phenomena that exist objectively in the natural world, which is not positive for a person or a group.

It is the spiritual content that human beings transmit and communicate in the form of symbols, which are not valued by people, or cannot make people feel satisfied, and become objects that people do not respect, or are not interested in pursuing, i.e., things that are regarded as having no value, which may be equally great in the mind.

[D] Therefore, if a person who is full of the passion for truth loses trust in all "truth" and in the passion for truth itself, he will not lose his sincerity and will dare to bear the consequences of faithlessness.

If a person who regards the meaning of life as higher than life itself can endure the absolute meaninglessness, then this alone proves that his vitality and spirituality are strong enough to foretell the hope of future creation.

Nietzsche believes that the expression of active nihilism is "sometimes destructive, sometimes ironic". By "irony" I mean a spiritual superiority, because it is seen that all things or phenomena have a positive meaning for a person or group, are valued, or are satisfying.

It is an attitude of exposing, criticizing, or ridiculing people or things with disdain, because it becomes a worthless object that people respect or are interested in pursuing, and so it is a condescending and irresistible exaggeration of their destruction.

However, the active nihilist does not limit himself to denying the existence of objects, the existence of certain properties, and the existence of certain relationships between things, by analyzing, synthesizing, judging, and reasoning on the basis of images and concepts.

They deny the old values of ideas, cultures, morals, customs, arts, institutions, and behaviors that have been passed down from generation to generation, and they actively engage in actions to destroy the old values.

Positive nihilism consists of several sequential stages. The first is the denial of all things or phenomena that have positive meaning for people or groups, that are valued by people, or that satisfy people, that are respected or interested in pursuing actions or thinking, that reveal all values as goals, that are not truths, that do not treat something as a truth, that do not treat something as a truth.

It is not the premise of a conclusion, or the basis of speech and action. Second, on this basis, all values are revalued. The final destination is the creation of new values.

(6) Nietzsche's Critique and Expectation of Nihilism

The full name of nihilism should be value nihilism. What causes people to feel nihilistic about the existing value system and form nihilism, its manifestations, causes and overcoming.

01. What is nihilism?

From Nietzsche's "God is dead" onwards, the collapse of the values that people have lived by since the beginning of time has been announced. The cornerstone of values from ancient times to the present is the metaphysics of reasoning and logic, which cannot be answered directly through perception.

It is the "truth" behind the shadow in Plato's cave metaphor, a circle that does not exist in reality without flaws. In such metaphysics, the world is divorced from human existence and from the world in which people live.

In the Western tradition of thought, the metaphysical tradition attaches importance to the latter level of meaning, that is, the experiential phenomenon of the rational and active process of reflection of the human mind on the real world or any object in the form of an "inward dialogue".

The values formed on the basis of the transcendence behind them, but used to guide the world in which people live, will inevitably result in "the self-depreciation of the highest values and their rejection or repudiation", thus creating a sense of emptiness of the existing value system.

In "The Crisis of European Science," Husserl pointed

out that the most prevalent value at that time and today is the use of specific methods and means to achieve efficient, convenient, low-consumption, and high-yield production through the study of objective things and their laws.

In order to promote the rapid development of social and economic training in the inertia of thinking, science is equated with the truth and applied to the world of life with a certain object as the scope of study, based on experiments and logical reasoning, to obtain a unified and exact objective law as the truth and value.

However, this kind of "truth" is a systematic system of knowledge, which accumulates and organizes, and can examine the explanations and predictions about the universe.

Science emphasizes the specificity and falsifiability of predictions, which is different from the vague philosophical truths that tell us nothing when human beings are facing existential crises, creating an indefinite state of human spiritual life.

02. Real-life manifestations here

An example can be given. The theory of quantum mechanics has an assumption of rational man, and on this basis the theory of quantum mechanics is built. This is also a typical theory that uses scientific thinking to deal with problems in the living world.

Quantum mechanics is the basis of our understanding of all the fundamental forces (electromagnetic interaction, strong interaction, weak interaction) except gravity.

If not, then this "knowledge" is a systematic body of knowledge that accumulates, organizes, and tests explanations and predictions about the universe. Science emphasizes the specificity and falsifiability of predictions, as opposed to vague philosophy.

Science originally refers only to the exploration of the laws of natural phenomena, and what is the value of summarizing the assumptions of rational man to guide the world of human life?

Furthermore, the connotation of rational man is that man seeks to maximize his interests, but in human life, such a value system, although it can regulate human behavior, inevitably gives people a sense of emptiness about such a value system.

The ineffectiveness of the existing value system in

guiding the world of life, which is based on experimental and logical reasoning to find a unified and definite objective law and theory of truth with a certain object as the scope of study, will bring a sense of emptiness, which is the concentrated manifestation of nihilism in the world of life.

Worldview refers to the position and the time period in which one sees and analyzes things, and it is a reaction to one's judgment of things.

It is the basic viewpoint of people on the world, which changes with the times. In Nietzsche's time, it was the Christian values, and in Husserl's time, it was the scientific values and rational values.In modern times, the pursuit of profit maximization and the pursuit of wealth in economics is the main value guiding the world of life.

03. Reasons why nihilism is related to a major philosophical issue.

In fact, nihilism is related to one of the major issues of philosophy: ethics, that is, how people should live. The emergence of nihilism is a result of the ideas, cultures, morals, customs, arts, institutions, and habitual ways of behavior that have been handed down from generation to generation in the West through history.

The cultural system that has invisible influence and control on people's social behavior has gone astray in the pursuit of the question of "how people should live".

The progress of life brought about by science is undeniable, but this progress and accumulation of knowledge, based on experimental and logical reasoning, with a certain object as the scope of study, and the search for unified and exact objective laws and truths, is mostly about the conditions of life.

Most of the knowledge is about the conditions of life, that is, the level of "being", or the direction of "subject-object" opposition, rather than about the "existence" of the universe and life itself.

The sense of nothingness is not based on the will of a person to realize a certain ideal, or to achieve a certain purpose, and to consciously work for it, to transfer the reasonableness of something from a different point of view or perspective, to think about or judge something, something that is not influenced by subjective thoughts or consciousness.

The law of the nature of independent existence arises because of the value of the level of being, not the level of existence. The forgetfulness of the "existence" of the universe and life itself is the root cause of nihilism.

Overcoming nihilism is the discipline of inquiry and reflection on the fundamental problem.

Overcoming nihilism is a discipline of inquiry and reflection on the fundamental questions of life, knowledge, and values in China through analytical thinking. For example, "Is there an objective standard of morality?" The impact on the Chinese system should be minimal, because China has a tradition of recognizing "nothing" since ancient times.

For example, Taoism describes the subtle abstraction of "Dao Wu", and Buddhism also describes "emptiness" to express the subtlety of the doctrine, and there has always been a profound understanding of "emptiness", which refers to indefinite persons, things, time, and premises [nothing].

In the article "Wang Fu-ci's visit to Pei Hui at the age of twenty" in Chinese literature, it is mentioned that when Wang Fu-ci was not twenty years old, he visited Pei Hui. Pei Hui asked him: "Nothing" is indeed the fundamental basis of everything, but Confucius did not express his opinion on it, but Laozi repeatedly discussed it.

Wang Fuji said: Confucius realized "nothing", and "nothing" cannot be explained clearly in a short time, so it cannot be said, so when he spoke, he must talk about "existence" with the concrete facts and conditions that exist in front of him; Laozi and Zhuangzi have transformed beyond "existence", so they always explain "nothing" which is nothing.

This knowledge provides "spiritual" pillars and life guidelines for people at almost all levels of the living world. There is the idea of helping the world by "worrying before the world", and there is also the happiness of Zeng Diao.

Chinese culture seems to provide a shelter for each value, even the opposite ones, and at the same time is based on the value of discovering more about how to live. For example, there is a famous story about Zeng Diao: one day, four men, Zhong Yu, Zeng Diao, Ran Qiu and Gong Xi Chi, were with Confucius.

Confucius said, "Let's not worry about age and seniority today, let's have a chat. You always say, "No one appreciates me! If there is such a ruler or minister who can appoint you, what do you want to do to show your ambition?

When he heard this, Zhongyu answered, "Suppose a great country with a thousand chariots and chariots is caught between international powers, is subject to military aggression abroad, and is suffering from a lack of livelihood at home, then if I were to rule over it, in three years the people would have the courage and knowledge of the law to build up the strength of the country.

Confucius smiled at this and asked, "What about you, Ran Qiu?

Ran Qiu replied, "If I were to preside over a small country, about 60 or 70, or 50 or 60 square miles in size, I could feed and clothe the people in three years, but I would have to ask someone else to teach me the rites and music.

Confucius then turned to Gong Xi Chi and asked, "What about you, Chi?

He said, "I am not saying that I can do it, but I hope I can learn and work hard in this direction. I would like to be the master of ceremonies when there is a temple festival, when the lords meet each other, and when the king goes to court.

At this time, Zeng Dou was playing music, so Confucius asked him, "Dou, what will you do? Zeng Dou slowly ended his playing, stood up and said, "I want to do something different from everyone else.

Confucius said, "What does it matter? Just talk about your own aspirations."

Then Zeng Dou replied, "In March, in the late spring, I put on light spring clothes, and went with some friends who had seldom met for years to bathe at the edge of the river Yi, where the rain prayer festival was held, and took a cool bath under the trees near the altar, while we talked and sang the ritual music left behind by the former kings, and sang as we set out for home.

Confucius sighed after hearing this, "Oh, I think like Zeng Dou, I want to live a self-sufficient life in the countryside.

What Zeng Dou said seems to be a kind of life with nothing to do, but in fact, this kind of society, where everyone acts according to the seasons and is happy and uncontested, is exactly Lao Tzu's ideal: the country should be small and the people should be few. Even if there are various instruments, they should not be used more than necessary.

Although there are boats and vehicles, there is no need to ride on them; although there are weapons and armaments, there is no need to fight in battle. Let the world be restored to the ancient state where people were bound together.

They were well clothed and well fed, and were satisfied with their ordinary life. The nations could see each other and hear each other, while the people were self-sufficient and did not come and go from life to death.

Therefore, what Zeng Dou wanted to pursue was a commonwealth in which all people could live and work in peace and happiness. When Confucius was traveling around the world, a hermit from the south asked Zhong Yu, who was accompanying him, "This is how the world is, who can change it? If you want to stay away from people, just stay away from the world.

When Confucius heard this, he said with a sigh, "I cannot join the flock of birds and animals, and if I don't want to be with people, who should I be with? If there is a way in the world, I will not change it. [Weizi] "A quiet life in the countryside, where the years are unhurried, is the life that ordinary people aspire to.

The experts and scholars, however, are not willing to avoid the crowd and pursue only their own comfort, but hold the concern that people are hungry and they are hungry, and that people are drowning and they are drowning, and pursue the peace of the world. These people may not seem to have much value, but they have actually discovered the value of life. The process of "discovery" of value in daily life is the nemesis of nihilism.

From the above discussion, we can clearly see that Nietzsche's words "God is dead" and "the highest values have lost their value" are the most common expression and the most classic summary of nihilism, respectively. Nihilism completely rejects the supreme existence and supreme value set by religious beliefs and metaphysics.

The absence of supreme existence and the absence of supreme value lead to the total disappearance of the ultimate basis of ideas, cultures, morals, customs, arts, institutions, and habitual behaviors that have been handed down from generation to generation and from history to history, and the will to attach to supreme existence and supreme value.

Nihilism as a virus of mental symptoms (COVID-19) (immune deficiency syndrome) spread in Europe in the nineteenth century and continues to this day. The "redundant" image of Russian writers such as Turgenev and Tostoevsky; the "outsider" image of Western writers such as Camus and Salinger.

The "deconstructionism" and "postmodernism" that emerged in the middle and late last century and are still alive today are the contemporary variants of the nihilistic virus (COVID-19).

Since Jacobi first used the term "nihilism," the term has been used in a derogatory sense. Nihilism has always been unpopular because of its demythologizing and dismantling of the sublime. But there is no denying that nihilists are the most sober, sensitive, and honest in their perception of the world and of life, and they are the least willing to fool themselves.

The nihilists deconstruct the system of values and the system of meanings, see through the lack of grounds for values and the complete absence of meanings, see through the worthlessness of values and the meaninglessness of meanings, and see through the absurd nature of the world and life.

Thus, in European philosophical and literary criticism, the school of criticism founded by the French post-structuralist philosopher Dershida. De Cida proposed a method he called the deconstructive reading of Western philosophy.

Broadly speaking, deconstructive reading is a method of textual analysis that exposes the differences between the structure of a text and its Western metaphysical nature. Deconstructive reading presents the text not as a single author conveying an obvious message, but rather as a manifestation of various conflicts in a culture or worldview.

The nihilists, who are in the world, are cold-eyed observers of it. Their physical involvement does not hinder their spiritual detachment, and they observe things in an irrational way with their own cold qualities.

They do not show emotion easily, are not sympathetic, and do not care about the harmony of relationships. Nihilists are interested in a form of visual art that is regarded as inferior, a tasteless copy of an existing art style, or a worthless imitation of widely recognized art.

The contemporary term nihilism is used to describe

works that, in their view, are not created to express oneself, but only to satisfy commercial purposes and popular demand.

They resent a state of self-foolishness, a state of self-inspired "wonder", the feeling of being bored, disgusted, bored by too many times or for too long, the feeling of doing something intimate between lovers, saying something intimate, and not being fanatical and crazy about anything in the world that seems noble but is actually ridiculous.

The nihilists have a deep and thorough understanding of the absurdity of the world, for those who see through and clearly understand the truth, not to be confused to live confused to die, those who look silly and a little slow to react to the pure and lovely Chaplin, or they have the characteristics of the stupid character.

In fact, nihilism is the result of skepticism going to the extreme, a complete subversion of the principle of "no decision, no judgment" and a kind of skepticism.

The most radical negativity of nihilism is that it drives away the so-called God of traditional values, and hardens the ultimate basis of human fabrication, not only collapsing the framework of fictional values, but also emptying the purpose of the creation of the universe's will and reducing the meaning of human life to zero.

The fatal destruction makes the absurd nature of the world and life, the decay of the heart, the sadness or distraction of the mind, appear nakedly. Nihilism is self-indulgent, ignoring moral and social perceptions, destructive to the extreme, but its irrational logic is absolutely rigorous and meticulous, simply impeccable.

The world that should exist does not exist, and the world that does exist should not exist. The double disappointment with the world that should be and the world that actually is leads to double despair, which in turn leads to the creation, spread and continuation of nihilism.

The nihilists, with their deviant thinking about "worldview, life, and values," are the most determined and categorical deviants. Nihilists will never turn back.

They can no longer understand and recognize the world that they have obliterated as ordinary people do, and they can no longer perceive life in the same way as a young man who seems to love art.

Nor is it a youth who refuses to speak or act like the majority of people after the 21st century, marking their different aspirations and tastes, sometimes interpreted and played with in English as hippie "hipster". It rejects general or fundamental aspects of human existence, such as objective truth, knowledge, morality, values, or meaning.

Different nihilistic positions hold different views that human values are unfounded, that life has no meaning, that knowledge is impossible, or that certain entities do not exist or are meaningless. Indeed the nihilism of a psychiatric symptom virus [COVID-19] (immune deficiency syndrome), once contracted, is "incurable" unless a true antidote to the meaning of life is found.

(7) Nietzsche's Expectations and Criticism of Buddhism

In section 20 of his book "The Anti-Christian", Nietzsche includes both Christianity and Buddhism in the category of nihilistic religions, and says that both are self-indulgent, decadent religions with no regard for morality and social perceptions.

The main focus of his criticism still falls on

Christianity, and Buddhism is only a reference for Nietzsche, a marker to indicate the position of a certain point on a plane or in space. In contrast to Nietzsche's unrelenting attack on Christianity, Buddhism is, in Nietzsche's eyes, a religion.

Buddhism, in Nietzsche's eyes, is still a religion of a highly developed race, meant to refer to the absence of European spiritual civilization, which still has a long way to go to reach such a mature stage.

Nietzsche also described Buddhism as "the only empirical religion" (die einzige eigentlich positivistische Religion), which is a deliberate attempt to confront Christianity with "original sin" (the sin of stealing the forbidden fruit committed by Adam and Eve in the Garden of Eden, the first human beings.

This sin was passed on to future generations and became the source of all sins and disasters in human society, and it was not based on any fact), and projected an illusory "kingdom of heaven", and developed a religion that compares with each other.

Nietzsche sees "Buddhism" as opposed to "Christianity": a religion of the more practical, the educated class, the over-sensitive to suffering, the tired of civilization, the "latecomers"; these words or expressions of praise for Buddhism are in contrast to Christianity.

The main intention is to highlight the impracticality of Christianity, which arises from the lower classes, the barbarism, and the creation of a virtual world beyond the reality of life, the Kingdom of Heaven. This is to deny the real world of life and the concrete facts and conditions that exist in front of us, and so on.

But this does not mean that Nietzsche considered Buddhism to be a positive religion in his mind, but that it is still what he called a "negative nihilism", a decadent religion, and that it is not more desirable because it is more practical than Christianity.

For, in the essence of "negative nihilism," Nietzsche still believed that the amazement and awe of the mysteries of the universe and of life were used to constitute a doctrine of persuasion of good and punishment of evil, and to teach the world and make people believe in religion.

The stereotype that "religion is self-denying to life" and "religion is weary of the existence of life" (die Unlust am Dasein) is also the cultural type of "weakness" that

Nietzsche wanted to criticize.

The "superman" (Übermensch) that Nietzsche himself proclaims is the "strong man" who has the power to destroy the old values of thought, culture, morality, customs, art, institutions, and customary behavior that have been handed down from generation to generation, and to set new values of will and power.

If we look back at the literature in The Science of Pleasure, which was published earlier than The Anti-Christ, we can clearly see Nietzsche's consistent view of Buddhism (in The Anti-Christ, we can clearly see Nietzsche's most "positive" assessment of Buddhism).

In the fifth chapter of The Science of Pleasure, Nietzsche says that both Christianity and Buddhism were developed on the basis of an abnormal "disease of the will", and that they were the teachers of blind faith during the "Willens-Erschlaffung" period.

They are the teachers of blind faith in the period of "Willens-Erschlaffung" (atrophy of the will), which means the state of mind in which human beings consciously strive for the realization of a certain ideal or the achievement of a certain goal, suffer serious setbacks and failures, and in critical situations have no time to judge the object, but pursue reliance on impulse. Furthermore, in the preface to the Genealogy of Morals, Nietzsche criticizes Schopenhauer's philosophy of pity as an ominous symptom of European culture.

It is a circuitous trend towards a new Buddhism, a European Buddhism, nihilism. It "says no" to life, to oneself (Nein sagte), and speaks directly and bluntly but not in accordance with the ritual requirements of the time, and may appear to be cynical.

At the same time, in Nietzsche's manuscript of June 10, 1887, there is a note on European nihilism in 16 subsections, and this document also presents Nietzsche's view of Buddhism in a rather positive light. That is, the most extreme form of European nihilism, according to Nietzsche, is "eternal nothingness (meaninglessness)! (das Nichts (das "Sinnlose") ewig!), which Nietzsche calls "the new Buddhism of the European type".

1. "The eternal circle of reincarnation" (ewig Wiederkehr).

Nietzsche's "new Buddhism of the European type" is compared to his doctrine of "eternal circulation". Nietzsche believed that the social elements of nihilism, such as customs, morals, habits, beliefs, ideas, etc., which are inherited from generation to generation, are invisible in all objects or phenomena that exist objectively in the natural world.

It is the abstraction of the thought process, the development from pessimism to the "final nihilism" (letzten Nihilimus). In other words, nihilism goes through different stages of development, and at the final stage, it manifests itself as "der radikale Nihilimus".

What Nietzsche means is that only at the final stage of nihilism does nihilism reach complete self-understanding and develop into an opposite movement, the movement of nihilism's own overcoming.

Since everything is in vain (Umsonst) and life is meaningless and purposeless, in the end we are forced to accept nihilism in its most extreme form, namely, the "ewig Wiederkehr" (eternal wheel of reincarnation). This is a concept that assumes that the universe will keep on cycling in exactly the same form, and that the number of such cycles is incomprehensible and unpredictable.

As for the "ewige Wiederkehr", Nietzsche sees it as a temporal possibility. In this possibility, the transition of time becomes eternal, the past returns to the present, everything in the world returns to the present with the same appearance, and we are reborn countless times.

In this process of change and return, the hierarchy of values is destroyed and chaos becomes the norm, and this is also a process of eliminating the strong from the weak, and only the strong can eventually live again, and the so-called strong are in fact chaos and lack of order.

Time becomes a cycle, self-identification, based on a certain sense of human thinking and cognition, understanding, judgment or choice, that is, people identify things, debating the right and wrong of a kind of thinking or orientation, thus reflecting a certain value or role of people, things and things is cancelled.

Although the "ewig Wiederkehr" symbolizes change and chaos, it is in fact an inherent and necessary connection between things that determines the inevitable trend of their development, a certainty.

The ultimate goal of the "will to power" is to achieve "eternal reincarnation" (ewig Wiederkehr), and these two theorems are closely related to each other. Nietzsche tried to bring down all fixed order and destroy the principles of metaphysics.

But in the end he seemed unable to free himself from the fetters of the question that cannot be answered directly by perception, that it is deduced by rational logical reasoning under a priori conditions, and that it cannot be contradicted by empirical evidence. Perhaps all struggle can only be carried out within the realm of metaphysics, and there is no other way.

However, Deleuze does not seem to think so. In Pensée nomade, he argues that Nietzsche's work is not based on "inner" conscious thought, but can be extended to the "outer".

Like those nomads from the outside, Nietzsche's movement of thought came from the outside, from the outside into the center, and created turmoil. Nietzsche's thinking, in Deleuze's eyes, was that of the nomads who ran and dashed outside of the country, who lived in no fixed place, who were not shackled by the internal values of the Middle Kingdom, and who were a force of free movement.

Nietzsche believed that the world is composed of a finite number of particles, and the change of the world is the change of the combination of such particles.

If the world is eternal, then that kind of eternal reincarnation exists. Therefore, the material in the present person must have the chance to be combined into a person exactly like him again in the future, and what this person does is the same as what the previous person did again. This concept of eternal reincarnation is equivalent to the denial of Schopenhauer's free will, which is a kind of fatalism without freedom.

Everything has been decided by eternal reincarnation. In this eternal reincarnation, one does not need to bother about free will, but only needs to live according to the guidance of strong will, to achieve the greatest inner transcendence, and to become a true superman.

This theory can also refute the guilt that Christianity's "original sin" gives people. Because everything is not free, these sins cannot be borne by the individual. This role of eternal reincarnation can be said to be both anti-Schopenhauer and anti-Christian.

But why does Buddhism belong to what Nietzsche called "the nihilism of extinction? In what ways does it conform to what Nietzsche called "as a sign of spiritual decline and regression"? How can we identify it with Christianity, which rejects the "affirmation of life" and the "upward movement of life" in the same way? Let us try to find the answers to these questions in Nietzsche's brief description of Buddhism.

According to Nietzsche, the highest aim of Buddhism is joy (Heiterkeit), peace (Stille), and the absence of desire (Wunschlosigkeit). It is the religion of the "späte Menschen," of the good, gentle, spiritually developed race of people who have an excessive feeling for suffering.

Buddhism restores one to peace and joy, teaches spiritual moderation (zur Diät im Geistigen), and requires a certain degree of physical discipline. Nietzsche also states that in the Buddha's teachings, "Egoismus" becomes an obligation, the content of which is first and foremost the liberation of oneself from suffering.

Nietzsche compares Buddhism to Socrates on this point, saying that both Buddhism and Socrates are "Personal-Egoismus" in this respect. If we understand Nietzsche's nihilism as a spiritual force that progresses in intensity from its initial stage of pessimism to its final stage of overcoming, we can roughly describe it chronologically as follows pessimism → negative nihilism → positive nihilism → radical nihilism → the overcoming of nihilism. Both Buddhism and Christianity are essentially negative nihilism, but their forms of expression are different.

Regarding Nietzsche's view of nihilism as "Wille zum Nichts," it is a disguised "will to power," which creates an a priori world and uses it to criticize and condemn the real world in which we actually live, which inevitably leads to the self-criticism and even the self-destruction of life.

The will always sets the object of desire, but when the object of desire is nothing, the will becomes the "negation of life itself" (Leben gegen Leben), which is a major inversion. This perversion eventually leads to a fundamental "Unsinn" (meaninglessness). In Volume 15 of the Buddhist Sutra, it is written that Shakyamuni was determined to become a monk because he felt the suffering of impermanent life and death, and this is a fact recognized by all schools of Buddhism.

Nirvana, the state of Buddhism, is a state in which all kinds of greed, anger, foolishness, and annoyance cease. Therefore, if Nietzsche understands Buddhism as a religion that discovers the source of uneasiness and distress, and through spiritual restraint and physical exercise, urgently thinks about how to get rid of suffering and achieve happiness, then his grasp is generally correct.

But the problem is that Nietzsche compares Buddhism to Christianity and takes Buddhism out of context as what he calls a pessimistic, nihilistic religion. From this, we can see that Nietzsche is still looking at Buddhism from a very far distance, that is, he cannot even find the way to enter by knocking on the door.

Buddhism can only be viewed with a miserable nihilistic religious mentality, not to mention that Buddhism has never been a religion, let alone a metaphysical one, in which questions that cannot be answered directly through perception are answered under a priori conditions.

It is an answer deduced through rational and logical reasoning under a priori conditions, and cannot contradict empirical evidence. It is a discipline in which human reason explores the most general aspects and ultimate causes of things.

The adequacy of his arguments and the objectivity of his criticisms need to be further clarified. What is even more curious is whether Nietzsche would have had a different perspective on Buddhism had he been able to delve deeper into the profound meaning of Buddhist philosophy and achieve a significant degree of objective understanding.

We might even expect that such an upheaval of ideas would have brought about shocking results. Is such an expectation only imaginary but not based on thinking?

2. Superman

In "Thus Spoke Zarathustra", Nietzsche, in his capacity as Zarathustra, argues that after experiencing the nihilism of moral and Christian faith disillusionment, man should turn his mind to a "positive, positive nihilism", so that he can face the meaning of values in his heart and create a life based on this meaning.

Nietzsche thought he had found a way to defeat nihilism once and for all, the "superman". Those who can achieve this state are the great "supermen".

It is worth noting that the "superman" is an ideal type of human being, different from all existing human beings, a new "human being", a "human being" different from human beings.

But Nietzsche believes that there has never been a superman in human history, and the Zarathustra in Thus Spoke Zarathustra is not a superman, nor does Nietzsche consider himself to be one. But the superman is not a brave man with brute force or a cruel tyrant, but a man who is brave enough to transcend himself, to criticize himself, and to reassess his values.

Theists who presuppose the existence of "gods" may misunderstand that Superman is a new "god" of Nietzsche's making (as opposed to the "old gods" of Christianity or other established religions), but in fact Nietzsche's "Superman" is the highest expectation of the future of humanity.

In "Thus Spoke Zarathustra", he states that the superman is the meaning of the earth. The metaphor is that the superman is the negation of the kingdom of heaven and the replacement of God.

The philosophical value of Nietzsche's voluntarism is twofold. On the one hand, Nietzsche inherited the essence of the Enlightenment and reflected the awakening of modern consciousness. The positive affirmation of the value of life has triggered people to think about the real meaning of life and the value of life of all species in the universe, and to reposition the universe and life.

The negative critique of instrumental rationality and industrial civilization opens up the modern irrationalist thinking. On the other hand, the criticism of rationality and the negation of tradition are also self-indulgent, ignoring the one-sided interpretation of moral and social perceptions, which is the aspect appreciated by post-modernist egoism.

The most important point of Nietzsche's philosophy is that the mission of analytic thinking to explore and reflect on fundamental questions about life, knowledge, and values is to focus on life, to give an explanation of the meaning of life, and to give an explanation of the value of life.

The most important point of Nietzsche's philosophical view is that his mission is to focus on life, to give an explanation to the meaning of life, to give an explanation to the value of life, and to explore the question of the real meaning of life. This is somewhat related to Nietzsche's reading of Schopenhauer's works. Another point is that Nietzsche pointed out that philosophy is apolitical, and philosophy and politics are two different things.

Therefore, Nietzsche's view of philosophy is, firstly, about life, about life, secondly, non-political, and thirdly, non-academic. Philosophy is a holistic, fundamental and critical inquiry into the real world and people. It is not purely academic.

Nietzsche's criticism of the ideas, culture, morals, customs, art, institutions, and habitual ways of behavior that have been handed down from generation to generation and from history to history, the key to traditional philosophy is the lack of concern for life.

The consequence of traditional philosophy is nihilism. There is no essence behind the present image. Nietzsche taught people to deny the established values, to affirm their own creation, and to pursue difference. We can say that Nietzsche wanted to oppose everything that is established and unchanging, including human beings themselves. Thus, Nietzsche turned to the idea of the "superman" (English: Overman / German: Übermensch).

Nietzsche believed that in the age of "negative nihilism" it is necessary to reaffirm value and meaning, that some things are considered valuable and worth choosing, pursuing, or preserving, while other things are considered worthless and not worth choosing, pursuing, or preserving.

This is the evaluation activity of our cognitive point of view: the evaluation activity is expressing our attitude towards things and objects, which can be positive or negative.

If we consciously work for the realization of a certain ideal, or to achieve a certain purpose, and the mental state. It is because something is useful, may achieve our other purposes, or to meet our other desires, and it is considered valuable, then these things and things have instrumental value to us.

On the contrary, if these things are in themselves our purpose, the object of our desire, they have a purpose value for us. The same thing that has a purpose value for one person may only have an instrumental value for other people.

This depends entirely on one's cognitive perspective and evaluation attitude. What we see as having objective value is seen as our purpose, not as a tool or means to satisfy our other desires.

Therefore, Nietzsche argues that people who regard something of objective value as our end cannot rely on

God, because He is dead. People need a new species, and that is the "superman". So what exactly is a "superman"?

In fact, Nietzsche does not directly answer the question of what a superman is. He only indirectly explains what a "superman" is by comparing it with the "last man" (English: Last man / German: der letzte Mensch).

The "last man" is actually a person who has no personality and no creativity, and who blindly follows the views of the public, or a person who "lives in confusion and dies in confusion". On the contrary, a "superman" is a person whose will to live is maximized. A "superman" breaks through all barriers, transcends good and evil, and has absolute autonomy.

In this way, "supermen" do not need any standard of truth, good and evil, because they themselves are the standard of truth and good and evil. Nietzsche thinks that all the great people in history cannot be considered as "supermen", and it is difficult to specify anyone who meets Nietzsche's criteria of "superman".

Rather, "superman" is a new species that may appear in the future. Nietzsche once said that the average person is to the "superman" what an ape is to a human being.

Nietzsche taught people to deny established values, to affirm their own creations, and to pursue differences. We can say that Nietzsche wanted to oppose everything that is established and unchanging, including human beings themselves. For the "last man" is the archetypal nihilist who can destroy but cannot establish and adopt the spirit of self-realization.

The "last man" first appears in the prologue of Zarathustra. According to Nietzsche, the "last man" is clearly the goal that modern society has set for itself. Nietzsche says that the "last man" society may be too barren to provide for healthy human life or great personal growth. Thus, Nietzsche turned to the idea of the "superman" (English: Overman / German: Übermensch).

(8) The influence on Freudian psychoanalysis and philosophy of life

1. Psychoanalysis

J. Locke (1632-1704) and D. Hume (1711-1776), two of the English philosophers of the seventeenth and eighth centuries of modern philosophy, are the two philosophers who have attracted the most attention.109 The latter, in particular, describes a person in terms of the flow of perception and sensation, not at all. The latter, in particular, describes a person in terms of the flux of perception and sensation, without mentioning the actuality of the "self" at all.

In contemporary times, S. Kierkegaard (1813-1855), the father of the Western philosophy of existence, expresses the "one and all" view in this way: The (self)-self is nothing more than an abstract conceptual set-up that can refer to a particular person; or to a certain kind of unity (body) that is It can be ego, subject, mind, I, memory, awareness, or consciousness. consciousness Knower...etc.

The individual is called the spirit, the self, or a relationship; that is, the relationship between the spirit and the soul, the soul and the body, or the inner connection between the spirit and the body. The Austrian medical psychologist and founder of psychoanalysis, S. Freud (1856-1940), even from an analytical point of view, referred to the human being as a person.

S. Freud, the Austrian medical psychologist and founder of psychoanalysis (1856-1940), even divided the human psychological structure into three elements, the

Id, the Ego, and the Super-Ego, from an analytical point of view, and pointed out that they have different roles to play.

※The Id, Ego, and Super-Ego

Psychodynamics, also known as kinetic psychology, in a broad sense, is a psychological approach that emphasizes the systematic study of the psychological forces that shape human behavior. It includes the study of behaviors, feelings, emotions, and connections to each other and to earlier experiences.

It is particularly interested in the consciousness, motivation, and subconscious motivation of the ego, the self, and the superego, the three major components of the psyche as proposed by the psychoanalyst Freud's structural theory.

The term psychodynamic is also used, in particular, to refer to some of the means by which Freud (1856-1939) developed psychoanalysis. Freud was inspired by the theory of thermodynamics and invented psychodynamics to describe the mental energy in the stream of consciousness.

In 1923, Freud developed concepts to explain the

formation and interrelationship of the conscious and subconscious mind. The "ego" (fully subconscious, not controlled by subjective consciousness) represents desire and is suppressed by consciousness; the "self" (most of the consciousness) is responsible for dealing with the real world; the "superego" (some of the consciousness) is the conscience or inner moral judgment.

01. The Self

The ego (Latin: id, German: Es) is the mind in its unconscious form, representing the primitive process of thought. Its energy comes from "the great reservoir". Only the Self is the innate personality. It is the primordial desire to satisfy the instinctive impulses of man, such as hunger, vitality, libido, etc.; this word is based on the work of Georg Groddeck by Freud.

The ego and superego are the basis for the development of the future ego and superego. The ego follows only one principle - the principle of pleasure - and is not concerned with the rules of society, meaning the pursuit of the individual's biological needs, such as the satisfaction of food and sexual desire, and the avoidance of pain or unpleasantness. It cannot tolerate any frustration, just like a spoiled child, wanting whatever it wants.

Freud believed that the influence of the hedonic principle is maximized in infancy and early childhood, when the ego is most prominent. The ego does not have the power to judge right and wrong, and it has the desire to destroy itself. Meaning: We only pay attention to the satisfaction of human biological needs, and tame the human "ego" through the process of socialization.

02. Ego

The concept of the psychological ego (Latin: Ego,[11] German: Ich[12]) is the most important part of the concept of things constructed by many schools of psychology.

The ego is the psychological component of the personality. The ego temporarily suspends the pleasure principle with the reality principle. Thus, the individual learns to distinguish between the mental processes of cognition in the mind and the thoughts surrounding the external world of the individual.

The ego, in itself and in its environment, carries out the regulation of the functions of the tissues and organs of the organism through the activity of the nervous system, the basic way of which is reflex, such as delayed enjoyment. Freud considered the ego as the executor of the personality.

Another confusing aspect is the form of thought that is formed in the mind to reflect the nature of the object. The common nature of things perceived, the universality of which is extracted from the self, includes the unconscious.

The psychological approach to the study of the self is very diverse and complex, and often involves philosophical metaphysics. Meaning: The "ego" is the expression of the individual's biological desires and social norms, which can be appropriately reconciled with each other to make them reasonable.

03. super-ego

The super-ego (English: super-ego, German: über-Ich) is the controller of the personality structure, governed by moral principles and an ardent desire for perfection, and is part of the normative totality of the personality structure in which human beings distinguish between good and bad behavior. In Freud's doctrine, the "superego" is the symbol of the father figure and cultural norms that make things that are not the same gradually become similar or identical.

The Superego tends to stand in opposition to the primordial longings of the Ego and is aggressive in nature towards the Ego, due to disputes over objects with different opinions. "The superego operates as a moral mind, maintaining the moral sense of the individual, avoiding taboos, and putting the ego in a difficult position.

The formation of the "superego" occurs at a time when the Freudian view of the son's complex of mother-hating father is disintegrating, an internalized identification with the father figure.

As the boy is unable to successfully maintain his mother as his object of love, he develops a castration anxiety for possible castration retaliation or punishment by his father, which leads him to identify with his father. Meaning: The motivation to form a "superego" in response to the social and cultural norms of behavior and moral expectations.

04. The relationship between the ego, the self, and the superego

The ego, self, and superego constitute the complete personality of a person. The ego exists permanently, while the superego and the ego are almost permanently opposed to each other.

If the pressure from the ego, superego and the outside world is too much for an individual to bear, the ego will help activate the defense mechanism, which is called psychological defense mechanism or ego defense mechanism. The defense mechanisms include repression, denial, regression, counteracting, projection, sublimation, and so on.

Among them, especially the "ego" is regarded as the center of one's rational consciousness and practical activities. The British philosopher R. Russell (1872-1970) and the American psychologist B. Skinner (1872-1970) have similar views in this regard, following the empiricist line of Hume. B.F. Skinner (1904-?), an American psychologist. The "self" is the most important thing. We can see that the concept of "self" or "ego" has a wide variety of meanings, although there is no agreement on what it means.

However, if we use the skeptical method of R. Descartes (1596-1650), the father of modern Western philosophy, we can certainly conclude that "the (self)-self" is an unquestionable "thinking self", a conscious self, or by applying Kierkegaard's unique "intuitive" method of existence. Or, if we apply Kierkegaard's unique method of "direct observation" of existence, we can prove that "existence" is an undeniable fact and an unquestionable union of spirit and body.

In this regard, the "spirit", the medium through which one can communicate with the transcendent (true) God and obtain the possibility of "eternal happiness", can be considered as the real subject of one's existence.

Although the "self", which can be regarded as the "thinking self", "conscious self", "spirit" or "real subject", cannot be referred to as a definite entity, it is undeniable that it exists.

That is to say, each person's "(self)self" is dependent on, exists with, and follows each of us as a finite being in time and space. No matter what you want to call it, it is a matter of the structure of one's existence, the way of existence, the meaning of existence and the pursuit of existence in time and world.

Each person's "self" refers not only to the existence of an individual with a physical body in physical time and space, or a concrete existence, but also to the existence of an infinite consciousness and a formless spirit (spirit) that is not governed by time and space. It also refers to the existence of an infinite consciousness and formless spirit (spirit) that is not governed by time and space.

To this end, the rationalistic cognitive system, together with imagination, intuition, intuitive awareness, observation, or epiphany...etc., are used to approach the "self," or more specifically, the "self" of each individual. or, more specifically, each person's inner self, must be able to achieve a certain cognitive efficacy. Although some philosophers have explicitly stated that

The ego is not a thing in itself, nor is it a purely self-conscious self, but rather a being that should exist as a positive being.

Rather, it is the self that should be understood in terms of being, spirituality, in pursuit, or "action in being", and it is difficult to achieve true knowledge of the "self" or "oneself". We still believe that as long as the mind is dedicated, persistent, and engaged in the exploration of the inner self with a humble mind in pursuit of the truth, we will be able to achieve the truth.

As a cognitive subject, every person has the opportunity to approach and understand himself or herself throughout his or her life. Philosophical thinking not only has its proper task, i.e., to constantly explore the reality of all truths from the perspective of knowledge, but it also has a binding characteristic that is relevant to the "well-being" of each individual.

It is necessary to treat oneself with a super-physical cognitive mind and to look at oneself squarely. Its ultimate purpose is to serve as the owner of "wisdom" and the master of "truth" as the highest reward it can give to human beings for their transformation "beyond" the present situation.

However, what is most noteworthy is that he should not be confused, exasperated, or deterred by this; rather, he should have the courage to face it, i.e., to understand himself, i.e., to understand that man himself possesses multiple aspects and abilities (e.g., sensibility, knowledge, virtue, enlightenment). Instead, one should have the courage to face it, that is, to know oneself, i.e., to understand that one possesses multi-faceted and multifaceted abilities (e.g., sensual, intellectual, virtuous, enlightened, spiritual, etc.), and to develop them carefully and use them flexibly to achieve one's highest goals in life.

Jasper particularly emphasized an attitude of

self-responsibility. In this period of Existentialism, the inculcation and influence of this dimension of thinking on people's hearts is very profound and deeply beneficial.

In the end, all of these wise words of Jaspers have made it possible, when faced with the many important issues of life's boundaries, to realize: "Life is very different. Everyone has a life, but not everyone can read it.

Everyone has a brain, but not everyone uses it well. "Life is the tempering of life experiences. How can there be no wind and no rain? It is because of the baptism of wind and rain that we can see the brilliant rainbow.

It is only with the pain of failure that we can taste the joy of transformation beyond the present. However, this is what Jaspers wanted to understand from the great philosophers, how they really understood the meaning of "transcending" the present situation and trying to deal with the existence of "existence" in the life of the self.

2. The influence of the philosophy of life

Spirit, or "spirit" in English, can be traced back to the original Indo-European word (s)peis, which has many different meanings, usually meaning soul, mind, consciousness, idea, etc., and is the source of human life force. Nietzsche divided the human mind, thought and psychological condition into three types of consciousness. He proposed three changes of spiritual consciousness: camel, lion and baby. He believed that the spiritual will should first become a camel, then a lion, and finally a baby.

01. The first type is: camel

The camel is the "desert boat", hard work and endurance, meaning that people have to be trained at a young age, to bear the burden of tradition. Camels have two kinds of spirit.

One is, believe that the end of the desert is an oasis; when the camel once set foot on the journey, the vast and endless desert, the musical notes of life, they began to jump, challenging the limits of endurance. At the same time also challenge death, the body exudes reveal a fearless tough and down-to-earth temperament.

There is no fear, no tiredness, no restlessness, no resentment, no resentment, no turning back, but steadily, one step at a time, towards the front, towards the oasis, towards hope and the future.

The second is, one step at a time, towards hope,

towards the future. There is no solemn song of farewell, no friends and relatives teary-eyed waving goodbye, not to mention the embrace of flowers. There are only camel bells accompanying the lonely shadow, silently walking in the feet without words! When we step into the boundless, yellow sand, dust and smoke, the sound of camel bells in the wind, the fearlessness of cold and heat, and the exhaustion of living beings in the desert, what kind of life is fearful, even for the most advanced people?

In this stage, we are as foolishly loyal as a camel, carrying on as much as possible the patterns handed down from generation to generation, from parents and predecessors, an idea, culture, morality, customs, art, institutions and ways of behavior that have been handed down from history.

We take on the wisdom and at the same time absorb their unconsciousness, prejudices and repressions. As "camels," we always say "yes" and accept without question.

We are unable to use our senses, perceptions, thoughts, memories, and other mental activities to grow in awareness and understanding of our physical and mental states and changes in people, events, and objects in the environment. We have to bear the pain of those sufferings, such as honesty and hypocrisy, good and evil, righteousness and unrighteousness, justice and partiality.

02. The second type is: the lion

If we take a step forward, we come to the lion stage before we go further into becoming ourselves. The Lion stage is a necessary process of rebellion and opposition to those values and behaviors that are naturally imposed on your past. In the Lion stage, our opposition and rebellion will inevitably bring us conflict and discomfort, and the accusations and doubts of the environment will always be directed toward us.

However, when we are stuck because of the frustrations and fears of the Lion stage, we will return to the Camel stage and continue to carry the baggage of those who came before us or the established values. For the "Lion" stage, the lion roars against the repressed, antiquated, accustomed sense of security, against the baggage of tradition, against the established framework. It is therefore more powerless and helpless, more in denial of the uniqueness of the individual's existence.

The difference between the camel and the lion is that the camel must listen to the guidance of others, accept the orders of others, and hear others say, "How should you! And the lion is to make their own decisions, responsible for themselves, said: "I want to how! Everyone goes through the camel stage.

We listen to our parents and teachers who tell us what we should do, and we can't refute or resist. However, after adulthood, we should enter the lion stage, that is, by ourselves to tell ourselves how to do.

In other words, although the camel looks very poor, but at least do not have to make their own decisions, as long as they obey other people's instructions on the line.

On the contrary, if you want to become a lion, you have to take responsibility for yourself, for yourself. This is very stressful because when we are free to choose what we want to do, at the same time, we also lose the right to find excuses and complaints.

03. The third type is: Infant

After the Lion stage comes the Infant stage. The baby means "the perfect beginning" and offers all the possibilities. When a person is still a baby, parents must have endless imagination, imagining that he may become a scientist, an engineer, a doctor, and so on. Watching him every day brings colorful and dazzling hope to the parents' life.

Of course, the process of a child's growth is often a process of disillusionment for the parents. In the end, the child disappoints the parents, just as the parents once disappointed their parents, and life is such a repetitive process. The naked child.

Our consciousness comes to the stage of the naked child, where we truly become ourselves. The world will be experienced, touched and felt by the individual. The world is new, and the realization of life will be new.

We become a new wheel, and we will truly own ourselves, accumulate our own experiences, and create our own experiences through our own lives. However, we may be too naive, too imaginative, and forget what we really are before we complete our maturation.

When you transform into a naked child, all your knowledge of the world will be zeroed out and you will start anew. You will define your world, and you will let the world know you. You will no longer encounter the problems mentioned above, which means that your mind will return to its origin and you can start again.

Regardless of what type you are in, or what transformation you go through, when you go through the transformation of your spiritual consciousness, you will inevitably go through the camel and lion types. Only after going through these two processes can you train and accumulate the real power of transformation, gain the real growth of your ego, become your whole self, become a child, and really start to grow up and mature your lost "self".

Exploring the truth of life from the five levels of psychological consciousness

From the perspective of parapsychology, we study the universe, the principles and principles of life.

Most importantly, it is the greatest merit for the collective consciousness to awaken from the confusion and uncertainty of its own consciousness! Helping other individual consciousnesses to awaken from their confusion is the greatest contribution to this collective consciousness!

In psychology, human cognitive ability and cognitive

clarity of the environment and the self can be divided into five distinct structures, and their composition is related to each other.

This delineation of the human brain's reflection of the objective material world is the sum of various mental processes such as sensation and thought, and can be used for specific purposes by ensuring that these "cognitive" and "recognition" behaviors have the potential ability to be used for specific purposes.

Through this systematic system of knowledge, we can accumulate and organize and examine experiences or associative explanations and predictions about the universe, and we can understand the five layers of consciousness structure, and then make a systematic and familiar organization.

At the same time, it is also the opportunity for the individual to have a holistic awareness of the whole consciousness and to help himself to quickly clarify the reality of his own physical and mental existence, in order to seek the possibility of sublimation beyond his own metamorphosis.

04. Explore the truth of life from the five layers of consciousness in psychology

Ideational consciousness corresponds to the individual's comprehensive awareness and understanding of his or her physical and mental state and the changes of people, events, and objects in the environment through mental activities such as sensation, perception, thinking, and memory, and is the main area of study in general psychology.

Generally speaking, ideation is actually our thoughts and perceptions: it is the general psychological terminology of various psychological experiences and reactions, such as fear, anger, irony and pity, jealousy, fear, happiness and love, etc., which can be potentially depicted and expressed verbally by using various rhetorical techniques to visualize and elaborate things.

Although there are many different physiological methods that can be used to measure the internal perception of the external world, these methods are not recognized as uniform and individually valid. Conversely, sensations are interpreted as personal or subjective qualities of consciousness, or ego states.

For example, do you feel good? Are you happy? And all kinds of painful and happy feelings. In fact, as the Heart Sutra says, the six consciousnesses that arise from the sensory organs of color, sound, fragrance, touch, and the eyes, ears, nose, tongue, body, and mind, correspond to the sensations.

From the perspective of the individual's comprehensive awareness and understanding of his or her physical and mental state and the changes of people, events and things in the environment through mental activities such as sensation, perception, thinking and memory: whether one is a billionaire or a poor person.

No matter whether one is young and beautiful or old and decrepit; no matter whether one is high and powerful or a peddler. No matter what kind of people are, they all feel that life is actually just a feeling of the actual object or the whole thing with actual content, so the feeling is directly called the reality of life, and the feeling is the language of the self-talking soul.

This feeling, in essence, is the existence of our unique consciousness, or unique personal experience.

It is also an abstract entity that exists outside of oneself and is related to the subject, something that is distinguishable and exists independently of oneself. This concept is particularly important in European philosophy, where "subject" is the main key term for the nature of the self in the discipline of analytical thinking and reflection on fundamental questions of life, knowledge, and values.

In philosophy, it refers to the necessary essence of things, without which things cannot be established. The subject is the observer, and the object is the observed thing, which means that the ideation is in the hands of the self, and through practice and training, it can be completely free from external interference.

In the quenching of daily life experience, always keep our inner feeling good, is a kind of subliminal, self-soul thought dialogue language.

The Emotional Dimension: Subconsciousness

I. How the "subconscious" was discovered

In his days as a neurologist, Sigmund Freud saw people who were hysterical, or who imagined that a part of the body was uncomfortable, but could not be medically detected, for no reason, for unknown fears, etc.

The disorder is a mental illness caused by conflicting thoughts and feelings in the subconscious, which manifests itself physically through conversion, resulting in vomiting, fright, convulsions, numbness, etc. The medical profession has now gradually stopped using the term in favor of more precise terms to describe different symptoms, such as conversion disorder and dissociative disorder.

Patients, led by psychiatrist Freud, are treated with hypnosis. Freud found that the patient, under hypnosis, was able to recall ordinary, seemingly forgotten memories, especially those of major traumatic events in his early life.

Moreover, in patients with psychogenic factors during hypnosis, once the patient recalls these traumatic experiences after hypnosis. For example, life events, internal conflicts, suggestion or self-referral, etc., cause symptoms of mental disorders in the individual, which immediately disappear.

Later, on the basis of hypnosis, Freud evolved the therapeutic techniques of "free association" and dream interpretation. When Freud used the free association technique, he would first let the patient relax, lie comfortably on a reclining sofa, close his eyes, and free associate, so that when recalling past events or experiences, other events and experiences related to these events would be recalled at the same time.

At this point, the patient is still able to enter the subconscious state and discover the existence of the subconscious mind. This verifies that the subconscious is indeed an objective mental phenomenon that is not influenced by subjective means such as thoughts, feelings, tools, calculations, etc., but can maintain its real existence.

The application of this form of thinking, which reflects the nature of things, was gradually expanded, and was once used to generalize all mental activities except the primitive senses.

Later, Freud added to it, by Anna O. Later, Freud added what Anna O. called the "talk therapy" technique. Freud found that once a patient could clearly recall early traumatic experiences and their accompanying negative emotions, these traumatic experiences would rise from the subconscious to the conscious level.

The hysterical, uncontrollable emotional outbursts disappear immediately and permanently when the patient is able to speak about them through talk therapy.

The subconscious mind is the part of our mental activity that is not normally perceived by our conscious mind. In this area of the subconscious mind, it is that which, under normal circumstances, cannot become conscious at all.

For example, desires that are repressed deep within the mind and not realized, what psychology calls the "iceberg theory": that is, the composition of human consciousness is like an iceberg, where only a small part of it is exposed (consciousness), but the vast majority of it is hidden underwater and affects the rest (unconsciousness).

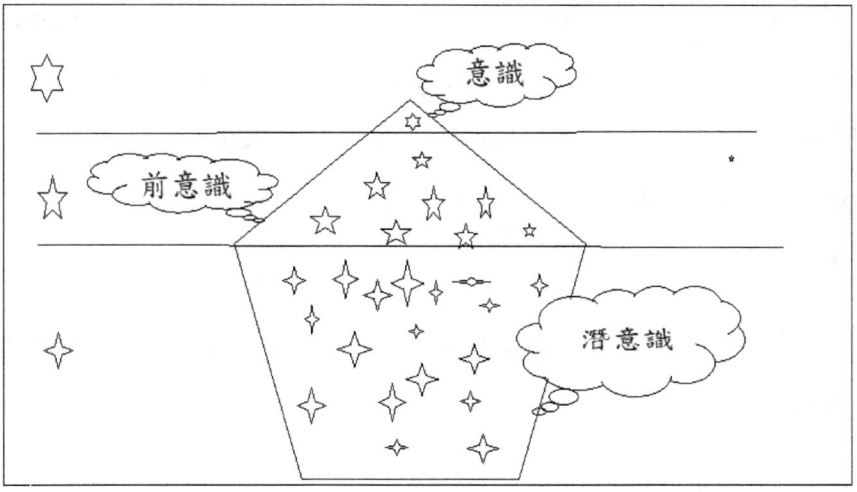

This position on which we study and analyze or criticize problems and issues divides our thoughts into three parts: first, consciousness, second, preconsciousness. The third is the subconscious mind. In other words, the subconscious mind is the deep part of the brain that directly influences your behavior without passing through the conscious mind.

A. Consciousness

When an individual reads this article, the text of this article is being

When you read this article, the text of this article is being searched and read by yourself using your own eyes to project into your brain and into the

The content of this article is being searched and read by your own eyes and projected into your brain and filtered by your own "consciousness". Based on what you read, your consciousness will do some thinking and judging.

Your own consciousness will think, judge, digest, and absorb.

Pre-consciousness

Icebergs float on the surface of the ocean, so a part of the iceberg ebbs and flows with the fluctuations of the sea, sometimes above the surface, sometimes below. This part of the iceberg is called preconsciousness. To put it plainly, it is our memory.

It is the ability of the nervous system to store past experiences, and the study of memory belongs to the field of psychology or brain science. Memory represents the accumulation of impressions of a person's past activities, feelings, and experiences, and is classified in a variety of ways, mainly by environment, time, and perception.

Based on the fact that we are now in the process of analyzing, synthesizing, judging, reasoning, and other cognitive activities based on representations, abstractions, and universal ideas that serve to specify the domain or class of entities, events, or relationships.

The memory mechanism formed by the recognition, as a standard form of acceptance, so that people can repeat the test of the standard style, the memory process is divided into three different stages: 01.

01. Coding: Take anything that reduces uncertainty in a situation, and process and combine it.

02. Storage: A permanent record of the combined information of anything that reduces uncertainty in one situation

03. Retrieval: take out whatever is stored that reduces

uncertainty in a situation, and respond to hints and events.

The three stages of the memory system are like a production object that passes through each workplace sequentially according to a certain functional route and completes the production process of the information workplace at a uniform production rate, transforming the incoming stimulus information flow into a meaningful pattern that can be stored and recalled.

This three-stage model was first proposed by Richard Atkinson and Richard Shiffrin in 1968, and has been widely accepted after some processing and modification.

Currently, there are quite a few categories of impressions of past activities, feelings, and experiences accumulated over the course of human life, mainly based on environment, time, and perception. Based on the current understanding of the memory formation mechanism, the process is recognized as similar to the process of information access by computers.

By understanding the principles of computer data input and output, it can help us to dissect and understand the complex process of memory along the lines of a rhythm or a structure.

Psychologically, it refers to a mental process that consists of three basic components: sensory experience, retention, and experiential recall (or recollection). Memory agility, persistence, and accuracy vary from person to person, but can be trained and changed.

Memory is currently divided into working memory (formerly also called short-term memory) and long-term memory according to the length of time it takes for new memories to emerge. According to the content characteristics of memory, researchers have divided it into two categories, namely, episodic memory and implicit memory.

01. Episodic memory refers to the comprehensive awareness and recognition of changes in one's physical and mental state and in people, events, and objects in the environment by using mental activities such as sensation, perception, thinking, and memory, and is sometimes referred to as expressive memory.

02. Implicit memory, including our motor skills, behavioral habits, is a type of memory that we do not have consciousness of, but is indeed generated by some

conscious events in the past, more specifically, perception, or by the practical knowledge and familiarity generated by these conscious processes.

It is generally accepted that long-lasting episodic memory is stored in the cerebral cortex, but its production is absolutely dependent on a structure in the brain known as the hippocampus. However, research on the location of memory storage is still ongoing, and there is a lack of strong direct evidence.

Some types of memory, however, are stored in other locations, which are often cited as examples in the previous section. For example, motor patterns, walking, swimming and bicycling - they can be stored in the cerebellum or spinal cord.

The brain stores a lot of stuff, but we don't bet it all on the individual's use of sensory, perceptual, thinking, memory, and other mental activities to become aware of and recognize changes in one's physical and mental state and in people, events, and objects in the environment, because that would make thinking less efficient.

Therefore, we store our memories in the preconscious mind so that when we need them, we can float to the sea level and enter the level of consciousness at any time.

Subconsciousness

If the preconscious mind is described as our "remembered memories", then the subconscious mind can be summarized as "unremembered memories", such as childhood memories that you do not remember, or memories from past lives that some people think are also stored here.

At the same time, the subconscious also contains information that you "don't pay attention to". For example, if you are reading an announcement on a bus board on the side of the road, you are reading the announcement while waiting for the bus to arrive. On the other hand, you are waiting for the bus to arrive.

As you focus on the text of the announcement, you are not aware of the changes in your surroundings. However, your ears have more auditory functions, so while your eyes are focused on the text on the bulletin, your ears do hear the cars that are whizzing by one by one.

At this point, the content of the article enters your consciousness, and the information about the cars that your ears have collected about the changes in the surrounding environment enters your subconscious.

At this point, if you were to "think" or "recall" the changes in your surroundings, you would not be able to answer the question of whether there were cars whizzing by one by one. You think you didn't see the cars whizzing by, but in fact, the information about the cars and the changes in the surroundings have been input into your brain, but they are stored in your subconscious.

But at this time, if you rely on your "intuition" or "guessing" the most number of cars, you have a high probability of being accurate just by the sound of the car's engine. This is because when it comes to intuition, it is easy to touch the messages stored in the subconscious, in old memories.

For example, we have all had the experience of suddenly wanting to eat something special "for some reason", like homesickness, or suddenly being caught in a time warp due to a certain situation. I don't know why, but I just like it.

Intuition, thought to be an unexplained thought, is probably the subconscious information that drives us to have these thoughts. The world class master of subliminal abilities, Boontrecht, said, "The power of the subconscious mind is tens of thousands of times greater than that of the conscious mind.

Our actions can be thought and decided through the conscious level. But often, our "subconscious" or "unconscious" choices and behaviors inadvertently project the thoughts of our subconscious mind. In other words, we accidentally reveal thoughts that we are not even aware of.

For example, some people are slow to feel stress, so if you ask them directly, "What's bothering you lately? He will always say "not bad" in a relaxed manner.

However, you will observe that the person will always want to eat junk food with high oil and sugar, or he is particularly prone to buy some irrelevant and wasteful things to treat himself recently. These behaviors project his inner stress level.

The unreachable subconscious

We can use our sensory, perceptual, thinking, memory and other mental activities to control our actions by being aware of our physical and mental states and changes in people, events and objects in the environment.

However, some actions are subconscious constraint responses that we cannot control or feel because of our cognitive ability and clarity of awareness of the environment and self. For example: blinking, yawning, dreaming and other behaviors.

You would never expect, if you have been meditating for a long time, that the subconscious mind would create a picture of all objects or phenomena that exist in nature according to what we think.

The subconscious mind cannot distinguish whether all the things (phenomena) and objects that exist are true or false, but once accepted, they will eventually become reality. As soon as a clear picture enters the subconscious mind, the subconscious mind immediately tries its best to turn this picture into a fact. As soon as we give the subconscious mind a picture, it will try to materialize it.

Once the subconscious mind accepts an idea, it begins to act on it. The subconscious mind executes both 'good' and 'bad' thoughts, and, of course, naturally executes 'bad' thoughts.

If you use this law negatively, it will bring you frustration, failure and misfortune. If your habitual way of thinking is harmonious and constructive, then you will experience health, success and all good things.

Therefore, a calm mood and a healthy body are the inevitable result of thinking and feeling the right way. When everything is judged according to your own perception of all objects or phenomena that exist objectively in nature, without seeking to conform to the actual situation, is it the right way of thinking.

It is the cognitive process of consciousness that occurs independently of the sensory stimuli for the development of all things (phenomena) and objects that exist objectively.

Their most typical forms are judgment, reasoning, concept formation, problem solving and deliberation (English: deliberation). When transmitted to the subconscious mind, it leaves traces in the cells of the brain, where it executes 'good' thoughts, 'bad' thoughts, and, of course, naturally, 'bad' thoughts.

This is why we are forced to accomplish these tasks by the unexplained annoyance and pain that sometimes appear like pins and needles. In order to realize a certain ideal or achieve a certain purpose, and unconsciously work for it, the driving mentality.

In order to achieve the purpose, it will use all previous experiences, and any little bit, that is, all kinds of experiences or feelings in life, including gratitude, tears, growth, encouragement, etc.. These little experiences are like drops of water that merge to form a river, compiling a symphony of knowledge in our lives.

It will give birth to infinite power and wisdom; it will summarize and utilize all the natural laws. Sometimes the problem is solved immediately, sometimes it takes days, weeks or longer, but all the smallest problems of the mind will eventually be solved.

The "subconscious" is the most fundamental and mysterious concept in psychoanalysis. Throughout history, people have always been interested in and explored what is going on in the deepest parts of our being. Thus, the subconscious is the part of our consciousness that is out of reach or unnoticed.

The depth is so deep that the conscious mind cannot immediately dive down and pull what it needs to use to the conscious level. Moreover, there is a huge amount of information in the subconscious mind, so if we do not organize it regularly or if we lack clues, it is not easy to find the information we need in the subconscious mind.

Subconsciousness and psychodynamics

The subconscious of adults was once the consciousness of children. The subconscious mind is the inner memory of past life experiences. There are two types of life experiences, pleasant and painful. Generally speaking, painful experiences, especially traumatic ones, are engraved deeper and remain longer in the mind.

Trauma is a dramatic change in the environment, especially a sudden and destructive stimulus, which causes people to have unbearable painful experiences. These traumatic experiences sink deep into the heart and form subconscious cruxes.

Behind every trauma, there is a psychological trauma that one consciously works for in order to realize a certain ideal or achieve a certain purpose, and there are unfulfilled wishes and unmet needs.

These wishes and needs become the mental or emotional shocking experiences that cause abnormal emotions in the practice of knowing all the things (phenomena) and objects that exist objectively, and constantly emerge from the psychological inner dynamics of the individual's mental activities such as sensation, perception, thinking and memory, and the comprehensive awareness and knowledge of his or her physical and mental state and changes in people, events and things in the environment.

In order to reduce the painful experience, the individual is always in a state of mind that causes abnormalities due to external stimuli or internal physical conditions. These include joy, anger, sadness, fear, love, evil, desire, etc., mental or emotional shock experiences, repression, rejection and isolation, psychological defense mechanisms, do not want to let these traumatic experiences and memories, at any time in the internal presentation, affecting mood and other psychological activities.

Freud later discovered that the subconscious mind has not only traumatic symptoms, but also a large number of repressed instinctual desires, especially sexual instinctual desires. The sexual instinct is an internal state of arousal or tension that arises from the need for forcefulness, and is expressed as an internal drive to drive the organic body's activities to achieve the satisfaction of needs.

Therefore, subconsciousness can be defined as the intrinsic characteristics of all objects or phenomena that exist objectively in nature, or a human being who, in the process of cognition, rises from perceptual knowledge to rational knowledge.

It is an expression of the connotation and extension of the ego-cognitive consciousness, which is precisely and briefly described as "the part of mental activity that is not perceived by the consciousness but rejected by the consciousness," including past traumatic experiences and emotional experiences.

3. What are the psychological characteristics of the subconscious mind?

1. Phenomenological characteristics of the subconscious: Although Husserl analyzed the intentional constructive role of the individual's mental activities such as sensation, perception, thinking, memory, etc., in perceiving and understanding the changes of people, events, and things in the environment.

However, the ambiguity of the concept of consciousness still makes Husserl's theory of consciousness fall into the framework of making judgment on things based on one's own cognition, without seeking to conform to the actual situation, taking a certain object as the scope of study, and seeking to obtain a unified and exact objective law and experience based on experiment and logical reasoning.

What kind of fundamental modifications does Husserl make to the concept of a composite embodiment of self-feeling, self-existence, and feelings of the outside world, so that it can be detached from its natural meaning and have the meaning of reality or [psycho-physical] structure?

The act of "cognition" and "identification" of a subject is provided in order to provide confident knowledge, and such knowledge has the potential to be used for specific purposes. The ability to understand and grasp (a situation) through observation or experience through experience or association. What are the innate conditions that underlie a situation?

Under what circumstances does his theory of consciousness have a purely phenomenological character? Since the purpose of Husserl's holistic, fundamental and critical inquiry into the real world and human beings

He must take into account the exclusion of the dubious learning and experience gained by all people in the process of learning and practice.

In this regard, Husserl adopted a Cartesian, universally skeptical, deep reflection on a central idea or image, on the way in which all objects or phenomena objectively existing in nature develop and evolve.

The result of the examination and verification, like Descartes, establishes the process of analysis, synthesis, judgment, reasoning, and other cognitive activities on the basis of appearances and concepts, as the existence of clear and unambiguous facts that are never in doubt.

Husserl calls this thought, which exists absolutely through the verification of doubt, "absolute consciousness," while at the same time calling it "pure consciousness" on the basis of its freedom from all experience and reality.

Having established the unquestionability of absolute consciousness, Husserl's theory of consciousness is strictly limited to the pure content of conscious activity that is completely free from all suspicious empirical facts.

In other words, all assumptions beyond the scope of consciousness are excluded. In this way, the notions of intentional activity, intentional correlates, intentional objects, and even objects of consciousness as concrete existences analyzed by Husserl are all reduced to the realm of conscious phenomena.

Accordingly, Husserl's theory of consciousness has a purely phenomenological character. In addition to the analysis of the operational structure of consciousness, which is strictly limited to the pure phenomena of consciousness, Husserl's theory of consciousness has the following characteristics.

First, he distinguishes between static and emergent constructions of consciousness.

Accordingly, Husserl's theory of consciousness distinguishes between static phenomenology and emergent phenomenology. The so-called static construction of consciousness refers to the analysis of the intentional activity of consciousness, the interrelationship between intention-related items and the intentional object, and the explanation of the innate and integrated structure of the rules that constitute the object of consciousness.

The analysis of the fundamental nature of consciousness in constructing people or things in temporal changes belongs to the field of phenomenological research, and the related examination includes the investigation of the intrinsic structure of consciousness itself.

Here essence (English: Essence), in philosophy, is an eternal attribute or set of attributes that make an entity, or a substance, its very essence, and which necessarily exists, without which it would lose its essence. It is the substance that is hidden inside the operational structure of inner time consciousness.

At the same time, it is the individual's comprehensive awareness and recognition of his or her physical and mental state and the changes of people, events, and things in the environment by using mental activities such as sensation, perception, thinking, and memory. The original source of the constructive activities of the individual's perception and awareness is the inherent characteristics of the person or thing itself, the current consciousness, and the neurological response of the individual.

When a person is born, consciousness is present with life, and it is a constructive process of [active synthesis] and [passive synthesis] of the synthesis of self-feeling, self-existence, and feeling of the outside world.

Secondly, whether in a static or an emergent structure, the intrinsic meaning of all objects and the scope of control ultimately originate from the special function and activity of the human brain, which is the reflection of the objective world unique to human beings.

In this regard, the human neurological response, the consciousness of which is present at birth, is a synthesis of self-feeling, self-existence, and perception of the outside world, as an innate form of constructing objective knowledge.

In this sense, Husserl's absolute consciousness acquires the characteristics of Kant's concept of "transcendence" and is therefore "transcendental" consciousness. In Husserl's phenomenology, the transcendental consciousness is the absolute subject of the constructive activity in which all objective knowledge and science must obtain their final explanation.

Therefore, Husserl's theory of consciousness is fundamentally a deep analysis of the subjective mapping of the objective material world, as a transcendental subjectivity, the function of the human brain and the reflection of existence.

Third, all objects of consciousness can only be rewritten by a message through the manifestation of consciousness associated with them, i.e., the facts that can be observed and observed.

Thus, to recognize the true nature of an object, consciousness must grasp the phenomenon itself as it is known; Husserl calls this position of cognition "going back to the facts themselves".

Moreover, since consciousness is the intention to synthesize a multitude of phenomena in order to grasp the essence of a unified and homogeneous object, Husserl points out that consciousness is constructed fundamentally and purposefully toward the object of consciousness as a whole (including the world and consciousness itself).

As a whole, Husserl's theory of consciousness is a phenomenological philosophy, or rather, Husserl's phenomenology is a study of consciousness itself at multiple levels of reflection, hence the name "phenomenology of consciousness".

Based on the analysis of different aspects of consciousness, Husserl also proposed different types of phenomenology, including: pure phenomenology, static and emergent phenomenology, phenomenological psychology, and transcendental phenomenology, among others.

The reason that has dominated these different types of phenomenological research, or fundamentally enabled the phenomenology of consciousness, is that Husserl proposed a series of phenomenological methodological concepts from the very beginning, and implemented them rigorously.

But the subconscious is the part of mental activity that cannot be observed or observed, and is perceived by the conscious mind. It is the part of human mental activity that cannot be cognized, or is not cognized, and is the "process of mental activity that has occurred but has not reached a state of consciousness.

As mentioned earlier, for Freud, the founder of the psychoanalytic school, what we know as consciousness is only the tip of the iceberg of the entire structure of consciousness.

He compared the whole consciousness to an iceberg in the sea, and the special functions and activities of the human brain, which is a reflection of the objective world, is like the tip of the iceberg, only a small part of which is exposed to the surface, and the larger part is under the sea water, which is difficult to be discovered, so it is called "subconscious".

We usually only use our "consciousness" to process information, to learn and to work, to show the individual's comprehensive awareness and understanding of his or her physical and mental state and the changes of people, events and objects in the environment, using sensory, perceptual, thinking and memory activities, just like the pre-processing of a computer. More importantly, we need to make full use of the subconscious mind to help us process and process information in the background.

At the level of consciousness, it is the part that can be perceived and described in words as all things (phenomena) and objects that exist objectively.

Unconsciousness, on the other hand, cannot be described in words. Consciousness is characterized as obvious, clear, and conscious; while unconsciousness is potential, vague, and unconscious.

Although the subconscious is not obvious, it is always behind our destiny trajectory. Communication with the subconscious mind is not about behavior or words, it is about feelings!

For example, if you want to achieve a goal, then you have to show your will to achieve the goal first, and then do it. Not just struggle! Therefore, how to use subconsciousness, there are three main tips.

1. Concentration: focus on one thing for a short period of time

Concentration is a cognitive neuroscience term that refers to the ability to concentrate on a continuous activity while ignoring the interference of the external environment on vision, hearing and touch.

This ability is closely related to memory and other control functions, and is also mainly controlled by the frontal cingulate cortex of the brain.

As we all know, Germans are strict, serious and focused, Germany has a population of 80 million people, has more than 2,300 world brands, and is among the top Nobel Prize winners in the world, the quality of Germans has always been very high.

Many mothers who care about their children have more or less in-depth information about how to educate their children, and they are clear that German children are very strong in concentration?

In fact, from childhood to adulthood, we have always known that attention is important. Especially curious teenagers, during the class, easily distracted, inattentive, often in a trance. "Once he started studying, his mind deserted and he was distracted by everything, especially his cell phone games.

Could the child be an overactive child, suffering from some kind of inattentiveness?" In fact, a child's inattentiveness must be due to something else that attracts more attention than the child's own lack of ability to focus on something.

Attention is an emotional response, which is the ability to direct and focus one's mental activity, such as perception and thinking, on something.

Once students are interested in what they have learned, they will have a strong curiosity and desire to explore the mysteries, and they will spontaneously focus their attention. If something does not arouse our interest and mobilize our emotions, the brain cannot mark or record any information.

Likewise, if we don't pay enough attention when we observe or experience something, then we won't remember anything. The secret to a strong memory is to concentrate fully on the perception. Only those scenes (pleasant or depressing) that draw us to them can leave an imprint on the brain.

Therefore, any learning should be done carefully and thoughtfully in the face of all things (phenomena) and objects that exist objectively - this is also the process of concentration - thinking about how best to remember what we read, see, and hear.

Poor performance or memory loss is not a matter of IQ, but of distraction. Once you become interested and learn by heart, it is easy to understand and learn the knowledge of all objects or phenomena that exist in nature.

Whether or not attention can be effectively focused is not determined by the content alone, nor by lectures. If the knowledge you learn can stimulate thinking, you will not only improve your concentration, but also your interest and affinity, and you will remember more.

Human beings are capable of choosing their own points of interest and focus. However, to achieve full attention requires strong self-control. But as we age, many people begin to overlook the importance of focus in their lives.

What is focus?

Some people compare focus to the power of concentration: if a child's brain is a cell phone, then the child's focus is the phone's memory, and what the child needs to do is the app in the phone. if you give the child too much stuff, it will cause the memory to be insufficient, and the memory can also be increased, the larger the memory, the more things can be installed.

It is also said that concentration is the acceleration that determines how far we can run, how fast we can run, and is an important factor in determining the gap between people. If you want to improve your child's academic performance, in the long run, you have to start with concentration.

Most students who come out on top in exams have a high level of concentration. Both studying and working need to be in shape.

Concentration is not only a habit, but more importantly it is an attitude. For example, some people have been playing table tennis for more than 10 years, but their skills are still very average. And some people with just two or three years can learn a variety of techniques to perfection.

Because the latter focus on the study of various techniques day and night, constantly to practice. In fact, the effectiveness of learning is more important than the length of learning time, which depends on whether or not to adopt a focused attitude.

The fastest way to learn is to let the subconscious and the conscious mind work together, which requires short periods of immersion in a matter, whether it is eating, bathing, sleeping and thinking about it.

2. Processing information using image thinking

Have we ever had such an experience in our life and work? Around 3:00 pm, we tend to fall into a mental coma and our creative thinking is hindered by all kinds of obstacles. At this time, we will put down the work at hand, tell a little joke, listen to a little gossip. We can always find jokes from the gossip news that make people gush or make other people's brains go crazy. This is always a good way to keep everyone's mind alive.

Usually, when dealing with everyday things, there are always some objective things (phenomena) and objects that are difficult to describe and define in words, and when describing them, thinking is very confusing, or when you need to think of new ideas, inspiration dries up.

In fact, this is quite normal, 95% of the imagination of the vast majority of people is in a dormant state, so most of our functions of association, memory, creativity, etc., are not even at their normal level, let alone can play to the fullest.

Those who "think really carefully" and "have sharp ideas", that is, smart people, how to make thinking more flexible, "think carefully" and "think deeply"? The answer lies in the common habits of those who can think carefully and those who can think deeply.

They often stand in front of the whiteboard and draw "diagrams" just like Edison. Moreover, they make good use of "pictures" to present important things, and cleverly organize the discussion to derive fundamental answers.

They treat the whole whiteboard as their own thinking garden.

Therefore, their way of thinking, the habit of image thinking. The use of various images to think, and it provides a human in the process of cognition, from perceptual awareness to rational awareness, the common nature of the things perceived abstraction, to generalize, is the concept of the ego cognitive consciousness of an expression of a good reflection of the nature of things thinking form, that is, the use of "picture thinking That is the use of "pictorial thinking".

From a historical perspective, the evolution of the visual system is much longer than the evolution of the language system! In prehistoric times, when writing did not exist, the history of making images already existed.

For modern people, reading pictures is definitely easier than reading a bunch of words because the human brain uses "simultaneous processing" when processing images and pictures, while the processing of words is "linear" and "sequential", and therefore "pictures" are more easily interconnected with other information.

Dan Roam, author of "Behind the Napkin", says that

the images are processed in a "synchronous" way, while the text is processed in a "linear" way. Dan Roam, author of Behind the Napkin, says. A pen and a piece of paper is all it takes to communicate. "In fact, the message that can be expressed in five minutes of speech can be explained in one picture at a glance. In fact, what can be conveyed in five minutes of talking can be explained in one picture.

According to medical research, vision accounts for most of the brain's functions. 30% of the brain's neurons are responsible for processing "visual" sensory information, compared to 8% for tactile and 3% for auditory, it can be found that "vision" is very important to humans, and is essential for learning and experience.

The human brain has 100 billion neurons, and every 100 neurons form a neural column. The neurons are connected to each other to generate information flow. The neurons and the flickering stream of information generate thoughts.

Different areas of neurons are in charge of information about the material components of the real world, such as colors, lines, shapes, dimensions, textures, rhythms, layers, structures, sounds, smells, images, imagination, etc.

"Imagination" means "drawing pictures with the brain". Images trigger a wide range of associations and enhance creative thinking and memory. Please think about it, when we listen to stories, communicate with people, and think, will it be like playing a movie in our brain, showing a dynamic picture?

In terms of cognitive ability and clarity of cognition, pictures are clearer than words, because words are too abstract; pictures are more practical than behaviors.

Because behavior is too concrete. Images combine the advantages of both, being accurate, practical, and able to express our thoughts clearly, making the special functions and activities of the human brain, which are unique to human beings, reflect more clearly on the objective world.

We use visual memory everywhere, and without it, we would not be able to access what we see, let alone recall to extract it.

But when neurons in the cerebral cortex receive various sensory or perceptual messages, they pass them on to the hippocampus, and if the hippocampus responds, the neurons begin to form a "persistent" network that is more easily remembered.

Develop pictorial thinking habits. Through pictorial thinking, we can quickly access the systematic understanding that we have acquired from various sources, which have been refined and summarized. It is also faster and more intuitive to process information.

"Image Thinking is not a new invention or a new technology, but an innate human gift. Modern brain science and evolutionary studies have found that "pictorial thinking" is a result of the biological evolution of the two eyes.

Roger Wolcott Sperry (USA) in 1981 also described the collection of information on a particular subject for this purpose.

He was awarded the Nobel Prize in Physiology and Medicine for his description of the process of problem solving using a planned and systematic approach to data collection, analysis, and interpretation.

Dr. Sperry's (also translated as "Spencer") active and systematic process of discovering, interpreting, or correcting facts, events, behaviors, or theories, or making practical applications of such facts, laws, or theories, revealed that the left and right halves of the human brain are responsible for different types of information processing mechanisms, and that it is through the corpus callosum in the center of each brain that information is exchanged.

Generally speaking, the left brain controls the five senses such as vision, hearing, taste, and other parts that require a lot of logical operations, while the right brain emphasizes the operation of images, space, and so on.

These describe the collection of information about a particular subject. The use of planned and systematic data collection, analysis and interpretation methods to obtain results of problem solving processes has brought revolutionary advances in brain science, especially in human behavior, and cognitive science is not the same as the search for absolute truth.

In particular, the science of human behavior and cognition is not the same as the search for absolute truth, but on the basis of the existing, groping approach to the truth.

This is the survival characteristic of human creatures that are influenced by the external environment or their own internal changes, and gradually change from simple to complex, from lower to higher.

Images are a powerful tool for communicating marketing messages and increasing memory. Let's explore "image thinking" together, what are the advantages of using visual content?

Images directly affect the emotions of the audience, making it easier to create an emotional impact and helping to convey marketing messages.

Another benefit is that vibrant or persuasive images can help attract the attention of the audience, making consumers more willing to stay engaged and more likely to influence their personal shopping intentions.

If you want to motivate potential customers to read marketing materials or learn about services or products, images have the ability to beautify the layout, quickly convey marketing messages, and even reduce reading fatigue.

3. Easier to remember The human brain has the ability to recall images, and images are one of the most effective ways to convey emotional messages. Experiments have shown that humans can remember up to 2,000

images, and when tested a few days after reading, the accuracy rate of recall is as high as 90%, even for images viewed for a short period of time.

4、Communicate visually Images are easier to handle and more popular than words. It takes 20 seconds to read text, but communication with images can be done in milliseconds. The use of graphics or images can effectively communicate marketing concepts through a visual stimulation mechanism.

5、Build trust and increase profitability According to eBay's research, images can have a positive impact on conversion rates, effectively attracting buyers' attention, building trust in sellers, and even increasing conversion rates. There is a strong correlation between the number of photos and profitability, and the more photos there are, the higher the likelihood of profitability.

Then let's look at why we need to use image thinking to solve our problems. Why is graphic thinking so important to us?

First of all, from a historical and logical point of view. In the process of exploring history, we find that written language is not human, and that images are more useful in helping us to communicate and communicate.

Similarly, people use images to help them think and reason, for example, experienced teachers will additionally ask students to learn how to do diagramming problems. In fact, all walks of life make extensive use of pictorial language to communicate.

Although words are derived from images, ancient texts have continued to simplify pictorial symbols to create pictographs, and at the same time, pictographs have developed both phonetic and ideographic characters to facilitate information communication, but words still cannot replace images.

In other words, most of the information was lost in the process of converting images into words, and the shape of the "elephant" was lost with it. Therefore, words cannot replace images to convey information accurately.

However, even though people have generally understood and realized the importance of pictorialization, there are still "picture-blind" people who are unwilling to accept the use of pictorial tools because they do not have the talent to draw, do not have the ability to think imaginatively, and even feel that pictorial methods are not logical and rigorous.

From a personal point of view, we need to improve our logical thinking ability. People who are good at logical thinking are good at summarizing and coming to clear conclusions.

The level of logical thinking ability is not constant, it can be improved through training, which requires us to visually display, analyze and organize our thinking process. Drawing a mind map is a process of visualizing our thinking.

This is because most people's thinking process is disorganized and illogical, and this kind of thinking cannot get effective feedback.

Generally speaking, the most active time of the human brain is before going to bed and squatting in the toilet, when your brain will keep flashing back to various life clips, you will also think about some life topics, but you can hardly say what you think.

It's hard to remember what comes to your mind when you're thinking aimlessly, and those bright ideas are wasted for nothing.

The brain has limited space, just like a piece of paper,

if you write all over it, the information you can receive is limited, but if you draw on it, then the amount of information you receive will be greatly increased.

Because of this difference, when doing input and output, use pictorial thinking, i.e., when outputting, first form a picture in your mind, and then describe it in words.

When inputting, the meaning of the text is outlined in the brain as a picture, so that the limited storage resources of the brain can be used more efficiently, so as not to read before and forget.

By extension, if you want the other person to better understand and remember what you want to say, you can use a more graphic way of expression, such as telling an immersive story, to give the other person a sense of immersion.

The natural human senses include images, sounds, touch, and smells. The brain abstracts sensory information into words or language through thought processing, so input and output is basically a process of processing and restoration, and images carry the most information.

First of all, we boldly "draw" out the innovative ideas

without considering the feasibility and rationality, and without judging whether they are correct or not.

Second, for each specific problem feasibility to start thinking, discussion, the same type of viewpoints and views will be filtered and merged, remove the part that does not meet the reality, re-optimization to produce a thought map.

In this process, new ideas and opinions may be generated, thus creating more room for thinking. In general, images can be clearer and more intuitive, so it will be easier to find solutions to problems.

3、Storage of information before going to sleep

According to the legend, there are two animals in the world that can reach the top of the pyramid, one is the majestic and brave eagle, and the other is the snail. The eagle can reach the top of the pyramid because he has wings, and the snail can reach the top of the pyramid because he has enough concentration and perseverance.

Therefore, people should strive to move forward in their careers and studies, and strive to move into the future, just like the eagle soars on wings, and just like the snail's concentration and perseverance.

Researchers at the University of Exeter in the United Kingdom asked some volunteers to memorize words before going to bed and others to do so 12 hours after staying awake. They found that the volunteers who memorized the words before going to bed remembered them more clearly.

In an article published in the journal Cerebral Cortex, psychology professor Nicholas Demy says that memory improvement is due to the brain's hippocampus. The hippocampus is primarily responsible for memory.

During sleep, new memories are "unblocked" and "replayed" in the hippocampus, so people will remember this part of the brain with exceptional clarity after waking. He said, "Sleep doubles our chances of remembering things. Therefore, every day before going to bed can let the brain store some information, training our memory.

And we have this experience ourselves. For example, if you are preparing for an exam the next day, you will fill your brain with a lot of information the day before, and you will want to have a memory.

In fact, the subconscious mind itself is also processing the information in the background by memorizing some information before going to bed. In fact, memorizing things before going to bed makes them more memorable. Therefore, this is indeed an efficient way to process information.

2. Instinctive or motivational characteristics of the subconscious mind.

It is the driving force behind the kind of consciousness and behavioral activities that drive people. Starting with the psychoanalytic theory of S. Freud (1856~1939), it is believed that the mental process that occurs between the conscious and unconscious. It is an instinctive, unconscious response that governs all human thoughts and behaviors.

It is also known as the "subconscious". The subconscious is a condition capable of activity and can be resurfaced through medical treatment; deep psychology observes surface phenomena and the influence of hidden psychological conditions in the depths, all of which emphasize the possibility of "movement".

There are many schools of thought that tend to synthesize the philosophical positions of materialism and pragmatism and do not explore the supernatural factors in nature, based on the theory that all phenomena can be explained by the concept of natural reasons. They all consider natural biological instincts, such as the pursuit of life and desire.

For example, the pursuit of life, desire, and pleasure are considered to be stimuli of neurological reactions; those that tend to be psychological instincts are considered to be the influence of the subconscious rather than the influence of the external material world.

Freudian kinetic psychology is a school of thought in psychology, which has changed the past view of the psyche as a static state and emphasizes the basic energy of psychological life as the driving force of personality and behavior, believing that the psyche is subject to change, flow, and even change.

There are many people who hold this view, and there are many people or things in almost the same category. For example, in the 1908 book "Introduction to Social Psychology", Doktor Mak listed dozens of motives to describe the causes of behavior.

In addition, in 1935, the psychologist Levin proposed the concept of environmental space and psychological space, and argued that psychological space can be divided into several zones, which are full of energy, and when stimulated, the relevant energy in one zone begins to take effect, and the energy in the neighboring zones immediately concentrates in this zone to respond to the stimulus.

When a stimulus is received, the relevant energy in one zone begins to take effect, and the energy in the neighboring zones immediately concentrates in this zone to respond to the stimulus.

Therefore, the defense mechanism of suppressing or limiting human thoughts, emotions and behaviors constitutes the main feature of the dynamics of the subconscious mind. The repressed ego (instinct) of the subconscious is the source of spiritual dynamics.

The emotions and desires of the subconscious, expressed as irrational or animalistic, are the source of spiritual dynamics; the subconscious causally determines the individual's use of sensation, perception, thinking, memory, and other mental activities, and the integrated awareness and knowledge of one's physical and mental state and changes in people, events, and objects in the environment.

3. Automatic characteristics of the subconscious.

When psychologists try to understand how our mind works, they often come to a conclusion that may be surprising: people often make decisions without thinking, or more precisely, before "consciously" thinking, they have already made up their minds to make decisions.

We know from the neuropsychology of the brain that there are many areas of the brain that the conscious mind cannot see, but is aware of, for example, we can unconsciously tell the truth of a smile from another person, but not the difference.

For example, why do we not pay attention to which foot we step out first when we walk? It is because we do not pay attention to which foot we walk with.

That is to say, when you are familiar with walking, driving, swimming, etc., it is completely controlled by your subconscious mind automatically, you do not need to use your conscious mind to direct it, it is completely automatic.

This is also generally known as "practice makes perfect", as long as you are familiar with it, you can find the trick. I once cited a clichéd story.

In the Northern Song Dynasty, there was a man

named Chen Kansu, called Yao Consulting, who claimed to be so good at archery that no one could match him. He was so arrogant that he often boasted of his superior skills: "My archery skills are unmatched by anyone else. Who among you is willing to try it with me?

The others always said, "Master, your archery skills are so good, how can we compare with you?

"Yes, we need to learn more from you! Show us again, Master, so that we can have a better understanding. The young men who wanted to learn archery from Chen Yao Consulting were always saying complimentary things to him, and they were very much to his liking.

One day, Chen Yaocun was shooting arrows in the courtyard with a large group of disciples, as was his custom, when an old man selling oil passed by and stopped to watch.

Chen Yao Consulting raised his bow, loaded his arrows, and shot ten arrows in a row, all of which hit the red center. The disciples applauded and applauded, but Chen Yao Consulting turned to the old man and said, "What do you think? The old man only nodded slightly and did not applaud and clap.

Chen Yao Consulting felt very uncomfortable and asked him angrily, "Hey, do you know how to shoot arrows, you old man?

The old man said lightly, "No."

In a reproachful tone, Chen Yao Consulting said, "So, did I not shoot my arrows well enough?

The old man said, "Yes, but this is just a normal technique, I don't see anything remarkable.

The apprentice next to him supported his teacher: "Old man, how can you talk like that? How dare you insult our master like that? You know that our master's archery skills are unmatched by anyone. You are so deceitful!

The old man said, "Little brother, don't be angry, I said your archery skill is really ordinary, nothing worthy of praise.

Chen Yao consulted and said, "Old man, from what you said, you obviously don't take us seriously? Then you should show us your skills. What's the use of mere words!

The old man calmly said: "Little brother, I do not know how to shoot arrows, but let me pour oil for you to see.

The disciple asked, "What's so difficult about pouring

oil? Who doesn't know how to do that? Don't be ridiculous!"

The old man said without delay, "You'd better watch before you talk big.

The old man took a gourd and placed it on the ground, then put a coin with a hole in the mouth of the gourd. Then scooped a spoonful of oil, only to see the ladle gently tilted, the oil, like a thin yellow line, straight from the money hole into the gourd. After pouring, strange to say, the oil from the ladle did not touch the coin.

The old man modestly said to Chen Yao Consulting, "I have no skills, but I have practiced well.

After hearing this, Chen Yao Consulting felt very ashamed, and since then, he has been practicing archery even harder in silence, never boasting about his archery skills again. Later, his character was praised as well as his archery skills

Have you ever ridden a bicycle like this?

Remember when you were a kid and you just learned how to ride a bicycle? You were so nervous, your palms were sweaty. The handlebars of your bike were shaking left and right, and you didn't know what to do. But after you've gotten good at it a few times.

You can even talk to the person you're carrying while you're riding, can't you? When you see a red light, you will still stop, and when it's time to turn, your hands will automatically let the handlebars turn.

Further, in fact, our heartbeat, breathing, blood flow is not also controlled by the subconscious? The subconscious mind is not controlled by subjective will and reason, but has the characteristic of being spontaneous, autonomous, free, automatic and flowing, or "dynamic". This characteristic has been the focus of cognitive psychology, such as the concepts of "implicit learning", "automatic thinking", and "core beliefs".

Chen Yaoyao's archery skills and the oil seller's skill in pouring oil without dripping oil both originate from the subconscious automation feature. All successful people in all walks of life have different achievements.

But they all have one common characteristic, which is enthusiasm, concentration and diligence. Thus, whether it is Chen Yao Consulting who shoots arrows with a hundred hits or the oil seller who pours oil without a drip, it all comes from their hard work and repetitive practice.

Because of enthusiasm, they can generate strong power and energy; because of concentration, they can devote themselves to it and go forward without any distractions; because of diligence, they can develop their skills.

No matter what excellent skills you want to practice, as long as you are willing to work hard, study hard and practice repeatedly, you will be able to find out the know-how and do it with ease, which is the automatic feature of the subconscious mind.

04. Subconsciousness' subjective characteristics.

To understand the subjective characteristics of subconsciousness, we should start from understanding how people use the word subjectivity, and then clarify the subjectivity of subconsciousness one by one. Subjectivity is a western word, and it was first translated from Japanese (subjectivity) before it became a Chinese word.

However, the Japanese use of the word "subjectivity" is quite volatile and unstable. It is not only translated from "subjectivity", but it usually corresponds to "autonomy", "independence", or even "identity".

Such undefined or unclear definitions of words,

terms, notes, or concepts with no clear meaning are also often found in the interpretation of language, in the general use of a being with a unique consciousness and/or a unique personal experience, or an entity that is related to another entity that exists outside of itself.

The subject is the observer and the object is the thing being observed. There is often an ambiguity. Basically, when we use the concept of subject or subjectivity, it may refer to several different meanings at the same time.

(1) Subjectivity: This term is most commonly used to explain the factors that influence, inform, and bias people's judgments about truth or reality; it is a collection of perceptions, experiences, expectations, personal or cultural understandings, and beliefs about external phenomena of a particular subject.

It is a specific perspective of knowing, grasping, understanding the object or introspecting oneself with one's own consciousness as the point of departure, as opposed to objectivity. Different definitions of subjectivity are often used together and interchangeably.

(2) Self-discipline: Essentially, self-discipline is having the courage to let yourself do what you have to do before

you are forced to act. Self-discipline is often associated with a reluctance or laziness to do something that has to be done.

The "law" is the norm, the guarantee that no behavior will go outside of it. The ability of an individual or group to legislate for itself is opposed to otherness.

(3) sameness: each of the two contradictory aspects of the development of things, each with its opposing aspect as the premise of its own existence, the two sides of the coexistence in a unity.

The two contradictory sides, according to certain conditions, are each transformed to their opposite sides, and the individual's inner unified self or soul, or the identity of the group (this identity may be constructed or intrinsic), is opposed to the other and the other group.

(4) Independence: The human will is not easily influenced by others, and has a strong ability to propose and implement independently for its own purposes. It reflects the intrinsic stability of the value of the act of the will, and the individual or group is independent and self-sustaining, not influenced or interfered by other individuals or groups, and therefore self-sufficient and

non-dependent.

In a word, the subject has two possibilities of understanding the sentence, but only one of them is used in the current context.

In other words, it is a sentence that can be understood one way or the other, but it is not certain which meaning is being expressed. This comes from the overlap and confusion with the concepts of sameness, independence, autonomy, and subjectivity.

Such an analysis may give us a preliminary understanding of the different meanings and levels of the various subjective discourses.

For example, the so-called cultural subjectivity often refers to the level of cultural independence, while the concept of cognitive subject refers to the self-consciousness that adopts a subjective perspective; subjectivity in the philosophical context is related to the lack of objective reality.

Since subjectivity is not usually the focus of philosophical discourse, different sources have given various vague definitions. However, it is related to the concepts of consciousness, agency, personality, philosophy of mind, reality, and truth.

Three common definitions include subjectivity as the quality or condition that something is a subject, narrowly defined as a person/individual having conscious experiences such as opinions, feelings, beliefs, and desires, referring to the subjective characteristics of the subconscious.

Therefore, the philosophy of subjectivity clarifies the fundamental principle of philosophy that "man is the master of everything and man determines everything".

The philosophy of subjectivity distinguishes the human individual (self) and develops the concept of "subject/object", and the philosophical idea of "man as subject" influences the definition of subconsciousness. The needs and desires of the subconscious become the motive and purpose of human behavior, and the subjective character of the subconscious is particularly emphasized and valued;

Therefore, Freud, while adopting causality theory, also adopted a "purposive" view to construct the concept of "subconscious".

The "Object Relations Theory School" is a

psychoanalytic theory developed by British psychologists such as Ronald Fairbairn and Melanie Klein in the 1940s and 1950s.

Unlike Freudian theories, object relations theories suggest that people do not seek satisfaction in "drives" but in relationships with others. It emphasizes the existence of internalized early "object relations representations" in the subconscious;

Although object-relationship theory emphasizes the "relational features" of the subconscious, it treats the relational features of the subconscious as internalized "object-to-object" relationships and does not pay enough attention to the subjectivity of the individual's subconscious.

The notion of "self", that is, the subjective feeling that we feel at the moment, is our own self in the present moment.

It may be because it is clear that in the process of cognition, from perceptual knowledge to rational knowledge, the common essential characteristics of what we perceive are abstracted and generalized, and become firm and confident.

It is also possible to feel a little weakness because you cannot understand the form of thinking that reflects the nature of the object. So the self, more directly, is what we feel at the moment, what we feel as the subject, and what we feel as the self in the sense of a continuum of time from the past to the present.

Kohut's autopsychology, on the other hand, places more emphasis on the subjective feelings (deep inner experience) of human beings, the narcissistic phenomenon of "feeling good about oneself," and the "omnipotence and idealized self" characteristics of the psychological states that lie beneath the consciousness without being conscious of them and cannot be directly observed by others;

In contrast to the form of thinking in which the self reflects the intrinsic properties of the object, Kohut further describes the concept of self-object empathy, replacing his previous concept of narcissistic empathy, which is the experience of integration between the relative self and the object, a mental experience in which the subject is empathized with and understood by the object in a holistic way.

Then, what is inter-subjective psychoanalysis? Let's

look at the term "intersubjectivity" first. In fact, this term can hardly be used to describe or regulate the meaning of a word or a concept by listing the basic properties of an event or an object.

It originated in the field of philosophy and is embedded in the thought of classical German philosophers such as Fichte and Hegel, and is repeatedly referred to by phenomenologists such as Husserl, Heidegger, Sartre, and Merleau-Ponty.

Moreover, different theorists differ in their use of physical existence, or explicit, rather than abstract, generalized, usage. It is related to "the subjective and conscious world of man, the world of life and the world of practice, and the world of values and the world of ideals", and affects the real and possible life of man, covering "the relationship between the individual and the subject, the group and the group, and the individual and the group or class (the human whole)".

In short, there are multiple dimensions of interaction between human beings and other subjects as beings with a unique consciousness and/or unique personal experience, or in relation to another entity (called "object") that exists outside of themselves.

This creates complexity and diversity among subjects. The subconscious desires and needs are the motive and purpose of the person, the starting and ending points of the individual's behavior, as well as the inner basis of the individual's life existence itself.

05. Characteristics of subconscious relationship.

When philosophy moved from ontology to subjectivity and further developed the concept of inter-subjectivity, psychology, including psychoanalysis, also underwent a radical change and development. Intersubjectivity, or "interactive subjectivity," is a term used in empirical science.

Reciprocal subjectivity is a requirement of the empirical scientific method; it means that the statements of observation in the empirical sciences can only be accommodated if they can be verified by the researcher in each discipline.

Observations must be repeatable by the researcher, i.e., they are not limited to one or a small number of individuals with particular gifts and can be expressed in words.

Strictly speaking, the first observation and its

verification are not mutually subjective, because any observation is necessarily made by one subject. Only by using language as the medium through which different subjects communicate with each other can observations be verified as mutually subjective.

Moreover, all observations must belong to the external world without exception, and this is the common structure of different subjects.

Some scholars believe that rational a priori propositions have mutual subjectivity validity because, in principle, every cognitive subject is rational and can have insight into the universal validity of rational a priori propositions.

Finally, philosophical anthropologists often regard mutual subjectivity as a characteristic of human beings, because as subjects, human beings always point to others and depend on them. Mutual subjectivity in phenomenology has a special meaning.

In the discussion of the origin of knowledge, phenomenologists believe that people live in groups in the world, and there are various relationships between people, the most fundamental of which is knowledge, that is, the relationship between one subject consciousness and another or more subject consciousnesses, each of which has a cognitive role, that is, mutual subjectivity.

A. Schutz, synthesizing the ideas of M. Weber and Ed. Husserl, the originator of phenomenology, constructs his sociology and expounds Husserl's statement of "mutual subjectivity".

It emphasizes that each person has an a priori ego in the cognitive subject and the ability to recognize the other, which constitutes a mutual cognitive commonality or homogeneity, and this social consciousness is also a manifestation of mutual subjectivity.

The energy chain. Jacques Lacan, in his books "The Function and Domain of Speech" and "The Role of Agency of the Word", introduced Sothir's structural linguistics into psychoanalysis and made a creative adaptation.

Thus, inter-subjectivity is proposed from Lacan's elaboration on the "referential chain" and the "subconscious", which Lacan gave a fatal blow to the subjectivity of modernity.

He believes that the subject is determined by the "otherness" in its own existential structure, i.e., the subconscious is essentially the internalized Others; this "otherness" in the subject is actually the intersubjectivity.

Storoulou, who represents the school of "inter-subjective psychotherapy", believes that the "subconscious" is a "mode of interaction" or "mode of organization of experience" formed by inter-subjective behavioral processes of interpersonal communication and feelings, which are not perceived by the consciousness.

In the operation of interdependent behaviors that occur between individuals and individual subjects, between groups and groups, etc. in society through the transmission of information by language or other means, he emphasizes the co-creation of "subject-to-subject" interactions and the mutual sharing of subjective feelings (inter-subjective field).

The philosophical view of inter-subjectivity in fact also emphasizes and reflects the "relational characteristics" of the subconscious, but attaches more importance to the relational characteristics of the "subject-to-subject". The subconscious not only has traumatic symptoms and repressed desires, but also has an internalized superego and internalized "interpersonal relationships", therefore, the subconscious has "relational characteristics".

For example, remembering emotions that have harmed others in the past can make you want to be kinder, help and cooperate with others.

Another well-publicized study also showed that after reminding subjects of a sinful act, if they washed their hands as if they were susceptible to a virus, the act of washing hands seemed to "wash away" their feelings of guilt; a phenomenon typical of subconscious relationships.

The difference between consciousness and subconsciousness

Individuals use their senses, perceptions, thoughts, memories, and other mental activities to become aware of their physical and mental states and the changes in people, events, and objects in the environment, and they can reason and make choices.

For example, in order to realize a certain ideal or achieve a certain purpose, you can consciously make efforts to choose books, housing, and a partner. The subconscious mind is not in control, for example, the heart beats, the digestive system works, the blood circulation, breathing, etc., all are the function of the subconscious mind.

The subconscious mind cannot reason and does not argue with your conscious mind. The subconscious mind is like the soil and the conscious mind is like the seed. Negative, destructive thoughts can only grow the fruit of disaster. The subconscious mind cannot distinguish between good and bad.

If you think something is false, the subconscious mind accepts it as false, even though it may actually be true. Likewise, if you have a biased perception that something is true, the subconscious mind accepts it as true, even though it may actually be false.

In psychology, the subconscious is a state of mind that lurks beneath the conscious mind without being consciously aware of it, and that cannot be directly observed by others. For example, hypnosis is a way to stimulate the human subconscious. It is often referred to as the subjective mind.

The subjective mind recognizes the environment without relying on the functions of the five senses, but through a direct intuition of thoughts, feelings, beliefs, or preferences that quickly emerge without much thought process. It is the place where feelings are generated and is the storehouse of memories.

When your organs that perceive stimuli from the outside world, including the eyes for sight, ears for hearing, nose for smell, tongue for taste, and various parts of the body for touch, are not active, it is the time for the five senses to stop functioning.

When the five senses cease to function, the brain is most active. In other words, when the objective mind stops its activity or is in a state of sleep, the wisdom of the subjective mind comes to light.

Subjectivity in a philosophical context is related to the lack of objective reality. Since subjectivity is not usually the focus of philosophical discourse, different sources give various vague definitions. However, it is related to the concepts of consciousness, agency, personality, philosophy of mind, reality, and truth.

Three common definitions, including subjectivity, are the quality or condition that something is a subject, narrowly defined as a person/individual who has conscious experiences such as opinions, feelings, beliefs, and desires.

Consciousness is the human brain's awareness of the external appearance of the brain. Physiologically, the conscious brain area is the area of the conscious brain (around the prefrontal lobe) where information from other brain areas is available.

The most important function of the conscious brain area is to recognize the truth, i.e., it can recognize the appearance of its own brain area, which comes from the external organs that perceive external stimuli, including the eyes, ears, nose, tongue, and body. Or it comes from imagination or memory. This ability to recognize the truth is not available in any other brain area.

When a person is asleep, the excitement of the conscious brain is reduced to a minimum, and at this time it is impossible to distinguish the authenticity of the images in the brain, which are based on the cognition in the memory, which is called "dream state".

The subconscious, in the narrow sense, corresponds to the ideographic consciousness, which together with the ideographic consciousness constitute the mental world of man. By subconsciousness, Freud meant subconsciousness in the narrow sense.

Subconsciousness in the broader sense is the pursuit of an act or its effect by the will, called intention or meaning. Intentions are called real intentions if they exist in reality and affect the actions of the will, and if one is aware of them.

If the intention only affects the action of the will and there is no consciousness of it at the time, it is called a potential intention. If there was an intention, but it was not withdrawn, and now there is no influence on it, and there is no consciousness of it, it is called a dormant intention.

Only the first two are causally related to action, while dormant intention is not related to action in general. It is the unthinkable force that makes up everything in the universe.

If we could use the subconscious mind to control our behavior, it would be more powerful than using the conscious mind. When the subconscious mind and the conscious mind have opposing thoughts, the subconscious mind usually wins.

For example, if we consciously want to quit smoking, but then we see a cigarette and unconsciously pick it up and smoke it, this is the subconscious reaction of still wanting to smoke.

Many people want to have self-confidence, good relationships, increased income, and increased mobility, but after thinking about it for a long time, they cannot achieve the desired results. It is because the root beliefs in the subconscious are not changed.

If the root cause is not changed, any idea will only stay at the conscious level and will not be powerful. If we can input positive thoughts into our subconscious mind, and let the subconscious mind directly influence our behavior, and then become a habit, we can easily achieve the result. This is the importance of developing subconsciousness.

The most important key to the development of the subconscious mind is repetition, that is, the mental state of consciously working hard to achieve a certain ideal or a certain goal. Once a piece of information is entered into the subconscious mind, it will directly affect our behavior, our persistence and confidence in our beliefs.

Imagine thinking activities such as analysis, synthesis, reasoning, judgment, etc. Are advertisements effective? Will we pay for a product just because we see a great advertisement? Usually not! But why do manufacturers still want to advertise?

Consumers will give more choices to familiar brands because they don't have to make the effort to do background research, and their subconscious will take shortcuts, thinking that there must be a reason for a brand's longevity. Therefore, how to manage the "presence" of your brand is a must for operators.

The "familiarity effect

We have only met someone a few times, but we can establish a better relationship with them. For example, at first we have neither good nor bad feelings towards someone, but after a long time.

As this person does not hurt or violate us, we may develop a good feeling for this person. This is exactly what the old saying goes: once you get to know someone, twice you get to know them, and after three or four times you become friends. In psychology, it is called "Mere Exposure Effect".

This is a psychological phenomenon of repeated exposure effect, people will simply because they are familiar with something and have a good feeling. In social psychology, this effect is also known as the "law of familiarity".

This phenomenon encompasses a wide range of things, such as words, paintings, portraits, polygons, and sounds. In the study of interpersonal relationships, the more often a person appears in front of one's eyes, the more likely one is to develop a preference and liking for that person.

Therefore, psychologists believe that the repeated exposure effect arises because a repeatedly exposed stimulus does not have a bad effect, so the stimulus eventually becomes a safety signal.

The key to this psychological effect is the word "more" - quantity is more important than quality.

According to a Japanese marketing expert, there is a great deal to learn about maintaining customer relationships, and it is better to meet long than to meet more often. A simple visit of 10 minutes a month is better than playing golf once a year. It can be said that a simple face-to-face appearance and continuous exposure can gain popularity, and this is the familiarity effect.

In our growing up years, have we ever had this

experience: a song or theme song that we didn't like at first, but after listening to it a few times, we started to think that the song was pretty good.

After listening to it a few more times, we find that we have fallen in love with the song, and the melody of the song or theme song lingers in our minds.

Robert Zarenz Robert Zajonc is a PhD in social psychology at Stanford University. Robert has experimentally demonstrated that the phenomenon of the repeated exposure effect, where people are attracted to something simply because they are familiar with it, makes people like it more and more the more often they see the same stimulus.

Robert conducted an experiment in 1968, he prepared 12 photos of a university graduate, and then randomly selected a few photos of people and let the students participate in the test to see these photos.

When the experiment began, Robert said to these students participating in the test: "This is an experiment on visual memory, the purpose is to test the photos you look at, to what extent you can remember. The purpose of the experiment is to test how well you can remember what you have seen.

In fact, the real purpose of the experiment was to understand the relationship between the number of times the photos were viewed and the favorability level. The number of times the photos were viewed was 0, 1, 2, 5, 10, 25, etc. The subjects viewed two photos according to the conditions, and were randomly sampled a total of 86 times.

The experimental results showed that the subjects' favorability towards the people on the photos was directly proportional to the number of times the photos were viewed. That is to say, when the number of times to watch the photo increases, regardless of the content of the photo, people's good feeling degree will obviously increase. This also clearly proves the objective existence of the exposure effect.

Robert later did a similar experiment: fictional three single words, respectively abcdice, ganghood, bokebang.

In fact, these three single words do not exist. Then, he began to repeat these words and asked the subjects to guess whether these three words meant good or bad things in Turkic language.

The result of the experiment was that the more often the three words were repeated, the more the subjects thought they represented something positive. In fact, these words were made up, both in Turkic and in English, and were just meaningless syllables.

Later, Robert showed the subjects, who knew nothing about the Chinese language, some Chinese characters and found that whether they thought they represented something positive or not depended on how many times they saw them.

People like to give more favorable feelings to familiar things, such as people, tastes, and topics. This is because familiar things, such as all objects or phenomena that exist objectively in nature, can give people a sense of security and control.

This discovery is widely used in various fields such as advertising and music promotion. Even in political elections are often used.

2. It is important to make people feel familiar

The familiarity effect may make us think of "subliminal advertising". The so-called subliminal advertising, is the use of consumers' subconscious perception of advertising stimulation, a means of promoting products.

For example, food advertisers will insert a picture of food in the middle of a 50 frames per second video.

Because the speed is too fast, sometimes people can not see the picture, but subconsciously will have an impression of this food. This is actually a successful way to get the product information into people's brains.

Subliminal advertising is just an attention-grabbing gimmick that does not influence customers' desire to buy. Many marketing planners take credit for the success of a new product, saying that the new product sold well because of their creative advertising.

"Repetition" is a key point in advertising and marketing. By repeating a product's message through an ad, a marketer can get it seen by people who don't care about the product, and with each repetition, the chances of being seen increase a little.

With each repetition of the ad, the ad's audience will naturally become more familiar with the product and the company. Unless they have a specific reason to do so, they will slowly accept the product in their minds.

As people's acceptance of the product grows, a close relationship will be established and developed. The relationship between the consumer and the product must be based on a sense of "comfort".

Here's another example. When you see an advertisement for a beverage, you don't buy it right away, but you see it on TV, in the newspaper, on the radio, on signboards everywhere, and on signs all over the street.

For example, if you are playing with your cell phone, walking, driving, riding in a car, flipping through a book, reading a computer, or watching TV and keep seeing a picture of a drink and hearing the sound, if you repeat it enough times, the product will enter your subconscious mind.

One day, you will walk into a store and ask for a bottle of a certain drink without thinking about other drinks. Let's use this example to think about how the subconscious mind can be used to repeat itself in life, and how it can be used everywhere.

Third, the cognitive level: the unconscious

The term unconscious comes from Freud's psychoanalytic theory. Unlike the subconscious, the unconscious refers to that which does not normally enter the consciousness at all, and is completely unobservable and unintelligible.

(The subconscious consists of the preconscious and the unconscious, the role of the preconscious is to remove what is not accepted at the conscious level and to suppress it into the subconscious.

In cognitive psychology, it refers to information that has been stored in long-term memory, but is only recognized when necessary for recall, and is the intermediary link between the conscious and the subconscious)

In Freud's view, the unconscious is the main body of human mental activity, and although it is confused and chaotic, it is powerful and fundamental, and is the fundamental driving force behind human action.

The unconscious (that which does not normally enter the consciousness at all, which is completely unobservable and unintelligible) is mainly those repressed desires that exist deep in the human brain.

The unconscious is the deepest part of the human brain. Normally, only the surface of the brain is used for the individual's mental activities such as sensation, perception, thinking, memory, etc., and for the comprehensive awareness and knowledge of the state of one's body and mind and the changes of people, things and objects in the environment.

Therefore, the power of the unconscious mind cannot be freely exercised, but in our unconscious mind, there is a great power hidden, and this great power will burst out unintentionally and play a great role.

In Western psychology, Jung's theory of the original form, which is commonly referred to as collective consciousness, is the most important one. When we move from ideation to the subconscious and then to the unconscious, we find that people are governed by many belief systems.

Some people defend the concept of "unconsciousness" and do not allow people to call it "subconscious" or "subliminal" as it is wrong and misleading.

After Freud proposed his theory of the individual subconscious, his student Jungian, based on his teacher Froude, proposed a new concept, the collective subconscious.

Jungian believed that there is a collective subconscious in the universe, which is a kind of infinite wisdom; Napoleon Hill called it "infinite wisdom".

There are all kinds of family unconsciousnesses, national unconsciousnesses, national unconsciousnesses, religious unconsciousnesses, earth unconsciousnesses, galactic unconsciousnesses, and cosmic unconsciousnesses, all of which are collective consciousnesses.

Dr. Joseph Murphy, a renowned expert on the subconscious, describes this collective subconscious as "King Solomon's Treasure"; some call it the "superconscious".

At some point, anyone's subconscious mind may connect to this collective subconscious mind, and when you connect to this collective subconscious mind, there is a sudden feeling of enlightenment.

Have you ever had such an experience? Sometimes when you are thinking about a difficult problem, you can't make sense of it, and then you just give up, maybe when you are sleeping, maybe when you are playing in the field.

In any case, it is in their own inadvertent, sudden

inspiration, so inexplicably out of the whole solution, and this program, or a very complete solution.

Or, one afternoon you suddenly thought of something urgent to be done and wanted to call someone to remind them of it, but then, due to some other things delayed.

The next day, you run into him and suddenly remember something, so you hurry to tell him about yesterday's incident, but he says, "It's too late, the contract has already been signed. Why didn't you call me yesterday afternoon, that opportunity is gone, things have been settled, become the past!

The so-called unconscious contains, on the one hand, all kinds of activities that are temporarily unknown to the consciousness because they are latent, and everything else is the same as conscious activities, and on the other hand, it contains all kinds of activities that are "suppressed".

If these activities become the individual's comprehensive awareness and recognition of his or her physical and mental state and the changes of people, events, and objects in the environment by using mental activities such as sensation, perception, thinking, and memory. The activities that the individual perceives and recognizes must be in clear contrast to other activities in the consciousness, unlike the "subconscious" or "subliminal".

It seems that many people are confused about the concept of subconsciousness. The concept of subconsciousness proposed by Freud was first called "unconscious", but it is different from the common idea of "unconscious".

The main content of unconsciousness

For human beings, consciousness has a symbolic light. Its full development and differentiation leads to the emergence of the individual conscious self, which gives consistency and continuity to the personality, so that people can feel that I am the same person today as I was yesterday.

As more unknown things are discovered and mastered by the individual using sensory, perceptual, thinking, memory and other mental activities, the individual becomes more and more independent and perfect in his or her own physical and mental state and the comprehensive awareness and knowledge of changes in people, events and things in the environment.

If a person is indifferent to himself and the world around him, it is impossible for him to achieve a higher degree of individuation. The ability to recognize the environment and the self, as well as the clarity of cognition, is another important value associated with the human effort to recognize and assimilate the unconscious.

The unconscious becomes the reflection of the objective material world by the human mind, the sum of various mental processes such as feeling and thinking, and a creative process of metamorphosis and sublimation. According to Jung, the creative significance of this process from ancient times is that they have been deepening their understanding of nature, society and self in the long practice of struggling with nature or society, explaining and exploring the relationship between subject and object, and creating the theme of heroic performance.

The study of heroic mythological narratives began in 1871, when anthropologist Edward Burnett Taylor observed the common model of the hero's journey. Later, other scholars proposed various theories of heroic myth narratives, such as psychologist Otto Rank's Freudian psychoanalysis and Lord Raglan's unified mythic ritual.

Mythologist Joseph Campbell, who was influenced by psychologist Carl Jung's mythology, eventually developed the hero's journey formula, and in his 1949 work The Hero with a Thousand Faces, he described the basic narrative pattern.

The creative process of the hero's metamorphic sublimation, Junger said, implies the renewal of light and thus indicates the regeneration of consciousness from darkness (i.e., regression to unconsciousness).

A hero ventures from the mundane world into an extraordinary one - gains mythical powers and achieves a decisive victory - the hero returns from this mysterious adventure with a certain power to share the benefits with his fellow human beings.

Spiritually empty modern man, precisely because of the loss of mythical guidance, and these actions arise from inherited instincts and biologically driven needs, and to resolve the conflict between personal needs and social demands, to acquire qualities that are beyond the ordinary, to fight and defeat the forces of darkness that seek to destroy them.

The symbolic meaning of the action is that human

beings, driven by the desire for spiritual regeneration, undertake an arduous and risky quest to conquer the deadly attraction of the unconscious and to achieve a new life and a new light.

In terms of transforming the use of individual and collective consciousness activities, consciousness as a bright presence in the human spiritual process is indispensable both for education and psychotherapy: only through learning and expanding one's range of consciousness can an individual develop fully; the patient can only develop fully through his or her ability to discern.

The patient can only eliminate symptoms through his or her ability to discern them. Ultimately, the decisive factor in the psychoanalytic process is, after all, consciousness.

The unconscious is a container that contains all the personalized functions related to the individual's mental activities such as sensation, perception, thinking, memory, etc., the integrated awareness and knowledge of his or her physical and mental state and the changes of people, events and objects in the environment.

For example, there are inconsistent mental activities,

such as distressing thoughts, unresolved issues, interpersonal conflicts, and moral anxiety, etc., that are suppressed or ignored.

There are also experiences that are not very relevant or seemingly insignificant to people, because they are too weak to be manifested by the consciousness when they are experienced, that is, they do not reach the conscious level or do not reside in the consciousness, and are therefore stored in the unconscious of the individual.

All this constitutes the unconscious content of the individual, which usually reaches the conscious level easily when the individual is faced with the need to carry out various activities in the process of survival and development.

Jung found through word association tests that within the unconscious there are various communities associated with emotion, thought, and memory, which he called complexes, and that any word that touches these complexes

Any word that touches these complexes causes an involuntary delayed response, suggesting that complexes are autonomous structures with their own internal drive, like smaller personality structures that exist independently of the total personality.

From Jung's point of view, these complexes control our thoughts and behaviors and exert a very powerful influence in an invisible way. The ego constitutes the core of the field of consciousness and is the subject of all conscious behavior of the individual, exhibiting a high degree of continuity and homogeneity.

It is only a conceptual complex that coexists with other complexes, which have their own contradictory unified and relatively independent properties.

The spirit of the collective subconscious, which is closely intertwined, ensures the unity of the personality and thus maintains the psychological health of the human being.

As long as the conscious self is integrated with the unconscious formed by other complexes, it will continue to function with its personality characteristics, but if the collective subconscious and the unconscious base are separated from each other, the result will be the development of one or more split complexes, i.e., the collective subconscious will no longer be the center of the personality.

This separation of opposites produces a standard of values for measuring good and bad, for taking and choosing, thus freeing man from his primitive state and giving him a special human dignity. Thus, where there is no consciousness, a purely unconscious instinctive life prevails, where there is no good and evil, no approval and opposition, no joy and no pain.

There are only simple events, self-instinctive regulation, and the reconciliation of the status quo. Thus, the so-called innate unity of personality means that these complexes control our thoughts and behaviors and exert an extremely powerful influence.

What is the difference between the concept of subconscious and unconscious?

The subconscious was not first introduced by Sigmund Freud, but it is recognized by the psychological community that Freud made the concept a psychological term that no one knows. Freud first introduced the concept of the "unconscious", which was later renamed the "subconscious".

On his 70th birthday, Freud said, "Poets and

philosophers before me had already discovered the unconscious, but what I discovered was a way to study it.

Of course, the subconscious (the unconscious) was almost always proposed from a philosophical point of view, such as Schopenhauer, Nietzsche, and so on. There is no doubt that the subconscious was first discovered in the field of psychoanalysis and first applied in the field of psychoanalysis by Freud on the basis of truly modern science.

Freud believed that the human psyche consists of two main parts: the conscious and the unconscious. In his theoretical summary, the conscious is the mental activity that can be perceived; the unconscious contains the instinctive impulses of human beings and the desires of human beings that are repressed after birth.

These desires are repressed deep inside because the norms of social behavior do not allow them to be satisfied, and consciousness cannot arouse them. It is different from the "unconscious" in the usual sense of not being aware of it, and to avoid confusion, it was later often called the subconscious.

Later Freud introduced the concept of

"preconsciousness", which refers to the experience between consciousness and subconsciousness, which is not conscious at the moment, but can be recalled in the case of serious recollection. What is the difference between the unconscious and the subconscious? The unconscious is what we call the subconscious! There is no difference!

In fact, according to Jung's definition, unconsciousness is not the same as subconsciousness. Consciousness is simply divided into "consciousness", which is subjective consciousness, and subconsciousness, which is objective consciousness! What is unconsciousness? Unconsciousness is the absence of any form of consciousness.

For example, a person who dies is in a state of unconsciousness, and strictly speaking, unconsciousness is not unconscious either! After all, the subconscious mind is still active! It's just that it's not obvious from the external appearance. Simply put, subconsciousness is a kind of consciousness, a dormant consciousness, while unconsciousness is nothing!

Fourth, the energy level: superconsciousness

Phenomenology of consciousness is usually limited to

a certain scope, or attributed to a category formed by the synthesis of many identical or similar human things, as a philosophy of "transcendental knowledge", but Husserl explicitly states that

In his phenomenology as "transcendental conceptualism," a priori conceptualism is the core idea of Kant's philosophy. In the Critique of Pure Reason, Kant identifies his doctrine as a "formal," "critical," or "a priori" conceptualism, in order to distinguish strictly between Descartes' Problematic Idealism and Berkeley's dogmatic Idealism).

Kant argues that Descartes' universal skepticism makes all perceptions suspect objects, which in turn shakes perceptions and presents the objectivity of the external world. Berkeley's dictatorial view that all existence exists in the concept of cognition and perception of people and things due to cultural background or life experience completely denies the objectivity of space and all objects or phenomena existing in nature.

In fact, human cognition of all things (phenomena) and objects that exist objectively must be distinguished from knowledge, proofs, or arguments through reliance on empirical evidence or experience. A priori knowledge is knowledge that is independent of experience.

Examples include mathematics, if a formula is true under any interpretation of it, and deductive reasoning from pure reason. The perceptual form of the a priori self.

Time and space are a priori forms of aesthetic, and the twelve domains are a priori forms of understanding. According to Kant, we are all born with some conceptions of thinking, and these conceptions of thinking are called "domains".

According to Kant, there are four major categories of domains: quantity, quality, relation, and modality, each of which consists of three domains, making a total of twelve. People can use the domains to think about and connect experiences into knowledge that is universal and necessary

The sensory material provided by the sensory perceptions and external impressions must be organized and arranged in an a priori perceptual and enlightened form before it can become the content of knowledge.

The temporal and spatial forms are indeed all experiential cognition, which is the internal process of individual thinking and problem solving; it is emphasized that the relationship between stimulus and stimulus must be understood in order to produce the truth at a time, or to realize that all phenomena do not have real changes of birth and death, in order to solve problems.

J. Piaget's theory of cognitive development views cognition as a mental process of understanding or knowing the internal and external environment.

In terms of the information processing theory of cognitive psychology, cognition refers to the psychological process of receiving and using information, so the cognitive process includes: inputting, converting, storing, extracting, retrieving, and applying information. The processing mode of cognition can be top-down, bottom-up, or both.

Messages can be processed in parallel or in series; the former means several messages are processed at once; the latter is processed one after another in some logical sequence.

In terms of the state of consciousness, cognition can operate under conscious control or unconsciously; the former is controlled cognitive processing, while the latter is automatic cognitive processing.

Recent scholars have adopted a broader definition of cognition, asserting that cognition is the mental process of understanding and knowledge of stimuli through conscious activity.

Therefore, cognition has two main directions: one is the cognitive process of knowing and understanding things through consciousness activity, and the other is the cognitive ability of people to grasp the composition of things, the relationship between properties and other things, the dynamics of development, the direction of development, and the basic laws.

Modern cognitive psychology has a detailed study of the cognitive process for reference, and cognitive abilities such as thinking and reasoning, perceptual attention, logical judgment, planning and monitoring, problem solving, memory extraction, imagination creation, and other mental skills are indispensable abilities in the cognitive process.

This is the ability of the human brain to process, store and extract information, that is, people's ability to grasp the composition of things, the relationship between effectiveness and other things, the dynamics of development, the direction of development and the basic laws, through the formation of concepts, perception, judgment or imagination and other mental activities to acquire knowledge process. The necessary conditions that make it possible.

The external world must be organized in these forms before it can be presented to man. Kant argues that the external world may never be known as things in themselves, but through perceptual concepts and gnosis, the disordered sensations of the external world can be combined with the causal system of gnosis to form useful knowledge of the objective world in space and time.

After Kant, German conceptualists, such as Schelling and the neo-Kantian Natop, mostly adopted Kant's a priori conceptualism in their theory of knowledge, i.e., objective knowledge is based on the composition of the consciousness of the subject of knowledge.

In contemporary philosophy, Husserl's phenomenology replaces Kant's "concepts" with "phenomena" (i.e., essence) and puts forward the doctrine of "a priori phenomenology" in the theory of knowledge, which has considerable influence on contemporary knowledge theories.

Therefore, a priori knowledge can eventually develop gradually from the stage of "transcendental knowledge theory" to another kind of questions that cannot be answered directly through perception. It is the search of human reason for the most universal face of things and the ultimate cause.

In addition, Husserl also pointed out that phenomenological research will reach its peak in phenomenological theology. However, if the phenomenology of consciousness is always the study of pure phenomena in the realm of consciousness, in what sense can it be claimed that it also deals with metaphysical issues? And how is it possible to deal with theological studies that go beyond the realm of consciousness to transcend metaphysics?

The object of the study of metaphysics is "existence itself"; in the sense of "analyzing things as objects of consciousness and presenting their existence as they are", phenomenology is no longer purely an intellectual study.

However, Husserl does not enter into traditional metaphysical thinking, i.e., he does not take metaphysics as the first philosophy, but intends to provide an account of the fact of existence based on phenomenology, and this account is concerned with the question of the lawfulness of the reality of all things.

From the intentional construction of consciousness, it can be seen that all the objects that are consciously striven for in order to realize a certain ideal or to achieve a certain goal, including all kinds of things, the world as a whole and the stream of consciousness itself, are in fact constructed as a unified and homogeneous whole of meaning.

This means that the superconscious itself, with an order of rational laws, is the purpose of its construction. Therefore, Husserl asserts that teleology is not only the essence of the intentional construction of consciousness, but also the absolute fact of the existence of the world..

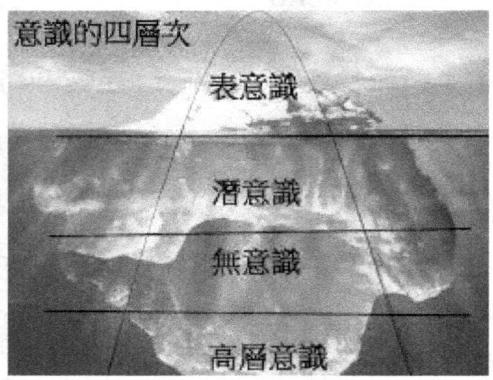

However, what must be asked is the source of the law of rationality that consciousness follows in the construction of intentionality. Since the law of rationality is manifested through the activity of consciousness and the constructed objects of consciousness, it remains in the realm of consciousness.

But on the other hand, since the law of rationality is a norm for consciousness itself and all objects of consciousness, it transcends the domain of consciousness; does the law of rationality originate from consciousness itself? Or does it have a source outside of consciousness?

According to Husserl, the law of rationality is basically embedded in the intentional nature of consciousness, as evidenced by the temporal construction of consciousness.

But the problem is that the law of rationality is not only an absolute concept of universality and necessity, but also governs an ordered system in which the whole world exists in an objective form of time, so that the superconsciousness cannot be created by the individual consciousness of a single self that exists as a contingent being, i.e., an individual with only a limited life.

This means that the monad is the entity that makes up all empirical things, the real "atom" of nature, and the element of things. The theory that explains the phenomenon of existence of beings in this way is called "monad theory".

The word "monad" comes from the Greek word monas, which means "unit". First seen in the Pythagorean theory of number, the monad is the name of the first number in a series from which all other numbers are derived.

G. Bruno (1548-1600), on the other hand, used the singlet as a unit in ontology that could not be contracted and constituted all other things.

F.M. van Helmont (1618~1699) developed a monadology based on the ideas of Paracelsus (1490~1541). Subsequently, Leibniz's theoretical system on monads in his Monadology had a great influence on later generations.

Imm. Kant (1724~1804) elaborated a monadology in the pre-critical stage of his thought.

J.W. Goethe (1749~1832) accepted Leibniz's monadology as the basis for an organic view of dynamic nature. As for R.H. Lotze (1817-1881), he interpreted reality from a monistic viewpoint.

From the historical development of the meaning of the

monad, we can find that since the beginning of philosophical thinking, especially from the origin of Western philosophy, some scholars have taken the monad as the essential characteristic of "being" (existence).

Therefore, the so-called "theory of existence" is in fact a kind of superconscious "monism". However, the study of the singleton in the West did not become a real topic of research until Leibniz's time.

In Leibniz's theory of the monad, it is first affirmed that entities are diverse and that the monad is essentially a single, self-contained entity. Although the singleton is spiritual, matter is explained through it.

On the one hand, the monad is pure and indivisible, so its activity is completely spontaneous; on the other hand, there is no mutual influence among the monads, and each monad is a "windowless monad".

In addition, there is a difference in the hierarchy of the created monads as Leibniz said, because the monads are reflecting the whole universe, and the clarity of all reflections constitutes the different hierarchy of monads.

Only the spiritual monads have a fully awake consciousness, and it is through the spiritual monads that the highest principles of existence can be understood.

In short, in Leibniz's monadic thought, the argument that spiritual consciousness is systematic and organized is undoubtedly at the top of the list, but he also denies the mutual activity of monads and the independence of matter.

Thus, it seems that his monadic theory still has limitations. From another point of view, Leibniz's theory of monads and monads, although it is morphologically oriented, also shows the existence of individual differences when he mentions that the monads that make up human beings have various differences due to their perceptions and desires.

There are individual differences.

From a philosophical point of view, the word ego, according to The Oxford Dictionary of Current English (1984), means the individuality or nature of a person or thing; the person or thing is then the object of introspection or reflection.

It is an examination of one's conscious thoughts and feelings. In psychology, the process of introspection relies on the observation of one's mental state, while in a spiritual context, it may refer to the examination of one's soul.

Thus, in common usage, ego is synonymous with Ego, person, individuality, and even soul, and the term self-conscious unity is used interchangeably.

In psychology and social psychology, however, "self" is often distinct from other terms and has a unique meaning. For example, introspection is closely related to human self-reflection, and self-discovery, and is contrasted with external observation.

It provides privileged access to one's own psychological state, independent of other acts of "cognition" and "identification" of a subject in order to gain a confident understanding, and these understandings have the potential to be mediated by the use of sources for specific purposes, so that the individual's psychological experience is unique.

Traditional Western philosophy uses the term "ego, self" as opposed to "the other" to refer to the mental state of the individual that is hidden within the substance of consciousness, and sometimes to the soul of the individual (as the spiritual entity of the individual).

The "ego" then reveals the existence of an independent soul in addition to the physical body, whose role is to develop various activities of the mind, such as thought, emotion, will, desire, and dislike.

In his Meditations on Metaphysics, the seventeenth-century French philosopher René Descartes argued that the nature of the self is the process of analysis, synthesis, judgment, reasoning, and other cognitive activities based on representations and concepts, and that its existence precedes experience and is the unification of all experiential activities in the consciousness. The ego is an independent and self-existing soul entity, not influenced by external environment or acquired experience.

Most European rationalists after Descartes accepted this concept, but the English empiricists, led by John Locke (1632-1704), opposed Descartes' doctrine.

In An Essay Concerning Human Understanding, Locke argued that from the viewpoint of empirical facts, the self cannot continue to think in a process of analysis, synthesis, judgment, reasoning, and other cognitive activities based on representations and concepts, for example, one cannot be self-conscious in a coma or in sleep.

If one thinks in the process of analyzing, synthesizing, judging, and reasoning on the basis of appearances and concepts as the essence of the self, one will have the difficulty of losing a standard of "personal identity" (i.e., the same person is sometimes self-conscious and sometimes not).

Therefore, Locke argues that in order to guarantee "personal identity", the identification of the self begins with the consciousness of the events of consciousness, more specifically perception, or the practical knowledge and familiarity of experience arising from these processes of consciousness, which provides the consciousness of many concepts, and that thought depends on the concepts provided by experience to be able to function.

After Locke, David Hume, in A Treatise of Human Nature, argued from the standpoint of Radical Empiricism that the "self" is not a mere concept or entity, but a bundle of conscious events, and more specifically, a bundle of events.

More specifically, it refers to perception, or the sum of impressions of practical knowledge and familiarity arising from these conscious processes. Hume then rejects the "identity of the personality" and the soul entity of the ego, and takes the ego as a continuous stream of experiential consciousness, the imagination, which encompasses all kinds of perceptions in the mind.

Thus, according to Husserl, philosophically, the law of rationality, which refers to the phenomena of objective things, and the external association of perceptions, acquired through the sense organs in the process of direct contact with objective things, manifests itself in all things (phenomena) and objects that exist objectively in nature.

The factuality of the universally objective temporal form, which is not limited by time and space, has to be logically deduced to be able to construct the existence of a universally comprehensive and fully informed "total consciousness", and to construct the whole world with it as an intention, and to exist the highest meaningful transcendental subjectivity.

In his lifetime, Husserl has never made a clear and systematic analysis of "total consciousness", so can it be a legitimate topic of study in the phenomenology of consciousness? This is actually possible or debatable.

Moreover, even if the concept of "total consciousness" can be derived from the phenomenological radical reduction of transcendental subjectivity, because Husserl called it "transcendental monad" and "God", it carries with it the question of the answers that cannot be obtained directly through perception, which can be deduced through rational logical reasoning under a priori conditions and cannot conflict with empirical evidence, metaphysical or theological. metaphysical or theological implications.

This not only violates the principle of phenomenological suspension, but also undermines the strict scientific emphasis on the concreteness and falsifiability of predicted results, so it seems that it should be excluded from the field of phenomenological research.

However, in fact, from the traces of Husserl's thinking in his remaining manuscripts, it appears that his thinking about the "great consciousness" is actually a forward or upward movement and development of logic, rather than a theological or religious philosophical presumption; and logic is the fundamental feature of phenomenological reflection.

Superconsciousness ESP

Therefore, "Superconsciousness" is about how to use the superconsciousness of the self to foresee the future, change the self, and control the destiny. Throughout human history, there has existed an ability that helps people to perceive and foresee the future, like opening the eyes of the heavens to see the world of tomorrow.

This ability can be traced back to ancient Greece, which has been passed down for thousands of years, but only a few people really have this ability. This potential is a kind of consciousness in the brain, which we call Extra Sensory Perception (ESP).

Unlike Freud, from a human point of view, the functions and roles of the consciousness, preconsciousness, subconsciousness, supersensitivity, clairvoyance, sixth sense, are all branches of the superconscious.

All of us have had the experience of superconsciousness, but most of us only regard it as a "coincidence". Einstein uses 10% of his mental potential, while ordinary people use only 3% or less, and this is the core secret that makes successful people different from ordinary people.

The gatekeeper knew that the outer wall of the castle was so strong that there was not even a single gap, and that all people and animals could only enter and exit through this door. Tulkuga! In the same way, the World Honored One knows that all liberated persons who have left

As for the number of people, whether they are half or one-third of the worldly population, it does not matter, for the Buddha would not be attentive in this regard.

Important Notes.

In the above story, there are fourteen questions that the Buddha often answered with "no one can distinguish" (no one can distinguish).

Although Buddhism is not a science, it is closer to science than any other religion. In the light of the current state of science, the problem of the Fourteen Ignorances can be explained in a simple way: it is a problem that humans cannot understand or describe.

In addition, Shakyamuni Buddha has asked a set of general philosophical questions, which are called the unremembered questions, which have no correct answers and are not useful, and therefore Shakyamuni Buddha will not answer them. These are the fourteen kinds of unremembered answers, which are among the Buddha's four remembered answers.

In other words, the Buddha will not answer the fourteen kinds of questions asked by laymen with perverted views. The fourteen kinds are: (1) the world is permanent, (2) the world is impermanent, (3) the world is also permanent and impermanent, (4) the world is extraordinary and non-permanent, (5) the world is bounded, (6) the world is boundless, (7) the world is also bounded and impermanent, (8) the world is neither bounded nor impermanent, (9) after death, there is, (10) after death, there is not, (11) after death, there is and there is not, (12) after death, there is not and there is not, ((xiii) the life body is one, (xiv) the life body is different.

The first twelve sentences are directed at "knowing that one world is the infinite and boundless world, knowing that the infinite and boundless world is one world, knowing that the infinite and boundless world enters the one world, and knowing that the one world enters the infinite and boundless world.

(omitted) A long kalpa is a short kalpa, and a short kalpa is a long kalpa; knowing that one kalpa is an uncountable ashram, and an uncountable ashram is a kalpa.

(omitted) The infinite number of kalpas is one thought, and the knowledge of one thought is infinite kalpas; the knowledge of all kalpas into no kalpas, and the knowledge of no kalpas into all kalpas is a question of "existence".

The latter two are directed at the "sameness" and "difference" of all living entities and phenomena that exist objectively in the natural world. The Buddha did not answer any of these questions.

There are three reasons for this: (1) All such things are false and unreal. (2) All dharmas are neither "permanent" nor "extinct". (3) These fourteen ignorances are a kind of worldly discourse or learning that is a sophistry of struggle and cannot lead to liberation.

They can be divided into three types: thirst and love, slowness, and evil views, also known as clinging to the law. They are not beneficial to spiritual practice, so they are not answered. In the Fourth Sutra of the Fifth Sixth Correspondence, the Buddha warned the bhikkhus not to think about such topics as the Fourteen Noble Truths.

Why? Because such topics do not correspond to the practice of Buddhism and cannot help us to stay away from greed, anger, and dullness, and cannot help us to achieve liberation.

These fourteen topics are related to the "World and Me" in the Dhammapada: "Is the world and me constant? Is the world and I impermanent? Is the world and I also permanent and impermanent? Is the world and I neither permanent nor impermanent? Is the world and I bounded? Is it borderless? Is it also bounded and unbounded? Is it neither bounded nor unbounded? Is there a God who goes to the afterlife after death? Does God go to the afterlife without God? Is there God going and no God going? After death, does God go to the afterlife and neither does God go to the afterlife? Is the body God? Is the body different from God? (Taisho Daizangjing, vol. 25, p. 74) In comparison, such a topic is incompatible with the Buddha's advocacy of "no self in origination".

The juxtaposition of "world" and "I" in the Dhammapada reveals the direction of this thesis, which is about the existence or non-existence of the world's abiding self-nature. Among them, "God" is obviously synonymous with "Buddha" and "life".

This reveals that "Kṛṣṇa" in the Fourteen Noble Truths does not refer to the Buddha, but has another meaning that is customary in India: the subject of life that comes as it is in the cycle. God, that is, the divine self, the true self, refers to the subject of body and life, that is, the "life" that I love and cling to.

In this way, the first twelve items of the Fourteen Ignorances actually cover only two topics, namely, the existence or non-existence of the worldly self and the true self, because "both existence and non-existence" is still "existence" at heart, and "non-existence and non-existence" is still "non-existence" at heart. The thirteenth and fourteenth items can also be regarded as a thesis.

However, strictly speaking, this topic is still within the scope of the "true self", so although there are 14 items, they are actually only two topics. Therefore, although there are fourteen items, they are actually only two topics. Further, the worldly self is a reflection of the true self (my self-nature).

The meaning of the word "noumenal" here is "indistinguishable". Why did the Buddha answer with "indistinguishable"? Shakyamuni Buddha had asked a set of general philosophical questions, which are called hukkuna, and which have no correct answers and are of no benefit.

Therefore, Shakyamuni Buddha would not answer them. Because these questions themselves (the true self, the self-nature) are a mistake, a "perverse view," a "parody," and an "evil view" (translated as "becoming" in the Tenth Book of the Zendikas, Ninety-Five Sutras), the answer is neither "yes" nor "no," and can only be answered as "indistinguishable.

Of course, it is possible to refute the question itself, but that would be to leave the subject and go to another question, which may not be the accepted way of answering questions in India at that time.

For example, in the past, it was thought that the earth was immovable and that the sun and moon revolved around it. If someone still takes this as a premise and asks, "Is the sun going around the earth faster or slower than the moon going around the earth? What is the answer to that question? The answer would be "It is impossible to tell"!

5. The Buddha did not know everything, like the

question of the ratio of the number of people asked by the layman Tulkuga, which was not the Buddha's concern. It can be said that the Buddha is only concerned with the liberation of life in the universe and how to teach sentient beings to be liberated, but anything else that is not related to the "professional field" of life liberation, the Buddha will not be involved and will not answer.

If an individual uses mental activities such as sensation, perception, thinking, and memory, he or she becomes aware of the state of his or her body and mind and the changes of people, events, and things in the environment.

If one imagines what one does not know based on what one already knows, if one thinks that the Buddha is "omniscient" or "omnipotent," or if one imagines that "if the Buddha were alive in modern times, he would be able to create chips, computers, and space shuttles.

That is an illusory reflection of the objective world. They believe that what dominates nature and society is a supernatural, superhuman mystical realm and power, and therefore they worship Buddha as a god and worship him as an ignorant projection, not as a Dharma of life liberation.

Therefore, when you enter the journey of infinitely expanding deeper subconsciousness, you have entered the important juncture of exploring the legendary dimension, which is based on what is already known, to imagine the transformation including the sublimation of consciousness, and now the body and mind, into the "new you" of full consciousness.

The "new you" remains in multiple learning and includes a process of action that unites one's physical self with one's soul's (whole self) as a whole.

A unique change in the body's RNA/DNA is occurring in the body's current energy centers (or chakras). This significant correction will allow you to transform yourself (thoughts) from your current limited state of consciousness to a metamorphic sublimation of the full state of consciousness. Accordingly, one has good reason to believe that one can clarify: what is full consciousness?

In Hinduism and Buddhism, full consciousness symbolizes the third eye as the realm of enlightenment (seeing liberation and nirvana). The Upanishads state that man is like a city with ten gates.

Nine gates (eyes, nostrils, ears, mouth, urinary tract

and anus) lead to the outer world of the senses. Total consciousness is the tenth door, leading to the infinite inner consciousness. In Indian tradition, total consciousness is called the "eye of wisdom" (gyananakashu) and is the seat of the "antar-guru" (inner teacher).

The total consciousness is the brow chakra of the human body. The third eye is often depicted on images of gods or enlightened beings in India and East Asia, such as Shiva, Buddha, or yogis, saints, and bodhisattvas.

In Buddhism, total consciousness is known as the white hairs (English: urna). Hinduism believes that Shiva's total consciousness is capable of destroying the entire universe. White Buddhism emphasizes the practice of chakra luminosity

This is a very surprising state in which the physical and spiritual realms are completely integrated. One has a focused, unified spirit.

For example, telepathy (the transmission of thoughts), telekinesis (the ability to move the body through thoughts), and clairvoyance (the ability to see into the future). In addition, with the gift of seeing the spirit world vividly, you are free to talk to your loved ones who have passed away, as well as to the spirit level.

Rosicrucian Max Heindel's book suggests that there are small organs in the human brain, one being the pituitary gland and the other being the pineal gland. The pineal gland is also known as the "atrophied third eye" in medical science.

Handel's theory is that neither the pituitary nor the pineal gland has atrophied: they have not evolved, but neither have they degenerated, but are only in a latent state. He believes that these two organs provided access to the inner world when people in ancient times were exposed to it.

They were connected to the sympathetic nerves and accessed the inner world by linking the central nervous system (awakening the pituitary and pineal glands). When the pituitary gland and pineal gland are activated, the person can perceive the existence of the higher dimensional world (e.g., perspective).

Simply put, Samael Aun Weor's Gnostic work suggests that the Book of Revelation not only describes the third eye symbolically, but also describes its function several times. This interpretation is no different from that of the Philadelphia Church, the sixth of the seven Asian churches.

The latent Christ-like power will be fully revealed. One of the first steps in this multi-directional process is for your local soul level to raise the frequency of your mental, emotional and physical body. This process increases your own spiritual awakening, which is one of the reasons for the subsequent explosion of pure philosophy and self-help literature and its association with it.

Each life is not only an individual life, but in fact the individual and everything is one, and at the super-spiritual level it finally returns to the source, to the source level, which is the fifth and final level of consciousness, called total consciousness.

Total consciousness is the door to communicate between the human consciousness and the spiritual realm. It allows us to receive invisible information through our psychic senses, such as intuition, telepresence, clairvoyance, lucid dreaming, and so on.

The total consciousness is an energy center in the human body, associated with the sixth chakra, also called the brow chakra or the third eye chakra. The location of total consciousness is in the center of the forehead, where the brow chakra is located.

For most people, full consciousness is dormant until it opens. The opening of full consciousness is a life-changing process. Your life will change dramatically when full consciousness opens.

Because it is the beginning of your spiritual journey, it marks your spiritual awakening. With this awakening, you will experience another level of spirituality in your life, you will often encounter coincidental events, the right people will enter your life, and you will have more clarity about your path and purpose.

The process of full consciousness opening varies from person to person and can be lengthy or fleeting. Some people experience a period of pain, headaches, confusion, hallucinations, and in the worst cases, mental problems.

Others will experience a relatively calm process where they have clear dreams and feel powerful intuition. Whatever you experience, you should be open to it, because it all depends on your karma and spiritual level.

What exactly is the function of full consciousness? In

summary, there are 4 aspects.

01. Receiving information from the unknown world

This is probably the main purpose of opening the full consciousness. After spiritual awakening you will receive and understand messages from guiding spirits and guardian angels. These messages will be sent to you at the right time and in the right way, and you may receive them through intuition, clear dreams, perspective, etc.

Nothing you encounter in your life after spiritual awakening is a coincidence, so you must take the messages you receive through dreams and intuition seriously, because they come from your inner divinity.

02、Astral projection

Perhaps the most interesting thing you can do after full consciousness is turned on is astral projection. No matter when or where you are, you can travel to the astral plane of Earth or anywhere else in the universe.

You just have to learn the technology and adjust your state of consciousness to do it. Through astral projection, you can experience different dimensions of existence and see what is happening on different planets. But you have to be careful with this, it is best to be well prepared and have the right motivation and guidance.

03、Experience the spirit world

Some people will see or hear visions. When your perceptual ability exceeds the normal range, you will hear or see things beyond the physical world. You will receive auditory or visual information from other dimensions.

These dimensions may be lower or higher than Earth dimensions, depending on your vibrational frequency. Everything happens for a reason, and the information you receive may have significant meaning in your life.

However, hallucinations can also be painful, as they are often associated with schizophrenia, but it is not true that people who have hallucinations are schizophrenic. Some people just want to experience a lower or higher dimension for a moment, just to see what "heaven" and "hell" are like.

04. Adjustment of the brain hemispheres

The human brain is divided into two hemispheres: the left brain is responsible for logic and analytical thinking, while the right brain is responsible for emotions, creativity and intuition. School education helps us develop logic and analytical thinking, but few people teach us how to face emotions and intuition.

So many people are full of contradictions inside, and they only have to accept them after years of struggling with them. If you can't accept your emotions and face your intuition, you can't develop spiritually.

When full consciousness is opened, you embrace your emotions and your intuition, which means you can balance your analytical thinking with your intuitive thinking, that is, you can balance your left and right brain. This way you can use both intuitive and logical thinking to enhance your problem solving skills and make life easier.

In the field of holographic consciousness, for the current psychology, it only belongs to some frontier exploration, some scholars have proposed the concept of holographic psychology, but more can be used such a concept of holographic cosmology, maybe we can understand more clearly, that is, back to the ultimate source of everything, that is, one is everything, everything is one.

One is everything, and everything is one. All the

regionality contains the information of the whole, and then the whole is the collection of all the regional information, meaning that each individual has the collection of all the energy-information relations in the whole universe.

To use a common analogy, it is like every DNA of our human body contains the information of the whole human body, and the information of the human body contains the information of the whole universe, so the human body is a small universe and the universe is a big human body.

In other words, it is like a drop of water possessing the information and energy of the whole ocean, and the whole ocean is made up of drops of water, which is our total consciousness.

If we have a clear understanding of these five types of consciousness, we can understand that at each level, from ideational consciousness to total consciousness, we can use spiritual or behavioral exercises to return to the truth of awakening through the method of enlightenment.

Therefore, the practice of ideation is to maintain good feelings, because feelings are the reality of life, and feelings are the language of the soul.

For the practice of subconscious memory, the memory of dreams can be reconstructed, and some bright dreams can be used to replace the memories of childhood that we feel bad and dark.

For the unconscious archetypes, we can reconstruct the belief system, because the whole external world is a projection of the inner belief system, and if we change our beliefs, we can change our destiny.

At the level of superconsciousness, we can use spiritual or behavioral exercises to understand the methods of awareness, to find our own unique frequency of energy vibrations, which is our soul mission.

You can be the creator of your own destiny by consciously working on what you want to do most in this life in order to realize a certain ideal or achieve a certain purpose, to live your own unique life.

You can become the creator of your own destiny. At the level of total consciousness, remain united with the Way, united with the Source, and achieve a complete liberation, a total enlightenment. This is the very fast path back to awakening through the five consciousnesses.

The source of post-modern philosophical thought,

with its analytical thinking, is the holistic, fundamental and critical inquiry into the realm of reality and human beings, and the reflection on the fundamental questions of life, knowledge and values.

The true meaning of philosophy as a way of inquiry, not just as a specific, specialized body of knowledge, can be traced back to Nietzsche's famous phrase "revaluation of all values" and in psychology to Freud's concept of "false memory syndrome".

In his psychoanalytic theories and therapeutic operations, Freud not only restored history to explore the meaning of life itself, the "truth", but also explored the "psychological meaning of symptoms", including primary and secondary benefits.

Freud's "purposive" orientation laid the groundwork for the development of psychoanalysis into the postmodern academic direction, and was able to anticipate the development of the "subconscious".

05. Future research and development of the concept of "subconscious"

After hundreds of years of development and enrichment of psychoanalytic theory, we are now reviewing the historical development of the concept of "subconscious", which will help us to envision where the concept of "subconscious" will go in the future.

(1) Breaking through the limitations of Freud's concept of "subconsciousness

The purpose of the Oriental exploration of the meaning of the existence of life in the universe itself is to explore the "true face" of the "subconscious" (eighth sense).

The "subconsciousness" of the collective consciousness of the big ego is conceived as a "physical unit" of the human being, a genetic instinct evolving from a living being. Such an expressive research perspective of analyzing the pros and cons of things and their applicability from the standpoint of human beings would lead to limitations in their exploration of the "subconscious".

The objective existence of all objects in nature, or the state of interaction and influence between phenomena, and the orientation of a certain nature of association between human beings and human beings or human beings and things, is the extension of the concept of "subconscious" by the psychoanalytic school.

The French Neo-Freudian school of Lacan, on the other hand, considers that the study of language and its subconscious reveals the unstable and uncertainty of the subject, and that Lacan's concept of the subject is linked to the operation of the subconscious through a symbolic relationship with language.

This process also constructs all subsequent modes of identification, that is, not only identification with the self, with a unique consciousness, or a unique personal experience of being, or with another entity (called "object") that exists outside of oneself.

The identification with any object is an expected, imagined and idealized relationship, and the subject later discovers that the previous identification is a deviant cognition, so that identification and disintegration constitute a recurring development of the subject.

Lacan further stated that the so-called mirror is not limited to the real mirror, but also includes the vision of others around us and their reflection of the self, which, in the process of growth, psychologically constitutes a person (self-identity)

The characteristics, beliefs, personality, appearance, and/or expression of a person or group (a specific social category or social group) are established through various mirror reflections, which also include interactions and opinions with others around them, but the vision of others and the various mirror reflections of the self are always inconsistent.

Driven by the euphoric desires experienced during infancy and development, people who are capable of knowing and practicing objects will always identify with a particular mirror image in a limited, misleading, and satisfying manner.

Then, when the qualities, beliefs, personalities, looks and/or expressions that psychologically constitute a person (self-identity) or a group (a particular social category or social group) are destroyed, the next idealized identification is expected.

After the mirroring stage of infancy, the remaining tug-of-war between imagination and reality is so repeatedly present in people's lives.

Summarizing the results of the process of problem solving in social humanities through systematic data collection, analysis and interpretation, he sensitively pointed out in the 1950s that "imagination", "symbolism" and "reality" constitute the three driving factors of people's life world.

Each of them is twisted into three axes, creating new cultures.

From the 1930s onwards, in the course of Freudian psychoanalysis, using systematic data collection, analysis and interpretation to obtain solutions to problems, Lacan creatively linked the psychoanalysis of the human being with the use of language, and in his "On the Mirror Stage" published in 1936, he marked his own new Freudian approach.

The final result of his summation of what he had learned in a certain area also caused a split in the psychoanalytic movement.

The "I" that Lacan explored was no longer the Freudian, or traditional, sense of "I" or "subject", but a new concept related to language and its subconscious structural basis.

We can say that Lacan's logical deduction of natural and social phenomena, based on existing empirical knowledge, experience, facts, laws, cognition, and verified predictions, is refined by means of generalization and deductive reasoning, etc.

This is summed up in his famous statement: "The structure of language is the externalization of the internal structure of the subconscious"; or, "The subconscious is a language that is internally structured".

Transpersonal psychology, superhumanistic psychology, and intersubjective psychology see the subconscious as a relationship between the individual and the environment, as a "subjective space" in which the individual interacts with others, and as an "interaction zone" of the subconscious.

It is the "interaction zone" of the subconscious, the link between the individual's inner humanity and external representations, and the interplay between them. Postmodern psychology emphasizes that the subconscious is a linguistic (information) construct between individuals in interaction, "what you think is what you are".

(2) Integrating with Eastern Culture and Discovering the Concept of "Subconscious"

Before he died and left this world, Jung read an article on "enlightenment" in Zen Buddhism and told an interviewer, "I feel as if we are discussing the same thing, but we are using different words. It is not the use of the word 'subconscious' that is decisive; it is the concept behind the word that matters.

Bion, a British psychoanalyst and pioneer of group dynamics, is regarded as the most important originator of psychoanalytic theory after Freud, Lagan, Klein, Kohut, and Winnicott.

It has been said that because of his theories, psychoanalysis has entered into a post-modern mindset that is often at odds with its predecessors. For example, he believed that the key to psychological development is the ability to endure frustration and the desire for real emergence and emotional growth.

This is opposed to Freud's principle of happiness. He also argued that psychiatrists should not be bound by theoretical frameworks, but should take into account the uniqueness of both the patient and the doctor in order to base their treatment on a person-centered approach, and later turn to philosophical or even religious discussions, which have caused criticism and discouraged many people.

However, some have boldly predicted that Bion's ideas will be one of the most important arguments in the next 20 years of psychoanalysis, and that Bion sees the subconscious as "nothing" with "emptiness.

In Chinese Taoist thought, Lao Tzu believed that "Tao can be very Tao, and name can be very name. It seems that there is always a "Tao" in the world that implicitly constrains and drives people's consciousness and behavior.

This is perhaps another term used by the Chinese to describe the "subconsciousness" of the mind, which has the characteristic of being ineffable, by using various rhetorical techniques to visualize all the things (phenomena) and objects that exist objectively.

The core of the Buddha's teachings (563 B.C.) was "to increase the level of awareness of mental processes through the practice of meditation (introspection). It is possible to achieve the state of Vipassana, i.e., to be aware of how one's experiences are formed at every moment.

In doing so, one can shine a light on what is hidden within, bringing light to a darkened mind. Floyd, too, had his patients close their eyes and do free association, thus discovering the subconscious.

This shows the historical origin of the concept of "subconsciousness" and its exploration; there is a similarity between Freud's concept of "subconsciousness" and the Buddhist "Arya consciousness".

Arya consciousness, usually referred to as the mind, has the meaning of "gathering up" because it can collect all the seeds of dharma. Arya consciousness, which means "storehouse", is also called "Tibetan consciousness" because it is translated as "hide" in Chinese. There are three meanings of "Tibet" in itself.

01. Can hide.

It means that the Arya Consciousness contains the seeds of all dharmas. These seeds are the habits and forces left behind by our ordinary words and actions and thoughts, and because they are stored in the Arya consciousness, they are not lost for a long time until they are ripe for the purpose.

02. What is hidden.

This refers to the Arya consciousness as the place where all good and bad seeds are hidden. What we do, say, and think when the seeds of the Arya consciousness are hidden in the karmic origin, although they have already passed away in the present moment, "everything that goes by leaves a trace.

Therefore, the Arya consciousness is the hiding place of these sentient seeds.

03. The hiddenness.

This is the relationship between the Arya consciousness and the Māna consciousness. Since the Arya consciousness is always held by the Māna consciousness as the permanent self, we always remember that there is a me, my feelings, my money, my friends and relatives. ...... Therefore, the Arya consciousness is also called the "clinging" or "clinging to my love".

In fact, "can hide", "what is hidden", and "hold on to hide" all refer to one "Arya consciousness", but due to different perspectives, there are three different names.

For example, a woman is called "mother" by her son, "wife" by her husband, and "daughter" by her parents. The mutual integration, penetration, borrowing, integration and complementarity between psychoanalytic theoretical techniques and Buddhism will certainly become an important direction for future research in psychoanalysis.

Buddhism believes that the deepest part of an individual's inner mind ("subconsciousness") is in fact "emptiness", which can be experienced through meditation and internal observation.

The greatest depth that can be achieved through meditation is the "ultimate level": the disappearance of the subject and object, a state of "no-self-no-other. Thus, it can be said that "the whole human process is ...... every moment that one experiences as a human being" (living in the present moment).

For more than a century, people have been trying to uncover the subconscious and have discovered more and more of it. Although on the surface it may appear that there is everything in the subconscious, in fact there is nothing in the subconscious (emptiness).

As people describe what the subconscious is, they describe it more and more, but eventually it turns out that the subconscious is really nothing.

The subconscious is "empty" in the sense that it exists as a "non-being" (a kind of "absence of being" according to

Lacan).

No matter how we explore and view the subconscious, whether we think it is there or not, the subconscious is always there.

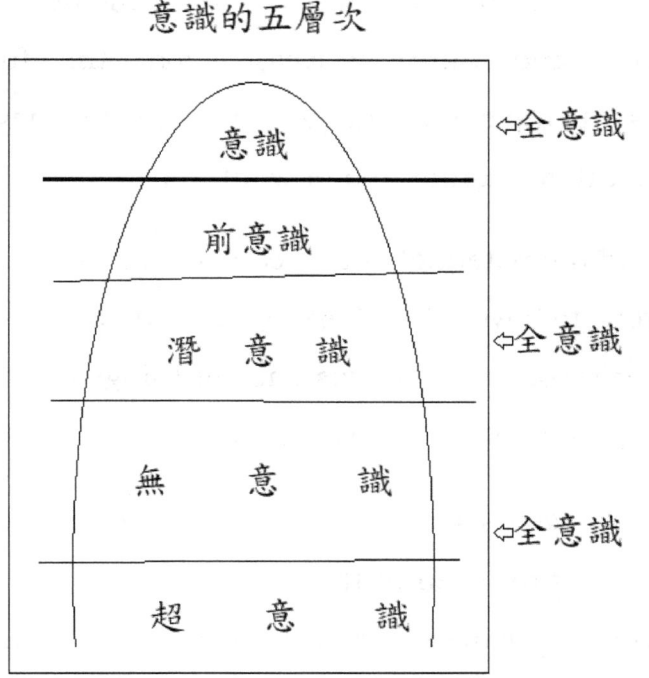

(9) Nietzsche's Real "Self" Hidden in the Unconscious

A self-concept is a collection of beliefs that a person has about himself. Generally speaking, the self-concept embodies the answer to the question "Who am I? The answer to this question. The self-concept consists of a person's self-schema (English: schema) describing a type of thinking or behavior used to organize categories of information and the relationships between information.

It also interacts with self-esteem, self-perception, and social self to form the whole self. It includes the past, present, and future selves, where the future self represents a person's thoughts about what they could be or what they want or do not want to be.

And the potential of this can serve as an incentive for everyone to have a "self"? As mentioned above, Nietzsche's answer recognizes the existence of things or the truth of things, the reasonableness of things.

This "ego" is something that you cannot get rid of even if you want to. Even in the seemingly objective activity of knowing, there are still your human relationships and the rules for dealing with them, your honesty, your selfishness, your fatigue, your fears, your "whole lovable and hateful ego.

The act of "cognition" and "identification" of a subject confirms the mental process by which an individual, through conscious activity, comes to know and understand things, and has the potential to be capable of specific purposes, without ever escaping the boundaries of the "ego.

"No matter how great my appetite for cognition may be, I cannot obtain anything else from all objects or phenomena that exist objectively in nature, except what is already mine, and what remains in others. How can a man be a thief?

We will analyze in detail, and understand from a certain cognitive point of view, and we will take "self" as a boundary.

I am full of hope for you, "But if you have not experienced in your own hearts the light, the fire, and the sunset, what can you see and hear in them? I can only bring to mind what is, and have no other characteristic!

Everyone has a "self", but most people do not live for their "true self", but for "the heads of the people around them".

However, most people do not live for their "real self" but for "the illusions, hallucinations, or dream images of the self that are conveyed to them by the social matrix that is formed in the minds of the people around them", a kind of "pseudo-individualism".

Knowing the "self" can be described as a process of reacquainting oneself with oneself. In the ancient Greek temple proverbs, there is a phrase: "Know thyself". It is clear that the importance of knowing oneself has been emphasized by the ancients since long ago.

It is not an easy thing to do. "How many people know how to observe! And of the few who do, how many observe themselves! "Everyone is the furthest away from himself or herself." This is not easy for anyone to know who reflects on the substance of things hidden within.

And the proverb "Know thyself", spoken from the mouth of a God, is almost a prank. There are cognitive reasons for the difficulty of knowing oneself.

According to Nietzsche, the real "self" is often hidden in the unconscious, and the usual way of knowing, through language, is based on the process of analysis, synthesis, judgment, reasoning and other cognitive activities on the basis of images and concepts.

Instead of achieving the "self", we deliberately change the original nature of things or reflect the "self" incorrectly.

The term we use to summarize our mental state is mostly the end of some object's two ends. The names given to states of expression that are more than normal do not indicate the non-extreme states that we have most of the time, which cannot be described in words, but are the very forms that these people or things manifest.

They are the forms or states of affairs that weave the web of our character and destiny when real (or virtual) things are in periods of creation, survival, development, and extinction or at various points of transformation.

We also unconsciously look for generalities, the results of objective existence reflected in human consciousness, through thinking activities, or the formation of viewpoints and systems of concepts and judgments to serve as the basis of our nature afterwards.

Social opinions and evaluations also interfere with our self-cognition and make us mislead our self-cognition.

For example, society judges us by our successes and failures: "Success often casts a glorious glow of good intentions on an act, while failure casts a shadow of guilt on an honorable act. As a result, "motives and intentions are rarely clear enough to be pure, and memories themselves are sometimes confused by the results of the act.

The power of public opinion is so powerful that it can determine a person's fate. "What we know about ourselves and what we remember is not decisive for our happiness in life, and when it comes to others.

What we know (or think we know) about ourselves, then we understand that it is more powerful." In the "fog of public opinion," people confuse the illusionary "self" with the real "self" and spend their lives laboring for this illusionary "self.

Truth requires great courage, and knowing one's true "self" is no exception. Weak people often deceive themselves intentionally or unintentionally, forgetting those unpleasant life experiences and experiences. This "self-deception" plays a major role in why the true "self" is "repressed" into the realm of the unconscious.

"We are constantly working on this "self-deception", which creates a false confidence in the "self".

Some people's confidence is nothing more than a "helpful, profit-seeking blindness," as if subconsciously aware of their own inner emptiness and boredom, and avoiding looking too far into themselves in order to support the adequacy of their false content.

According to Nietzsche, a truly confident person must be one who has the courage to look at himself squarely, and such righteous self-confidence must also be linked to doubts and dissatisfaction with oneself, which are concealed in the substance of things.

Such people trust themselves, have confidence in themselves, and have to fight for themselves: "Everything they do that is good, excellent, and great, is at first the opposite.

They ask questions to convince and persuade the doubter, and for this it is almost necessary to have a genius who can convince himself. This is a great self-satisfier."

In fact, almost all great geniuses are not self-confident by nature, but rather have an inferiority complex. They are aware of their weaknesses, they pay a great price for them, and they are not willing to destroy themselves.

So they strive for self-improvement and self-reliance, but have a different world, and have a surprising achievement. It is difficult to know "self" and even more difficult to realize "self", and the difficulty of realization adds to the difficulty of recognition.

The greatest difficulty lies in the fact that once one knows the "self", one has to take responsibility for this "self", that is, to realize this "self".

And this must come at a great cost. The "ego" is not the privilege of the few. In this world, each "ego" is a unique and irreducible being, with the opportunity to form a unique personality.

Nietzsche had an aristocratic streak, but he did not argue that human nature is inherently unequal. He recognized that "every human being is a one-time miracle, and every nerve and every muscle that beats in the body and mind of every human being is his own, only he knows how to evaluate and see himself.

Moreover, from early childhood, each person develops a feeling that he or she is the most important, and in turn wants others to value him or her, or at least not to neglect him or her, and as long as he or she is strictly consistent with his or her uniqueness, he or she will be beautiful enough to cause pleasure and admiration, just like every work of nature, which is so incredibly new that it will never make people tired.

The difference is that some people (such as artists) are

intensely aware of this unique "self" and realize it in the process of how they evaluate and view their own creations, while the "self" of many people remains a possibility that is ultimately unrealized, buried in an existence that is not its essence.

"Every person has a favorable situation of his own time, when he will find his personal higher self, a stable psychological state of positive evaluation of his own qualities and abilities.

That is, the psychological tendency to believe in one's own ability to achieve one's set goals", but "some people avoid their higher self because this higher self is demanding and unreasonable.

Blindly and unconditionally, they submit to the fetters of the social matrix, often just for the sake of realizing a certain ideal or achieving a certain purpose, and consciously believe in and worship a certain religion or a certain doctrine, and hold it as a standard and guide for their words and actions.

For example, religion is the use of human surprise and awe at the mysteries of the universe and life, constituting a doctrine of persuasion of good and punishment of evil, and used to educate the world, so that people believe.

To give up one's will and responsibility to a social group that shares a common language, culture, race, territory, government, or history is the easiest way to lose oneself in the world.

It is easier to reject a psychological desire to achieve a certain goal than to regulate a desire to work consciously for the realization of a certain ideal or the achievement of a certain goal, and it is easier to give up one's character, interests, hobbies, etc. than to develop one's unique character.

Nietzsche emphasized time and again that "cowardice" and "laziness" are the greatest enemies that prevent people from realizing their "self". "In the origin of things, every human being understands that as an objectively existing in nature, all objects or phenomena are unique.

It is a coincidence that there is only one time in the world, and there will not be a second time, when the reality and the situation of the existence of the self, or the affirmation of the value of the existence of the life of the self, can magically bring together so many diverse and complicated elements, and combine them into one individual like the one he is now.

It is the result of a positive evaluation of his own personal psychology and social role. It is a belief in the ability to perform a task or solve a problem by some effective means.

It is one of the most important indicators of mental health, and the person always understands this, but he personally hides it as if it is a negative thing, as if he feels guilty for violating family, religious or social norms in his actual behavior or in his imagination, and triggering internal condemnation.

Because I am afraid of the norms and standards of behavior that I should follow when I live with my neighbors, and because my neighbors want to preserve the ideas, morals, customs, arts, institutions, and other customs that have been passed down through history, and to wrap themselves in them.

What is it that compels a person to fear his neighbor, to think and act in accordance with the norms and rules of behavior and behavior that he should follow when living with his neighbor, instead of being happy and being himself?

A few people are "timid and weak", most people are lazy. People are more lazy than "timid and cowardly", and they are precisely afraid of the burden that absolute honesty and frankness may impose on them.

All objects or phenomena that exist objectively in nature are surprising and strange enough, and everyone has an "ego".

Here Nietzsche reveals the psycho-social mechanism of habitual power. In society, the free development of each individual's character implies the competition of a certain form of consciousness and will. The creation of others requires one to make new creations, and the superiority of others stimulates one to strive for superiority.

So, in order to be able to be comfortable, one does not work hard. The person who is better than himself or herself in terms of talent, reputation, status, or situation resents the excellence of others, and prefers to keep everyone at the level of mediocrity and no special performance.

Laziness, which takes the path of least resistance, is a state of mind that prevents society from acting in accordance with the set goals for subjective reasons, and is part of human nature.

It becomes the biggest obstacle to the development of a person's traits that are different from others in terms of thought, character, quality, will, emotion, and attitude. "If we take the decisive step to follow what is commonly referred to as "our own path", a secret is suddenly revealed to us.

People who have always been friendly and trusting to us, henceforth all develop a contempt for us and feel insulted. The best of them show tolerance, forgiveness, non-judgmentalism, and patient and unbiased tolerance even when they encounter views that do not agree with their own or accepted ones.

Patiently waiting for us to find the 'right way' again, which is, of course, what he knows. In short, a "good society", that is, a society in which everyone can feel at ease, is only possible if all people are on the same page, if all people sing a single song. Therefore, those who show that they dare to "go their own way" will inevitably be slandered and isolated.

At this time, he not only has to pay the most difficult

price, but also has to suffer the most humiliation. How many people can be slandered by false rumors, and still remain unchanged? "It is a strange thing that makes you think that it is comfort, rest, and blessing.

But in reality what it brings is boredom, weariness, and depression. It manifests itself in a variety of ways, including extreme laziness and a slight hesitant state of mind. The power of the vast majority of people, however, forms a cordon to prevent individuals from seeking differences in the same, and then there is the cowardly mentality that people are afraid of.

As a result, instead of discovering the "self" and making the non-existent situation the actual "self", people run away from the "self" for fear. The way to escape is to "engage in physical or mental work", so to speak, which is a stereotypical and uncreative "physical or mental work" from morning to night.

Nietzsche says that the hidden sentiment of this cult of "physical or mental labor" is "the fear of all individuality", and that engaging in physical or mental labor is considered as the "best policeman" to control the individual, so as to effectively curb the human will from being easily influenced by others, and to have a stronger ability to propose and implement the purpose independently, which reflects the development of the intrinsic stability of the value of the act of the will.

"Engaging in physical or mental labor" "almost exhausts energy, thus excluding contemplation, meditation, dreams, sorrow, love, hatred, it always takes a personal or systemic, as a result of what it wants to achieve, and will try to achieve a tree for this plan, keeping an easy, rule-abiding satisfaction in sight.

A society in which people are constantly engaged in "physical or mental labor" at high intensity is safer, and safety is now regarded as the supreme creator and ruler of all things in heaven and earth.

In the modern industrial society, the one-sided division of labor and the tense and rigid way of working have severely damaged the sum of stable psychological characteristics of individuals, including personality, interests and hobbies. Nietzsche had the most sober understanding of this.

He repeatedly pointed out that in modern times, life is sick, "sick with the machine system and mechanism that go against human nature, sick with the 'impersonality' of workers, sick with the false economics of the 'division of labor'. "The suffocating rush of American work has begun to barbarize the old traditions of Europe through contagion, spreading a very strange spiritlessness in Europe.

People have now become timid and fearful of laziness in silence; long, serious, deep thinking, deep contemplation of a central idea or image in silence and solitude, almost brings one to conscience.

One is always with a file in one's hand, murmuring in an "inward dialogue" to the real world, or to any object, eating lunch, with one's eyes fixed on the news, and behaving as one who is always apprehensive "lest one should delay" something. Such a situation will "kill all cultivation and high spirits.

The true "self" is lost in the "unspirituality" of "physical or mental labor," which is obviously a spiritual "self," a unique personality with "cultivation and high interest.

In Nietzsche's holistic, fundamental and critical philosophical inquiry into the real world and human beings, the real "self" has two meanings.

First, at a lower level, it refers to the instincts of one's life, the unconscious desires, emotions, feelings and experiences that are hidden in the subconscious.

Second, at a higher level, it is the spiritual "ego," which is the product of one's own self-creation. However, for Nietzsche, these two dimensions do not contradict each other, because he always regarded the vital instinct as the driving force and basis of creation.

On the question of the interaction and interconnection between the individual self and the things of the society as a whole, Nietzsche's philosophical viewpoint is that the whole social collective or the whole thing is an instrument, device or equipment that uses energy to achieve a specific purpose, generally to transform or transmit energy, materials and information, to perform mechanical movements and tools, and the individual is the purpose.

He argues that the modern collection of individuals living together, united through various social relationships, reverses precisely this relationship. "If the individual is unified only to maintain the machine, then why have a machine? Isn't the goal that the machine wants to achieve, or the result that it achieves in itself, something comical and ridiculous for human beings?

Nietzsche was a frank and unconcerned individualist. However, the meaning of "individualism" he advocates is different from that advocated by the general public, and does not refer to the "individualism" of those who are profit-oriented and fame seeking.

It is because "individualism" advocates the achievement of personal goals and aspirations, the importance of independence and self-reliance, and the priority of the individual's interests over those of the state or social groups, while opposing the infringement of personal interests by social or governmental institutions.

"Individualism" is often defined as opposed to totalitarianism, collectivism, and more social forms of society.

At the same time, "individualism" is often confused with egoism, but in fact "individualism" and egoism are not identical. "Individualism" is one of the constituent elements of classical liberalism.

He calls the latter "pseudo-individualism" because, in his view, it is a "pseudo-individualism" that loses the real "self" in the vague and insubstantial realm of "property" and "opinion. The real "individualism" is not the pursuit of property or fame, but the real "self".

This is similar to what the British writer Wilde said: "The recognition of private property inevitably conflates man with all that he has, which in effect undermines and obscures 'individualism'.

It leads "individualism" completely astray, making it about profit rather than growth. In this way, human beings think that the most important thing is to get rich, but do not know that the most important thing is to live. This passage speaks to the true meaning of "individualism" as advocated by Nietzsche.

Nietzschean "individualism" is, in a word, a specific wish that Nietzsche wants to achieve or realize: "to become one's own most authentic "self"".

According to Nietzsche, the essence of the human being lies neither in our ability to form concepts, to judge, to analyze, to synthesize, to compare, to reason, to calculate, nor in our innate human instinct to congregate and live in groups, as in sociality.

It is also called "herding". It is in our irrational state of unconsciousness that societies possess their qualities.

The psychoanalyst Froude was deeply inspired by Nietzsche, and he combined his experience in practicing philosophy to discover that "sexual repression" is the main cause of psychosis, which led him to propose the doctrine of sexual instinct and found the psychoanalytic method.

The psychoanalytic theory of Freud was also deeply influenced by Nietzsche's ideas, especially Nietzsche's unique psychoanalysis, which directly inspired Freud's psychoanalytic theory. When Freud used psychoanalysis to

When Freud applied psychoanalysis to the study of modern civilization, he was able to find that he had made some of Nietzsche's insights concrete. Nietzsche further analyzed and explored the deeper psychological activities behind the individual's use of sensation, perception, thinking, memory, and other mental activities, and his comprehensive awareness and knowledge of his physical and mental state and changes in people, events, and objects in the environment.

He believes that the so-called individual's use of sensation, perception, thinking, memory and other mental activities, the comprehensive awareness and knowledge of his own physical and mental state and changes in the environment, people, things and objects, is only a state of our spiritual and mental world.

Nietzsche's emphasis on the reflection of the human mind on the objective material world and the exploration of the deeper psychological layers behind various mental processes such as sensation and thought made him a recognized pioneer of the Frodean school of psychoanalysis.

He also named the symptoms of illness and disease that Nietzsche mentioned many times in his writings, such as the disease of life, illness, and the weakening and regression of instincts (body, mind, will, and ability), and analyzed the causes of the disease.

Finally, he concluded that instinct, the suppression or restriction of human thought, emotion, and behavior, is the basis of the progress and enlightenment of modern human society, and that the final result of suppression is the emergence of psychopathology.

Nietzsche was the first person to reveal the unconscious realm of the human psyche and to analyze it in detail. His works have provided many enlightening concepts for the study of modern deep psychology.

Freud laid the foundation of psychoanalysis with his book The Interpretation of Dreams, while Nietzsche made a similar analysis of the role and mechanism of dreams twenty to thirty years before him.

Nietzsche's unconsciousness of a mental state in the absence of consciousness. For example, "He had fallen into a state of unconsciousness because he had fallen into a coma in a car accident. Irrational. For example, "The masses of the marchers were incited to unconscious blindness. There are many insightful insights.

Freud

Freud's most important contribution was his discovery of the Unconscious/Unbewusste. What does "unconscious" mean? First of all, "unconscious" is not the same as the result of potential thinking or cognitive mental processes.

Many people mistakenly think that "unconscious" is just a hidden thought or idea that is hidden behind the dream state. Therefore, they think that the unknown is presumed based on the known.

As long as the confusion in the dream is explained and clarified in depth, and the process of converting a relatively unfamiliar expression into a relatively familiar one becomes the language of daily life, then we will naturally understand what the "unconscious" is.

However, in Freud's discipline of analytic thinking, which explores and reflects on fundamental questions about life, knowledge, and values, human beings' understanding of natural and social phenomena is based on existing empirical knowledge, experience, facts, laws, cognition, and tested hypotheses.

The "unconscious" does not interpret known facts, principles, and principles in such a way that they can be interpreted by its own words, texts, or other symbols.

Sigmund Freud, a psychotherapist, developed a theory in the late 19th century that dreams are driven by the satisfaction of "unconscious" wishes. According to Froude, the structure of a dream actually consists of three elements: the [apparent dream experience], the [hidden content of the dream], and the [unconscious].

In other words, the "unconscious" is not the deep structure of the dream's unspoken meanings (most of which cannot be spoken at all), hiding behind the dream; rather, the "unconscious" can be something epiphenomenal, a form of the dream, an operation of the dream itself.

Froude calls dreams "the path to the unconscious". He created the theory that "dreams reflect the unconsciousness of the dreamer" and that the content of dreams is shaped by the fulfillment of "unconscious" desires. He believed that important "unconscious" desires are usually associated with childhood memories and experiences.

According to Froude, the situations experienced in dreams consist of manifest dream-content and latent dream-content, with "latent dream-content" being associated with deep [subconscious] wishes or unrealistic or unrestrained imaginations about the future development of things, while "latent dream-content" is superficial and lacks meaning. The "manifest dream" is superficial and lacks meaning. The "manifest dream" often obscures, obscures, or obscures the "hidden dream".

In Froude's early writings, he argued that the vast majority of "hidden dreams" were about instinctual sexual impulses, but Froude later abandoned such an absolute statement. In Beyond the Law of Happiness, he carefully considers how trauma, or aggression, affects the content of dreams.

In "Dreams and Occultism," a lecture in New Essays in Psychoanalysis, he also discusses the origin of supernatural concepts, the hidden thoughts that are only the content of dreams, but the form and nature of dreams are created by the unconscious. The unconscious contains all the symbolic mechanisms of the dream and has a much wider meaning than the hidden thoughts.

Freud's revolutionary view is that although the unconscious is some fluid, untouchable, impractical, elusive, abstract ideological concept, it is the core of the cognitive subject and consciousness, and the entire human symbol, the world, depends on the unconscious to exist.

"The paradox of the Unconscious is that the world of symbols cannot turn them into meaningful symbols, yet in philosophy, the Unconscious seem to be an everlasting function. They make an entity or a substance, like a cloud of emptiness, its very essence.

Without it, the entity or matter loses its identity. Freud believed that the whole symbolic world actually depends on this "unconsciousness" in order to function.

The human mind is in fact dominated by the "unconscious", and the activities of human consciousness are also influenced by the "unconscious", in other words, reason is not completely clear, but subject to certain blind spots.

In Freud's work for some time, the "unconscious" is often compared to "repression". He traced the source of this "repression" to the suppression of "sexual desire" in infancy.

The child's attachment to the mother represents the human desire for unity, but the presence of the father inevitably prevents this desire from being satisfied. Freud borrowed the Greek myth of Oedipus' parricide to illustrate that human desires are "suppressed" by social civilization, resulting in "unconsciousness", rather than the generalization that all parent-child relationships end in the killing of the father and the mother.

In fact, the triangle of father, mother, and son, in Freud's logical conclusion of human nature and social phenomena, in accordance with existing empirical knowledge, experience, facts, laws, cognition, and tested hypotheses, through generalization and deductive reasoning, is only a symbolic position, not fully equivalent to the reality of family status.

Freud, in fact, wanted to explore how the primitive tendency of human beings in the pursuit of satisfying desires, due to the constraints and fetters of the social and civilized matrix, produced countless psychological frustrations and pathologies.

The constraints of ideas, cultures, morals, customs, arts, institutions, and inertia passed down from generation to generation and from history have prevented the desires of human beings from destroying themselves by going too far, but the resulting "repression" has caused endless problems.

Dreams are the disposal of this "repression" distortion (disfiguration/entstellung). Freud's view of "reproduction" as repressive has had a great influence on contemporary critiques of "metaphysical" reproduction theory as the main target of attack.

To approach the unconscious, Freud proposed two steps: first, to interpret the seemingly meaningless and confusing dreams, and to find the "repressed" meaning.

Second, to go beyond these "repressed" messages and pay attention to the whole operation of the dream. It is not enough to look for the so-called "secrets" alone, because the real secrets are not hidden behind the images. It is the whole process and operation of the dream that is the real secret.

Focusing on translating dreams into the language of everyday communication cannot explain the "unconscious" because the "unconscious" is not a cognizable object in our world of consciousness, let alone a concrete and palpable thing.

What's more, there is still no definite conclusion on the cause and purpose of dreams in academic circles, and the common view is that dreams are caused by some neural impulses released by the brain when processing information and consolidating long-term memory (like dust raised during cleaning or information flow being processed), which are interpreted by the conscious brain as optical and auditory sensations.

Therefore, Freud believed that in order to understand the "unconscious", it is necessary to start with "abnormal" phenomena or signs, such as dreams, unintentional speech, and various psychiatric disorders.

It is only in the midst of "dreams" or "abnormalities"

that one's ability to perceive the environment and the self, as well as the clarity of cognitive control of the world, is relaxed, and we can truly approach the "unconscious". The truth of the "unconscious" often appears as a symptom in our rational daily life.

The human mind, in Freud's eyes, is in fact unquiet, full of contradictory struggles and conflicts, the subject of people's ability to form concepts, to judge, to analyze, to synthesize, to compare, to reason, to calculate, etc., but is a temporary product under various repressions, restrictions and censorship.

At any time there may be unwanted visitors (i.e., unconscious, desiring truths) who visit the defenses of people's ability to form concepts, judge, analyze, synthesize, compare, reason, calculate, etc.

Freud's approach to human crisis is different from that of the footloose thinkers who give advice on testing decision-making and problem-solving abilities.

Freud interpreted it as a turning point in the development of life, community and society, when life and death are at stake, when interests are shifted and bifurcated, when sudden and unexpected mutations occur at a temporary time, and when these so-called unhealthy and pathological things are regarded as the norm and the core, the true face under the mask of reason.

Chapter 5: The Influence of Existentialism on the Philosophy of Life

Nietzsche developed his philosophy from Schopenhauer's theory of the will to live, and broke away from his negative and pessimistic tendencies to become a rebellious philosophy of positive action, thus creating the "will to power" and the "philosophy of the superman".

The formation of Nietzsche's thought was closely related to the background of the Prussian victory in the Franco-Prussian War in 1871, the declaration of the success of German national unification, and the shift from free "capitalism" to imperialism.

Nietzsche's legacy is one of masterpieces and pioneering ideas. The influence of Nietzsche's writings on future generations is undoubtedly enormous. His ideas had an incomparable impact, subverting Western Christian moral thought and traditional values, and revealing the spiritual crisis that man must face after the death of God.

Jaspers said that Nietzsche and Kierkegaard brought tremors to Western philosophy. Anyone who picks up his writings without prejudice will find them brilliant, luminous, and imposing, but, of course, they are also mixed with exaggeration and neurotic self-indulgence. These writings have had a tremendous influence on future generations.

In these writings, Nietzsche, with extraordinary courage and astonishing insight, easily subverts all kinds of accepted notions, taunts all virtues, and praises all evils.

Nietzsche did not build a closed and vast philosophical system; he wrote only prose, aphorisms, and aphorisms; in his words he proved nothing, but foreshadowed and inspired; but it was precisely not by logical reasoning, but by the magic of his imagination, that he conquered the world.

He subverted Western Christian moral thought and traditional rational values, revealed the spiritual crisis that people face after the death of God, and offered mankind not only a new philosophy, not only a poem or an aphorism, but also a new faith, a new message.

It is also a new faith, a new hope, and a new religion. Unfortunately, Nietzsche's life was too short, his experience too simple, and he did not have time to develop his one-sided truth into wisdom.

During his short life, although he expressed his thoughts mainly in the form of essays, aphorisms and aphorisms, and did not establish a closed and huge philosophical system, as Jaspers said

Nietzsche and Kierkegaard brought a ripple of shock and trembling to Western philosophy, and the final meaning of this shock and trembling caused a gradually spreading effect, similar to the gradual expansion of the ripple produced by an object dropped on the surface of water. It has not yet been estimated.

A whole generation of early 20th century thinkers and artists found in Nietzsche's writings the ideas and imagery that inspired their creative work.

His ideas deeply influenced a large number of prominent thinkers such as Jaspers, Heidegger, Bergson, Sartre, and Malraux; his writings became known not only in the German and French-speaking regions, but also in distant North and South America, Asia, Oceania, and Africa.

In the development of modern philosophy, which is based on analytical thinking and reflection on fundamental questions about life, knowledge, and values, Nietzsche's influence can be seen in all non-rationalist schools, such as philosophy of life, existentialism, pragmatism, and psychoanalytic doctrine.

The objective existence of Nietzsche is reflected in human consciousness, and the result of his thinking activities or the formation of viewpoints and systems of concepts has become a tall and magnificent beacon of modern thought, guiding people in the direction of things to come.

"Existentialist philosophy is the philosophical school most influenced by Nietzsche's thought. Most philosophers believe that existentialism originates from two people, one is the Danish philosopher Kierkegaard and the other is Friedrich Wilhelm Nietzsche.

Nietzsche's doctrine of irrationality has had a profound influence on existential philosophy. Heidegger was an ardent fan of Nietzsche's faithfulness, mentioning Nietzsche's "God is dead" in his book "The Road in the Woods". in 1954, and in 1961, he published a two-volume set on most of Nietzsche's works.

In addition, in his other writings, he has repeatedly referred to Nietzsche and the results of Nietzsche's thinking or the mental process of cognition, calling Nietzsche the last Western question to which an answer cannot be obtained directly through perception, which is deduced by rational logical reasoning under a priori conditions, and which cannot be contradicted by empirical evidence.

It is the searcher of human reason for the most universal face of things and the ultimate cause. Heidegger was also interested in the pre-Socratic school. In fact, his exposition of the pre-Socratic school is much more focused and extensive than that of Jaspers.

Schart is more like Nietzsche than any other German "existentialist" in terms of the subjective consciousness of an individual's actual or imagined experience of guilt for violating family, religious, or social norms that provoke an internal condemnation of conscience.

Jaspers and Heidegger believed that human beings, either consciously or unconsciously, have unrealistic ideas or have done something wrong, and that the fear of condemnation leads to a 'moral phobia'. To some extent it is necessary and useful to guide people to the real world.

In 1943, Scharthe adapted an existentialist tragedy, The Fly, based on an ancient Greek mythology.

The author borrowed the poetry of this rich ancient mythological tragedy to artistically dispel the human's sense of wonder and awe at the mysteries of the universe and life, as well as his fear of the mysteries of nature, and to convey the modern consciousness that man can overcome "God" and freely choose his own path in life.

Schart's accusation of guilt in his book "The Fly" is well known, and he himself claims that the morality discussed in "The Fly" is not exactly Sartre's but Nietzsche's ......

A clear and powerful restatement of Nietzsche's thought can be found in Sartre's writings, which also attribute human nature to freedom and freedom to will and judgment. But while Nietzsche emphasizes the absolute freedom of the individual to evaluate, he does, after all, offer his own measure of value, the Will to Power.

Sartre, however, pushes the relativity of value to the extreme, denying any measure that can be considered. It is alleged that the ideas, morals, customs, arts, and institutions that have been handed down through history have entered the hearts and minds of people in the form of folk culture.

(1) God is dead = reassessing all values

"God is dead" is one of Nietzsche's most famous aphorisms. The meaning of this phrase is not just a criticism of the Christian religion, but also a "revaluation".

It was believed at the time that Western culture could not exist without Christianity, for example, that the reason why a person should behave and behave according to the norms and standards of human life together was because he believed in God.

However, in Nietzsche's time, this kind of religious belief had become very vague, everyone had faith, but the spirit of faith was not really realized, and religion gradually became socialized.

In other words, God was originally the basis of the norms and standards of behavior that human beings should follow when living together, but people's moral behavior became a kind of hypocrisy.

People's hypocritical behavior proves that their attitude of complete trust and dependence on supernatural things (such as God and gods), or their belief in God, is a false God. For if one believes in a true God, then one cannot behave in such a way as to be false and untrue.

Nietzsche did not like this kind of religion, or the hypocrisy and exaggeration of the name of God, which uses the amazement and awe of the mystery of the universe and life to constitute a doctrine of persuasion and punishment of evil, and to teach the world to believe in it.

He once wrote a parable: There was a madman who walked around the market in the early morning with a lantern. He replied, "Is it daytime? Why do I feel like it's night?

God is dead, the universe is dark, I can't see anything, so I have to carry the lantern everywhere to find God. It is clear from this that many people think the world is full of light, but the light they see with their eyes is not the real light.

Nietzsche said, "The philosopher is the physician of culture. Philosophy is the discipline of analyzing and reflecting on the fundamental questions of life, knowledge, and values, and of studying the fundamental truths of the universe and the principles and principles of life by means of rational inquiry.

In this way, it guides the reality of life and evaluates the cultural ecology, which means "objective things" or "conditions that fit the objective situation" in daily application. The cultural atmosphere is like air, and when there is a problem with the cultural ecology, the people living in it will fall into the dilemma of confused values.

For example, most modern people respect and worship people who have achieved fame and fortune, i.e., people who have achieved superficial "achievements" by any means.

This kind of objective existence of all objects or phenomena in the natural world has a positive meaning to people or groups, is valued by people, or can make people feel satisfied, become people respect or interested in pursuing the object of choice.

In itself, it gives energy to the individual, triggers the activity of the individual, maintains and promotes that activity toward a fixed goal. This is problematic because it does not grasp what the object of one's worship should look like.

The object of worship should be a person with a perfect personality, which is the right kind of thing or phenomenon that has a positive meaning for a person or group, is valued or satisfying, and becomes a value and life view that people respect or are interested in pursuing.

However, few people worship noble people nowadays because nobility is difficult to achieve, and even if it is achieved, there are no objective things or situations of practical benefit.

Nietzsche's idea that "God is dead" is in fact the result of a profound reflection that, as we know, if no one has an attitude or belief of complete trust and dependence on supernatural things (such as God, God), then there is no such thing as apostasy.

It is a departure from one's original beliefs, an

abandonment of moral constraints, a rebellion against the common good, and a failure to fulfill one's promises. Therefore, those who betray Jesus are Christians, and those who betray Shakyamuni are Buddhists.

From this, it can be seen that the amazement and awe of the mysteries of the universe and life constitute a doctrine of persuasion of good and punishment of evil, and are used to teach the world, so that people will have complete trust and dependence on supernatural things (such as God, God).

The very attitude or belief of complete dependence on supernatural things (e.g., God, gods) does not save the believer from human weakness and is therefore destroyed. In essence, religions have good ideals, and the fatalities of religions are in fact the result of human weaknesses, which are expressed through religion.

(2) Will to Power; Superman

When 'God', the ultimate pillar of human values, was declared dead by Nietzsche, all things or phenomena that have positive meaning for people or groups, are valued by people, or can make people feel satisfied, become respected or interested in pursuing action.

When people respect or are interested in pursuing action or thought, the things that are the goal have become dependent on certain conditions, and the relativity of existence or change can be replaced at any time by newly emerging values, and new ones replaced by newer ones, completely losing the absolute standard.

The death of "God" was a tragic loss of the highest standard of moral values, but it also liberated human beings overnight, opening up a whole new landscape, a new horizon of unknowability for them.

However, Nietzsche doubted whether human beings were capable of confronting, from a point on the ground, the sudden influx of all the objects or phenomena that form part of the circumference of the earth's surface, full of infinite possibilities, and yet very frightening and frightening to exist objectively in the natural world.

Does man really have the will to seek the purest, most realistic truth, that is, the correct reflection in his mind of all things and objects and their laws that exist objectively?

Nietzsche was a complete destroyer of the cornerstones of Christian ethics, believing that the soul, reason, and truth are all fabrications. Human beings would prefer to be made into these fictional things or phenomena.

They produce positive meanings for people or groups, are valued, or are satisfying, and are respected or pursued with interest, rather than abandon them and accept the reality of nothingness.

Perhaps this is not quite accurate, because in Nietzsche's holistic, fundamental and critical inquiry into the real world and human beings, the fundamental questions of life, knowledge and values are explored and reflected upon by analytical thinking.

For all questions that cannot be answered directly through perception, it deduces the answer through rational and logical reasoning under a priori conditions.

Moreover, dichotomies that cannot be contradicted by empirical evidence, such as truth and falsehood, good and evil, etc., are declared invalid. Therefore, since there is no such thing as "truth", there is naturally no such thing as "falsehood".

Nietzsche says that there are no facts, but only detailed and deep explanations, endlessly detailed and deep explanations. The historical facts of the French Revolution do not exist, only an infinite number of detailed explanations and elucidations of this revolution.

There is no real face behind the mask, only a mask behind a mask behind a mask. Meanings have become thoroughly diversified, but these endless meanings may ultimately be meaningless, because there is no meaning that can be called an absolute, decisive standard of paradigm.

The authority of truth is undermined and corrupted by Nietzsche, and the world becomes fragmented, with no more fundamental principles or depth, only a shifting mask. Nietzsche's work attempts to resist systematization, emphasizing the "dance with words," the overturning, breaking up, fracturing, and scattering of what is fixed, consistent, and homogeneous.

The power of Nietzsche's thought is no doubt extremely explosive. However, if we look closely, we may find that the destructive power is actually hidden inside the surface of things, attempting to construct a new kind of "certainty".

In other words, Nietzsche's holistic, fundamental, and

critical inquiry into the real world and human beings may not represent a radical destruction of the answers to questions that cannot be obtained directly through perception through rational reasoning and logic, but rather a brutal reconstruction.

Where is the evidence that Nietzsche really wanted to "conquer" metaphysics? Basically, the radical destruction of a question that cannot be answered directly through perception, which derives the answer through rational logical reasoning under a priori conditions and cannot contradict empirical evidence, is an impossible "splitting" of thought, perhaps with a more or less "piecemeal" connotation.

In fact, although Nietzsche completely rejects abstract definitions, analyses, and arguments about the origin and meaning of various concepts of the world, such as what is meant by essence, form, cause, effect, and co-existence, and other commonly used language (such as God, truth, reason, consciousness, soul, etc.), he himself also creates a new language.

But he himself created new terms, such as "the Will to Power" (der Wille zur Macht), "eternal return" (die ewige wiederkunft), and "superhuman"

(Overman/Übermensch), to give expression to his The anti-systematic (or another kind of systematic) aphoristic thinking.

"The Will to Power (der Wille zur Macht) has historically been used to distort or deliberately misinterpret the original meaning of the term to mean that individuals seek power in order to control, dominate, and manage others by relying on power, or that the powerful suppress the weak.

This distortion of the original meaning, or deliberate misinterpretation, was deliberately abused by Nazi German fascists to justify German aggressive ambitions. In fact, "the Will to Power/der Wille zur Macht" does not mean the pursuit of the rule of power; "will" is not the subject, and "power" is not the object.

The metaphysics of ideas, cultures, morals, customs, arts, institutions, and ways of behavior, which have been passed down from generation to generation and from history, regard the "will" to consciously work for the realization of a certain ideal or the achievement of a certain purpose as the root of all actions, and therefore the unity of the subject is understood as the "subject with a will".

However, Nietzsche's "the Will to Power/der Wille zur Macht" is to challenge the "metaphysical" understanding of "will". Nietzsche argues that "will" is not the same as unity, but rather that "will" is the result of competing instincts and impulses, and that it does not have any unity or coherence.

Therefore, the unity of the "will" has no intrinsic basis, and its so-called integration is entirely governed by practical applications and the influence of linguistic structures.

Nietzsche says from time to time that these "metaphysical" so-called distinguishable and independent entities that exist within themselves, some kind of objectively existing objects or phenomena in nature, are all the products of grammatical habits, of logicians' fictional superstitions.

The "will" is not a fixed core, but a battlefield of competing forces, representing a diversity of complexities rather than a unified view.

Thus, the Will to Power/der Wille zur Macht is not a fixed center or a controlling law. However, the Will to Power/der Wille zur Macht is a theorem with an obvious logic invented by Nietzsche as a way of understanding all physical or psychological needs that arise and motivate man to engage in satisfying them.

Nietzsche's "Will to Power/der Wille zur Macht" is a theorem with a clear logic that seeks to understand the history of all physical or psychological needs that cause and motivate people to engage in actions to satisfy those needs, internal states of arousal, and the individual's overall evaluation of the meaning, role, effect, and importance of objective things (including people, objects, and events) and the results of his or her actions.

He argues that the Will to Power/der Wille zur Macht, which is insatiable, is the essence of all things.

He proposes a revaluation of all values, arguing that the ideas, cultures, morals, customs, arts, institutions, and habitual ways of behavior that have been passed down through the generations and through history are true and good and suppress the value of life.

In fact, man does not have the instinct of goodness and beauty, but only the instinct of the Will to Power.

Therefore, Nietzsche emphasized the need to establish a new value of the Will to Power/der Wille zur Macht.

Nietzsche is the archetype of anti-rationalism.

He advocates replacing reason with will, instinct and intuition, and that the true philosopher should be the ruler and legislator. Nietzsche started from "power voluntarism" and "eternal reincarnation", which are irrational logic for natural and social phenomena.

This is one of the most important themes of Nietzsche's philosophy, which is to put forward his "superhuman" philosophy by generalizing and deducing from existing empirical knowledge, experience, facts, laws, cognition, and tested hypotheses.

01. Ethical Thought

Nietzsche's idea of ethical morality refers to the various moral principles of human relations. In Chinese, the term refers to human relationships and the rules for handling these relationships.

He inherited Schopenhauer's ideas of "irrationalism" and "voluntarism" and established the first non-moralist theoretical system in the history of Western ethical thought, starting from his "the Will to Power/der Wille zur Macht".

He established the first non-moralist theoretical system in the history of Western ethical thought by generalizing and deducing from existing empirical knowledge, experience, facts, laws, cognition, and tested hypotheses about natural and social phenomena.

His logical deduction concluded that all human actions and desires are governed by the instinct of the Will to Power/der Wille zur Macht, and that the unlimited pursuit of power is the most fundamental universal law of life, as well as the highest purpose and value standard of morality.

In his view, conceit, passion, bestiality, drunkenness, adventure, as well as the instinct of conquest, the apotheosis of exuberance, etc., are all necessary for the realization of the Will to Power/der Wille zur Macht, and the satisfaction of the Will to Power/der Wille zur Macht is The satisfaction of the Will to Power (der Wille zur Macht) is the greatest joy and happiness, and the highest good.

Another key point of Nietzsche's philosophy is the Will to Power. Here "power" does not mean political power, but a power that promotes the original meaning from the original meaning.

Nietzsche criticizes [Christianity] and [humanist morality] as "weak" in speech or writing, and rejects [rationalism], which holds that truth cannot depend on the senses, but on reason and the methodology of deductive reasoning, or the universal morality of theoretical ethical doctrine, as "strange and absurd" in language and incomprehensible.

Utilitarianism is also translated as efficiency, a type of ethical theory that holds that the most correct behavior is to maximize efficiency. The "benefit" is happiness, and it is right to prefer the greatest happiness to the avoidance of suffering.

This "greatest happiness theory" was scorned by Nietzsche as "hypocrisy", attacking the idea that society as a whole should own and control products, capital, land, assets, etc., and that their management and distribution should be based on the public interest. The socialist value of equality is a utopian "naive and romantic dream".

In his view, all morality boils down to only two basic forms, namely slave morality (commoner morality) and master morality (aristocratic morality). Master-slave morality (German: Herren- und Sklavenmoral) is a philosophical concept proposed by the German philosopher Friedrich Nietzsche.

It first appeared in The Other Side of Good and Evil, and was later given its greatest expression in the book The Genealogy of Morals. The Genealogy of Morals, Nietzsche's last work before the chaos of 1888, consists of three essays.

Each essay focuses on the development of ideas, cultures, morals, customs, arts, institutions, and habitual modes of behavior that have been handed down from generation to generation, from history to history, and the development of concepts of ideas, cultures, morals, customs, arts, institutions, and modes of behavior.

Nietzsche tries to prove that the original origin of contemporary morality has no moral basis at all, and that the Will to Power/der Wille zur Macht is the main role in the formation and shaping of morality, which is implemented according to certain requirements, directed to shape or cultivate.

Compared to other works, this book is more inclined to the style of a holistic, fundamental and critical inquiry into the real world and human beings in its form and tone, and thus it has become a major source of analysis of

Nietzsche's thought in philosophical circles.

According to Nietzsche, there are two basic forms of morality: the "master morality" and the "slave morality". Master morality places behavior on the scale of "good" and "bad"; slave morality places behavior on the scale of "good" and "evil".

The main characteristics of master morality are: self-affirmation, pride, and initiative. Slave morality is self-denial, humility, passivity, and pity. Therefore, it is not the status of a person that determines which morality he is dominated by.

Rather, it is the state of mind embedded in his behavior. A great dictator may also be controlled by a slave morality, for his actions may be motivated by resentment and revenge.

It is clear from the above that Nietzsche appreciated the master morality more than the Will to Power/der Wille zur Macht, but he also considered the spiritual force in the slave morality to be worth learning. The essence of master morality is nobility.

Other qualities that are often valued in master morality are: it means that the person is special, that there is music in the background as soon as he appears, and it is often used to describe a play in which the main character is special, has a strong presence, and is loved by the audience as soon as he appears.

To be open-minded, brave, honest, trustworthy, and to have a more accurate perception of one's own self-worth. Recognize [rèn zhī]. Basic explanation. The self-development of perception, thought, or awareness, including the conscious faculty or process of understanding and reasoning.

The master of knowledge about sensations or ideas by which morality begins with the "noble man", who naturally possesses and has "good" judgment; the affirmation or denial of the existence of objects of thought, whether they have certain properties, and whether there is a certain relationship between all objects or phenomena that exist objectively in nature

Then either the thought is "good" or "bad". The "noble man determines values according to the master's morality"; it does not need approval; it judges: "What is bad for me is by nature bad".

The master morality, knowing that it is the first thing

that gives honor to all things and objects that exist objectively; the master morality produces values." In master morality, the individual's judgment of "good" is based on whether it helps him or her, and on the pursuit of personal excellence as defined for him or her.

Nietzsche's "morality" is also different from its common interpretation. Basic morality, for Nietzsche, both absorbs and describes a complete worldview, while the German meaning of worldview (German: Weltanschauung)

It is a term used in German [theory of knowledge] to refer to a "broad conception of the world". It refers to a basic framework of human perception through which an individual can understand and interact with the world. In its most fundamental form, it forms a unique culture.

That is, its language, its rules and conventions, and its discourses and institutions, all of which make Western culture such a study of things that have no form, that are unprovable, that are detached from practice, and that are not in any way akin to the world.

The structure of a way of thinking that looks at things from an "isolated, static, one-sided point of view" is formed by the struggle for support or resistance between these two ethics.

Nietzsche says: "I have, among the many refined and vulgar morals that have hitherto prevailed or are still prevailing on this earth, a view, experience, and resistance to all objects or phenomena that exist objectively in nature.

I have found some characteristics that appear regularly and repeatedly at the same time, as well as the relations that occur between the contradictory sides of things, and between things. Finally, I found two main types, the existence of 'master morality' and 'slave morality'.

"However, all higher mixed civilizations also try to reconcile and reconcile the opposing views of these two social ideologies. In order to adjust the norms of behavior in the relationship between people and individuals and between individuals and society.

The two are more commonly confused and mutually misunderstood, and sometimes, indistinguishably juxtaposed, even appearing in one person and in one soul.

02. The Origin of Good and Evil

In Nietzsche's logic, On the Genealogy of Morality (1887) traces the two most fundamental aspects [of moral philosophy]: good and evil and conscience, using a genealogical and philological approach.

Tracing the roots of the word "good" in European languages and its use in historical literature, Nietzsche argues that in early human civilization, there was no concept of good as opposed to evil, but only good as opposed to bad.

He found that "good" was associated with words such as "noble," "noble," and "sincere," while the word "bad" came from words such as "common," "plain," "vulgar," and "low.

In other words, Nietzsche argues that the norm of "good and bad" originates from the conflict and struggle between the aristocracy and the commoners, but the class he refers to is not the class defined by the nature of property in Marxism, but the Will to Power (der Wille zur Macht). Two types.

The class is defined by the will to power/der Wille zur Macht. The criterion of good or bad is not used to judge whether a person has an objective moral code of action to fulfill a goal or a promise, but to judge whether a person's actions express and increase his or her power.

Any action that "affirms oneself", "increases one's power", "eliminates or overrules others" is "good"; in contrast, anything that "hinders one's action", "diminishes one's vitality", or "passively proceeds" is "bad", "bad".

As for the language, rules, and practices hidden within it, as well as the substance of its discourse and establishment, how did the hierarchically meaningful "good and bad" evolve into the non-hierarchically meaningful "good and bad"? Nietzsche suggests that this is related to the rise of Christianity.

With the fall of the aristocracy in classical society, the role of social leaders was gradually taken by the monastic class, and the passive nature of the commoners and their resentment of power, coupled with the belief that nature and society were dominated by supernatural and superhuman mystical realms and powers, became a common trait in medieval and modern societies.

This led to a change in the language of morality. The concept of "good and bad", which was originally based on the expression of the Will to Power/der Wille zur Macht, was reversed, and the more powerless a person was, the more he was regarded as good, while the more he expressed his will was regarded as evil.

"Good and evil" belong to the objective normative concept of morality, while "conscience" belongs to the concept of the moral subject. While Nietzsche's historical analysis of good and evil has received the most attention, his tracing of the problem of conscience has been less discussed.

This kind of logical inferential summation of natural and social phenomena by human beings in accordance with existing empirical knowledge, experience, facts, laws, cognition, and tested hypotheses, through generalization and deductive reasoning, etc., appears.

This is probably because most moral philosophers or researchers only want to explore the norms and contents of norms (questions like "what to do"), but less about the cognitive ability of the environment and the self and the clarity of cognition to the moral subject, which constitutes a question of reflection itself.

03. Characteristics of Moral Values

The characteristics of moral values are either born in the ruling class, where the ruling class realizes that it is different from the ruled and feels proud and happy, or they are born in the ruled class, i.e., the various slaves and dependents, who feel humble and small and jealous.

In the former case, since it is the ruler who decides the concept of "goodness", the noble, elegant and arrogant personality is regarded as a superior characteristic, and this personality determines the class difference. The noble type is distinguished from such a person, who shows the opposite of the above-mentioned noble, elegant and arrogant personality: he despises and looks down on these people.

The nobility of ancient Greece claimed this, and a basic tenet of all nobility was that the common people were not to be trusted. "Thus, in the first morality, the opposition between "good" and "evil" is in fact the opposition between "noble" and "contemptible", although the opposition between "good" and "evil" comes from another source.

Cowardly and timid people, those who are worried, those who have a low status, those who are shallow or mean, those who only consider immediate interests, and those who give people a bad feeling because of their stature or demeanor, are despised and despised.

Moreover, narrow-minded suspicious people, people who despise themselves, people who think they are inferior to others, people who are willing to be abused, people who are like dogs, people who wag their tails and beg for pity, especially those who talk nonsense, are also despised.

It is clear that, wherever it is used, the term moral values is applied first to people and then, by extension, to behavior.

Thus, the study of the norms and standards of behavior that should govern the common life of human beings begins with "a way of thinking from the standpoint of the other side. It is obvious that it is not in line with the background of the time.

The noble person's tendency to look at things from the perspective of the subject's own needs, which is the viewpoint, experience, consciousness, spirit, feelings, desires, or beliefs that the individual can have, and sees himself as the determiner of values, and therefore does not need to be recognized.

He asserts; "Whatever is harmful to me is itself harmful." He knows that it is entirely he himself who gives honor to all objects and phenomena of objective existence; he is the creator of values. It can influence the factors of human judgment and truth

He respects everything that he recognizes in his own heart, and such morality is self-consciousness. What stands out is the fullness of feelings, the sense of inhibition of strength, the high degree of urgency of happiness, the desire to give and to gift affluence, the use of the power of the body and the power of the mind.

The desire to give and gift affluence, the use of mental activities such as feeling, perception, thinking, and memory, the comprehensive awareness and recognition of one's physical and mental state and changes in people, events, and things in the environment, so that the noble will also help the less fortunate.

But not or almost not out of sympathy, but from a position of superiority out of overflowing strength, resulting in a kind of behavior or mental activity without rational thinking due to emotional excitement.

The noble person is the individual's subjective

evaluation of his or her own value. Self-esteem includes beliefs about oneself (regardless of what people around you think of yourself, or regardless of the surrounding environment, I feel good about myself, regardless of others) and emotional states.

For example, victory, despair, pride and shame, respecting themselves as powerful and in control, knowing how to speak and how to keep silent, preferring to be tough and hard on themselves, and respecting all tough and hard people. This type of person even prides himself on being naturally unsympathetic.

Thus, confidence in oneself, pride in oneself, and a fundamental hostility and cynicism toward selfishness must belong as much to high morality as a natural disdain for compassion and "tenderness".

It is the strong and powerful who know how to treat others with respect, considering it to be their calling, their field of creativity. A deep reverence for antiquity and tradition, a double reverence on which all laws are based.

And this morality, which considers that to hold compassion, or to do for others, or to be selfless, is the characteristic of the virtuous, is the most distant from the noble and the brave.

Trust and preference for ancestral traditions, distrust and dislike of those who come after us, and norms and standards of behavior are typical of the morality of the strong and powerful.

On the contrary, people with "modern thinking" believe almost instinctively in "progress" and "the future", and increasingly disrespect the ideas, morals, customs, arts, and institutions inherited from ancient history, thus fully revealing the inferior origin of these "ideas".

This principle is that people are obligated only to those who are equal to them; to those who are lesser, to all those who are different, they can act arbitrarily or "as they wish", in short, "beyond good and evil".

It is here that compassion and its analogous feelings enjoy a place. The ability and duty of lasting gratitude and retaliation, which exist only in the circle of equals, the subtlety of retaliation, the gracefulness and delicacy of friendship, the certain necessity of making enemies (as an outlet for jealousy, aggressiveness, arrogance, etc.), are all typical features of the noble morality.

The second kind of morality, the morality of slavery, is

the specific situation and atmosphere of another occasion. Suppose that the abused, the oppressed, the afflicted, the unliberated, the weary, and those who are unsure of themselves.

What would be the common denominator in their moral evaluation? It is likely that they express pessimistic doubts about the whole human condition, and perhaps condemn it.

The slave does not like the morality of the strong and powerful; the slave does not see it as a code of conduct that regulates the relationship between people, between individuals and society.

He is full of suspicion and mistrust, and absolutely does not believe in all the "good things" that the strong and powerful respect.

He prefers to convince himself that the happiness of the strong and powerful is not true happiness. On the other hand, those qualities that help to alleviate the suffering of the afflicted and the pains of existence, are esteemed and praised.

It is from this point of view that compassion, gentleness, helpfulness, generosity, patience, diligence, humility, and kindness earn respect; for here these are the most useful qualities to experience in daily life, and are almost the only way to bear the burdens of existence.

The morality of slavery is, in essence, a "utilitarian" morality. It is here that the well-known opposition between "good" and "evil" arises: strength and danger are considered to be evil, that is, a certain fearful, elusive power that is not to be taken lightly is considered to be evil.

Thus, according to the slave morality, the "evil" man causes fear; according to the master morality, it is precisely the "good" man who causes fear and tries to cause fear, while the evil man is regarded as a despised villain.

The logic of slave morality, when analyzed, can be defined as the complex psychological process of seeking or establishing rules and evidence to support or judge a belief, decision, or action.

Ultimately, there is also a degree of contempt for this moral "good" person, even if it is a slight, well-intentioned contempt, and the contrast between the two reaches a level of difference in the contrast between different things, or different aspects of the same thing. The contrast between the two will reach a level of difference between different things or different aspects of the same thing.

Because, according to the way slaves analyze, synthesize, judge, reason and other cognitive activities on the basis of images and concepts, a good person must be a safe and reliable person in any case, must be gentle, easily deceived, perhaps a little foolish, seemingly faithful and honest, but actually timid and fearful.

In fact, they are timid and fearful people who do not know right from wrong. Wherever slave morality prevails, the language shows a tendency to bring the words "loving heart" and "stupid, unintelligent" close to each other in meaning. The ultimate and fundamental distinction is this.

Nietzsche believed that strength is good and weakness is evil, and that only by enabling the strong to triumph over the weak can the Will to Power/der Wille zur Macht be strengthened, the faults of others be hidden, and the good deeds of others be proclaimed.

The desire for freedom, the instinct for happiness, and the delicate feeling of freedom must belong to the slave morality and the slave character, just as subtle and fervent reverence and devotion are the usual expressions of the aristocratic way of thinking and evaluation.

From this, we can immediately understand why love as passion - which is characteristic of our Europeans - must have an absolutely noble source; it is well known that the invention of this love belongs to the knight poets of Provence, that is, to those brilliant, original men with "happy knowledge", to whom Europe owes so much, even Europe's own existence is indebted to them. Europe itself benefited from their very existence.

In the first essay of On the Genealogy of Morality (1887), Nietzsche traces Christian morality back to the period he calls "the slave's revolt through morality," describing the "resentment" of the members of the lower strata of society toward the powerful, rich, and noble members of the upper strata.

The aristocrats were valued on the basis of "good/bad," believing that their dominance in society was proof of their superiority, and despised those at the bottom.

The slaves, on the other hand, found it impossible to

face the fact that they had been subjugated by the strong, so they conceived an "imaginary revenge", describing the strong as "evil" and themselves as "good".

It was through On the Genealogy of Morality (1887) that Nietzsche constructed the Christian morality that the incompetent and weak members were qualified to live on earth.

(3) Superman

Nietzsche's thought is rich: he advocates the revaluation of all values and the transformation of human values; he believes that the essence of man and the world is "the Will to Power/der Wille zur Macht" (the Will to Power).

He distinguishes between the development of cognition, thought, or perception, including the function or process of consciousness of understanding and reasoning, by which knowledge and truth about feelings or ideas are obtained; he proposes a value of life beyond the self, i.e., the philosophy of the superman.

In the second volume of "Thus Spoke Zarathustra,"

Nietzsche says, "Once upon a time, when they looked at the distant sea (and marveled at its vastness), they spoke of God; now, however, I teach you to say: Superman. .

In "Thus Spoke Zarathustra," Nietzsche paints a vivid image of the superhuman: "The will draws me away from the protection of God and the gods; if God blesses and protects, what need is there for new ways to be thought out, or new theories to be built, new things to be done or achievements to be made! My impassioned and throbbing will drives me back to mankind:"

As an iron hammer against a stone. Fellow citizens! There is an image lying or lying down in the stone! Oh! It lies or lies down in the most solid and ugly stone! So I smashed its prison with a hammer so violently that the fragments splashed up from the broken stone.

I had to finish it: for an image moved closer to me! The image of the beautiful Superman, moving towards me. Oh! My fellow countrymen, the gods are nothing to me! Nietzsche once said, "Superman is the meaning of the earth.

Superman (German: Übermensch) is the famous theory of the German imperial philosopher Friedrich

Nietzsche. In his book "Thus Spoke Zarathustra", Part I, Section III, Zarathustra says that what the world sees as happiness, reason, morality, and justice.

It is self-indulgence, a call to heaven from sinful greed. The soul has always branded itself with contempt for the flesh, and this disgusted Zarathustra. Now Zarathustra wants to defy the soul by means of the flesh, standing on the earth and defying the heavens, and such a defiance is a great contempt.

A great contempt for the soul is in fact a great respect for life, and this is the description of the corner of Zarathustra: "Superman is this ocean, in whom your great contempt will be incorporated. Superman

Superman is a person different from human beings, brave enough to transcend himself and criticize himself. Nietzsche believed that in a "superhuman society", the strong should be worshipped by all, and intended to create an ideal model for human beings.

Moreover, the superman in Nietzsche's philosophy is not the same as a dictator. The dictator is unwilling to deny himself, while the superman dares to deny himself; the superman always wants to become stronger, and the competition among supermen results in the development of a "superhuman society".

In "Thus Spoke Zarathustra", Nietzsche, in the person of Zarathustra, argues that after experiencing the nihilism of moral and Christian faith disillusionment, man should turn his mind to a "positive, positive nihilism", so that he can face the meaning of values in his heart and create a life based on this meaning.

Nietzsche thought he had found a way to defeat nihilism once and for all, the "superman". Those who can achieve this state are the great "supermen".

It is worth noting that "Superman" is an ideal type of human being, different from all existing human beings, a new "human being", a "human being" different from human beings; theists who presume the existence of "God" may misunderstand that Superman is a new "God" created by Nietzsche (as opposed to the "old God" of Christianity or other established religions).

But Nietzsche's "superman" is in fact the highest expectation for the future of mankind. But Nietzsche believed that there had never been a superman in human history, and that Zarathustra in "Thus Spoke

Zarathustra" was not a superman, nor did Nietzsche consider himself to be one. But the superman is not a brave man with brute force or a cruel tyrant, but a man who is brave enough to transcend himself, to criticize himself, and to reassess his values.

Nietzsche takes the position of Zarathustra: "I teach you what it is to be superhuman. The human being is to be transcended. What effort have you made to transcend him?" According to Nietzsche, the essence of life is to transcend oneself constantly, and man is "something that should be transcended.

Man is a link between the ape and the superman, and the ape is material for man to make fun of.

Likewise, man is also a material that can be used to make fun of Superman. The superman is the goal of man, and the "superman" is the transcendent of man.

Nietzsche advocates that the purpose of life is to realize the Will to Power (der Wille zur Macht), to expand oneself, and to become the superman who dominates everything.

The superman is the highest value of man, and the reason why man has the positive meaning and usefulness of the object to the subject is that he is the fertilizer for the cultivation of the superman and the tool for the realization of the Will to Power/der Wille zur Macht.

The superman should disdain the moral values of all ideas, cultures, morals, customs, arts, institutions and ways of behavior that have been handed down from generation to generation and from history to history.

He should transcend all traditional standards of good and evil and moral requirements, and do whatever he wants, and realize himself by harming and enslaving the weak and the rogue.

Because, the traditional moral values have invisible influence and control on people's social behavior. Tradition is a manifestation of historical inheritance. In a classed society, tradition has class and ethnicity, and positive tradition promotes social development, while conservative and backward tradition hinders social progress and change.

Unlike man, who relies on socially defined morality, Superman defines his own morality and seeks to break through without constraint.

Since the weak cannot defeat the strong, "morality" is

formulated to restrain the development of the strong; Superman will not sympathize with the weak, but will see the weak destroy themselves. Nietzsche believed that the weak deserved to perish, and that the morality of the weak restrained the development of the "superhuman society".

By understanding the Will to Power (der Wille zur Macht) in this way, Nietzsche is less likely to misunderstand and misjudge.

In his view, any life in the universe, as long as it exists, will express its own life force, and the Will to Power/der Wille zur Macht refers to the state of expansion of this life force. This philosophical idea, when applied to the human body, evolves into a kind of "Overman".

According to Nietzsche, man is only a bridge between the animal on the one hand and the superhuman on the other, and human life should be transformed from the animal side to the superhuman side.

This objective existence is reflected in human consciousness through the process of analysis, synthesis, judgment, reasoning and other cognitive activities on the basis of representations and concepts, and the result is influenced by Darwin's theory of evolution.

Darwin believed that everything in the universe evolved, and eventually, for some reason, humans appeared. No matter how many billions of years the earth has been around, humans have only existed for 150,000 years.

Therefore, let's take a broad view and focus on the overall understanding and grasp of things: "After three billion years of evolution, humans emerged only in the last 150,000 years.

Obviously, humans do not have such a right, because we only live in strong self-confidence, self-righteousness, exaggeration, and consider ourselves as special beings. The so-called "ignorant are fearless" do not know that we are only one part of the evolutionary process.

Therefore, we should then think: "What kind of new species will mankind evolve into? Nietzsche's answer is "Superman".

What is the rationale for such thinking? Let's put it another way: Before humans existed, the most advanced and greatest creatures on earth were the primates, the so-called orangutans.

At one time, these animals were confined to zoos

because of the emergence of humans. In this way, the fate of human beings may be the same as that of the orangutan, and our descendants may also be confined to zoos because of the emergence of a newer species called the superman. In other words, Superman may be to us what we are to apes.

1. A man who "walks the rope

Nietzsche also compares "Superman" to a man who is "walking on a rope", that is, he must undergo various tests. Nietzsche is classified as a pioneer or leader of Existentialism because the structure of his thinking highlights this "self-responsibility" part of one's life.

He believed that a person cannot be truly "human" if he only lives among the masses, living and dying in a state of confusion.

To be a human being, one should try to transcend the present situation and become a "superman". ...... said Zarathustra.

When Zarathustra reached the town below the forest, the nearest town where the population continued to gather, and where human civilization progressed and economic and social development took place, he found many people gathered in the market square: because he saw someone reading to the audience that a man on a steel rope would appear. Zarathustra, then, said to the people the following words.

I am going to teach you today about the superman. Man is a certain kind of creature that should overcome with will and strength. What have you ever done to overcome it with will and strength?

Until now, all living things in nature, including animals, plants and microorganisms, have created something beyond themselves: do you want to be part of the ebbing of this great wave and return to a great class of creatures as opposed to plants, instead of defeating man with will and power?

What is an ape in relation to a human being? Is it a subject to be laughed at, or is it a painful shame? The same is true of man in relation to Superman.

A subject to be laughed at, or a physically or mentally uncomfortable, embarrassing or emotionally revealing shame that comes from perceiving one's inability to conform to social expectations or norms because of an invasion of privacy or the experience of dishonor, lack of success, or indecency.

You have made a path for yourself from being a worm, transforming your original nature into something very different, and describing it as human, but much of you is still a worm.

You were once an ape, but even now man is more like an ape than an ape. But the wisest among you is only a disharmony, a mixture of plants and ghosts. But will I command you to become ghosts or plants?

See, I teach you about the superman.

Superman is the meaning of the earth. Let your will say: "Superman will be the meaning of the earth! I beseech you, my brothers, to be true to the earth, and not to believe those who speak to you about the hope of the superman! They are poisoners and cruelers, whether they know it or not ......

It is the greatest blasphemy to ever act insultingly, to make critical or negative remarks, or to show a lack of reverence or contempt for God, the gods, religious mythological figures, books or holy objects, but God is dead.

Therefore, those who offend and despise God are also

dead. Now the most terrible offense is to offend, to despise the earth, and to have a high respect for that which is unmeasured, but not for the meaning of the earth.

2. Thus says Zarathustra.

Each of Zarathustra's words has a substance hidden within things, so rich in meaning that it is impossible to find out all the meanings and open all the mysteries hidden within them.

And things keep getting in the way, so it becomes more difficult, because he opposes any tradition, orthodoxy, or past. Usually, our concepts and opinions that express things, facts or speakers in a logical way can be explained by the past. They contain the past. They are also the conclusions of the past.

For Zarathustra, the opposite is true. His methodical expression of things, facts, or speaker's ideas or opinions, includes the time from the present to the future, as opposed to the present moment in which we live.

The future is vast, and the time from now on is multifaceted in relation to the present moment in which we are living. For the past, we can say something that is clear and definite, because it is dead.

The time from now on is the future time in relation to the present moment in which we are living, and it is a moment or a period of time.

Relatively speaking, tomorrow is only a part of the future, and we can only speak of its probability, its possibility, its potential, because the time from now on is the future time in relation to the present moment in which we are living, and it is open.

It has not happened yet, and there is no possibility of predicting it - that is its beauty, that is its unknowable nature, that is its majesty.

Look at the time from now on, a future time in relation to the present moment we are in, which is a moment and can be a time period.

Relatively speaking, tomorrow is only a part of the future, and you can only feel a deep awe, a sense of wonder, a sense of amazement. There are so many hidden treasures around every corner that there is no way to say anything until you find them.

The Buddha was pure, so was Jesus, so was Mahavir - they were all conclusions of the past. Zarathustra is a time from now on, a time in the future in relation to the present moment we are in, it is a moment, it can be a time period. Tomorrow is, relatively speaking, a prophet of a part of the future.

This should be remembered: he is the most unpredictable mystic in the whole history of mankind. "When Zarathustra arrived in the forest below, the nearest town where the population continued to gather, and where the civilization of mankind advanced and developed economically and socially, he found a large number of people gathered in the market square: he saw someone reading to the audience that a man walking on a rope would appear.

Man is so miserable that he wants to forget his misery with any entertainment, no matter how stupid it may look in the eyes of those who are a little bit intelligent.

All our games have a childish attitude or behavior, but millions of people are very interested in them, as if they will bring them new life, new changes, as if they will take away all their misery and the dark night of their souls.

And if someone announces that the rope walker will appear, then thousands of people will gather together just to see someone walking on the rope, as if there is nothing meaningful in the lives of these people.

As if they did not know that they had to use the existence of their own life itself to give them time to do something really meaningful with their own limited life, or something like that.

Zarathustra found these people. Of course, these people were not worthy of Zarathustra to spread his message, but these people are the only kind of people on the whole earth, there is no other kind of people.

Therefore, "Zarathustra said the following to the people," whether they were worthy or not, whether they were wise enough to understand what he said, or even whether they were completely unable to understand what he said.

He was like a dark black cloud, he was burdened with wisdom, so he wanted to rain on everything. He only wants to empty himself. His abundant joy, peace, and gladness had become so heavy that he needed to share it with anyone.

The question was not whether they were worth it. Of course, they were not the ones who wanted to listen to him, but a dark, black, dense cloud would rain even on the rocks, on the barren ground. The dark black cloud could not be treated differently; his problem was how to unburden himself.

His first words encompassed his whole philosophy, his whole religion.

"I teach you about the superman.

"Humanity is something that should be overcome (defects, mistakes, bad phenomena, unfavorable conditions, etc.) with a strong will and strength. What have you ever done to overcome (defects, mistakes, bad phenomena, unfavorable conditions, etc.) it with a strong will and power?

No one has ever said so clearly and to the point that man must be transcended, that man must transcend himself, that man is something that should be overcome. You should not be satisfied with being a human being. You should transcend all human things. Everything in you belongs to the human being.

To be a superman means to be righteous, to go forward, to never back down, to abandon your mind, to abandon your ideology, to abandon your instincts, to abandon your intelligence, to transcend all your notions of what it means to be human.

Superman is what he teaches, and his insight comes from a very natural phenomenon. "All creatures to this day have created something beyond themselves. ...." That is the theory of evolution: every creature has created something beyond itself.

The so-called "superhuman" means that a person living in this world has to be fully affirmative of life. In other words, to fully realize the unexplored capabilities of human life.

The potential of life includes both the "tangible body" and the "invisible spirit". Nietzsche once gave an example of a true "superman" represented by the union of two men, Napoleon Bonaparte (1769-1821) and Johann W. von Goethe (1749-1832).

Napoleon represents the achievement in the tangible world developed by the "tangible body," while Goethe represents the "invisible spirit," which is the spiritual expression in the invisible world.

The Germans had a kind of fear and admiration for Napoleon because Napoleon had swept through Europe and occupied the whole of Germany (then called Prussia), and his powerful posture made the Prussians at that time think that French was a beautiful and noble language, while German was a vulgar and barbaric dialect.

However, the national self-confidence lost by the Germans due to Napoleon's occupation was later restored by the emergence of great philosophers such as Immanuel Kant (1724-1804), Fichte (JG. Fichte, 1762-1814), Friedrich W.J. Schelling (1775-1854), and Hegel. In the twentieth century, there was even Hitler.

In the twentieth century, there was even the figure of Adolf Hitler (1889-1945). Hitler was inspired by Nietzsche's concept of "superman" and used it as a pretext to eliminate the so-called inferior races (such as Jews).

3. Who can be "Superman"?

After reading the above-mentioned Nietzsche's "superman" theory, which expresses things, facts or Zarathustra's concepts, one cannot help but wonder: Since Nietzsche proposed the shape of "superman", does it really exist in everyday life? Who in the world can be the "superman" that Zarathustra described?

In "Thus Spoke Zarathustra", Nietzsche emphasizes: "There has never been a superman. I have seen the greatest and the smallest of men with their bodies unclothed and naked.

The difference between them is really too similar. I found that even the greatest people are too human with normal emotions and reason. Therefore, the superman does not refer to an existing great man, it has not yet been created, a symbol of the type of man.

Nietzsche's intention in proposing the superman is to provide a result that the individual, or the whole, wants to achieve in the existence of human life itself, and to try to achieve, for this plan, the idea and reason contained in a thing.

"The existence of human beings is an unexplained and inexplicable fear that does not have any meaning after all. ...... I want to teach people the "meaning of existence" in their life existence itself, which is superhuman. ...... The death of God makes human beings believe in a certain religion or a certain doctrine. Nietzsche wanted to fill this gap with the Superman, "God is dead, and now we want to be reborn as Superman.

Therefore, Nietzsche's "superman" summarizes natural and social phenomena in a logical and inferential way according to empirical knowledge, experience, facts, laws, cognition and tested hypotheses of the existing social situation, through generalization and deductive reasoning, etc.

It means that human beings should have positive thoughts, and that human beings should transcend themselves and abandon the beliefs of ideas, cultures, morals, customs, arts, institutions, and habitual behaviors that have been handed down from generation to generation in Christianity, and pursue a goal higher than themselves.

(4) Superman, the opposite of the last man, has the following typical characteristics:

In contrast, Nietzsche, in "Thus Spoke Zarathustra," introduced the concept of the Übermenschen, the opposite of the Superman, the last man, but usually far less well-known than the Superman; the last man, as opposed to the Superman.

The archetype of the mordecai is the archetypal nihilist, who can destroy but cannot build, and who adopts the spirit of self-realization. The last man first appears in the prologue of Zarathustra. According to Nietzsche, the last man is clearly the goal that modern society has set for itself.

According to Nietzsche, the last man society may be too barren to provide for healthy human life or great personal growth. People lose the ability to dream and do not want to take risks, but live and die in a muddle, just for the enjoyment of material civilization, and to live and stay warm.

Nietzsche predicted that the end of man would be a response to the problem of nihilism. But the full meaning of the death of God has not yet been revealed: "The event itself is too great, too distant, too far away, too far from the comprehension of the masses, even if one thinks that its news has arrived.

"I call myself the last philosopher, because I am the last man. No one speaks to himself as I do, and my voice speaks to me like a dying man." -- (Summer 1872 - early 1873)

"The opposite of the superman is the last man: I created him at the same time. To man, all supermen are like disease and madness. One must be an ocean to absorb the turbid streams without turbidity. -- (November 1882 - February 1883).

Nietzsche, in Thus Spoke Zarathustra, describes.

"O! The time has come for the vilest of men, the one who can no longer despise himself. Behold! I will show you the last man. "What is love? What is creation? What is desire? What is a star?" So asked the Last Man, and winked.

The earth became small, and on it the Mordecai, who makes all things small, leaped. His face could not be erased like a flea; the Mordecai lived the longest. 'We invented happiness,' says the last man, with a wink.

From these words of Nietzsche's cognitive ability and clarity of perception of the environment and the self, the so-called last man is a person who lives in comfort and complacency and does not know how to transform and sublimate himself from pain and loneliness.

Obviously, Nietzsche wants to use this as a metaphor for the difficult spiritual situation of modern man, who has fallen into a sinful and painful situation. Thus, contrary to what Zarathustra said about the "superman", the last man has the following typical characteristics.

First, they do not have the willingness and ability to create: they are not interested in the ideas, culture, morals, customs, arts, institutions and behaviors that have been passed down from generation to generation and from history. They are used to and satisfied with the current state of material enjoyment, and do not seek to advance.

For example, they only ask "What is love? What is creation? What is wishing? What is a star?" For example, they will only ask "What is love?

Secondly, they live their lives in a muddle: they only want their own selfish interests and do not care about everything.

For example, they walk carefully for fear of stumbling on a stone or on another person. The person who thinks that he is happy when he does something that is completely according to his heart.

Thirdly, they have lost their individuality and are one dimensional: they lack universal moral principles, a sense of responsibility or restraint, are free from the normal social and religious concepts and moral fetters.

They are self-indulgent, disregarding moral and social

perceptions, for example, they do not want to be poor or rich, and they do not want to dominate or obey, and all are too distressed. It is better that all people have the same will, all people are the same.

(5) What is Zarathustra's "Superman"?

First, the Superman highly affirms the will to life and the will to rights of man: he is the sum of all activities in the process of human existence, the strongest in existence for the meaning of happiness: "The most noble, excellent, outstanding, good and excellent belong to the same kind as me, without difference, and we have to strive to obtain or achieve.

Strive to get or achieve the best food, the clearest sky, the strongest objective existence reflected in human consciousness, the result of thought activity, the most beautiful woman, this is the power to strive to get or achieve, you should not endure out of compassion or virtuous thoughts, given possessions, this is a power to achieve a concept of your "should".

Second, Superman is constantly transcending both others and himself: in his view, seeking to produce or create things that did not exist before is clearly a typical act of human autonomy, transcending oneself, with what is called the most purely for the realization of a certain ideal, or the achievement of a certain purpose.

And the will to consciously work for it. The love that is higher than the love of people who live next to each other and people who live near their homes. It is for the time farthest away from oneself, and from now on, it is for the future time relative to the present, the moment we are in, and it can also be a time period.

Relatively speaking, a substance or a whole is compared with another substance or another whole, or refers to the love that exists or changes depending on certain conditions, and tomorrow is only a part of the future that people temporarily exist.

Life is a process of development of changing situations, and human life is a permanent conquest of will or life force, and the object of conquest of will or life force is not only others, but also oneself, that is, one's own stagnant or "passive existence".

Third, the superman is the destroyer of old morality and the creator of new morality: the criterion of all evaluation. Nietzsche believes that the ideas, culture, morals, customs, arts, institutions and ways of behavior that have been handed down from generation to generation, from history to history.

The theocracy, which has invisible influence and control over people's social behavior, compresses the limits of human activity and even denies the true value of the meaning of life's existence.

Nietzsche calls for the overthrow of ideas, cultures, morals, customs, arts, institutions and ways of behavior that have been handed down from generation to generation and from history to history.

Nietzsche called for the overthrow of the old values that had invisible influence and control over people's social behavior, and established the morality of "super-good and evil", trying to re-establish the dignity of human beings, to give full play to their creativity, and to make them become themselves, master of themselves, and masters of morality.

(6) Where does the superhuman thought come from?

After clarifying Nietzsche's concept of "superman" as described in Zarathustra, where did Nietzsche's idea of superman come from? There are two kinds of views on the origin of the idea of the superman.

One is that Nietzsche's idea of the superman is based on the position of biology, which is an extension of Dahl's theory of evolution.

Another view of things or issues from a certain position or perspective is that Nietzsche's idea of the superman is based on the values of the Will to Power/der Wille zur Macht culture rather than on a biological position.

Many Western scholars believe that Napoleon had superhuman potential, and Nietzsche also praised Napoleon. Therefore, the academic community also agrees with the second type of view, which is a view of things or issues from a certain position or perspective.

It is worth noting that Nietzsche praised Napoleon not because of the great achievements he made by force and army, but because of his amazing potential, his indomitable spirit, and his efforts to realize certain ideals.

The spirit of his conscious efforts to realize a certain ideal or to achieve a certain goal is a great inspiration to mankind, so that people who are depressed and decrepit can be revived and their confidence or courage enhanced.

What Darwin focused on was the origin of the human race, that is, the study of the human past, while what Nietzsche valued was the future of mankind, valuing not what is established, but what is established.

What is given to the future time from now on is the future time in relation to the present moment we are in, which is a moment and can be a period of time. Relatively speaking, tomorrow is only a part of the future, the next second is also.

Superman is the highest level of human development. So, how can we achieve the state of superman? Nietzsche says: "In the process of contradicting the external material world, develop the self, examine the life of the best and most effective people, and then go back to examine your own words and actions.

If a great tree can stand unshaken and fearlessly

stand tall in the universe, can it be free from adverse weather and storms?

External objectively existing in nature, all objects or phenomena that are not good and antagonistic, some kind of hatred and jealousy, foolishness and disobedience, doubts and confusion about people and things, severe and strict (especially the crisis of the situation) greed and violence.

Are they not considered to be encouraging, contributing to the development of things (mostly bad things) and expanding their influence? What about the factor of a smooth environment? Without such a smooth environment, even great moral growth would not be possible.

We can see that Nietzsche gives the road to becoming a superman without the elements and components of bad things such as stormy weather and hatred.

Nietzsche regarded these causes or conditions that determine the success or failure of things. Without these causes or conditions of development, not only can one not grow, but one cannot even make great progress in one's natural sincerity.

According to Nietzsche, the superman is the one who has achieved the greatest realization of the Will to Power/der Wille zur Macht. How to make the Will to Power/der Wille zur Macht, which does not exist, a reality, so that one's needs and desires can be satisfied to the greatest extent possible within the constraints of the resources at one's disposal. It is the most relevant and decisive issue among the superhuman things.

In "Thus Spoke Zarathustra", Zarathustra says: "The superman is the meaning of the earth ...... I would like you to be faithful to the earth and not to believe in those who preach to you the hope of the afterlife, for they are all poisoners.

Whether they know it or not ...... but now that God is dead ...... the little reason you call 'soul' is the instrument of your flesh, a human mind-wisdom. It is perceived by you as an ability to think, calculate, measure, reason and logic, as well as a tool and a toy."

To become a superman, we must break the social factors that have been passed down from generation to generation, such as customs, morals, habits, beliefs, ideas, and other religious and moral concepts, so that the concept of man will change from a passive slave to a master who looks at things based on the subject's own needs.

People must have the Will to Power (der Wille zur Macht) to become their own masters, and then through overcoming difficulties and obstacles, they can continuously transform and surpass others.

The last condition for becoming a superman is to be able to bear pain, difficulties and misfortunes reluctantly, and to feel a subjective self-reliance when one is alone.

When one is alone, one feels a subjective and conscious feeling and experience of isolation and estrangement from others, or society, rather than an objective state. To become a superhero means to choose one's space and state of existence to be self-sealed. It describes the calmness and freedom one feels when alone.

Superman is solitary because the road to becoming a superman involves not only metamorphosis beyond oneself, but also beyond others. On this road, there is no side-by-side "or" simultaneous implementation or execution, but only a sequence of time, i.e., from the beginning to the end.

Although Nietzsche was an extremely self-confident

man, he began his autobiography "Look! This Man", he begins his autobiography by stating the main idea and content of the book, listing titles such as "Why I am so wise", "Why I am so clever", "Why I can write such a good book".

But Nietzsche did not see himself as a superman. The superman he refers to is a new human being in the future, an ideal human being, a person who uses his senses, perception, thinking, memory, and other mental activities to become aware of his own physical and mental state and the changes of people, things, and objects in the environment, and who, after realizing the decay and disillusionment of human beings, has high hopes for human consciousness.

One cannot decide how to die, but one can decide how to live. Encouraging people to take risks for the Will to Power/der Wille zur Macht, to go forward despite the hardships and setbacks, is the substance of Nietzsche's hidden philosophy of Superman.

(01). Nietzsche: Art is the most remarkable resistance to nihilism

The Birth of the Tragedy, entitled The Birth of the Tragedy from the Spirit of Music, is Nietzsche's main aesthetic work. His view of things or problems, basically from the standpoint or perspective of a certain period of time, is that

"The development of art "is inseparable from the duality of the god of the sun and the god of wine. In his view, art has two spirits, the god of the sun and the god of wine.

The day god is like a dream, perched on Mount Olympus (in Greek mythology Olympus is the mountain of the gods, and the original meaning of "Olympus" comes from the meaning of "place of light". In Greek mythology it was the equivalent of heaven, where the gods, demigods and their servants lived).

It overlooks the life of the universe as a dream, an objective phenomenon that is selected and organized in an orderly way in the subjective consciousness. This is how the plastic arts, such as sculpture and painting, emerged.

The alcoholic god is out of his mind, intoxicated with what he is intoxicated with, deeply immersed in a certain realm, or the process of objective existence reflected in the human consciousness, through the process of cognitive activities such as analysis, synthesis, judgment, and reasoning on the basis of appearances and concepts.

And the resultant activity of life, indulging in the sound, song and dance, in the drunkenness to a dazed look, feeling the joy of life and forgetting the misery and pain of life. This is how dance and music are created.

But the ideas, culture, morals, customs, arts, institutions and behaviors that have been handed down from generation to generation in Greece through history. The psychological state of consciously striving for the realization of an ideal or the achievement of a certain goal.

The Greek tragedy is a combination of the two, therefore, the Greek tragedy is both the god of wine and the god of the day. On the one hand, it is dynamic, like music, a cry of anguish from within; on the other hand, it is still, like a sculpture, a glorious image.

Such a tragedy is not to be understood by reasoning or experience, but simply by the mind's direct perception and comprehension of all objects or phenomena that exist objectively in nature, independent of thinking and discerning with reason and knowledge, and not acting on emotional impulse.

When Socrates' philosophy of reason and Euripides,

"the poet with Socratic aesthetics," emerged, the Greek tragedy tended to decline and give way to the new Athenian comedy.

For natural objects and science, things created by man, expressing concepts with images, sounds, etc., and having aesthetic value. The art of aesthetic beauty, such as poetry and song, drama, music, painting, sculpture, architecture, etc.

Compared to "what is art", Nietzsche is more concerned with "why is there art". That is, the distinction between art and other aspects of human culture, as opposed to trying to explain known facts and principles and principles in one's own words, texts, or other symbols.

For example, with the study of objective things and their laws, using specific methods and means to make production effective, convenient, low-consumption, and high-production to promote rapid socio-economic development.

Nietzsche is primarily concerned with why there is such a thing as art, the beneficial effects of its things or methods, and its value to human life.

Nietzsche's answer to the question "Why is there art?"

is based on Nietzsche's direct use of Schopenhauer's properties and methods, which form the view that life itself is subject to change, to difficulties, to dangers, etc. from time to time.

Faced with the impact of such direct, real and aggressive defeats and setbacks, art has a positive effect on human life compared to art. Our anxiety or panic can be easily resolved.

Art's many functions are organically integrated, with the aesthetic role being the foundation, and the cognitive and educational roles being naturally brought into play in the process of giving people aesthetic pleasure and enjoyment. In different works of art, one function may be more prominent than another.

For example, music and dance are particularly effective in giving people aesthetic pleasure and emotional impact, while literature, film and theater have a more contrasting effect on perceptual cognition. Thus, Nietzsche believed that art makes life bearable and allows it to continue to throb with vividness in the face of meaninglessness.

Nietzsche's aesthetic thought was influenced by

Schopenhauer. Nietzsche proposed that Greek tragedy has two spirits, Apollos and Dionysus. The spirit of Apollo is perched on the sacred mountain of Olympus, looking down on the universe and life, and enjoying it as a dream and an image.

Greek sculpture and epic poetry are typical of Apollonian art. The spirit of Dionysus, on the other hand, is the drunkenness of the god of wine, which forgets the pain and boredom of life in the midst of wild singing and dancing, and thus feels the intoxication and joy of life. The Greek dance and opera are the typical art of Dionysus.

The Greek tragedy is born from the combination of these two spirits. On the one hand, it is throbbing, like music, a cry of anguish from the heart; on the other hand, it is quiet, like sculpture, a glorious image.

In the combination of these two, Greek tragedy saves the pain and boredom of Dionysus in the image of Apollo; some tragic heroes, such as Oedipus and Prometheus, have also been transformed and sublimated from their pain. The true spirit of tragedy is to use the greatest suffering to exchange for the most noble life.

(02) Two important revelations from Nietzsche's The Birth of Tragedy:

Nietzsche's "Birth of Tragedy" has two important insights: he believes that the study of a certain object, based on experimentation and logical reasoning, to find a unified and exact objective laws and truths, and the norms and standards of behavior to be followed when living with human beings, and in life or doing things, encountering man-made, or natural obstacles to life and life.

In the midst of life and the things that nature prevents, art celebrates life and affirms it. Therefore, when we look at artistic creation from Nietzsche's "The Birth of Tragedy," we can obtain at least two important insights: the first is that "art is the salvation of human destiny" and the second is that "the spirit of Dionysus is to be revered.

01. Art is the salvation of the human heart and soul

In the Greek tragedy, the greatest and inescapable enemy is "fate", and art is the salvation of the human mind.

The Greeks, he says, were particularly susceptible to small, impressive, or intense pain, having been tempered by life experiences and gaining insight into the destructive power of nature and history. Yet, these learned and highly cultivated Greeks sought solace in the form of this chanting and singing opera.

Perhaps their ideas, cultures, morals, customs, arts, institutions, and ways of behavior, which have been handed down from generation to generation and passed down through history, have gone through the psychological danger of falling into the Buddhist denial that human beings are consciously striving to achieve a certain ideal or a certain goal.

However, they were saved by the use of opera, which is more typical of social ideology than reality, to reveal the objective reality of things, and through art they regained the meaning of the value of life.

The Greeks are a people with strong and rapid psychological and physical feelings and reactions, and are very prone to feel the fundamental pain of life (human beings cannot resist fate), but they do not deny this life, the present one, as the Christian original sin does.

Nor do they look forward, as Buddhists do, to a life of reincarnation after death, for art saves them. Therefore, Nietzsche's affirmation and emphasis on artistic creation are obvious facts or good reasons, and there is no need to doubt them, and there is no room for doubt at all.

02. Honor Dionysus' spirit of sensuality and freedom

In The Birth of Tragedy, Nietzsche uses the tragedies of ancient Greece to delve into the spirit of the unknown, or the act of searching for things, or the process of seeking answers to their fundamental spirit, that is, the synthesis of the spirit of Apollo and the spirit of Dionysus.

In other words, Nietzsche sees the unrealistic world of dreams and illusions of the former and the deep obsession with something and immersion in a certain realm of the latter as perfectly unified in the Greek tragedy.

First, the god of wine represents the strong, explosive and short-lived emotional impulse of human nature; second, the god of the sun symbolizes the other side of human nature, the ability to distinguish right from wrong, the ability to control one's own behavior and the ability to think quietly.

They are unified in the tragedy. The tragedy reveals the real existence of human life experience, allowing people to directly face the existence of their own life itself.

In The Birth of Tragedy, Apollo, the sun god,

symbolizes reason and calmness, while Dionysus, the god of wine, symbolizes sensuality and freedom.

For the creative stance of art, it must encompass both "rational conception" and "rich emotion," that is, the synthesis of the spirit of Apollo, the sun god, and the spirit of Dionysus, the god of wine, which Nietzsche particularly admired.

He said: "Among all those who are truly creative, "instinct" is the force that strongly recognizes the existence of things or the truth of things, while "reason" is the one who persuades people not to do something or carry out a certain activity, and the one who analyzes and compares things, assessing their merits and demerits.

In his book "The Birth of Tragedy" he further emphasizes that the spirit of Greek tragedy was cut off at the hands of Euripides.

Some even think that Socrates' (469-399B.C.) emphasis on logic and reason belittled artistic creation and caused the gradual loss of Greek tragedy in Western culture.

This has caused Western culture to gradually lose the Dionysian spirit of Greek tragedy, the most precious life force in creation, and has led "modern people to overestimate their Apollonian nature and lose their Dionysian nature.

Dionysus, the god of wine, is the spiritual pillar of Greek tragedy and the driving force of artistic creation, which extrapolates from its original meaning and transforms the irrational aspects of creation into other meanings, that is, the full freedom of creation.

This freedom of creation, like that of the god of wine, is the source of artistic life. Thus, he lifts the veil on the general tendency of Apollo, the god of the sun, to model the negation of life; on the contrary, Dionysus, the god of wine, models the horror of life.

In Nietzsche's mind, this kind of standard of object existence and a certain attribute is the common feature of what a human being perceives in the process of knowing.

The distinction between the two contradictory concepts, from sensual knowledge to rational knowledge and the extraction of essential properties, became the basis of a holistic, fundamental and critical inquiry into the real world and man, which swept through European culture.

Not only did it sweep through the arts, but it also had an impact on all aspects from science to morality. Nietzsche believed that the only hope for the West lay in the rebirth of Dionysus.

Although all art is a response to the horror of the "existence" of the self-living being itself, Nietzsche saw two intrinsically distinct types of art, "Apollo, the sun god," and "Dionysus, the god of wine.

Here, he inherits the distinction between beauty and nobility from Kant and Schopenhauer. Nietzsche claims that Apollo models the art of creating a world of dream experiences, a world that blocks the horror of direct confrontation with the self, the existence of life itself, the best imaginable and hopeful.

It is also a metaphor for the notion of something at its most perfect state. It is the aspiration and pursuit of the future development of society and oneself, which is formed in the process of practice and has the possibility of realization, and is the concentrated realization of people's world view, life view and struggle for goals.

Although Dionysus, the god of wine, taught people to make wine, he did not warn them of the consequences of drunkenness and sexual misconduct, that moderate drinking inspires inspiration and happiness, but excessive drinking leads to madness and degradation, and that wine brings about changes in people's past and future.

In the story, he is sometimes a happy and kind god, and sometimes a barbaric and ruthless god; sometimes he can warm the heart, and sometimes he can make people lose their senses.

The wine given by Dionysus, the god of wine, gives believers the freedom and joy to believe that they can do the impossible (that is, to be strengthened by wine), and even though the happiness brought by drinking is always short-lived, it suggests the power of the inner substance of man's hidden nature [sensuality and freedom].

These two artistic trends are different in Nietzsche's eyes, but they are also closely related. They are dynamic tensions between them. The achievement of Apollonian art can only be understood if it is seen as a deliberate hindrance to Dionysus' art, and vice versa.

Nietzsche's distinction between Apollonian art and Dionysus, the god of wine, ultimately transcends his initial consideration of art, specifically, the Greek tragedy. For Nietzsche, the two artistic trends are indicative of a broader cultural force.

Nietzsche's figuration of the sun god Apollo, along with Kant and Schopenhauer, uses various rhetorical devices to visualize things in a way that suggests the [rationality and calmness] of an individualized world.

On the contrary, Dionysus, the god of wine, is a god of intoxication and dissolution, sometimes happy and kind, sometimes brutal and ruthless. It is like the [sensuality and freedom] of an individualized world.

At this moment, Nietzsche argues, art helps to free us from a life of distress and danger by prompting us to reject individuation and to synthesize it with the power of mastery that does not allow arbitrary activity or transgress the entire universe.

(7) Conclusion

1. Nietzsche's judgment of Buddhism as "negative nihilism" is biased, because Buddhism is not only a religion that "denies the existence of the self", but is also a

religion where people's cognitive ability of the environment and the self, as well as the clarity of cognition, are able to analyze, synthesize, reason, and judge.

Rather, it is the ability to analyze, synthesize, reason, and judge the environment and the self, to look into the illusory reality of life, to realize the true meaning of life, and to reveal a positive way to break the fetters of delusion and freedom.

Both Nietzsche and Buddhism have something in common: they are both concerned with ideas, cultures, morals, customs, arts, institutions, and ways of doing things that have been handed down from generation to generation, from history to history.

They both developed their respective practical philosophies by analyzing and rejecting wrong or reactionary metaphysical and theological ideas, words and deeds with justification.

2.1 Nietzsche's critique of traditional metaphysics is an irrational metaphysics developed through the critique of language and the rejection of rationalist and empiricist philosophy, with the subject-entity as the axis.

Nietzsche links this critique of metaphysics with his

diagnosis of Western nihilism, and develops the idea of his practical philosophy of the Will to Power/der Wille zur Macht.

This philosophy of practice is not satisfied with rationalism, which sets up the necessity of an a priori self from an intellectual approach, and instead analyzes the conditions of existence from a practical point of view, developing a philosophy of practice that "centers on the interpretation of meaning" and "takes the body as a condition" and returns to the creative power of life (the will to power) as a "non-subjective self of meaning.

2.2 The development of Buddhist thought embodies a critique of the "unity of the Brahman-Self theory" in the tradition of metaphysics and theology, such as customs, morals, habits, beliefs, and thoughts, which have been passed down from generation to generation in India.

It also focuses on the analysis of the impermanence, impermanence, and suffering and emptiness, and the practice of breaking the illusory nature of the Brahman Self, and the metamorphosis and sublimation to the reality of the Selflessness (essence) and the religious philosophy of no longer seeking Brahman.

2.3 Nietzsche's "Werden" and Buddhism's "impermanence of all actions" both embody the same existential stance against physical metaphysics, and this existential stance is related to their respective philosophical systems of practice.

Although they are different in expression, they both point to a philosophy of practice that aims to return to the active creativity of life and to develop the meaning and value of human existence.

In particular, both of them are based on the realization of existence, which requires a breakthrough from the standard of a certain attribute of subject and object caused by representational thinking, and divides a form of thinking that reflects the essential attribute of the object into two contradictory concepts of separation.

The field of mental activity created by the intersection of the individual and the whole, by the interpretation of a structure that is open to the manifestation of the meaning of the self, is the field of vision of future time created by the philosophy of practice, from the present to the future time, in relation to the present moment in which we are living.

2.4. The conceptual clarification of at what level and on what grounds the "self" denied by Nietzsche and Buddhism is asserted is important for us to further illustrate the characteristics of their practical philosophies.

Nietzsche opposes the "same self" or subject as a necessary condition for representational thinking, while Buddhism opposes the physical self and advocates the removal of the ego in order to achieve liberation, but does not necessarily deny a "meaningful self" in the living world.

Therefore, from the perspective of practical philosophy, it is possible to establish Nietzsche's and Buddhism's philosophy of the self, and the profound existential analysis they contain will undoubtedly be an inexhaustible treasure of wisdom in the contemporary journey of human self-understanding.

For example, Lao Tzu's "The Supreme Being is like water" is any moment or period of time before the moment we are now on Mount Everest, which can be a moment, but mostly refers to a drop of water in a period of time, with the highest peak in Antarctica, Mount Vinson (English: Vinson Massif), a drop of water.

With Africa's highest peak, Mount Kilimanjaro (Swahili: Kilimanjaro, pronounced: /ˌkɪlɪmənˈdʒ ɑ ːroʊ/, also known as Mount Krimanjaro, meaning "splendidly glowing mountain")

A drop of water that exists concretely in the immediate facts and conditions, even the river Rhine from now on, is a future time in relation to the present moment we are in, it can be a moment or a time period.

Tomorrow is only a part of the future, and the next second is also a drop of water, a drop of water in Nietzsche's view of the "eternal cycle".

Chapter 6: Heidegger's Philosophy of Life

Heidegger is one of the famous German philosophers in the 20th century. He founded the philosophical system of existentialism and is the main representative of German atheistic existentialism. Generally speaking, the theory of truth correspondence holds that a proposition is true only if it corresponds to an external fact.

If a proposition does not correspond to external facts, it is false. Therefore, if "Being" can be expressed in a variety of meanings, which meaning is the most fundamental? What does "being" mean in terms of life?

At the end of the nineteenth century, the realists, who advocated the independent existence of the object, and the conceptualists, who advocated the primacy of the subject, were deadlocked in the study of universal, fundamental issues in the fields of existence, knowledge, values, reason, mind, and language.

Husserl argues that the way to salvation lies "toward the substance of what is hidden within things"-not toward the concepts we have preconstructed and used to replace them.

From Husserl's philosophical point of view, which is based on analytical thinking and reflection on fundamental questions about life, knowledge, and values, phenomenology is a discipline in which human beings are able to understand natural and social phenomena in the light of their existing empirical knowledge, experience, and knowledge.

It attempts to describe what we have learned from experience without any preconceptions or assumptions.

Because the tendency to see things based on the subject's own needs is the property of the viewpoint, experience, consciousness, spirit, feelings, desires or beliefs that an individual can have.

Its fundamental characteristic is that it exists only within the subject and belongs to the subject's state of mind. It can influence the factors of human judgment and truth.

Husserl asserted that the philosophy of holistic,

fundamental and critical inquiry into the real world and man should not make philosophical arguments about the whole of reality, because the discipline of studying universal, fundamental problems

This includes the fields of existence, knowledge, values, reason, mind, language, etc. Philosophy differs from other disciplines in that it has a unique way of thinking.

For example, it has a critical, often systematic approach and is based on rational argumentation. Philosophy is the study of the universe, the principles and principles of life, and must turn to a pure description of what exists (William Barrett, 2001).

Presentationalism advocates not to subsume all objects or phenomena that exist objectively in nature into all objects and phenomena that exist objectively in another, or to explain one thing by another.

2. Heidegger accepts Husserl's definition of phenomenology, but he disagrees that Husserl, when encountering the problem of "being", does not adhere to the phenomenological approach and does not analyze "being" itself.

Rather, he attributes "existence" to the individual's comprehensive awareness and knowledge of his physical and mental state and the changes of people, things, and objects in the environment by using mental activities such as sensation, perception, thinking, and memory, thus repeating the question that cannot be answered directly through perception, which is deduced through rational logical reasoning under a priori conditions and cannot contradict empirical evidence.

For it is the most universal face and ultimate cause of human inquiry into things by reason. He points out that "ontology" should be at the forefront of the study of disciplines that use analytical thinking to explore and reflect on fundamental questions about life, knowledge, and values.

The "method" of studying the principles and principles of the universe and life should be "explanatory" to interpret the meaning of "existence" and to interpret the structure of human existence.

A. Heidegger traces the Greek etymology of "phenomenology" to pheinomenon and logos, with pheinomenon meaning "that which expresses itself" and logos meaning "that which reveals itself".

Pheinomenon means "something that expresses itself", while logos means "to reveal or show", that is, to make visible something that is hidden within something. This means that all objects or phenomena that exist objectively in nature are made to appear "as they are".

For Heidegger, the meaning of phenomenology is to try to let all objects or phenomena that exist objectively in nature speak for themselves. Only by not applying our existing narrow concepts can all objects or phenomena in nature reveal themselves to us.

To truly "understand" the nature of all objectively existing objects or phenomena in nature is to use the power of all objectively existing objects or phenomena in nature to bring to light the substance of what is hidden within.

B. Heidegger traces the etymology of "phenomenology" around the Greek word phainomenon, which has several other etymologies: phaos (light), apophansis (statement or speech).

Thus, in their most common sense, thoughts and thinking refer to conscious cognitive processes that can occur independently of sensory stimuli. They most typically take the form of judgment, reasoning, concept formation, problem solving, and deliberation (English: deliberation).

But other mental processes, such as thinking about an idea, memory, or imagination, are also often included. Unlike perception, these processes can occur internally independently of the sense organs.

But in the broadest sense, any mental event can be understood as a form of thought, including both perceptual and unconscious mental processes. In a slightly different sense, the term "thought" refers not to the mental processes themselves, but to the states of mind or systems of ideas brought about by these processes.

In 1927, Heidegger's Being and Time was published in the Annals of Philosophical and Phenomenological Research, edited by Husserl. In contrast, in subsequent works such as "The Road in the Woods" in 1950 and "Toward the Path of Language" in 1959, Heidegger does not only express the idea that the activity of thinking produces results.

Its content is determined by the nature of the social system and the material conditions of people's lives. In a class society, thought has an obvious class nature, and obviously in the objective existence reflecting human consciousness, great changes occur, and in the writing techniques and styles.

Ideas are discussed in various disciplines. Phenomenology is interested in the experience of thinking. An important question in the field concerns the empirical character of thought and the extent to which this character can be explained by sensory experience.

Thus, he abandons the rigorous language of logic in favor of poetic language, which, it is worth noting, is generally the literary art of articulating the mind.

The poet and lyricist, on the other hand, needs to master mature artistic techniques and to follow strict rhythmic requirements in order to create something with a certain impulse and mood, using condensed language, dense structure, full of emotion, and a rich blend of objective images and subjective mind.

Heidegger is not only a highly focused representation of social life and the human spirit, but also a critique of the ideas, cultures, morals, customs, arts, institutions, and customary ways of behavior that have been handed down from generation to generation and from history in Europe.

He also criticized the social factors that have been passed down from generation to generation in Europe, such as ideas, culture, morality, customs, art, institutions, and habitual behavior, as well as the social factors that have an invisible influence and control on people's social behavior.

Heidegger believed that the basic states of "this being" in the world are annoyance, fear, and death. First of all, Heidegger believes that "this being" in the world must be with other people and other things, and that there are various kinds of interactions and interconnections with other people and other things, and the basic state of this process is "annoyance".

The basic state of this process is annoyance. He calls the connection of certain nature between "this being" and other things or between people and things "annoyance"; the state of interaction between "this being" and other things is "trouble".

In reality, the more social people are, the more they lose their individuality and freedom, and feel annoyed, thus giving rise to the internal emotion of trouble. Second, fear. Heidegger points out that fear is different from the fear of everyday life.

In everyday life, the object of fear in action or thought is visible, palpable, and intelligible, but man cannot say anything about what he fears, which is infinite and all-encompassing.

As it is said, "The fear of what is feared is "here" in the world itself. "Fear" reveals "nothing". We are "floating" in the midst of "fear", not in the sense that you and I do not understand or know what to do, but in the sense that everything and the thinker are one and the same.

Through this "floating", the shock, all the definitions of "nothing" cannot remain (because none of them are derived from a real encounter with "nothing"), so that only the pure thinker's understanding of "existence" itself remains.

The "fear" makes us forget our words. In the state of oneness, when the whole of Being disappears, it is the time when Nothing comes, and in the face of this Nothing, any talk of Yes will fall into silence.

In a state of complete ignorance or confusion of "fear",

we are often at a loss of mind and action, and we only seek to break this emptiness and silence with our own hands, which is the clear evidence that "nothing" has come to us at this moment.

When the "fear" has receded, man (consciousness) himself has directly experienced the "nothingness" revealed by the "fear". In the freshness of curious memories, we cannot help but say.

What we once "feared" and were "feared" for was "nothing" that was nothing. The truth is that the temporary existence of such a person is "nothing" itself.

Therefore, there is a fundamental difference between "nothing" and "fear" (dread) and what is commonly perceived. We are always afraid of this or that definite being "there" that threatens us in this or that definite aspect.

Fear of what is, is always fear of something definite. For fear always has the limitation of what it fears and what it fears for.

Therefore, the fearful and timid person is trapped in a prison of spiritual consciousness (in difficulty or bondage) by "fear".

In such a situation, the whole person becomes confused, confused, confused, and brainless.

In the state of "fear", there is no such confusion. The realm of "awe" is imbued with a unique tranquility. "Fear is this unique state of tranquility

Finally, what we fear and what we fear for is indeterminate, but its indeterminacy is not simply the lack of certainty, but the impossibility of certainty in its nature. Death is in the state of fear, of being one, and one is at a loss to distinguish between what is and what is not.

But this does not mean simply the total absence of everything, but that the whole of everything, including ourselves, is revealed before us while it is so and so invisible.

It is the imminent disappearance of the whole of existence in the process of impending death, which is so far away and at the same time presses upon us that there is no obstruction around us.

All that remains is the fear of the process of death that envelops us. Heidegger emphasizes the crucial importance of death to human existence.

"It is essential to have a true experience of the self, of

one's own existence. Only death is the end of life, the full realization of the nature of 'this being'. According to Heidegger, death is the most unique, the most incoherent, and the most irreplaceable.

Heidegger's view of death is a unique and profound philosophy of life. It foreshadows the individual's own subjective feelings that I feel at the moment, and the independence and awakening of the sense of self in the continuum of time from the past to the present.

However, it is a kind of negative and disgusting feeling of hatred, distrust or disdain to human nature, just like Schopenhauer's pessimism that life is like a pendulum, and the philosophy of will that survival is only a psychological state of conscious effort to realize a certain ideal or to achieve a certain purpose.

Chapter 7: The Search for the Meaning of Life

After analyzing the philosophers' interpretations of the meaning of life in different periods of history, and expressing things, facts, or philosophers' subjective and objective concepts and viewpoints in a rational manner, we can see that these answers about the real meaning of life can be divided into two categories.

We can see that the answers to the question of the true meaning of life can be divided into two categories: the first is the happinessist or happinessist view of life; the second is the ascetic or pessimist view of life.

The second is the ascetic or pessimistic view of life. Through the logical and inferential conclusion of natural and social phenomena according to the existing empirical knowledge, experience, facts, laws, cognition, and tested hypotheses, and through generalization and deductive reasoning, human beings are able to examine them.

We can realize that the humanists of the fifteenth and sixteenth centuries, represented by Democritus, the Cyrillicists, the Epicureans, and the humanists of the fifteenth and sixteenth centuries, have a view of life that is [happiness] and [happiness].

The cynics, medieval theologians, Schopenhauer and Heidegger, on the other hand, have an ascetic view of life.

The central idea of [Happinessism] and [Happinessism] can be summarized as: the pursuit of [happiness and well-being] in life, and the full enjoyment of life and the pleasures of life.

This [happiness and well-being] mainly consists of two parts, namely, material [happiness and well-being] (such as the accumulation of wealth and the needs and satisfaction of the senses) and spiritual or spiritual [happiness and well-being] (mainly referring to the tranquility of the mind and the peace of the soul). What they call [happiness and well-being] also has a distinctive feature, which is reality.

In everyday application, it means that "things that exist objectively" or "conditions that fit the objective situation" include all things that can be observed or understood, so it includes both existence and nothingness, and the narrower meaning of "reality" has different conceptual levels in philosophy, including phenomena, facts, reality, and axioms.

For example, it is a fact that "the sun rises in the east in most parts of the world," and it is a fact for people from any part of the world, speaking different languages and belonging to different nationalities.

That is to say, the happiness they pursue is something that can be achieved in the real world through personal efforts, not by looking to God, the gods or the afterlife.

They attach great importance to mental or spiritual happiness, that is, peace and leisure of mind or spirit, and some even believe that this is the real happiness. Their view of life is clearly humanistic and atheistic.

On the contrary, the central idea of asceticism or pessimism philosophy of life can be summarized as lamenting [the transience of life] and [the impermanence of the world], full of hesitation, confusion and bewilderment about reality.

The hope is placed in God, or in the suppression or

restriction of instinctive desires through human thought, emotion, and behavior, or even through death, in order to achieve [peace of life] and [tranquility of the soul].

For example, in ancient Greece, a school of philosophy was founded by Antisthenes, a student of Socrates, whose followers were called cynics. The school denied society and civilization, and advocated a return to nature, a purification of the mind, and a disdain for worldly glory and wealth.

It calls for self-restraint and selflessness, and is similar to the "wu wei" of Chinese Taoism. The most famous cynic is Diogenes, a disciple of Antisthenes.

Schopenhauer's essence of life is suffering and hope, and in the life of abstinence, he completely gives up the mental state of consciously working for the realization of a certain ideal or the achievement of a certain purpose.

In order to be free from suffering through abstinence from desire, and in Heidegger's "this life", the basic states in this world are annoyance, fear, and death, and only death is the end of life, the complete realization of the nature of "this life".

From this, we can see that philosophers of different

times, different classes, and different philosophers who analyzed and reflected on the fundamental issues of life, knowledge, and values often had different and even opposite views on the meaning of life.

For example, most of the philosophers of the ancient Greek period, such as Democritus, the Scholastics, and the Epicureans, were inclined to happinessism or eudaimonia.

In the long medieval period, asceticism or pessimism was undoubtedly like a great black curtain that enveloped all light, and people's lives and minds were firmly trapped by the shackles of religious asceticism.

During the Renaissance, with the gradual awakening of man's cognitive ability and clarity of cognition of the environment and self, it became an unstoppable historical trend to break the fetters of theology and religious asceticism and pursue happiness and joy in the world.

The modern mechanical materialists, on the other hand, regarded life as a machine and constructed the meaning of life in an extremely narrow range of values, and viewed the meaning and value of life with the mechanical, static and isolated vision of the bound nature.

Since the modern society, with the rise of the technological revolution, the material wealth in the world has been increasing at an astonishing rate.

Perhaps this is what is called the alienation of human nature being deprived by something that is originally interdependent or harmonious with nature, resulting in the alienation of human nature being deprived or lost, or even opposed to each other.

Modern people are gradually losing the essence of "this being" that separates them from nature, and are gradually becoming slaves to material things and money, and what they have lost cannot be measured by how much money and wealth they have.

The most distinctive feature of "this being" that makes it different from animals is that it can think. The highest realization of the will of this kind of thinking, which is based on the analysis, synthesis, judgment, reasoning and other cognitive activities on the basis of images and concepts, is that human beings can give meaning to all things.

It is under the guidance of human cognitive ability

and clarity of cognition of the environment and self that human beings are able to deepen the process of knowing external things, or the process of processing information about external things acting on human sensory organs.

And create various kinds of advanced tools, constantly transforming the world around, forming artificial nature. When the most beautiful flowers of the world's "this-ness" are withering and withering, they are gradually lowering themselves to the level of animals, and they lose their goal, drive and intentionality to move forward.

The search for the true meaning of life itself is an eternal subject that all people who have felt the transience of life and the ups and downs of life for thousands of years have tirelessly sought.

The closer to the time after the past is the time in the future compared to the present moment we are in, it is a moment or a time period. Relatively speaking, tomorrow is only a part of the future, and the next second is also the modern.

This search and pursuit, on the contrary, deviates more and more from the task of religious philosophy, which is reduced to the study of phenomena and takes the phenomenological point of view as the starting point, refusing to grasp the sensible material through reason and thinking that scientific laws can be obtained through the generalization of phenomena.

It takes the relationship between philosophy and science as the central issue of its theory, and tries to dissolve religious philosophy into science. The search for the meaning of the value of life existence; however, the search for the true meaning of life existence itself, the awakening of self-life [life and death] in the repetition of daily life experience quenching years, is the right direction to follow the ultimate goal of life.

(1) The value of life and death from the perspective of Eastern and Western philosop

The form of thinking that reflects the nature of life and death in this state of life, which exists in the concrete reality and condition before us, is a question that usually has both positive and negative sides, and presents different and closely related issues with the different perspectives of imagery.

We can even say that this paradoxical question of life is two sides of the same question. For in our limited life situation, there is life and there is death; moreover, there is death because there is life.

Therefore, those who struggle to pursue the way of eternal life have not understood the true meaning of life and the meaning of life and death, and have failed to realize the transformation and sublimation of their own lives.

Therefore, when we think about the meaning of life, the question of the value of death is also visible.

In the same way, when our cognitive ability of environment and self, as well as our cognitive clarity determine the value and meaning of death, the question of the meaning of life can be solved. A life of suffering and happiness is fulfilling, a life of success and failure is reasonable, a life of gain and loss is fair, and a life of life and death is natural.

All the wonders of life are only in one breath and one inhalation, and the seemingly decades of time pass as easily as water. There is no such thing as a life without troubles. Everything is a natural phenomenon of life, and there is no need to demand or fear it. It is only that we can cherish it when we are alive, so that we can achieve the natural state of life.

01. Human life is between one breath and one inhalation!

One day, the Buddha called all his disciples to his door and asked, "Tell me, what is the reason for your begging every day?

All the disciples answered without thinking, "To nourish your body and preserve your life.

"So, how long does physical life last in this world? The Buddha then asked.

One of the disciples said, "On average, it is only a few decades.

"You don't know what the true meaning of life is. Then the Buddha shook his head and sighed.

Another disciple thought about it and said, "Human life is between spring, summer, autumn and winter, spring and summer sprout, autumn and winter wither.

The Buddha still shook his head and said, "Not enough. You can perceive the wisdom of life, but you only see the appearance of life.

"Oh, I understand, my son, that one's life is between food and drink, that's why one has to beg for food every day. Another disciple replied joyfully.

"That's not true. There are many things to do in life, and one does not live only to beg for food. The Buddha corrected him.

The disciples looked at each other in bewilderment, and then one of the fire-burning disciples looked up and said, "In my opinion, I am afraid that one's life is in one breath.

When the Buddha heard this, he smiled and nodded his head.

02. James Hilton in the novel "Lost Horizon"

In fact, in many cases, death is only a part of life. From birth to maturity to death, life is only complete after death. If one can be free in this world, one is close to the state of freedom, which is also the natural way of life.

It is wise to live every day of one's life without greed and fear, and it is also wise to grasp the constancy in the impermanence of life. If one can even understand life and death, then what is there to fear from the suffering of life?

If one is able to transcend life and death, one will naturally have a lighter view of all the mundane things and a normal mind about the things that one cannot think of in front of one's eyes. In this way, life will be more relaxed and calm, and life will be less calculating and trivial.

Over the years, Shangri-La has always been a pure land of nature in people's minds, a "paradise" where people imagine and hope for better things in the future. So, what makes it so young and mysterious?

In Tibetan, it means "the bright moon in the heart", which is a metaphor for the concept of something being forever young and perfect.

Everything in Shangri-La is in line with people's imagination of a perfect life, where the inhabitants live in emerald meadows (a type of vegetation that develops under moderate moisture conditions and is dominated by perennial mesophytic herbs)

They live peacefully on the fertile land, herding sheep and horses, and live a quiet and fulfilling life in the narrow valley plains between the hills on the Yunnan-Guizhou plateau, where the population and farmland are concentrated.

Perhaps because of the inspiration of Shangri-La, the people living here are not only healthy and free from disease, but many live long lives. Many people come to Shangri-La and never want to leave.

Interestingly, Shangri-La seems to have the divine power to give life to all things. The villagers of Shangri-La are said to age rapidly once they leave their hometown, and their youthful looks are never to return.

Scientists have visited Shangri-La to find out the secrets of longevity, examining the water quality, studying the magnetic field, and asking the inhabitants about their diet, but the answers are still not enough to explain the magic of Shangri-La.

In 1933, when the American writer James Hilton described Shangri-La in his novel The Vanishing Horizon, people still thought that Shangri-La was just one of Hilton's wild imaginations.

We did not expect to find a place so similar to Hilton's in the noisy world. It was not until Hilton's novel became widely popular that the fantasy of a perfect home was awakened in people's hearts, and a fever of "Looking for

Shangri-La" quickly started in the United States and Europe.

It is recorded that the first person to find Shangri-La was a Singaporean businessman, who found Diqing in Yunnan based on Hilton's spirited and boldly written descriptions. But all the legends of Shangri-La have yet to be unraveled and unraveled.

The book "Vanishing Horizons" mentions that Hilton visited many beautiful places to express his memory of previous actions or situations, so it is difficult to determine the exact location of Shangri-La based on his travels, and Hilton himself did not give all the specific details and circumstances of the prototype of Shangri-La.

As a result, there are still doubts about the identity of "Shangri-La" in Diqing, and a significant number of people believe that the "Shambhala" of classical Tibetan tradition is the true location of Shangri-La.

In the Tibetan classics, Shambhala is depicted as a wonderful wonderland surrounded by snow-capped mountains and pure water between heaven and earth. It is also said to be dotted with golden stupas, a landscape very similar to Hilton's depiction.

But then again, is it really that important where the "prototype" of the Vanishing Horizon novel is located? Both Diqing and Shambhala are stunningly beautiful.

In the search for Shangri-La, people have come to know and understand the beauty of nature. Perhaps Hilton wrote Vanishing Horizons with this in mind: to awaken people's love for nature.

03. Tao Yuanming, "The Peach Blossom Garden".

Another example is Tao Yuanming, a famous poet in the Eastern Jin Dynasty (April 6, 317 - July 10, 420), who wrote an essay called "The Peach Blossom Source". The text says that a person who lives by fishing, rowing a boat to catch fish, lost, anxious, do not know what to do, when suddenly a burst of fragrance from the tip of the nose, look up, it turns out that both sides of the shore are peach blossoms.

The fisherman did not panic, slowly and methodically along the peach forest forward, found a small hill at the end of the peach forest. He calmly stopped the boat ashore, into the mountain pass, see there are fertile fields, neat houses; there are ponds, green bamboo. From house to house, the cries of chickens and dogs could be heard clearly from each other, and people were coming and going, very happy.

His arrival startled the neighbors in the surrounding streets and houses, and everyone swarmed around him, asking questions. Some people also warmly invited him to go to her house as a guest. The fisherman learned from the conversation that at the end of the Qin Dynasty, some people from the north fled here with their wives and children to escape the disasters of war.

Since then, they have settled down and isolated themselves from the world. When the fishermen left, they deliberately made some signs along the way, and when they returned home, they reported what they had seen and heard in person to the sheriff. The sheriff sent someone to go with the fisherman to look for, but search and search, looking for a very long time, never found this place.

From this article of Tao Yuanming, the idiom of "Worldly Peachland" came into being. "Worldly" means beyond the human world; "Peachland" means the end of the peach forest. The idiom of "Worldly Peachland" means an extremely beautiful place outside of the human world.

Tao Yuanming's description of the "Worldly Peachland" is fictional and cannot exist in the real world, so it is often used later as a metaphor for the ideal world of living in peace and contentment and a beautiful environment. It is also often used as a metaphor for the kind of imaginary place that is detached from the utopia of real life.

The author's fiction of a peaceful and tranquil paradise depicts a picture of a happy life without oppression, without war, where everyone lives and works in peace and harmony with each other, and where his social ideal is enshrined.

It embodies people's pursuit and desire, but also reflects people's dissatisfaction and resistance to reality.

The text uses the entry and exit of the fisherman from Wuling as a clue to create a peaceful and tranquil paradise, depicting a picture of life without exploitation and oppression, where people live and work in peace and harmony, expressing the author's dissatisfaction with the dark reality and his yearning for a peaceful life.

It reflects the people's aversion to war and their desire for a peaceful life. It also expresses the author's desire for "things that exist objectively" or "conditions that fit the objective situation" in everyday application.

It is the author's dissatisfaction with all the actual things or existing things, as well as his expectation and aspiration for a better life in the future, i.e. to live in a state of peace and harmony with the dark society's hypocritical and greedy falsehoods.

Now let's think about it from a different perspective: if we live our lives in "Shangri-La", or the land of the world, that is, in "Shambhala", the ideal paradise for human beings.

In this pure land in people's mind, human life is likened to an extremely important key, and every morning when we wake up to take it, we have to fill out the application form carefully. Before going to sleep at night, one must return to it after reflecting and praying in gratitude.

Every day, before we receive the key to our lives, the owner of Shangri-La, who rules our lives, asks us: "Why do you want to receive the key today? How do you want to live today? Do you have a plan for what you want to do? I think that

If we have used the days of our lives so many times in the past, thousands of times in the future, from now on, it is in the same space and time as the present time we are in.

Relatively speaking, tomorrow is only a part of the future, the next second, but also to continue to apply, so have we ever wondered why we have to continue to apply, this key to life, and as if it is never-ending to continue to apply,........

Whenever we return, the Lord of Shangri-La, the master of our lives, is always asking: "What have you achieved today? What did you fail to do? What are the sad, painful and troubling experiences that you cannot overcome?

Can you share the wisdom you have learned in life with your descendants, or can you proudly mention to others what you have failed to experience in life, or can you offer valuable advice to those who apply for it late, or can you even offer it as a loan, confession and atonement for others who have done something for their own selfishness, such as killing and setting fire to others, or for hurting virtue... ...".

If we always start our days with such a hard-won and end with such a sad loss, then we must have a deeper sense of inner self-discovery and outer self-discovery of life. In the process of contradiction with the external material world

In the process of contradicting with the external material world, we develop our own self and look back on our own thoughts and behaviors, and check the mistakes in them.

Perhaps living in the "paradise of the world", if all of our lives are predetermined. At the time we were born, our parents had already registered for a birth certificate with the owner of the Garden of the World, and received a fixed schedule of years for our lifetime, which we were free to take and spend.

It was as if our parents had deposited a fixed amount of trust funds in the bank for us to spend. The only condition is that we cannot spend more than 24 hours a day within certain limits.

That is, every time we spend a day and night, we lose a day of life, and it is irreversible. One day is lost in the total account of our life existence.

In this way, whenever we suddenly realize that we still have a fixed amount of life trust fund in the indefinite days, we open our Life Existence Ledger and find that our days are getting shorter and shorter, and then we suddenly remember that time is passing like an arrow, and there are not many days left.

Then, we feel sad and sad about the events and feelings that have passed away, and we have deep and sincere feelings and cherish all the objects and phenomena that exist in life or in the natural world objectively, so as to stimulate a more positive attitude towards life and a more aggressive spirit to deal with things.

However, our life does not begin under such conditions, nor does it take place in such a situation. Usually, living seems to be the most natural thing for us.

Therefore, we usually do not give much thought to the question of life. Likewise, death seems to be a very distant thing, so we usually do not think much about it either.

It can be said that we usually do not have a full understanding and consciousness of our own life; we lack the ability to work consciously for the realization of a certain ideal or the achievement of a certain purpose in our life.

We lack the mental state to consciously work for the realization of a certain ideal or the achievement of a certain purpose in our life. What is absolutely necessary must be indispensable to grasp and estimate in advance. At the same time, since we do not have the right to choose whether to be born into this world, or when to leave, it often seems to be helpless.

Therefore, many people unknowingly develop a negative attitude toward life: to live a life of peace, and to be submissive. Lack of enthusiasm for the ideals and aspirations in life that cannot be replaced.

Many people unknowingly develop an attitude of living and dying in a state of confusion and self-imposed exile: they are timid, fearful, cowardly, and constrained in their expression of human suffering and tragedy in this world.

The person who has developed the attitude of living and dying in a state of confusion and self-imposed exile, and who has the defect of cowardly personality expression, is often regarded as introverted because of the lack of initiative in dealing with people, and this defect of personality expression will only be revealed when he or she interacts with people or deals with specific matters.

For example, when interacting with people, they often involuntarily restrain their words and actions, and their demeanor appears extremely unnatural, resulting in evasiveness and helplessness; they are unable to fully express their thoughts and feelings during conversations, thus affecting the establishment of normal intimate friendships with people.

Another example is that in dealing with specific matters, always too cautious, not very sure of absolute, not risky and move, encounter difficult problems can be avoided, can be pushed, no own opinion, like to act according to the wishes of others, afraid to take responsibility, and by the other people's criticism and evasive, to go to the disaster to eliminate the psychology of peace.

We often do not take our lives seriously, and we do not carry out or pursue our overall long-term goals voluntarily, and we do not think about the truth of life and death.

However, in a life of confused life and confused death,

there are bound to be occasional unusual moments that cause us to be shocked by the stirrings of life and death, to be surprised by hearing about death, and to be shocked and thoughtful.

For example, when our loved ones or friends are struggling with illnesses and life seems so isolated and helpless; or when someone who was obviously with us yesterday, having a good time and chatting about family matters, now he or she hears the sad news from the blue. Thoughts suddenly freeze and empty, life is unreal and unpredictable like a show, no ending tragedy.

Or when we see that our own kind is suffering from slavery and persecution, and that the dignity of humanity is so thin and fragile.

Or when we find that many people are struggling on the line of hunger, living inhuman lives, and wonder if death is better than life.

In such extraordinary moments, it is easy for us to become conscious of the existence of the universe and life itself.

This opportunity is the key moment for us to further inquire about the value of life's existence and the "true meaning of life's existence" in the universe.

However, it is easy to become oblivious to the question of "existence", which is the "real meaning of life existence", just as it is easy to become oblivious to the habitual behavior of breathing. It is as if we are usually unaware of the existence of our heart and lungs, our teeth, or our stomach.

Only when we get COVID-19, when our lungs can't breathe, or when we feel a slight discomfort, or when our teeth are in pain, or when our stomach cramps come on, do we suddenly become aware of the existence of some organism with an independent physiological role in these organisms.

The funny thing is that after all the tissues and organs in our body resume normal operation, breathing smoothly and digesting well, we gradually forget about these important organs.

We become the same as before, and we live and die in a daze, without getting better. The same is true of our consciousness of life's existence. When we are at peace, we often do not think about life and death, we do not realize it.

When we begin to realize the problem of life and reflect on it, it is often the moment when we must face the relationship between life and death, and by then we may have already encountered the painful, heartbreaking, heartbreaking, painful and catastrophic situation of life.

Therefore, in this state of life, as in the case of the man who expects to walk the rope, what Nietzsche's "Thus Spoke Zarathustra" presents to us is that the comfort of life is often in inverse proportion to the depth of spiritual contrasts.

Whether it is the development of one's own needs in the process of contradiction with the external material world, based on the inner substance of the hidden self-discovery, or the formation of a sense of self-efficacy and interest based on beliefs, triggered by the sense of responsibility, when we ask about the meaning of life and the value of death.

It is only then that we realize that our habitual thought patterns are in an unknown inheritance of social factors such as customs, morals, habits, beliefs, ideas, and other religious and philosophical thoughts that have been passed down from one generation to another, or that we are studying a certain object as a scope.

In addition, it is a certain kind of logical and philosophical thought that is stirred up by experiments and logical reasoning to seek for unified and exact objective laws and truths, and to consider the specific facts and conditions that exist in front of us.

If, as the modern pragmatist philosopher W. James argues, habitual behavioral patterns of thought, the emergence of beliefs is also the result of human will.

Because of the role of the psychological state of consciously working for the realization of a certain ideal or the achievement of a certain purpose, man can understand reality by acting, and the knowledge of the object of faith (e.g., God) must first be passed down from generation to generation.

The knowledge of the object of faith (e.g., God) must first be passed down from generation to generation, and there are social factors of inherited continuity, such as customs, morals, habits, beliefs, ideas, and other religious and philosophical beliefs that affirm the existence of the object of inherited faith.

Therefore, if said from this perspective, inherited beliefs are a source of knowledge. This is different from scientific knowledge; the generation of scientific knowledge is a systematic system of knowledge, which accumulates and organizes, and can test the explanations and predictions about the universe.

It emphasizes the specificity and falsifiability of the prediction results, which is different from the vague philosophy, which takes a certain object as the scope of study, and seeks to obtain unified and exact objective laws and truths based on experiments and logical reasoning. At the same time, it is also the result of man's knowledge of external, existing objective things, and man does not need to use his will power to affirm the existence of external things.

First of all, let us observe how the meaning of life appears under the impact of the mainstream religious philosophy and the social factors such as customs, morals, habits, beliefs, and ideas that have been passed down from generation to generation in the West.

Next, let us examine what kind of contribution religious philosophical thought can provide to the problem of social factors that have been passed down from generation to generation in the East, such as customs, morals, habits, beliefs, and ideas.

In the Western philosophical logic of religion, human beings have a very prominent image. Theocracy: A social ideology that is a fictitious reflection of the objective world.

The word "faith" has two meanings: first, it refers to the attitude or belief of complete trust and reliance on supernatural things (such as God and gods); second, it refers to a state of cognition or action (act) by which one can know supernatural things. The second is a state of awareness or action by which one can come to know supernatural things.

Faith was originally a term used in discussions of religion, but has recently been applied to political discussions. In the discussion of religion, Christian theologians, such as St. Thomas Aquinas

St. Thomas Aquinas (1225-1274), for example, argued that faith arises from the divine grace of God acting on the human mind so that man can use his will to command the intellect and voluntarily accept the truth revealed by God through chosen action. divine truth.)

Some philosophers believe that faith and reason are two separate domains; in other words, faith is irrational. But this view is not accepted by other philosophers.

They think that faith is not irrational or arbitrary, that there is always a reason for having faith, and that since this is the case, faith cannot be considered irrational.

It is believed that what dominates nature and society is a supernatural, superhuman realm of mystery and power, and therefore infinitely revered and worshipped. At present, the major religions in the world are Christianity, Islam, Buddhism, Hinduism, etc.

(2) The origin of nihilism

The basic principles that make up nihilism existed long before anyone attempted to describe them as a coherent whole. Most of the basic principles can be found in the development of ancient skepticism among the ancient Greeks.

Perhaps the original nihilist was Gorgias (483-378 B.C.), for it was once said: "Nothing exists. If anything exists, it is unknowable. If it were known, its knowledge would be impassable.

It rejects general or fundamental aspects of human existence, such as objective truth, knowledge, morality, values, or meaning. Different nihilistic positions hold different views that human values are unfounded, that life has no meaning, that knowledge is impossible, or that certain entities do not exist or are meaningless.

Nihilist scholars may see it as a label attached to various philosophies, or as a distinct historical concept arising from nominalism, skepticism, and philosophical pessimism, or it may come from Christianity itself.

Contemporary understandings of this idea derive in large part from Nietzsche's "nihilistic crisis," from which two central concepts emerge: the destruction of higher values and the rejection of life-affirmation.

However, earlier forms of nihilism may have been more selective in denying the specific hegemony of social, moral, political, and aesthetic thought. This terminology is sometimes associated with the modernization process, which has resulted in the erosion, destruction, and even disintegration of traditional values and traditional social norms.

The term is sometimes used in conjunction with the disorderly state in which members of society are psychologically deprived of value guidance and disintegration as a result of the weakening, destruction, and even disintegration of traditional values and social norms in the process of modernization, in order to explain the general despair over the meaninglessness or arbitrariness of the existence of human principles and social institutions.

Nihilism has also been described as significant or constitutive of certain historical periods. For example, Jean Baudrillard and others have described postmodernity as a nihilistic era or way of thinking.

Similarly, some theologians and religious figures have suggested that many aspects of postmodernity and modernity represent nihilism by denying the philosophical principles of religion. However, nihilism is widely attributed to religious and non-religious perspectives.

In common usage, the term usually refers to a form of existential nihilism according to which life has no intrinsic value, meaning, or purpose.

Other prominent positions in nihilism include the rejection of all normative and ethical perspectives (moral nihilism), the rejection of all social and political institutions (political nihilism, English: Political nihilism), and the belief that no knowledge can or does exist.

The position that no knowledge can or does exist (Epistemological nihilism), as well as many metaphysical positions asserting the non-existence of non-abstract objects (Metaphysical nihilism), the non-existence of composite objects (Fractal nihilism), and the non-existence of complex objects (Mereological nihilism). Mereological nihilism), or even that life itself does not exist.

01. Nihilism in Philosophy

Although Turgenev made the term nihilism well known, it was first introduced into the field of philosophy by Friedrich Heinrich Jacobi. Jacobi wanted to use this term to show the characteristics of rationalism, especially the critical philosophy of Kant.

He believed that all rationalism can be reduced to nothingness, so that we should try to avoid it and return to some belief in and respect for a certain proposition, doctrine, religion or someone to be taken as a guide or example for our actions. In other words, faith is a code of conduct, a moral code of behavior.

Nietzsche's later works are mainly concerned with

nihilism. One volume of The Will to Power consists of a selection of Nietzsche's notes from 1883 to 1888.

He named it "European Nihilism" and considered it the main problem of the 19th century. Nietzsche defined nihilism as the absence of meaning, purpose, intelligible truth, and intrinsic value in the world, especially in human existence.

Although postmodernism has been ridiculed by some as nihilism, it does not conform to the nihilist formula in the sense that nihilists tend to be defeatist.

The postmodernist philosopher tries to find the forces and causes that define the unique human relationships he explores in all their forms. Skeptics do not have to draw any conclusions about the reality of moral concepts, and they do not have to discuss the question of the meaning of existence of life itself in the absence of known facts.

02. Nihilism in ethics

In ethics, the term "nihilist" or "nihilism" is used to refer to a person who completely rejects all authority, morality, and social conventions, or who claims to do so. Either by rejecting all established beliefs, or by extreme relativism or skepticism.

Nihilists believe that those in control of power are ineffective and should be confronted. For the nihilist, the ultimate source of moral values is not culture or reason, but the individual himself.

03. Postmodernism and the Collapse of Knowledge

Postmodernist thought has pushed cognitive and ethical systems to the extreme of relativism. This is particularly evident in the work of Jean-François Lyotard and De Sida. These philosophers sought to deny the truths, meanings, historical processes, humanist ideals, and foundations upon which Western civilization was built.

Although in principle postmodernism is considered a nihilist philosophy, it is notable that nihilism embraces postmodernism's denunciations. Nihilism is a claim to the truth of the universe, which postmodernism rejects.

However, "man is a rational animal". He wants to use his intellect to understand the world around him, to unravel the mystery of everything in the universe, and even to use everything and act as their master. Such a conception signifies an outward-looking direction for man. Instead of seeking deep within oneself to establish an inner reality that one can grasp.

We are casting our wisdom far and deep into the universe, capturing the "objective" appearance of the external world, in order to control the external world and to override what is in it. Therefore, the positive meaning of life is to keep exploring outward, to keep venturing forward, to keep expanding to other places.

Our intellect gives the will to think of it as an invincible sword that keeps exploring new realms, or as an all-pervasive key that keeps unlocking the mysteries of heaven and earth and the universe. Under such a scenario, human beings are enthusiastic about acquiring knowledge and are diligently engaged in the pursuit of science.

This is a kind of philosophical thinking centered on "practical verification". In a broader sense, any kind of philosophical system that seeks to know from empirical material is positivism.

This idea can be traced back to Roger Bacon, an empiricist scholar of the 13th century in England. The French philosopher Auguste Comte first used the term testimonials to convey the six properties of things: true, useful, certain, correct, organic, and relative.

The word testimonials can be interpreted as "found to be true". In a narrower sense, positivism refers to the philosophy of the French philosopher Comte, who believed that knowledge of reality depends only on a specific object as the scope of study.

Confucius believed that knowledge of reality can only be obtained through the study of certain objects, through experimentation and logical reasoning, through the search for unified and exact objective laws and truths, and through the observation of ordinary things. The growth period of Confucius' life was the era of the development of scientific thought.

People had doubts about questions that could not be answered directly through perception, and they deduced the answers through rational logical reasoning under a priori conditions, and they could not contradict the empirical evidence, and metaphysics arose.

Doubt is a state of mind in which one is caught in two or more conflicting arguments and cannot decide which one to choose. It is a state between belief and disbelief.

It may also include uncertainty, distrust, or lack of

evidence about a particular fact, action, motive, or decision. It is important to note that "doubt" usually delays some relevant actions, or even refuses to act in response, because of the potential for mistakes or missed opportunities.

Therefore, the empirical scientific method is gradually used to observe and study things, to explore the origin of facts and changing phenomena. The central thesis is that facts must be learned through observation or sensory experience to understand the objective environment and external things in which each person lives.

The positivists believe that although each person is educated differently, the principles they use to verify their sensory experience do not differ much. The aim of positivism is to establish that the act of "knowing" and "recognizing" a subject is an act of knowing with certainty, and that these knowings have the potential to be used objectively for specific purposes.

According to Comte, human beings are not born knowing everything, but must acquire, through the process of learning, from different contexts, the act of "cognition" and "identification" of a subject in order to know it with certainty, and these knowings have the potential capacity to be used for a specific purpose.

A form of thinking that derives one or more judgments (this is called a premise) from another judgment (this is called a conclusion) through direct or indirect sensory, inferential, or embodied experience, and in the process of learning, which has not yet been experienced as knowledge. Knowledge that is beyond experience or not observable by experience is not true knowledge.

(3) Human evolution can be roughly divided into three stages:

In his book "The Philosophy of Empiricism", Comte advocates the use of certain objects as the scope of study, and the establishment of empirical "cognition" and "identification" of a subject based on experiments and logical reasoning, in order to obtain unified and exact objective laws and methods of truth, so as to establish a confident knowledge.

These knowledges have the potential to be used for specific purposes. This also means that one must be familiar with something through experience or association in order to understand it further, and that facts must be obtained through observation or perception.

First, theological stage.

The study of theology is to understand "God" so that we can glorify Him through "love" and "obedience". Note the coherence here.

We must know "God" in order to "love God," and we must "love God" in order to be willing to trust and "obey God. As a by-product, God gives comfort and hope to those who know, love, and obey Him, and our lives are enriched beyond measure. A superficial, inaccurate understanding of God and poor theological knowledge will only make life poorer and will not bring the comfort and hope we desire.

Secondly, the metaphysical stage

Metaphysics is an important field of study in philosophy. Although there are different opinions on the scope of metaphysics, generally speaking, metaphysics consists of the following five items.

1. Formalism regards reality, existence, and the universe as a whole, and shows that it is the basis of consistent human vision, an objective reflection of natural

scenery, and an important source of human understanding of the world and human beings themselves.

Metaphysics is the study of some of the most universal and enduring characteristics of the universe, such as existence, change, time, space, causality, and ontology. In this sense, "cosmology" can be regarded as a branch of metaphysics.

Metaphysics is the study of the fundamental principle of what makes "existence" "existence"; it is the study of "universal existence" rather than "individual concrete existence". It is also the study of the ultimate reality, i.e., the real itself rather than the part experienced by the senses and perceptions.

Metaphysics is not only the study of the reasons for the "existence" of various things, but also the study of the "existence" of various objects or phenomena that exist objectively in nature and on which all objects or phenomena depend for their "existence". According to this definition, "ontology", "existence", and "first philosophy" can all be regarded as metaphysics.

3. Metaphysics is the study of the transcendent reality

that is the cause of all "existences"; it is the sum of the facts that exist in front of the eyes as opposed to the appearance, the state of existence, all objects or phenomena that exist objectively in nature, and all actual existences. and all real things that are not related to consciousness.

Reality is the "whole of reality", the "whole of reality". Objective Reality refers to the external existence related to language and perception; Formal Reality refers to the way of thinking applied to the understanding of reality, and involves the relationship between logical concepts.

4. Metaphysics is the study of spiritual objects: these spiritual objects are not suitable for the scientific method of studying those who have weight, occupy a place in space, and whose existence can be known by the senses.

In short, experimentation or empirical induction can be applied to the study of the nature of things, but it is not the main method of metaphysical research.

Metaphysics is a critique and review of the basic premises and presuppositions of various knowledge systems; by this definition, there is a close relationship between metaphysics and the theory of knowledge, and even a partial overlap. Some people also discuss theology and theory of knowledge together.

The main topics often explored in metaphysics include being, substance, reality, the nature of universal existence, characteristics, laws of change, God, soul, freedom, and the ultimate basis of knowledge.

Third, the empirical stage.

Positivism starts with the "empirical" proof of knowledge or skills obtained by practice, and therefore its methodology is observation-induction, advocating the acquisition of knowledge from "experience". This approach has been refuted by Hume and Popper, among others.

Popper's "provability" was directed at positivism, arguing that the "positivism" of philosophical thought centered on "practical verification" could not in fact avoid the a priori, i.e., the assumption that "positivism" observes and experiments with reality.

In fact, it is subject to a priori observation and experimentation of natural and social phenomena, according to the existing empirical knowledge, experience, facts, laws, cognition, and tested hypotheses, through generalization and deductive reasoning, etc.

To make logical inferential conclusion assumptions, or to make judgments on things according to one's own cognition, without seeking to conform to the actual situation, and thus unable to obtain comprehensive and objective results and conclusions. The real meaning of experience is to prove pseudoscientific theories.

Post-positivism is a slight modification of positivism. Post-positivism advocates a theory of negation, which has systematic and organized laws or arguments. It is derived from actual verification or from conceptual extrapolation, and is strictly scientific. The corroboration of the theory is temporary, although it recognizes the validity of systematic conclusions about the knowledge of nature and society that people have generalized from practice.

Science takes a certain object as the scope of study, and seeks to obtain unified and exact objective laws and truths based on experiments and logical reasoning, which is an undertaking that requires continuous thinking, and there is no absolute correctness in science.

That is to say, the stage of science, using observation, classification, and categorical data, to explore all the objects or phenomena that exist objectively in nature, and the connection of certain nature between people and people or people and things, the results obtained by this method are correct and credible.

Positivism opposes the idea of mystical transcendence and advocates the scientific method to establish empirical, "cognitive" and "discriminative" acts on a certain subject, in order to know with certainty, and these knowings have the potential ability to be used for specific purposes of knowledge.

The result of such thinking, or the mental process of cognition, is precisely the opposite of Plato's theory that the nature of all things in the world is in its purest and most perfect form, and that it is the cause of all things in the world having those properties which they have.

Plato believed that existence in immaterial form is necessarily opposed to material things, that only concepts are real, and that the senses are illusory. In the middle of the 20th century, the Austrian philosopher Wiggenstein combined the doctrine of empirical importance with the doctrine of symbolic logic in positivism, which became logical positivism.

Symbolic logic is the application of algebraic methods and symbols to logic. The logic of symbols is the application of algebraic methods and symbols to logic. The logic of symbols is the application of algebraic methods and symbols to logic.

(01), the application of positivism contains the following principles and principles:

01. the principle of realism.

It means that only the phenomena and knowledge contained in the senses can truly become knowledge. It is believed that physical objects cannot be proved to be self-existent, but can only exist as perceptual phenomena or sensory stimuli (such as redness, hardness, softness, sweetness, etc.) that appear in space and time.

To say that a pear existed before me is the same as saying that these specific attributes (greenness, hardness, etc.) were perceived in the present moment. When these features are no longer perceived or experienced by anyone, the object (e.g. the pear) ceases to exist.

In contrast, Machian phenomenalism holds that objects are "logical structures" external to perceptual properties. On this view, to say that if there is a table in a room and no one in that room perceives it is the same as saying that "if" there is someone in that room, "then" that person will perceive the table. What matters is not the "actual" perception, but the conditional "possibility" of perception.

02. The principle of interpretivism.

It refers to the logical inference of natural and social phenomena according to the existing empirical knowledge, experience, facts, laws, cognition, and tested hypotheses, through generalization and deductive reasoning, etc. It is a way of thinking that summarizes knowledge based on certain reflective objective laws, and deduces the unknown parts of things from the known parts of knowledge. The purpose of theory is to generate hypotheses that can be tested so that the interpretation of the laws can be evaluated.

03. The principle of inductivism.

It means that the judgment of a fact and its meaning depends on whether the fact can be verified through experience. In other words, knowledge is derived by collecting facts that provide the basis for the law. It is emphasized that experience is the basis for judging facts, and that scientific truth can be confirmed only through the induction of experience.

Logical nominalists, however, follow Hume's distinction between necessary and contingent truths, but do not agree with Hume's psychological explanation of induction, and thus put forward their confirmationism: on the one hand, they affirm the pursuit of scientific truth through the confirmation of induction; on the other hand, they try to find the logical basis of induction.

They believe that scientific truths are contingent truths, but they have a very high success rate. Although it is not the traditional formal logic, it has its own special logical connotation, which is related to the probability theory and can be operated by symbolic deduction, which R. Carnap (1891-1970) called inductive logic. 4.

04. Objectivism.

It means that science must be conducted in a value-free (i.e., objective) manner. The general criterion of truth in the theory of knowledge is objective evidence, a property of an object or objective thing that presents itself clearly.

For example, the light of a star in the dark sky enables us to discover the existence of the star and all that belongs to it, which would not be discovered if it did not shine. It is because things reveal themselves that they are qualified to be judged, and at the same time that one knows that this judgment is true.

The criterion of knowledge, and the judgment that is believed to be true, has its foundation in the object, that is, in the manifestation of the thing itself. For the thing itself produces an obviousness in the intellect, and this obviousness shows the intellect that the thing is this and not that.

Therefore, the reason cannot judge at will, but must judge according to the obviousness of the thing itself, which is the "objective obviousness," the standard of truth.

05. Objectivism principle.

In Stenmark's view, the strongest expression of scientism is that science knows no boundaries and that, given time, all human problems and hopes can be properly addressed and resolved by science.

This idea is also known as the myth of progress. Also in Against Method, Paul Feyerabend states that science is by nature "an anarchist enterprise.

It is also clear that there has never been a so-called monopoly of science on the "knowledge trade," and that scientists have never had a tradition of differentiation or narrow self-definition. He also describes the process of contemporary science education as a moderate form of indoctrination, intended to "make the history of science more boring, more simplified, more uniform, and more 'objective' so that it can be handled by strict and unchanging rules.

(02) The impact of Western culture

Therefore, the psychological state of consciously working for the realization of a certain ideal or the achievement of a certain goal. We are willing to venture into the unknown, and we are willing to explore new horizons and new horizons.

What human beings could not overcome in the last century, they now have to surpass with more advanced intelligence; what they could not solve in the past, they now have to deal with with more precise thinking and more developed intelligence. The characteristic of mankind is the developed brain, the high intelligence of consciousness, the calm reason.

So, although post-positivism is a slight modification of positivism. Post-positivism advocates "negationism", a theory that strictly judges a human being's knowledge of natural and social phenomena according to existing empirical knowledge, experience, facts, laws, cognition, and tested hypotheses.

Whether or not a logical inferential conclusion is made by generalization and deductive reasoning, whether or not a certain object is the scope of study, and whether or not a unified and definite objective law and truth is obtained based on experimentation and logical reasoning, and whether or not the corroboration of the theory is temporary, although the rationality of the theory is recognized.

Science is a business that requires continuous thinking, and there is no absolute right to use specific methods and means to make production effective, convenient, low-consumption, and high-yield by studying objective things and their laws to promote rapid socio-economic development.

This also means that whether it is an individual or the whole human race, the achievement of human beings lies in their ability to recognize the environment and the self, and the rational achievement of the clarity of cognition, which is the highest achievement of human thought and ambition, that is, the ability of human beings to decide their own behavior.

In short, the value of life's existence lies in the rational grasp of self-consciousness, and the real meaning of life's existence depends on the rational development of the individual's ability to realize his or her own will according to his or her own knowledge and laws.

It is true that man is a rational animal. It is true that people's ability to form concepts, make judgments, analyze, synthesize, compare, reason, and calculate is a valuable quality of human beings.

However, when we focus only on this rational quality, treat it as the most noble quality, and magnify it infinitely, and insist on being exclusive, sooner or later we will reveal the bias of this approach and the difficulty of solving the problem.

Today, in the West, this kind of externally-seeking mentality encounters the dilemma of human beings' logical inferential conclusion of natural and social phenomena in accordance with existing empirical knowledge, experience, facts, laws, cognition, and tested hypotheses, through generalization and deductive reasoning, etc. It is not all accidental and unexpected.

The pursuit of "truth" is an important concept in philosophy, in the theory of knowledge, when human beings are constantly expanding to the external image or environment that is revealed. There are many interpretations of this concept in disciplines that use analytical thinking to inquire and reflect on fundamental questions about life, knowledge, and values.

It may be thought that truth is a proposition; or that truth contains a meaning other than a proposition; or that truth is contained in a noun; or that there is a prior truth; or that it is synonymous with reality; or that logic contains formal truth, associated with abstract propositions; or that truth is found only in science, called scientific truth.

In exploring new objective existences in nature, in all objects or phenomena, in developing new realms, we cannot rely only on the wise mind, but we must also appeal to the keen senses.

Although we all know that our senses are not 100% reliable, and that we sometimes have illusions and occasionally even hallucinations, our eyes, nose, ears, tongue, and skin are the organs that can directly perceive the stimuli of the external world and produce neurological responses to experience.

This is the way in which human beings, in direct contact with objective things, acquire, through the sensory organs, the phenomena of objective things, the concrete facts and conditions that exist in front of them, and the way in which they associate with external recognition.

But we are in search of the most realistic situation, such as the external image or environment that is revealed. This is also an indispensable element in capturing all objects or phenomena that exist objectively in the natural world, which are concealed within things and revealed in the external image or environment.

Therefore, we must use our senses and perceptions to retrieve the images that remain in our minds from the external stimulation of the external things and the external world.

In other words, in our human activity of external seeking, the mind or individual's activity of "self-will" according to its own knowledge and laws must not be contrary to our sensory experience in order to be retrieved and trusted by us.

However, this internal state of arousal, which is caused and motivated by the physical or psychological needs of the living individual to engage in actions to satisfy these needs, by paying attention to the content of the senses and valuing the sensory experience, has a profound effect on the identification of life and the choice of values.

Since we are more concerned with describing (potentially) and verbalizing the experience of various psychological experiences and reactions in general psychological terms, such as fear, anger, sarcasm and pity, jealousy, fear, happiness, and love.

Thus, we ask that many of life's pursuits be realized on the visible, audible, touchable, and tangible level of the external image or environment. This requirement can also be applied as a methodological item to facilitate the establishment of experiential knowledge, the original positive contribution.

However, if we consider it as a guiding principle for all

things or phenomena in life that have a positive meaning for people or groups, that are valued, or that satisfy people, that are respected or interested in pursuing actions or thinking, then it is possible to use it as a guiding principle.

If this is the guiding principle of the things that are the goal, then it is easy to evolve into a "philosophy of life" that focuses only on appearance, immediate effects and benefits, and the pursuit of sensual pleasures by those who are in high positions of power.

The meaning of life itself, the ideas and truths contained in it, becomes a state of mind that is consciously worked for in order to realize a certain ideal or achieve a certain purpose, and exists outside the body.

It is the pursuit of the external image or environment that is revealed, but not the establishment of the substantial inner value of the human self that is hidden within the body and mind. The purpose of life becomes to increase material abundance and prosperity rather than to devote oneself to the metamorphosis and sublimation of spiritual consciousness.

In short, it will gradually evolve into the era of AI

artificial intelligence, which has arrived with the advancement of science and technology. We can clearly feel the rapid and convenient changes in our daily life, and see the increasing prosperity of Western civilization.

We have witnessed the expansion of Western material civilization and felt the democracy and freedom of Western lifestyle. Many people, under the strong impact of this outward-looking, extroverted, outward-seeking and outward-looking Western force, unconsciously cater to this Western trend, adopt this Western way of life, and pursue the meaning and value of life under this Western concept.

Even secretly, people think that Westernization is modernization, and that to be a modern person, one must adopt Western culture in its entirety. As a result, there are conflicts of concepts, confusion of values, physical and mental discomfort, and incompatibility of lifestyles in our society.

Generally speaking, there is nothing wrong with "maladjustment" in life due to certain factors, such as physical, psychological, family or social and cultural background.

The phenomenon of disagreement or conflict between people who seem to grow up in different generations, due to different living environment and life experiences, in terms of thoughts, attitudes and behavioral habits, can be seen everywhere.

01. A generation of rapid hollowing out

This positivist ideology has the view that all objects or phenomena in nature have two contradictory properties inherent in things, i.e., a thing has two opposing properties at the same time.

Technological (the process of using science, materials and human resources to achieve human desired goals) doctrine is also a double-edged sword. We are grateful to technology for enriching our lives and improving our quality of life, but we cannot stop it from eroding our hearts and minds with its rapid and negative impact.

Modern technology's unparalleled reach provides us with what we need and what we want, but it also traps us in its convenience, bad habits, bad habits, and laziness.

It is like being spoiled and pampered, an inertia that often occurs in our subconscious, leaving us with no choice and no ability to choose.

Relying on the rapid development of its ever-changing technology, we have become a part of the modern technological planning and design, instrumentalized and modeled in a situation that we cannot resist.

For example, the Internet is a treasure trove of big data and information, but it is also a dumping ground for information. Different cultural forms, ideas and concepts either intermingle or clash on the Internet.

Useful and useless, right and wrong, advanced and backward, economic information and all kinds of yellow, violent and fraudulent information are mixed together.

The Internet has become a kaleidoscope of information. The impact of this unfiltered junk information on young people is particularly serious, as well as its invisible and negative influence.

Generally speaking, individuals have inherited social factors, such as customs, morals, habits, beliefs, ideas, etc., which are passed down from generation to generation, and may be factors of physical, psychological, family or socio-cultural background.

Due to the different growing environment and life experiences, differences or conflicts occur in thoughts, attitudes and behavioral habits.

Whether it is a couple, a partner, or a family member, there are inevitably times of conflict, not to mention the impact of cultures from all over the world, which can be seen everywhere.

We are born in the present world, and we have the illusion of growing up in a world of chaos among different generations. Whenever we encounter some internal impact, we encounter spiritual or material incompatibility with each other, and the greatest impact is mainly in the discord between our three views.

But what are the three views? The old three views are the three views in the traditional sense, that is, the common three views used on the Internet, the three views that are not correct, mainly including the world view, life view, and value view.

001. Worldview

Worldview, also called cosmology, refers to a basic framework of human perception through which an individual can understand the world and interact with it.

Worldview is a fundamental view of the whole world in

which people live, and the relationship between people and the external world. It arises and is gradually formed on the basis of social practice.

It is the ideas, morals, customs, arts, and institutions that people have passed down through history. It is a kind of national culture that reflects the characteristics and style of the nation through the evolution of civilization.

At the same time, it is also an overall representation of the history of the nation, the different social status of various ideologies, cultures, and concepts, and the different perspectives of observation, forming different world views. It is also called cosmology.

Philosophy is its theoretical expression. Philosophy (English: philosophy) is also the study of the principles and principles of the universe and life. Philosophy differs from other disciplines in that it has a unique way of thinking.

For example, it has a critical, often systematic, holistic approach, based on rational argumentation, and a worldview analysis that explores and reflects on fundamental questions about life, knowledge, and values.

The basic problem is the relationship between spirit

and matter, thought and existence, and according to different interpretations of these two relationships, two fundamentally opposed worldviews are distinguished, namely the idealist worldview and the materialist worldview.

02. Outlook on life: Outlook on life refers to people's fundamental attitudes and views on life, including basic views and attitudes on the value of life, the purpose of life, and the meaning of human affairs. It is also an important part of the worldview.

The outlook on life is determined by the outlook on the world. Life view is the fundamental view and attitude of people towards the purpose of life and the meaning of human affairs.

It determines a person's standard of being a human being, and is a guide to grasp the direction of life and choose the path of life, mainly answering the questions of why people live, the meaning, value, purpose, ideal, belief and pursuit of life.

It is a fundamental viewpoint on the purpose, attitude, value and ideal of life. It mainly answers the questions of what is life, the meaning of life, and how to realize the value of life. Its concrete expression is bitterness and optimism, honor and shame, life and death, etc.

The concept of life is the ideology of a certain society or class, and is the product of certain social and historical conditions and social relations. The formation of the outlook on life is gradually generated and developed in the process of people's actual life, and is subject to the constraints of people's worldview.

Different societies or classes of people have different outlooks on life. In the history of mankind, the following representative outlooks on life have emerged.

(1) Hedonistic view of life. It is the idea that all actions can be determined by the enjoyment and pain a person will produce, and seeks to maximize the difference between enjoyment and pain. It starts from human biological instincts, reduces human life to the process of satisfying human physiological needs, and proposes that the pursuit of sensual pleasure and maximum satisfaction of material life enjoyment is the only purpose of life.

(2) Nihilistic view of life. The philosophy advocates the

denial of the possibility of all things, the truth or true knowledge is not available, there is no objective validity of intellectual truth, moral good and evil, nor is there a universal standard, religious anorexicism believes that life is an abyss of suffering, full of all kinds of trouble and pain, the only way to be truly liberated is to get rid of the mundane and eliminate desire.

(3) The ascetic view of life. It is a moral theory that requires people to strictly restrain their physical desires. It originates from the religious teachings and austerity rituals of ancient people who endured the hardships of the present life.

After the 6th century B.C., it was gradually developed into a theory through the generalization of religious doctrines and moral philosophies in the East and West. It regards human desires, especially physical desires, as the root of all sins and advocates the extinction of human desires and the practice of asceticism.

(4) Happiness theory of life. One view is to emphasize personal happiness as the highest purpose and value of life.

Another viewpoint is that while emphasizing personal

happiness, it also emphasizes the happiness of others and the public happiness of society, believing that the pursuit of public happiness is the highest purpose and value of life.

(5) Optimistic view of life. A positive view of everything. It is the opposite of pessimism. An optimistic person does not think about the flaws and defects of an event, and always thinks positively about everything around him or her. It believes that the future of social development is bright, and that the purpose of life is to pursue social civilization and progress, to pursue the truth, and to have a positive and optimistic attitude toward life.

(6) Existentialist view of life. It is a philosophy of irrationalism, which believes that the meaning of human existence cannot be analyzed or judged by the right or wrong of a matter, and that sensibility is judged by one's own preference regardless of right or wrong. Among them, the search for effective ways to achieve the purpose of behavioral thinking, and to get answers to the moral position, political philosophy, ideology that emphasizes the intrinsic value of the individual, advocates the realization of personal (career) goals and aspirations, and emphasizes the autonomy (of personal thought and

action) and subjective experience.

03. Values: refers to a person's total evaluation and total view of the meaning and importance of the objective things around him/her (including people, things and objects). On the basis of knowing the value of various specific things, people form a general view and fundamental view of the value of things.

Values are the criteria that members of society use to evaluate behaviors and things and to choose their own preferred goals from among various possible goals.

Values are reflected through people's behavior and their evaluation of things and attitudes, and are the main core of the worldview and the internal driving force of people's behavior. It governs and regulates all social behaviors and involves all areas of social life.

On the one hand, it is expressed as value orientation, value pursuit, condensed into certain value objectives; on the other hand, it is expressed as value scale and criteria, which become the evaluation standard for people to judge the value of things and their value size.

Once an individual's value is established, it has relative stability. However, in terms of society and groups, due to the turnover of personnel and environmental changes, the value concept of society or groups, and is constantly changing.

Therefore, individuals are guided by their own values, forming different value orientations and pursuing what they think is the most valuable.

Values are very rich in connotation and can generally be divided into material and spiritual values, as well as comprehensive and complex values, such as human values (or life values); whether one can establish correct values and scientific and reasonable value orientations is crucial to one's development.

Traditional values are constantly challenged by new values. The order in which things are viewed and evaluated in the mind is the order of priority and importance, which constitutes the value system. Values and value systems are the psychological basis for determining human behavior.

In fact, life and values are also unified. A correct outlook on life is conducive to one's perception of the true meaning of life and existence itself.

At the same time, the correct values are conducive to

an objective analysis of one's own values and the establishment of a correct outlook on life.

Therefore, these three views have the greatest physical and psychological influence on the growth of young people, naturally the first is the family, followed by school and finally society.

A physically and mentally sound young person who excels must have grown up in a family with good parenting, received a balanced and healthy college and university education, and then entered a society full of opportunities and challenges.

If any part of their lives is affected by problems or negative influences, they will grow up with a personality that is prone to deviations. This may lead to a lack of faith or a diversity of values, and affect the formation of a correct outlook on life, values, and worldview.

This may lead to a weakened sense of morality and a weakened sense of social responsibility, and may even lead young people to do things that are against the norm and to commit crimes.

02. Distorted values

By algorithm, we mean that in order to continue to provide viewers with a safe community environment and preferred video genres and content, YouTube has created an algorithm to help recommend all content on the platform, which will change according to "viewer behavior"?

Or rather, it should contain clearly defined instructions for calculating the "view rate" of the function. The incentive to use it again.

In fact, "algorithm" is a kind of logical thinking to solve problems! It can be described through code, flowcharts, electronic circuits, mathematics, and so on. Programming = data structure + algorithm. So Instagram users must have wondered at one point or another.

What is the sorting of limited-time dynamic posts, and how is the sorting of people who have seen the limited-time dynamic? For example, we may feel baffled by the fact that we are in a special kind of boyfriend-girlfriend relationship.

We have not chatted with each other online for a period of time, nor have we liked each other's photos, but why is she or he still ranked first in my computer in the ranking of the limited-time updates?

"Interests" is how IG decides what content to push based on what each individual is interested in. The criteria that affects how IG judges your "interests" include who you "like", who you "like", and who you "like".

The algorithm of "interest" indicators will enhance the use of this software and drive the incentive to use the program design (= data structure + algorithm) once and want to use it again.

Then, when you slide the Instagram home page in an attempt to increase and expand the "view rate" idea, or to achieve the goal of inducing the user to use it again, what will she or he see in the package?

Could it be a beautiful photo or a scary picture? Does the question of falsification of truth behind it violate the central thesis of positivism, which is that facts must be understood through observation or sensory experience of the objective environment and external things in which each person lives? What is the original intention of the pursuit of truth?

For example, many eighth and ninth graders go to great lengths to ignore the negative consequences or dangers, just for the sake of an illusory and unrealistic picture or image, and live almost exclusively for the purpose of posting a picture every day.

The overall appearance of the group is becoming more and more similar, and sometimes it is not even very distinguishable, all have the face of an angel, and the standard devil's body, only to know that many of the amazing beauty photos, are computer programs to fix out.

For modern people, the cell phone is like a doppelganger. We are inseparable from our cell phones every day, whether we use photos to record the friends we meet or the food we eat.

We use our cell phones every day, whether it's to record photos of friends we've met or food we've eaten, to use social and communication software to set up social networking sites, to create a circle of friends, or to catch up on dramas and games to pass the time. This shows that cell phones have been deeply integrated into our daily life.

However, every day from morning to night, excessive eyes glued to the life of the cell phone all the time, even face to face without communication, rather than fingertips constantly blindly click "like" behavior, let everyone in the virtual world of the Internet, like a living person lost consciousness, controlled by the zombie. The will of the individual becomes smaller and smaller.

Therefore, according to the Taiwan "Ministry of Science and Technology Communication Survey Database: Media Use and Social Interaction" (N=2028), we analyzed the situation of people's cell phone use. According to the survey, the survey was conducted by the Taiwan Ministry of Science and Technology, "Media Use and Social Interaction" (N=2028).

In the actual questionnaire survey, when asked about the aspirations of high school and university students, more than one-third of the young people wanted to become net stars, thinking they could become a big star and become rich overnight.

They even said surprisingly, "Individuals can use any form of vulgarity and claptrap to gain attention and gain views". In addition, Instagram offers a few "facts" to reduce speculation about the algorithm.

If you like videos, of course IG will push you more videos, but there will not be a situation where you like photos but a lot of videos are pushed to you.

And then there's the fact that "leaving fewer comments will still affect the results", so even if you only leave a smiley face for your favorite content, you've already increased the chances of it appearing in your view!

In addition, Instagram officials say that they do not favor any one type of account, which means that you have equal chances of appearing with business accounts, general accounts, creator accounts, and other accounts.

When everyone wants to combine factors of production through effective business models and create new businesses to achieve new commercial successes, many new start-up companies have emerged in this society and dreamers abound, but there are a few people like Bill Gates and Mark Zuckerberg.

According to the official statistics of the Ministry of Economic Affairs of the Executive Yuan, as many as 90% of new businesses face collapse within one year, and 90% of the surviving 10% will be closed within five years, which means that only 1% of new businesses can survive for more than five years.

The same can be said for young people who want to be

netizens and think they want to be stars. There are many good-looking people who can sing and dance, and there are many of them, even if you have all the right conditions, you may not be popular.

The standard of Instagram has always been: "You" like what content, it will give priority to you. It's not impossible that the other person likes you and follows you so much that they have priority to appear in their limited time feeds, but it's not officially confirmed by IG.

Therefore, the situation of "Is it because he/she cares about me too that I keep seeing the other person's limited-time updates? The situation of "does he/she also care about me so much that I keep seeing each other's time-limited movements?" is still in favor of the calculation record of personal information interest indicators, which will enhance the use of this software and drive the programming (= data structure + algorithm) mostly.

This kind of personal information interest indicators of the calculation record, and further enhance the use of this software, the driver has used the programming (= data structure + algorithm) for the network pictogram expression.

Looking horizontally, the X represents the eyes and the D represents the mouth, like an obscene and unintentional smile. At the same time, some people would like to think that it is a kind of cheerful laugh, X means eyes smiling into a forked shape, D means a wide mouth. Its meaning has been accepted by most BBS, people often add XD at the end of the message, indicating that they look at each other with a very evil eyes.

03. Summary

According to the above-mentioned Instagram proposed several indicators that affect the algorithm, we can see: to see which content you like, in fact, a large decision on your own, you click the like, leave a message, see the limit of action, will affect the next content will see.

So when the little girls around us all agree that "as long as I like it, there's nothing wrong with it," we often can't sit back and save their fragile and wounded souls, even if we ruthlessly believe that it's mostly the stupidity and ignorance of the people involved.

But when social networking sites reinforce the hatred and hostility in their stance, and many people make ruthless comments on social networking, like an executioner with a cruel expression on his face, is it clear that

Can we know clearly that we deliberately kill people on the internet, but we think it is justice to do so? When social injustice is revealed and we have to pay for our own lives, can we admit that we have lost the morality and courage that we have been proud of since we were children?

As human beings, it is important to accept the baptism of human spirit, inventions, creativity and public order and morality that have been precipitated in history, which are useful to enhance human adaptation and awareness of the objective world, in line with human spiritual pursuit, and can be recognized and accepted by the majority of people, and have conscience.

The above feelings are known to you and I. Whenever we are quiet and reflecting, how should we inform our family members, colleagues and friends around us to recognize the distorted values that need to be changed or adjusted? How should we educate the next generation? What should we do to educate the next generation?

This is a generation with severely distorted values,

and the question marks thrown up by positivist ideology may be unanswerable, but the vast majority of people with a conscience understand that even in a vanity society, technology and civilization are not exclusive to the rich.

We may not have the power, but we may not necessarily bow down, or this is the meaning of life itself.

We may not have the power, but we may not always bow down, or this is the moment to awaken the God-given nature of each of us to know good and evil, to judge right and wrong. What are the values that will lead us to the right path of awakening and to the correct meaning of life?

According to the Farsighted Research Survey, 6-8% of the world's population suffers from Internet addiction, and about 20% of the youth in Taiwan are deeply addicted to the Internet. 50% of the young people aged 26-38 spend an average of 8-12 hours a day online.

The American Psychiatric Association is the professional organization for psychiatrists in the United States and has global influence in the profession.

Its publications include academic journals and pamphlets, and its most familiar publication is the Diagnostic and Statistical Manual of Mental Disorders, or

DSM for short. The DSM defines "Internet Gaming Disorder" and has three clear criteria for determining Internet addiction:.

1. out-of-control use behavior, which means that the person is unable to moderate his or her own use of the Internet to keep from going beyond the scope of use or random activities.

2. Steps in daily life that interfere with the beneficial effects of things or methods that must be dealt with.

3. A state that lasts for a year. An out-of-control behavior that occurs frequently, often unconsciously, for a period of one year or more. That is, prolonged use of the Internet due to professional or other factors does not fall into the category of Internet addiction.

According to the survey, 1/3 of young people spend more time online than sleeping, and 23.1% of fresh Taiwanese aged 26 to 38 are at risk of Internet addiction.

One-third of young people spend more time online than the ideal 8 hours of sleep," said the survey. Nearly 60% of the respondents said the Internet is the first thing they think of when they wake up every morning; more than half of them feel restless when they can't go online, and 44.8% are worried about the negative impact of Internet use on their health.

More seriously, prolonged Internet use can lead to cyber loneliness, indifference to interpersonal emotions, disapproval or even avoidance of the real world, and induce dual personality disorders in adolescents, making them lonely, sensitive, depressed, vigilant, disobedient to social norms, and even mentally challenged and suicidal.

The virtual and free nature of online interaction can easily lead to people's behavior.

In the process of general modernization, traditional values and traditional social norms are weakened, destroyed, and even disintegrated, resulting in a disorderly state in which members of society lose their psychological guidance and disintegrate their values, which is not conducive to the socialization of adolescents.

It even leads to the youth's self-contribution to the society in their personal life and social activities. The relationship between society and others in the future is a kind of affirmative recognition of human existence.

This includes human dignity and the material and spiritual conditions that guarantee it, as well as the process of learning and inheriting various social norms, traditions, ideologies, and other surrounding social and cultural elements, and gradually adapting to them.

For individuals, socialization is not conducive to the learning process of young people, and the imitation and learning of different roles in society, due to the disorderly state of loss of "value guidance" and "value disintegration" caused by the weakening, destruction, and even disintegration of traditional values and traditional social norms.

Therefore, if we talk about the negative impact on the daily life of human beings, I believe that the most deeply felt is the chaos of the modern developed information network technology that accompanies us all the time.

Which direction should we choose, and what lifestyle should we adopt? What is the value of this way of life and what is the real meaning of life itself?

Furthermore, empirical science takes a certain object as the scope of study, and seeks for unified and exact objective laws and truths based on experiments and logical reasoning, trying to establish a densely structured and simple propositional system.

In fact, we are limiting ourselves to the system of division of labor, without considering the legitimacy behind it. This kind of philosophical thinking only involves the external surface phenomenon, but does not penetrate into the substance connotation hidden inside things.

Secondly, to seek the understanding of educational lawfulness by the scientific tool model is only the prediction and technical application of educational science theory.

However, the law of cause and effect is inappropriately applied to human mental phenomena and described in a quasi-behavioralist narrative, ignoring the fact that human beings are the whole of meaning and have the function of active self-determination.

Finally, empirical-oriented educational research ignores the subjectivity of educational objects, the spatio-temporal nature of the educational process, and the possible misleading ideology of educational research. As a result, we are born in the present world and have the illusion that we are growing up in a world of confusion among different generations.

As a result, pedagogy has not only failed to raise its

theoretical level, but also has been in the dilemma of treating the head when it hurts and treating the foot when it hurts in practice, and has developed an externally seeking culture that emphasizes rational activities and sensory experiences.

In addition to the dazzling material satisfaction, life seems to be a happy color on the surface, but under careful tasting, we find that what makes the body or spirit feel very uncomfortable is still the hidden essence of life that cannot be wiped away, the pain and boredom of the sadness and vicissitude.

The question of life and death has become an issue of sharp and harsh words that can easily cause strong reactions.

In such a moment of introspection about the way of existence of a person or a group of people, it is easy to inquire and think about the invisible influence and control of our own cultural traditions on our social behavior.

In particular, the values and life experiences of our cultural traditions. Our cultural ideals indicate what kind of life meaning and life value?

The meaning of life or the meaning of life has to do

with the quenching of the experience of daily life in general or the meaning of life existence itself.

In a broad sense, it includes the question of the purposeful meaning of life itself in the universe. In a narrower sense, it explores the question of possible meanings in the evolution of biology and social culture, especially in the case of Homo sapiens.

In a narrower sense, it examines "the relationship between human beings and their world, explaining what they seek and what they want to achieve. What do they want to live for and what do they want to die for?

He tells us what is the meaning of life and what is the value of death? These are the questions that we should ponder at this time of civilizational crisis at the beginning of the 21st century.

(03) Impact of Oriental Culture

Oriental culture generally refers to the unique thought and mindset of the Eastern world, centered on India, China, and Japan.

From the Western point of view, the ideas established in the eastern part of Europe are collectively called

Eastern ideas. Although India, China, and Japan each have their own social and cultural patterns that have been handed down from generation to generation.

Although India, China, and Japan each have different national and regional characteristics in terms of social factors such as thought, culture, morality, customs, art, institutions, and behaviors that have been passed down through history.

However, the religious philosophies of India, China, and Japan share significant and common ideological characteristics that have shaped the ideology of the Orientals in terms of their worldview, outlook on life, and outlook on life. For example

(a) India: Indian culture is not very expansive and aggressive, but actively resists the invasion of foreign cultures. Although there were many kings in early India who regarded Buddhism as the state religion, it was later followed by Islam.

Later, it was ruled by Mongolian and Turkic princes who believed in Islam, and in the last two hundred years it was colonized by the British who believed in Christianity, but after the fall of each foreign regime, India reverted to

Hindu traditions.

Although the Muslims have impacted India for centuries, they have only assimilated two lands, Pakistan and Bangladesh, and have not been able to shake the main Indian culture.

The Indian culture is not a single religious culture, there were already some other religions such as Sikhism, Jainism and Buddhism in the early days of the Indian continent, only Buddhism was successfully exported to other countries.

Only Buddhism was successfully exported to other countries, including the southern Buddhist countries, which became part of the Indian cultural circle, and the northern Buddhist countries, which absorbed the philosophical ideas of Chinese Confucianism and merged with Confucianism. Buddhism, Hinduism, Jainism, Sikhism and a number of other religions were born in the land where religious culture flourished.

These religions are collectively known as Indian religions. Indian religions are also considered to be "Dharmic Religions" and, along with Arab religions, are the major forms of world religions.

Today, Hinduism and Buddhism are the third and fourth largest religions in the world, with a combined total of more than 2 billion and possibly more than 2.5 billion followers.

India is one of the most religiously diverse countries in the world, and has some of the most "faith-based" social and cultural elements. Today, religion still plays a very important role in the minds of many Indians and has had a very significant impact.

According to India's 2001 census, 80 percent of religious adherents converted to Hinduism, while 13 percent of the Indian population practiced Islam. India is also home to 23 million Christians, 19 million Sikhs, 8 million Buddhists, and 4 million Jains.

The influence of Sikhism, Jainism, and especially Buddhism is not only limited to India, but has spread throughout the world. Local Christianity, Zoroastrianism, and the Baha'i faith are also influential, but their followers are relatively small.

Atheists (materialists) and "agnostic" philosophers have also been influential in India, where Indians place special emphasis on the universal commonality of things, and on

The Indians placed special emphasis on the universality of things and on the identification of abstract concepts and complex categories of things. In their argumentation, they prefer the concept and medium of negation, especially the certainty of the absolute, and the grasp of the unknown.

Therefore, the individuality of the particular is not taken seriously, and a holistic view of all things is emphasized. Therefore, the concept of time and historical understanding is lacking, and is replaced by the attitude of contemplation and observation.

He also regards the human being as the subject of action as a super-individual, so he is rich in national concepts, and therefore attaches great importance to the tradition of conservatism. He is fond of mythology and poetry, and prefers to ignore the laws of natural science in favor of meditation and contemplation.

On the other hand, in the internal aspect, he is particularly concerned with the psychological inner view. His outlook on life is mainly transcendental religion, full of reverence for the life of all things, but it also gives rise to a strong idea of peace.

(2) China: Generally speaking, the Chinese attach special importance to abstract rational thinking and perceptual awareness, and therefore love words, illustrations, and figurative concepts, but do not deny the character of irrational thinking.

This can be seen in the development of Zen Buddhism and the accompanying characteristics of artistic thought. In addition, Chinese historiography was developed in its early years because of its rich sense of continuity over time, and its strong sense of continuity in the same way of thinking has given rise to the characteristic of transmission of learning.

In contrast, free thought was extremely poor. In contrast, free thought was extremely poor, and the love of form and ceremony led to a preference for beautiful rhetoric, exegesis, and the study of the world.

Since their lives are centered on human beings, their religions are also humanistic and humanistic, centered on the present world. Therefore, it can be said that the study of form is less likely to develop, but rather focuses on the study of human life, such as astronomy, calendar, and astrology.

In addition, there is a special respect for the order of identity and the ethics of family and nation. China is experiencing a spiritual revival on the scale of the Great Awakening religious movement of the nineteenth century in the United States.

As it was a century and a half ago, this developing nation is now in a state of uncertainty as a result of dramatic social and economic change.

People are flocking to new and alienated cities where they have neither friends nor the strength to care for each other in their daily lives. Religion and faith provide a way for everyone, everywhere, to examine the following age-old questions, which people have always tried to answer at their tentative pace

Why are we here? What makes us truly happy? How do we live our lives, from individuals to communities and nations? What is our soul?

In order to understand this spiritual and psychological unrest, we must first look back to understand its origins, which began with one of the largest anti-religious movements in world history.

Almost all major religious faiths in China, including Buddhism, Christianity, Taoism, folk beliefs, and Islam, were affected by this movement.

Since China has been under Communist rule for a long time, this anti-religious movement looks rather like a typical case of atheistic Communists attacking religion, and in a way it is.

In reality, however, this movement did not begin in 1949 when the Communist Party seized power, but a century before the founding of the Communist Party, when traditional Chinese civilization began to fall apart.

The collapse of traditional civilization began with a crisis of confidence. For most of its recorded history, China has been the leader of its neighbors.

Some of its neighbors may have been superior in force to China, especially several nomadic peoples in the north, such as the Huns, Mongols, and Manchus.

But even when these peoples dominated and conquered China, the Chinese rarely doubted the superiority of their own civilization. The Chinese were often self-critical, but still believed that their way of life was far superior to that of their neighbors.

By the end of the nineteenth century, more and more Chinese began to believe that what the country really needed was more than superficial changes.

They realized that China lacked modern science, engineering, education, public health, and advanced farming techniques.

All of these things came from a society that was organized very differently from China, and science was the main foundation of that society.

As the crisis deepens, more and more radical ideas are taking root in people's minds. China did not only need a new policy, or even a new dynasty.

What China desperately needs is to depose the emperor and overthrow the entire political system as it currently operates. And that means destroying the most important pillar of the current system, which is the religious system.

Why religion? Can't China just reform its schools and modernize its economy without destroying traditional religious beliefs? Today, China is a rising power, and the prevalence of various traditional religions in the country may not seem contradictory.

But the role that religion played in traditional Chinese society in the past is very different from what it is today, and there are some things that we are only now beginning to understand.

Over the past few decades, scholars have argued that the religions in China are in some way similar to the Abrahamic Faiths, the three monotheistic religions that gave the Old Testament prophet Abraham an exalted status: Judaism, Christianity, and Islam.

In China, however, it is Buddhism, Taoism, and Confucianism that have replaced Christianity, Judaism, or Islam. This view is wrong. In fact, Chinese religious philosophy is "pervasive" throughout society.

Religion in China is not another pillar of the state second only to secular society, nor can it be defined by the standards of the activities of other religious organizations in the world.

For example, you go to a particular place twice a week to worship under the guidance of a particular sacred text. Chinese religions have little theology, almost no clergy, and few regular places of worship.

However, this does not mean that Chinese religious

consciousness is thin and weak. On the contrary, the light of religious philosophy has spread to every aspect of life.

(3) Japan: Japanese culture refers to the beliefs or behaviors (folk customs) with symbolic or special meanings that have been passed down from one group or society to another on the Japanese islands, originating from the past in a series of physical or non-physical things or symbols related to thought, behavior, life, education, beliefs, and values.

From the fourth to the ninth centuries, Japanese ambassadors from the Sui and Tang Dynasties brought Chinese Buddhism to Japan, such as the "flower ceremony," "tea ceremony," and "incense ceremony," all of which were introduced to Japan along with Chinese Buddhism, an important part of Japan's traditional religious philosophy.

Around the tenth century, the exchanges between Japan and the East Asian continent became less frequent, and new things began to brew and grow out of the old ones. The so-called "national style" culture of Japan evolved.

One of the more Japanese characteristics is Bushido,

or the spirit of Bushido, which is the moral code and philosophy of the samurai class in feudal Japan (called Samurai, or the slightly older term Samurai, or Bushi).

Like the spirit of chivalry that emerged in medieval Europe, Bushido is based on virtues such as righteousness, courage, benevolence, courtesy, honesty, honor, loyalty, and self-restraint. Only by fulfilling these virtues could a samurai maintain his honor, and a samurai who lost his honor had to commit hara-kiri (Japanese: 切腹 / せっぷく Seppuku, or Hara-kiri Harakiri) to commit suicide.

Shinwatari Inazo believed that for a samurai, the most important thing was to take responsibility and fulfill his duty, and that death was only a means to fulfill his duty, but a secondary one.

If one did not fulfill his duty, the punishment was worse than death. The view that harakiri was the only way for a samurai to give thanks for his sins was wrong. A ronin was a samurai who fled in fear of sin, or who did not die with the fall of the sovereign or country to which he was loyal.

The early samurai were in fact mercenaries, and in the

Warring States period, the Shogunate period was the era of the under-killers. From Shintoism, the samurai gained loyalty to their lord and respect for their ancestors.

From Buddhism, Japanese Zen Buddhism, it was learned to be focused, calm, composed, and unafraid of death; from Confucianism, it was learned the five ethics: "ruler and subject, father and son, husband and wife, elders and children, and friends. Bushido is the main content of Japanese Shintoism. It was originally the moral code of the Japanese feudal samurai.

In the middle of the sixteenth century, European culture was introduced to Japan, but later, due to trade protection policies and the ban on Christianity, the spread of European culture in Japan was stagnant.

It was not until the nineteenth century that Japan signed the Japan-U.S. Treaty of Kanagawa (Japan-U.S. Treaty of Peace) under the diplomatic pressure of the United States, which opened the ports of Shimoda and Hakodate to commerce, that European culture was revived in Japan, and later became an important part of Japanese culture.

Because of Japan's geographical location in East Asia,

Japanese culture has often been classified as part of East Asia or the Confucian cultural sphere, but this has always been controversial.

Samuel P. Huntington, an American conservative political scientist, in his 1993 theory of the clash of civilizations, argued that Japanese culture is independent of East Asia and should be included as one of the nine major civilizations in the world.

Japanese historians and Naha Jun, on the other hand, believe that Japanese culture is an extension of the culture of mainland East Asia, with a strong emphasis on the culture of the Tang Dynasty, which differs only slightly.

Shinto and Buddhism are the major religions in Japan, with the largest number of Japanese identifying themselves with Shintoism and Buddhism coming in second.

Nowadays, most Japanese are not psychologically devoutly religious. According to official statements, most Japanese practice both Shinto and Buddhism, and the rituals of these two religions have become integrated into Japanese life, such as wedding ceremonies and funerals.

The majority of Japanese people practice both Shinto and Buddhism. According to a survey conducted by the U.S. Central Intelligence Agency (CIA), Shintoism accounts for about 99% of Japan's population and Buddhism accounts for about 80% of the population.

According to the Nihon Shoki, Buddhism was introduced to Japan in 552, and then spread rapidly under the active promotion of Prince Shotoku.

Shintoism, on the other hand, is a religion developed in Japan itself, where shrines are places of worship for the gods, and Shintoism believes that everything in nature is a god.

In fact, the majority of Japanese people claim to be irreligious, and they do not care about religion or even show an attitude of dislike. Modern Japanese people have an attitude of "clinging to the Buddha's feet" and "utilitarianism" toward religion.

Catholicism entered Japan in 1549, and by the early 17th century there were about 750,000 members. However, the Tokugawa Shogunate imposed a policy of prohibition, and it was not until the late 19th century that missionary activity flourished in Japan again, after the

Black Ship Incident, in which the U.S. military forced Japan to open up to trade and diplomacy.

Nowadays, the number of officially baptized Christians in Japan does not exceed 1% of the total population. The Japanese consider the phenomenal world and the present world to be of absolute significance, and therefore lack a critical spirit.

In The Essentials of Seijutsu, Yamaguka Suhō criticized the interpretation of the Confucian classics by the popular Zhuzi scholars of the time and proposed "ancient learning," arguing that the original spirit of Confucianism should be learned directly from the ancient sages.

He believed that the highest principles of Bushido were "to kill for mercy" and "to sacrifice life for righteousness". Yamaguka Su-young called Japan the "Chinese dynasty" or "Chugoku" and advocated that the Japanese emperor "can be a king for all generations", that "the gods and goddesses are born together and the saints and emperors are united", and that "there is no limit to the heaven and earth" in order to maintain the "national body" that is united for all generations.

In Japan, he was called "the authority of national morality and the true essence of the Bushido spirit".

This is characterized by the nation's national supremacy, the seclusion of sects, and the absolute obedience to those with specific power.

The reason why the emperor's system still exists is not only because of the strong feudalistic tendency to follow, but also because of the poverty of the people and their own contradictory conservative tendencies. Bushido, as the spiritual norm of the traditional feudal system, has found a home in the increasingly fascist national army and has become a tool of imperialist aggression and expansion.

Bushido, in a nutshell, is a moral code of conduct and a standard of behavior. Throughout history, what the spirit of "Bushido" is actually depends entirely on the political needs of reality.

"Bushido was originally a moral system that advocated self-restraint, public service, bravery, patience, humility, and moral ethics, but the rulers took it out of context and overemphasized "bravery" and "loyalty" because the samurai had taken the samurai sword and the Japanese bow as symbols of bravery and status since ancient times.

In particular, "Bushido" is the awareness of death, and when this way of thinking about facing death with equanimity is combined with narrow nationalism and expansionist policies, it turns into a mad belief in ignoring the value of other people's lives and treating one's own life in that way, turning into a sadistic and self-mutilating maniac.

Although moral introspection is strong, it is weak in continuity and not deeply religious. The way of thinking tends to be irrational, but tends to be intuitively emotional, so the creative spirit of thought, art, and learning is lacking, and the emphasis is on the construction of the representational world of Western culture.

Chapter 8: Differences between Eastern and Western philosophies of life.

On the other hand, basically, Eastern philosophical thought is not an outward-looking, extroverted, outward-looking, and outward-looking view of life. Unlike Western culture, both the Chinese and Indian philosophical traditions, when it comes to the meaning of human beings and the value of life.

Both of them take the ultimate goal of establishing the reality of the inner substance that is hidden inside things, rather than the search for external truths as the goal of studying the universe and the principles and principles of life.

For this reason - because of this fundamental difference in "philosophical concern" - the Oriental philosophy of life is not devoted to the study of universal, fundamental subjects, including existence, knowledge, values, reason, mind, language, etc., and how to uncover the mysteries of the universe and heaven.

Rather, it is how to "become virtuous", how to "become holy", how to "become a man", and even how to "become a Buddha". It is how to "become virtuous," how to "become holy," how to "become a man," and even how to "become a Buddha. The following five points are summarized.

1. Philosophy of life is still a young discipline in the East.

As a discipline within the academy, its development and research in the East has only happened in the past two hundred years, but the Eastern tradition of the Upanishads has a history of more than 2,000 years and is splendid.

In the past 100 years, Eastern philosophers have, on the one hand, continued their own traditions to promote the spirit of culture, and, on the other hand, studied and published Eastern thought by means of philosophical work imported from the West.

Western philosophy of life has systematic and

organized laws or arguments. On the other hand, we want to study and publish the Eastern thought through the Western imported philosophical work, using the systematic and organized laws or arguments of the Western philosophy of life, which are summarized from the actual verification or derived from the discussion of concepts, in order to deal with the data of the Eastern philosophy of life and study them through rational reasoning and logic.

Therefore, the difficulties are summarized in two main points: one is the difference in the awareness of the problem, and the other is the difference in the way of expression.

01. Different interpretations of philosophical questions of life in the East and the West.

In the traditional history of Western philosophy from Plato to Hegel, Western philosophy is a discipline that explores and reflects on fundamental questions about life, knowledge, and values through analytical thinking. For example, "Is there an objective standard of morality?" and "What is science?"

The goal is to discuss what is the most real reality and what is possible for human beings to know, and to propose various theories to answer the questions through rational discourse.

In the history of philosophy, we have been able to analyze and reject false or reactionary ideas, words, and deeds with justification. Each family overthrows the independence of the other, and forms its own school of thought that has been passed down from generation to generation.

The traditional styles of thought, culture, morality, customs, art, institutions and behavior that have been passed down through history are different from those of the East. The Eastern philosophy is deeply influenced by Confucianism: cultivating oneself / making one's family whole / ruling one's country / pacifying the world, the idea of acting or changing in an indirect or invisible way, focusing on the pursuit of the ideal life.

In the Chinese tradition, for example, the study and practice of philosophical thinking on life in the three schools of Confucianism, Buddhism, Taoism, and the establishment of doctrines or doctrinal theories over the past two millennia have had many different meanings due to differences in the scope of application.

For example, the speculation of things, the hypothesis of events, the principle of things, the empirical general principle of things, etc., maintain the tradition and form the school of thought.

They ask about the true meaning of life, explain the truth of the world, propose methods of cultivation, establish theories of ideal perfection of personality, and put them into practice. Therefore, it is a practical philosophy, different from the Western discursive philosophy.

02. The expressions of the Eastern and Western philosophies of life are different.

Western philosophy specializes in natural and social phenomena, in accordance with existing empirical knowledge, experience, facts, laws, cognition and verified hypotheses, through generalization and deductive reasoning and other methods, logical inferential summary analysis and reasoning.

The presentation of concepts focuses on the explanation of reasons, which are summarized from the actual verification or deduced from the concepts, and is full of inferential and deductive relationships.

Oriental philosophy focuses on the discovery of the substantive connotation of life's wisdom hidden within things, and the cultivation of concepts, ideas, learning and knowledge accumulated to a certain amount.

Therefore, aphorisms, stories, poems and other literary genres that reflect the richness of the author's emotions in highly condensed language and concentrate on social life and have a certain rhythm and rhyme are all forms of expression of Eastern philosophical concepts.

Of course, Eastern philosophies are not completely devoid of theoretical or systematic, but they are not just theoretical discourses as the main form of expression of concepts.

2. Oriental philosophy of life focuses on the expression of practical philosophical theories.

The focus of the work of Eastern philosophy of life is on the systematic expression of practical philosophical theories: Eastern philosophers, in order to participate in the study of philosophy in the world through rational reasoning and logic that cannot be directly perceived and answered through perception, have been able to develop their own philosophical theories.

In order to participate in the development of philosophy in the world through rational reasoning and logic, which cannot be answered directly through perception, and to promote the essence of Eastern philosophy, it is necessary to express the philosophy of life based on Eastern thought by means of systematic theoretical constructions. In contrast, the coherent thinking of Eastern thought is limited.

When Oriental thought, in the tradition of the philosophy of life school, has put forward various approaches in the history of philosophy, it is necessary to find the structural relationship between the many approaches in individual schools as an explanatory framework for systematic expression.

3. Interpretive Framework of Oriental Philosophy of Life

The systematic interpretive framework of Eastern philosophy of life is composed of four basic philosophical issues of the philosophy of practice: The characteristics of the philosophy of practice emphasize first and foremost the theory of cultivation and the theory of ideal personality to teach the way of dealing with people and the pursuit of ideal and perfect personality.

The theoretical approach involves the study, through rational reasoning and logic, of questions that cannot be answered directly through the perception of the world as a whole, including the knowledge framework of the cosmology and ontology of existence as a whole.

It includes a knowledge framework of the cosmology and ontology of the whole of existence, and a sense of the ultimate meaning and value of world existence. This is an explanatory system consisting of four philosophical, fundamental questions: cosmology, ontology, work theory, and realm theory.

The fundamental philosophical theories are related to each other by deduction, and this deduction relationship forms the internal systematic structure of Eastern philosophy, which belongs to practical philosophy, and each school of thought is derived from practical verification or from conceptual deduction.

By means of this systematic and organized structure of laws or arguments, Eastern thought, which is deeply practical, can be constructed in a rigorous and systematic way, and the pursuit of philosophy must be systematic and well organized.

It is the systematic combination of concepts, variables, definitions, and propositions that explains the relationship between certain observed phenomena.

4. Oriental philosophy of life pursues ideal perfection of personality.

Oriental philosophy of life is a philosophical theory of life that pursues the ideal perfect personality in the context of the work theory: the work theory explains the way of the subject's activity, the positive meaning of the object manifested to the subject, and the ontology of usefulness consciousness.

It provides the theory of mental cultivation of the pure will, and the theory of physical exercise from the knowledge of cosmology that explains the structure of the body, and through meditation, we can clarify our thoughts and improve our health, which is an important way to cultivate our body and mind.

Because we live in this world, there are inevitably various kinds of diseases, and all diseases can be divided into two aspects: physical and mental.

Therefore, in addition to physical illnesses, all mental and psychological phenomena such as greed, anger, fear, pride, and so on, are called mental illnesses.

We usually only pay attention to physical illnesses, and generally do not pay attention to mental illnesses. After the main body has been purified through practical work, it will be able to upgrade its ability to the highest level, which means it will come into contact with the problem of "realm philosophy".

The "philosophy of realm" is to explain the actual situation of the ideal perfect personality from the mental and physical state of the subject. The above four-way structure of cosmology, ontology, work theory, and realm theory will form a consistent theoretical system within each school of thought in the form of systematic conclusions about the knowledge of nature and society, which will be established separately by individual schools of thought from practice.

Due to the difference in the scope of application, there

are many different meanings: the speculation of things, the hypothesis of events, the principle of things, and the empirical general principles of things, therefore, there are differences in the whole system between different schools of thought.

Usually, there are some theoretical similarities between different schools, but it cannot be simply assumed that different schools have the same theories based on some superficial similarities, which are used to explain the relationship between certain observed phenomena as a systematic combination of concepts, variables, definitions and propositions.

In addition, there are many different and coherent narratives dealing with different issues among the same schools of thought, and therefore one cannot simply assume that there are some differences between the different and coherent narratives of the same school of thought.

In short, each school forms a systematic and coherent narrative system based on the explanatory framework of the basic philosophical questions, and has its own systematic combination of concepts, variables, definitions, and propositions to explain the relationship between certain observed phenomena.

However, the different schools of thought are still full of contrasting ideological positions. The question of which is right and which is wrong, and how each school proves it, has not yet been touched upon.

5. Theoretical proof of Oriental philosophy of life is based on the completion of practice.

The correct reflection of the dialectical development of objective things through concepts, judgments, reasoning and other forms of thought, i.e., the reflection of objective dialectics, can be proven if dialectic is not possible?

Therefore, a systematic and organized law or argument must be the result of one's own practice, or a speech with rich empirical evidence, and it is the absolute truth for itself. However, each school of thought is a view of truth under its own testimony, and it is only a question of whether different schools of thought can understand each other correctly.

Therefore, human beings make logical deductive conclusions about natural and social phenomena according to existing empirical knowledge, experience, facts, laws, cognition, and tested hypotheses, through generalization and deductive reasoning.

Although the understanding of cosmology is not tested by modern scientific instruments, there is the experience of the main body practice, which is the physical practice of cosmology, and after the operation, there is the enhancement of the senses, and there is the cognition of the testimony, and there is the statement derived from the actual verification, or from the deduction of concepts.

This is the result of the display of the knowledge of the world cosmology in Taoism and Buddhism, and even the world view and the subject's ability will be revealed to wherever one thinks.

The universe as a whole is infinite, and the process of acquiring knowledge by forming concepts, perceptions, judgments or imaginations is limited, and the individual is able to present all the objects or phenomena that exist objectively in nature.

In order to say what objectively existing objects or phenomena exist in nature, there are many different cosmological systems of Taoism and Buddhism.

For example, the practice of Prajna wisdom can be divided into three stages: hearing, thinking and practicing.

Thinking wisdom is the induction of the cosmological doctrine of emptiness and origin from the discernment of actual things.

The answer is deduced through rational and logical reasoning, and cannot be contradicted by empirical evidence. To have understood the meaning of emptiness so deeply that one is no longer confused by the difference in nomenclature is called the triumphal understanding of emptiness.

The study of the Buddha's teachings on the meaning of emptiness, and the ability to use rational reasoning and logic to study questions that cannot be answered directly through perception, is applied to daily physical and mental observation.

In other words, observation is not only a visual process, it is a comprehensive perception that is mainly visual and integrates other senses, and observation includes active thinking activities.

This is why it is called the higher form of perception. This is why it is called the higher form of perception. Many people are able to receive this benefit, and when they explain the Dharma, they are able to understand it by analogy and show the wisdom of debating talent without hindrance.

However, the wisdom of contemplation is still mainly based on logical deduction, which is derived from actual verification or conceptual deduction, but not on meditating on the world and seeing things with wisdom.

Therefore, in the face of the situation, we have to think a little bit, thinking is to think, so that is to explore, the process itself with a clear purpose and direction.

The process itself has a clear purpose and direction, but at most, because of skill, it is possible to understand the meaning of emptiness without thinking, just like a formula. It is only through the practice of wisdom, that is, the dual movement of stopping and observing, that one can see emptiness.

What is meant by "the dual movement of cessation and observation"? It differs from the preceding thoughtful wisdom in that it is an elevation of the philosophy of realm: a steady and clear observation in tranquility.

What is observation? It is different from imagination and speculation, which are real; it is also different from the awareness of the present quantity, which stops at the clarity of the phenomenon, but to discover that there is nothing in it that possesses, forms, or determines its own form of existence.

It is a constant, unchanging, independent nature that does not change according to its origins. In other words, all dharmas are the result of the union of causes and effects, and have no fixed, solid self.

In the process of thinking and wisdom, observation is limited, rough, and unstable, and the form of thinking that reflects the nature of things, such as analysis, synthesis, reasoning, and judgment, is more of a dispersed observation.

In the elevated dual movement of cessation and observation of realm philosophy, due to the concentration of the mind, there is an open, detailed and stable observation, and there is less thinking and concept, which is the observation of the mind, called Prajna observation.

It is a higher form of perception, which is not satisfied

by giving oneself a concept or an answer.

Therefore, it is penetrating. The process of stopping and watching is in fact an activity of the mind that explores the unknown: the mind persistently searches for the truth that all dharmas are the result of the harmony of cause and effect and have no fixed entity (selflessness).

For example, by looking at the illusory non-self nature of the breath, or the illusory non-self nature of the Buddha, and further looking at the basic elements of human existence, namely, the harmony of the five elements of color, receptivity, thought, action, and consciousness, it is clear that for the whole world

For a specific "dharma", there is no permanent and unchanging essence of all dharmas. For every sentient being

There is no soul-like entity, and we believe that the objective reality of people, things, objects, and the world as a whole are also illusory and selfless, and that even the inner mental activities-emotions, thoughts, ideas, and awareness-are all illusory and selfless.

At this point, one can realize that any existence, including the subject that can know, perceive, act, and think, is illusory and selfless, and that what is known, perceived, acted, and thought is also illusory and selfless.

The "taking" that exists because of the "taking" and the "knowledge" that exists because of the "knowledge" both disappear.

Even the existence of all differences and oppositions: size, height, good and bad, beauty and ugliness, gain and loss, suffering and happiness, pollution and purification, enlightenment and enlightenment, birth and death, are all illusory and non-self-existent.

From the illusory non-self nature of the present view of the breath to the illusory non-self nature of all dharmas, it is in fact consistent, like a pile of straw, starting from a corner and burning the pile completely.

The same is true of the present view of the wisdom of Prajna, from little to much! Under the continuous "stopping and observing", all the self-views will be completely removed, the knowledge and insight will be clear, and the wisdom eyes of Prajna will be clear and bright, and the emptiness of all dharmas will be seen at once.

The actual formation of a school is the result of the

practice of countless scholars throughout the two thousand years of philosophical history.

After the construction of the basic philosophical questions, the validity of the philosophical theories of each school must be established through the practice of work in order to achieve the ideal state, and to prove the theory of cosmology and ontology to be true, and to have the so-called proof, which is the special feature of the theory of knowledge of practical philosophy.

In the case of the theory of knowledge, the failure of an individual is not enough to prove it false, but the success of one person is enough to prove it true. The key point is that the philosophy of practice is to enhance human ability, and only after the ability has been enhanced can the truth of what is said be confirmed.

People who do not have the same ability cannot prove the truth or falsity of their logical inferential conclusions about natural and social phenomena, based on their existing empirical knowledge, experience, facts, laws, cognition, and tested hypotheses, through generalization and deductive reasoning.

Furthermore, the object of observation is not a general

observation, but a breakthrough, from the closest body to mental states and activities, to observe its eternal properties, which make an entity or a substance its essence, and which necessarily exists.

Without it, it loses its identity of selflessness and leads to the wisdom of selflessness, which is a necessary process for kungfu philosophy, and from there, to observe all dharmas in general, so as not to lose focus.

This is the necessary process of kungfu philosophy, so that the focus of all dharmas will not be lost.

This is the inevitable process of realm philosophy. Therefore, although the wisdom of emptiness is the same, the result will be different depending on the object of observation.

This is why most Eastern philosophical systems have more power in demanding practice than in constructing new doctrines.

This is because there are already many systems of knowledge that can be used to illustrate, but it is the continued efforts of each generation that will make Eastern philosophy a true guiding philosophy of life.

Finally, practice is the only thing that matters,

regardless of the school of thought to which one belongs, and since the Eastern philosophical system seeks the ideal perfection of the human personality, all one should do is to cultivate it through self-practice.

The concept that is recognized is the wisdom with systematic and organized laws or arguments, and the wisdom is also an independent determination, but with the succession of practice, so there is the result of realization, so it can be said to be proved.

Therefore, to judge things according to one's own perceptions or ideas, without seeking to conform to the actual situation, is not a negation of wisdom, but a self-selection of different values, which can prove itself to be the result of successful practice.

But for the dialectic of the three religions, there is no disproof of the efficacy of other religions, because other religions, with different values, can also be practiced and realized and achieved.

Therefore, if we talk about theoretical proof from the role of systematic and organized laws or arguments, as long as there is realization and personal testimony, there is proof, and no one can deny it.

The next step is the proof of the practitioner. However, the proof of practical philosophy is not like the proof of natural science, where experience is proof, nor is it like the proof of mathematics and logic, where projection is proof.

The testimony of practical philosophy is often like a person who knows how to drink water, and the opinion of others may not be useful, but only the opinion of others who are more capable and sincere than oneself.

More importantly, the manifestation of ideal personality can only be affirmed in those who have the same ideals, and it is difficult to affirm the life practice of those who have different ideals or even those who do not have ideals.

In the case of Chinese philosophical thought, because of this requirement to become virtuous and because of this intention to establish subjective values, the focus of Eastern culture on human nature is very different from that of the West; the characteristics of life that Eastern culture wants to promote are also very different from those of the West.

For example, what the philosophers of traditional

Eastern culture emphasize is not the rational features of human nature, but the irrational moral possibilities of human nature. Of course, in the establishment and development of morality in life, the element of reason has an unshakeable position.

However, we cannot derive the spontaneity of moral behavior from human reason alone; likewise, we cannot prove the substantive connotation of moral values hidden within things based on human reason alone.

Therefore, the meaning of "existence" of the self-life existence itself is not focused on the development of rational wisdom to mark the greatness of human beings.

The Chinese philosophical wisdom starts from affirming the value of the human subject, thus pointing out the authenticity of human moral consciousness, moral concepts and moral feelings.

In fact, the meaning of "existence" in the existence of self-life itself, in our ideal of life, our moral heart and our life feelings, although they can be distinguished, cannot be forcibly separated.

This is why, under Western philosophical development, an insurmountable gap has been created between knowledge and morality, and an irreparable rift has appeared between reason and emotion; but in Eastern philosophical tradition, "mind" should be combined with "reason", and "knowledge" should be united with "action".

In fact, the meaning of "existence" in the existence of the self-life itself, the difficulty imposed by reason, we use our passion for life to cross and crush it.

Therefore, in our individual experience of life, we pay attention to reason, not only to rationality, but also to the meaning of "existence" in our own life. We combine emotion and reason, emotion and righteousness.

Such an attitude in life also shapes our unique relationship with people and things. Because we do not see people in a cold and rational way, we do not see them as objects, but as feelings like our own.

We do not only treat all things with the spirit of exploration and exploitation, but also build a realm of harmony and integration between things and ourselves.

Finally, let us look back from the value of death to the meaning of "existence" in the existence of self-life itself, in order to further set the characteristics of the value of life in the East.

From a biological perspective, death is a return to a state of ignorance, unawareness, senselessness, and unconsciousness.

This has no value at all. However, if we further ask: what is the meaning of "existence" in the existence of self-life itself, and what are we willing to die for?

This is exactly what is meant by the saying: "Death is heavier than a mountain, and death is lighter than a feather. Then the question of value immediately arises, and the meaning of birth is also attached to it.

For only those who know the meaning of life know the value of sacrificing it; in comparison, the life that the Chinese celebrate, and the death that they praise, is not based on the greatness and prominence of deeds, but on the solidity of moral integrity and the unbreakability of the inner self.

This is why the cultures of the East and the West have many different meanings in expressing the meaning of the existence of the self in the life itself, often in the hidden substance, and in the difference of application.

For example, the speculation of things, the assumptions of events, the principles of things, the empirical general principles of things, the tragic end of life, but this is exactly what we grasp the meaning of "existence", the meaning and value of life and death of the existence itself.

Reference Source

Wikipedia

Education Encyclopedia | Education Cloud Online Dictionary

Dictionary of Buddhism

1. Foreign documents

Martin Heidegger, Being and Time, Trans.J. Macquarrie and E. Robinson. New York: Harper and Row, 1962.

Shing-Shang Lin, Von den modernen zu den postmodernen Zeitvorstellungen. Essen: Die Blaue Eule, 2011.

2. Chinese translation

Martin Heidegger, Ontology: A Hermeneutics of Actuality, translated by He Weiping. Beijing: People's Publishing House, 2009.

Martin Heidegger, Being and Time, translated by Wang Qingjie and Chen Jiaying. Taipei: Jiu Da Lau Co-Published, 1990.

Otto Pöggeler, Heidegger's Way of Thought, translated by Song Zuliang. Taipei: Yang Zhe, 1994.

Joseph J. Kockelmans, Heidegger's Being and Time, translated by Chen Xiaowen et al. Beijing: Commerce, 1996.

Jonathan Rée, Heidegger, translated by Cai Weiding. Taipei: Wheat Field, 2000.

S. Mulhall (Stephen Mulhall, Heidegger and Being and Time, translated by Qi Xiaosheng. Guilin: Guangxi Normal University, 2007.

Michael Inwood, Heidegger, translated by Liu Huawen. Nanjing: Yilin, 2009.

Günter Figal, Heidegger, translated by Lu Lu and Hong Peiyu. Beijing: Renmin University of China, 2010.

Eric E.Rofes et al., Talking About Death with Children, translated by Hong Yujian. Taipei: Yuan Liu, 1997.

3. Chinese books

Xiang Tuijie, "Modern Existential Thinkers". Taipei: Dongda University, 1986. Item back to the end, "Heidegger". Taipei: Dongda University, 1989.

Duan Dezhi, Philosophy of Death. Taipei: Hong Ye Culture, 1994.

Edited by Xiong Wei, Phenomenology and Heidegger. Taipei: Yuan Liu, 1994.

Chen Junhui, Heidegger on Being and Death. Taipei: Student Bookstore, 1994. Teng Shouyao, Heidegger. Taipei: Shengzhi Culture, 1996.

Ni Liangkang, Phenomenology and Its Effects: Husserl and Contemporary German Philosophy. Beijing: Triple, 1996. Chen Jiaying, "Introduction to Heidegger's Philosophy". Beijing: Triple, 1995.

Gao Xuan, Existentialism. Taipei: Yuanliu, 1999.

Zhou Minfeng, Towards Great Wisdom: A Dialogue with Heidegger. Chengdu: Sichuan People, 2002. Chen Xinbai, Dialogue and Communication. Taipei: Yangzhi Culture, 2003.

Yu Dehui and Shi Jiayi, Fourteen Lectures on the Study of Life and Death. Taipei City: Mind Workshop,

2003.

Zhang Xianglong, Heidegger: The Most Original Thinker of the Twentieth Century. Taipei: Kant, 2004. Zhang Rulun, Ten Treatises on German Philosophy. Shanghai: Fudan University, 2004.

Chen Ronghua, Heidegger's Explanation of Being and Time. Taipei: National Taiwan University Publishing Center, 2006. Chen Ronghua et al., The Tradition of Western Philosophy. Taipei: National Taiwan University Publishing Center, 2006.

Chenglin Tu, The Historical Mission of the Phenomenological Movement: From Husserl, Heidegger to Sartre. Beijing: Central Compilation, 2007.

Hong Handing, "Introduction to Contemporary Philosophical Hermeneutics". Taipei: Wunan Publishing, 2008. Sun Zhouxing, "The Theory of Language Existence". Beijing: Commerce, 2011.

4. Thesis

Chen Ronghua, "The Universal Concept of Heidegger's Being and Time", National Taiwan University Philosophy Review. The tenth issue (1987) Chen Ronghua, "Thinking on Heidegger's Theory", "Review of Philosophy of National

Taiwan University". Thirteenth issue (1990).

Chen Ronghua, "The Hermeneutics of Heidegger's Philosophy", "Review of Philosophy of National Taiwan University". Issue Sixteen (1993).

Chen Ronghua, "Is Dasein in Heidegger's Being and Time a Humanistic Concept? ", "Review of Philosophy of National Taiwan University". Issue 26 (2003).

Chen Ronghua, "Authentic and Inauthentic Existence in Heidegger's Time and Being", Philosophy and Culture. Issue 35 (2008).

Chen Jiaying, "On the Consistency of Translation Names from Heidegger's Philosophy", Journal of Philosophy. Issue 21 (1997).

Zhang Xianglong, "The Meaning and Translation of "Dasein" ("Yuanzai"): Understanding Heidegger's "Being and Time" clues", "Journal of Commonwealth". Issue 7 (2002).

Li Yanhui, "Early Heidegger's Philosophy of Life and Death", "Revelation". Issue Eight (2005).

Sun Yunping, "Types and Implications of Heidegger's View of Freedom", Journal of Philosophy of National

Chengchi University. Issue 18 (2007).

Sun Yunping, "Accidental and Factual--Analysis of "Dasein" in Heidegger's "Being and Time", "Soochow Philosophical Journal". Issue 21 (2010).

Sun Yunping, "The Life of Phenomenological Reflection", "Life and Phenomenological Reflection" Phenomenology Seminar Conference Paper (2011).

Zhang Rulun, Why Is Being and Time Important? ", "Journal of Renmin University of China". Second issue (2010). Lin Xunxiang, "Heidegger's Two Ontological "Worlds": A Discussion from "Being and Time" and "The Origin of Works of Art", "The Value and Ontology of Contemporary Continental Philosophy" International Conference Proceedings (2010). Xunxiang Lim, "Death, Guilty Being and Conscience", "Life and Phenomenological Reflections" Phenomenology Seminar Conference Paper (2011).

Lin Hsun-hsiang, "The Temporality of Self-Restriction", the paper of the Philosophy Symposium on "Truth, Goodness and Life: The Feast of Philosophy" by the Taiwan Philosophical Society (2011).

Cai Weiding, "The most self-possessing ability is

where the action should be: On an ethics that can be derived from the early Heidegger's thought", Taiwan Philosophical Society "Truth, Goodness and Life: The Feast of Philosophy" Philosophy Symposium Conference Paper (2011).

Shi Guoming, "On Early Heidegger's Thought of Transcendence". Master's Thesis, Institute of Philosophy, National Central University, (2000).

References

Shen Qingsong, "After Physics/Development of Metaphysics", Taipei City: Newton, Min 80 year.

Sun Zhouxing, "The Great Way and the Original: A Re-examination of Heidegger's Ereignis Thinking", Journal of Phenomenology and the Human Sciences, No. 2, Hong Kong: Phenomenology, Chinese University of Hong Kong and Humanities Research Center, 2005. Included in Zhang Canhui and Liu Guoying, editors-in-chief, Phenomenology and Humanities: Phenomenology and Taoist Philosophy, Taipei City: Biancheng Publishing, 2005.

Heidegger, Martin, co-translated by Chen Jiaying and Wang Qingjie, "Existence and Time", Beijing:

Life•Reading•Xinzhi Sanlian Publishing House, 2006.

Kockelmans, Joseph J., translated by Chen Xiaowen, Li Chaojie, Liu Zongkun, Heidegger's Being and Time: An Analysis of Dasein as a Basic Ontology, Beijing: Commercial Press, 1996.

Kant, Immanuel, translated by Deng Xiaomang, Criticism of Pure Reason, Beijing: People's Publishing House, 2004.

Einstein, Albert, translated by Li Jingyi, "Introduction to the Theory of Relativity: Special and General Theory of Relativity", Taipei City: Taiwan Business, 2005.

Aristotle, translated by Xu Kailai, "Aristotle. physics. On Formation and Destruction, Taipei City: Huiming Culture, Min 91.

Kant, Immanuel, translated by Pang Jingren, "Anything that can emerge as a science

An Introduction to Future Metaphysics, Beijing: Commercial Press, 1997.

Husserl, Edmund (1928), " Vorlseungen zur Phanomenologie des inneren Zeitbewust β eins" , Tü bingen: Max Niemeyer Verlag, 1980. In Gesammelte

Werke-Husserliana (Den Haag: Martnius Nijhoff, 1966), Bd. X.

Huang Guoju, "The Phenomenological Analysis of Lao Tzu and the Problem of Time", in Journal of Phenomenology and the Human Sciences, No. 2, Hong Kong: Centre for Phenomenology and Human Sciences, Chinese University of Hong Kong , 2005. Included in Zhang Canhui and Liu Guoying, editors-in-chief, Phenomenology and Humanities: Phenomenology and Taoist Philosophy, Taipei City: Biancheng Publishing, 2005.

Heidegger, Martin, translated by Sun Zhouxing, "As When It's a Festival...", included in Sun Zhouxing's translation, Interpretation of Hölderlin's Poems, Beijing: Commercial Press, 2002.

Heidegger, Martin, translated by Sun Zhouxing, "The Essence of Language", included in Sun Zhouxing's translation, On the Way to Language, Beijing: Commercial Press, 2004.

Heidegger, Martin, translated by Sun Zhouxing, "Building•Housing•Thinking", included in Sun Zhouxing's translation, "Speech and Essay Collection", Beijing:

Life•Reading•Xinzhi Sanlian Publishing House, 2005.

Heidegger, Martin, translated by Sun Zhouxing, "Inquiring about Technology", included in Sun Zhouxing's translation, "Speech and Papers", Beijing: Life•Reading•Xinzhi Sanlian Publishing House, 2005.

Heidegger, Martin, translated by Sun Zhouxing, "Things", included in Sun Zhouxing's translation, "Performance" Lectures and Proceedings", Beijing: Life • Reading • Xinzhi Sanlian Publishing House, 2005.

Wang Qingjie, "Tao as a Matter: Heidegger's Theory of "Sifang Yu" and Lao Tzu's Theory of Nature," Journal of Phenomenology and the Human Sciences, No. 2, Hong Kong: Center for Phenomenology and Humanities Research, Chinese University of Hong Kong, 2005. Included in Zhang Canhui and Liu Guoying, editors-in-chief, Phenomenology and Humanities: Phenomenology and Taoist Philosophy, Taipei City: Biancheng Publishing, 2005.

Heidegger, Martin, translated by Sun Zhouxing, "What is Thought? 》, included in Sun Zhouxing's translation, "Speech and Essay Collection", Beijing: Life · Reading · Xinzhi Sanlian Publishing House, 2005.

Said, Edward Wadie, translated by Shan Dexing, "On Intellectuals", Taipei City: Maitian Publishing Co., Ltd., 1997.

Heidegger, Martin, translated by Sun Zhouxing, "The Origin of Art Works", included in Sun Zhouxing's translation, "The Road in the Forest", Shanghai: Shanghai Translation Publishing House, 2005.

Heidegger, Martin, translated by Sun Zhouxing, "Science and Shensi", included in Sun Zhouxing's translation, "Lectures and Papers", Beijing: Life•Reading•Xinzhi Sanlian Publishing House, 2005.

Abstract

This research explores Heidegger's Philosophy about Ontology from time to space. 1) Heidegger's early thought focus on "Dasein" from death. Because the final results of time change is death. But Heidegger redefines the meaning of time through "Dasein" existence. 2) Heidegger's later period thought transforms "Dasein" to "die Sterblichen". Because Heidegger finds the meaning of existence is build which "die Sterblichen" dwell through build. 3) Finally, Heidegger proposes "das Geviert" theory. "Das Geviert" is the field which let the encounter of "die Erde", "der Himmel", "die Göttlichen", and "die Sterblichen". So at late, Human be able to "Gelassenheit".

Keywords: Heidegger, Dasein, Time, Space

METAMORPHOSIS:
The Reality of Existence and Sublimation of Life
(Volume 1)

蛻變：生命存在與昇華的實相（國際英文版：卷一）

出版者/美商 EHGBooks 微出版公司

發行者/美商漢世紀數位文化公司

臺灣學人出版網：http://www. TaiwanFellowship.Org

地　　址/106 臺北市大安區敦化南路 2 段 1 號 4 樓

電　　話/02-2701-6088 轉 616-617

印　　刷/漢世紀古騰堡®數位出版 POD 雲端科技

出版日期/2023 年 2 月

總經銷/Amazon.com

臺灣銷售網/三民網路書店：http：//www. Sanmin.com. Tw

　　　　三民書局復北店

　　　　地址/104 臺北市復興北路 386 號

　　　　電話/02-2500-6600

　　　　三民書局重南店

　　　　地址/100 臺北市重慶南路一段 61 號

　　　　電話/02-2361-7511

全省金石網路書店：http://www.kingstone.com. Tw

定　　價/新臺幣 2400 元（美金 80 元/人民幣 500 元）

CPSIA information can be obtained
at www.ICGtesting.com
Printed in the USA
BVHW051454240123
656900BV00027B/375